# NATIONAL GEOGRAPHIC KiDS

# 5,000 AWESOME FACTS (About Everything!) 2

NATIONAL GEOGRAPHIC
WASHINGTON, D.C.

# CONtENTS

# 1

In 1889, the
**QUEEN OF ITALY,**
Margherita
of Savoy,
ordered the
first pizza
delivery.

(Follow the fact ticker at the bottom and count the facts!)

# 15 BRAIN-FREEZING

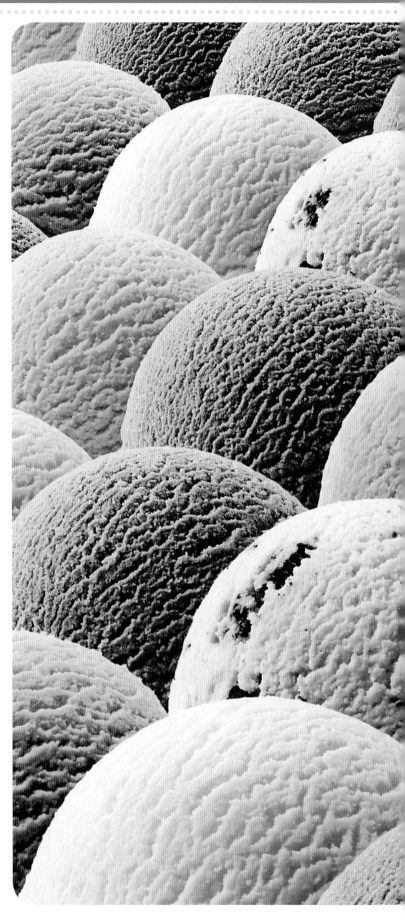

**1** A man in Italy once balanced **71 SCOOPS** of ice cream on a **SINGLE CONE.**

**2** You can buy **EEL-FLAVORED** ice cream in Japan.

**3** A microbiologist invented **DIPPIN' DOTS** in 1988 by using liquid nitrogen to flash-freeze ice cream.

**4** In late 19th-century England, a **HOKEY POKEY** was an inexpensive ice cream sold by street vendors.

**5** The actor who played **RON WEASLEY** in the **HARRY POTTER** films bought an ice-cream truck with some of his earnings.

**6** **NEW ZEALANDERS** eat more ice cream than **ANY OTHER PEOPLE IN THE WORLD**—an average of **7.5 GALLONS (28.4 L) PER PERSON PER YEAR!**

**7** It takes about a **GALLON AND A HALF** (5.7 L) of milk to make **A GALLON (3.8 L) OF ICE CREAM.**

**8** **BEN & JERRY'S** sells a special combination lock for its ice-cream containers that **PREVENTS ANYONE WITHOUT THE CODE FROM SNEAKING A SPOONFUL.**

**9** The **ICE-CREAM CONE** became popular after the 1904 **ST. LOUIS WORLD'S FAIR**, in Missouri, U.S.A., where ice cream was served **IN A THIN, CONE-SHAPED WAFFLE.**

# FACTS ABOUT ICE CREAM

**10** In **TURKEY,** ice cream is made with **GROUND ORCHID ROOT,** which makes the dessert STRETCHY.

**11** The **TOP-SELLING FLAVOR** of ice cream in the United States is **VANILLA.**

**12** Since there were **NO FREEZERS** to make ice, people in **16TH-CENTURY** Italy collected **ICE** from the **MOUNTAINS** to make **ICE CREAM.**

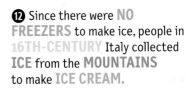

**13** Astronauts aboard **APOLLO 7** ate **FREEZE-DRIED ICE CREAM.**

**14** The first **BANANA SPLIT WAS SOLD IN 1904** in Pennsylvania, U.S.A., for **A DIME.** It was made of 3 scoops of ice cream on a split banana and topped with chocolate syrup, marshmallow, nuts, and a cherry.

**15** **SOFT-SERVE ICE CREAM** became popular in the 1930s after an **ICE-CREAM TRUCK BROKE DOWN,** and the dessert melted.

**1** All cats—domestic and wild—belong to the same family: Felidae.

**2** Endangered Scottish wildcats weigh about as much as 3 candy bars—4.5 ounces (128 g)—when they are born but can grow up to weigh as much as 450 candy bars.

**3** Abraham Lincoln was the first president to have a pet cat in the White House in Washington, D.C., U.S.A.

**4** Cats rub against you to leave their scent and mark their territory.

**5** Male lions in Tsavo, Kenya, don't have flowing manes. Scientists think it's a hormone thing, like men who become bald.

**6** Cats started living with humans about 12,000 years ago when people began storing grain. Cats caught the mice that the grain attracted.

**7** SMOKEY THE CAT HOLDS THE WORLD RECORD FOR THE LOUDEST PURR MADE BY A HOUSE CAT. A RECORDING OF HER PURR IS LOUDER THAN THE SOUND OF A VACUUM CLEANER.

**8** Although the bobcat is rarely seen, it is the most common wildcat in North America.

**9** Cats are intelligent. They can be taught to jump through hoops, walk on a high wire, and even "strum" a guitar.

**10** Snow leopards live at elevations as high as 18,000 feet (5,500 m). That's almost as high as North America's tallest peak: Mount McKinley in Alaska, U.S.A.

**11** The sand cat lives in the Sahara and doesn't need to drink water. It lives off of the body liquids from prey that it catches at night.

**12** A dog may be man's best friend, but cats are the world's most popular pet. More than 600 million live with people around the world.

**13** Cats were sacred animals to ancient Egyptians. A temple to the cat goddess Bastet in Alexandria contained some 600 cat statues.

**14** Clouded leopards are called tree tigers in Malaysia because they spend a lot of time in the trees.

**15** Cats were considered good luck to early sailors. Some thought cats could predict bad storms.

**16** SPRAYING PEE, LEAVING PILES OF POOP, AND SCRATCHING ON TREES ARE WAYS TIGERS SAY, "KEEP OUT. THIS IS MY TERRITORY."

**17** Cats have about 30 muscles in their ears and can turn each one in a different direction, 180 degrees.

**18** A cat spends two-thirds of each day sleeping.

**19** A cat named Towser was no slouch—she caught nearly 29,000 mice at the Glenturret Distillery in Perthshire, Scotland!

**20** In Japan, a small figurine of a cat with its paw up is called a *maneki neko*, which means "beckoning cat." It is said to bring good luck.

**21** From the ground, a mountain lion can jump as high as 18 feet (5.5 m) into a tree.

**22** Cats do not like prolonged eye contact, so don't stare at their eyes. They might think you are threatening them.

**23** Like many other animals, cats seem to be able to sense earthquakes before they happen.

**24** Ocelots clean all the feathers and fur off their food before they eat it.

**25** A cat's whiskers are the same width as its body to help it determine if it can fit through a tight opening.

**26** In one stride, a cheetah can cover up to 26 feet (8 m). That's as long as 9½ skateboards.

**27** A cat's tail contains nearly 10 percent of all the bones in its body.

**28** Jim Davis, the creator of the cartoon cat Garfield, modeled Garfield's behavior on the farm cats he grew up with and on some of his grandfather's personality traits.

**29** Cats usually have 4 back toes and 5 front ones. Cats with 6 or more toes are called polydactyls.

**30** Tommaso, a black cat from Italy, inherited about $13 million when his owner died.

**31** A clouded leopard can have canine teeth that are 2 inches (5 cm) long.

**32** Kittens as young as 3 weeks old are able to land on their feet even when falling upside down. A cat's keen sense of balance, flexible backbone, and lack of a collarbone make this possible.

**33** In the wild, lions live an average of 12 years. They can live up to twice as long in captivity.

**34** STEWIE, A MAINE COON CAT, HAS A TAIL THAT STRETCHES LONGER THAN THIS BOOK—ABOUT 16 INCHES (41 CM).

**35** Lions are the only cats that live in groups.

**36** The song "Here Comes Santa Claws," where cats meow the words, won an award from *Billboard Magazine* in 1995.

**37** The soft part of a cat's nose has a unique pattern, just like a human fingerprint.

**38** A 4-year-old cat that became lost while on a family vacation found its way home after traveling more than 200 miles (320 km) from Daytona Beach to West Palm Beach, Florida, U.S.A.

**39** Some mountain lions will eat porcupines—including the quills.

**40** In the first "Tom and Jerry" cartoon, Tom's name was Jasper.

**41** Is your cat mysteriously putting on weight? Maybe it's because someone else is feeding it. Tiny cameras attached to the collars of free-roaming pet cats have revealed that some "adopt" other families that they visit during the day.

**42** The Great Sphinx of Giza, a famous ancient Egyptian sculpture, has the body of a lion and the head of a human.

**43** Animal shelters use software that allows people to "play" with cats and other animals in the shelters from their home computers.

**44** THE FEUD BETWEEN TOM THE CAT AND JERRY THE MOUSE IN THE TOM & JERRY CARTOONS IS ONE OF THE LONGEST ONGOING RIVALRIES IN ALL OF AMERICAN ANIMATION.

**45** It seems the idea of cat doors has been around for quite a while. More than 600 years ago the English writer Geoffrey Chaucer wrote about one in "The Miller's Tale."

**46** Dr. Seuss' book *The Cat in the Hat* uses only 236 different words.

**47** Smarty, a pet cat, set a record by flying 92 times with its owners as they traveled back and forth between Egypt and Cyprus.

**48** The mountain lion and the cheetah share a common ancestor.

**49** Disaster, a black-and-white cat that had been missing for 2 years, was reunited with its owner thanks to a microchip in its ear and an alert "zombie," who works at a haunted house in New York City, U.S.A.

**50** Cats have claws for climbing but get stuck in trees because they don't think to back down after they climb up the tree.

**51** In World War II, a tuxedo cat named Simon was awarded a hero's medal for eating rodents and insects that might have dined on soldiers' food in the South Pacific.

**52** Lewis Carroll, author of *Alice's Adventures in Wonderland*, may have gotten the idea for his grinning Cheshire cat from cheeses made near his hometown in Cheshire, England, that were molded into grinning cats.

**Domestic kitten**

# 75 SU-PURR FACTS ABOUT CATS

**53** Fishing cats have webbed paws that help them swim and hunt in the water.

**54** The first international cat video festival was held in Minnesota, U.S.A., in 2012.

**55** Legend has it that the ghost of a black cat lives in the basement of the United States Capitol in Washington, D.C. It appears only before a major disaster.

**56** You can buy blingy collars, argyle sweaters, or even hoodies to outfit your kitty in style.

**57** In the famous photograph "Dalí Atomicus," it took the photographer 28 tries to capture artist Salvador Dalí, 3 jumping cats, and water tossed from a bucket in a way that makes everything in the picture appear frozen in midair.

**58** At the Calico Cat Café in Tokyo, Japan, you can enjoy a cup of tea as you pet one of the cats that hang out there.

**59** The Burmilla breed of cat came about by accident when a janitor left a door open and a Burmese and a chinchilla Persian cat mated.

**60** When running, cheetahs take about 3 strides a second. Olympic sprinters take just over 2 strides a second.

**61 A CAT WALKING ON YOUR COMPUTER CAN DAMAGE FILES AND EVEN CRASH YOUR MACHINE. NOW THERE'S A PROGRAM THAT CAN SENSE CAT TYPING AND BLOCK THE INPUT.**

**62** About 22,000 Americans come down with cat scratch fever every year, but many cases go unreported because they are so mild. The cause? Bacteria that cats can pass to humans.

**63** Models walk on a narrow stage called a catwalk. The longest one in the world is in Belgium. It takes 35 minutes to walk the whole thing!

**64** Lynx have back legs that are longer than their front legs.

**65 ALL CATS HAVE TONGUES COVERED WITH TINY SPIKES TO HELP THEM COMB THEIR FUR OR, IN THE CASE OF BIG CATS, TO TEAR MEAT OFF THE BONE.**

**66** Caracals can knock a bird out of the air by leaping 6 feet (1.8 m) straight up.

**67** Passengers can fly on a Hello Kitty airplane owned by Eva Air, based in Taiwan, China.

**68** Jaguars kill their prey by using their claws to pierce the animal's skull. Other big cats suffocate their victim.

**69** Cats purr at frequencies that can help heal their bodies and improve their bone density.

**70** People come up with some clever names for their cats, like Ozzy Pawsbourne and Cat Sajak.

**71** After humans, mountain lions have the largest range of any mammal in the Western Hemisphere.

**72** The Japanese island of Tashiro-jima has more cats than people.

**73** Cat shows have been around officially since 1871. The first one was held at London's Crystal Palace.

**74** In 2010, visitors to Antarctica saw a strange site when an iceberg shaped like a cat floated past Elephant Island.

**75** Leopards are able to hear 5 times as many sounds as humans can hear.

# 35 STICKY FACTS TO CLING TO

**1** SNAILS create a sticky slime from their muscular foot, which helps them CRAWL UP WALLS.

**2** The inventor of SUPER GLUE, Dr. Harry Coover, once lifted a TV game show host off the floor using just ONE DROP of the sticky stuff.

**3** MUSSELS make their own glue. Special proteins in the glue move water molecules out of the way so a mussel can ATTACH ITSELF to wet objects.

**4** The idea for POST-IT NOTES came to the inventor while he was in church. He needed a bookmark that wouldn't fall out of his songbook.

**5** During World War II, 3M—the company that makes SCOTCH TAPE—produced over 100 different kinds of tape to help seal, hold, protect, and insulate military parts.

**6** Your NOSE MAKES almost 2 gallons (7 L) of mucus every week. STICKY SNOT prevents dirt and other creepy crawlies from getting inside your schnoz.

**7** Sticky things are VISCOELASTIC. That means they behave like a liquid, flowing all over surfaces, but have some stiffness so they don't break easily.

**8** Stiffness is measured in a unit called a PASCAL. For something to be sticky, it must be less than 300,000 pascal.

**9** GLOWWORMS string 2-foot (0.5-m)-long twinkling lines from cave ceilings in New Zealand. The STICKY LINES attract insects, which become food for the glow-worms.

**10** Stone Age humans made GLUE by mixing RED OCHRE —a natural clay—and PLANT GUM. They used it to attach handles to their stone tools.

**11** EARLY HUMANS had their own version of GUM. A piece of 5,000-year-old black birch tar was found with teeth marks in Finland.

**12** Sugar-free chewing gum actually HELPS PREVENT tooth decay.

**13** In Sweden, October 4 is NATIONAL CINNAMON BUN DAY.

**14** The U.S. MILITARY is working on developing a STICKY FOAM that can be sprayed at tires of oncoming vehicles to stop them in their tracks.

**15** Police cruisers can fire GPS DEVICES THAT STICK to a fleeing car and report information about its location and movement.

**16**
In 1919, a MOLASSES tank EXPLODED in Boston, Massachusetts, U.S.A., sending a 30-foot (9-m)-high wave of the sticky stuff through the streets. Twenty-one people died.

**17**
The logo for ELMER'S GLUE is a cow because it was originally made from CASEIN, a by-product of milk.

**18**
BITUMEN is a sticky, black substance that, when heated and combined with sand and small pieces of rock, makes ASPHALT for paving roads.

**19**
Scientists have excavated over 3.5 million fossils of saber-toothed cats and other prehistoric animals from the LA BREA TAR PITS in Los Angeles, California, U.S.A.

**20**
It takes 10 gallons (38 L) of MAPLE TREE SAP to make 1 quart (1 L) of MAPLE SYRUP.

**21**
Astronauts took SILLY PUTTY to the moon in 1968.

**22**
Besides being sticky, HONEY has an ingredient that is good for FIGHTING BACTERIA. Scientists in New Zealand have developed a type that is being used to treat burns and halt infection.

**23**
Plasters, the first type of what we now call Band-Aids, were BRUSHED ON TO THE SKIN and covered with cotton strips.

**24**
BUBBLE GUM ALLEY, in San Luis Obispo, California, is a 70-foot (21-m)-long, 15-foot (4.6-m)-high alleyway with walls that are covered in bubble gum.

**25**
The BUMPER STICKER first appeared on a Ford Model A in 1927. It was made of CARDBOARD and METAL.

**26**
There's a type of SUNDEW PLANT that uses snap-tentacles to catapult insects onto a GLUE TRAP where the trapped victim is slowly digested.

**27**
A Johnson & Johnson employee invented the modern BAND-AID in 1920 to help heal his wife, who was always getting burned and cutting herself in the kitchen.

**28**
GECKO FEET have millions of tiny hairs that stick to surfaces with a special chemical bond and let them CLIMB WALLS and hang on by just ONE TOE!

**29**
CHEWING GUM may give you a quick MENTAL BOOST, make you more attentive, and even put you in a better mood—for about 20 minutes.

**30**
DUBBLE BUBBLE was the first successful bubble gum.

**31**
Someone with "STICKY FINGERS" is a thief.

**32**
VELCRO made a big hit with NASA in the 1960s when astronauts used it to keep things from floating away in a weightless environment.

**33**
A SPIDERWEB loses its stickiness after one day because it gets DUSTY. The spider may eat the dirty web before building a new one.

**34**
A DUCT TAPE company offers college scholarships for students who design and decorate the best DUCT TAPE PROM OUTFITS.

**35**
Do you VELCRO-JUMP? In this sport, you dress up in a Velcro suit and LAUNCH YOURSELF at a Velcro wall.

**Tokay gecko**

There are about 3 septillion (3,000,000,000,000,000,000,000,000) stars in the universe. 2. The sun is the closest star to Earth—93 million miles (150 million km) away. 3. **Stars are made up almost entirely of hydrogen and helium.** 4. The ancient Greeks called stars *asters*, which is where we get the word "astronomy." 5. **Astronomy, the study of the universe, is thought to be the most ancient of the sciences.** 6. **Sirius, the brightest star in the night sky, is known as the dog star.** 7. The sun is nearly a perfect sphere, like a beach ball. 8. **The largest star in the universe is more than 2,000 times the size of the sun.** 9. **The people of ancient Mesopotamia (now Iraq) are believed to be the first to chart the patterns that stars form in the sky and the first to name them.** 10. Later, the ancient Greeks and Romans changed the names of many constellations to honor the gods, goddesses, and other major figures in their mythologies. 11. Betelgeuse, the name of a bright red star in the Orion constellation, means "armpit of the giant" in Arabic. 12. **The International Astronomical Union officially recognizes 88 constellations.** 13. Constellations show people, real animals (like lions and dogs), and mythological animals (like dragons and flying horses) as well as other objects. 14. **The first-known star map may be 17,000-year-old markings on a cave in southern France.** 15. Since constellations appear at different times of the year, people have used them to tell time and to figure out the seasons. 16. Hypergiants—the biggest and brightest stars—release as much energy in 6 seconds as Earth's sun does in a year. 17. **Every star forms in a huge cloud of gas and dust called a nebula.** 18. If it could get close enough, a jet would take about 6 months to fly around the sun. 19. The temperature at the core, or center, of a young star is around 27 million degrees Fahrenheit (15 million°C). 20. **The hottest stars are white or blue, and the cooler stars are red or orange.** 21. Massive, 5,000-year-old animal-shaped mounds recently discovered in Peru are believed to be patterned after some constellations. 22. "Vampire" stars suck gases from another star to become bigger and brighter. 23. **It takes about 8 minutes for light from the sun to reach Earth.** 24. On a clear night in the suburbs, you can see 200 to 300 stars in the sky. In the city, you may see fewer than 12 because of all the bright lights. 25. Every star we see in the night sky is bigger and brighter than our sun. 26. **The Milky Way galaxy is so huge, you can see only about 0.000003 percent of it with the naked eye.** 27. Even the coolest stars are 15 times hotter than your oven set to the hottest temperature. 28. **The sun is 400 times larger than the moon.** 29. **The word "constellation" comes from the Latin word *constellatio*, meaning "with stars."** 30. Sky-watchers in ancient Greece made catalogs of the stars and constellations more than 2,000 years ago. 31. Astrology is the study of how the universe affects human personalities. 32. **Huge star explosions at the center of the Milky Way galaxy are so powerful, they'd wipe out any life on nearby planets.** 33. Star formation reached its peak 11 million years ago, when stars formed at a rate 30 times faster than they do today. 34. The light from a supernova, the explosive death of a massive star, is visible all the way to the edge of the universe. 35. **Some migrating animals, like ducks and geese, use stars to help them navigate at night—just like early sailors and explorers did.** 36. A black hole is formed when a giant star explodes. Its gravitational force is so strong that nothing can escape from it. 37. The closest black hole to Earth is about 10,000 light-years away. 38. **Some stars are more than 13 billion years old.** 39. The fastest stars in the Milky Way galaxy rocket through space at up to 2 million miles per hour (3.2 million kph). 40. Shooting stars, or meteors, are actually tiny specks of space debris burning up as they enter Earth's atmosphere. 41. **Meteors usually become visible to the naked eye when they're around 60 miles (95 km) above Earth's surface.** 42. A neutron star is so heavy that one teaspoon of the star weighs roughly around twice the combined weight of all the cars in the United States. 43. Some stars get brighter as they age. 44. **It would take more than 4 years for light from the sun to travel to the next closest star.** 45. The bigger a star is, the shorter its life. 46. The total mass of the Milky Way galaxy is equal to about 1.6 trillion of Earth's suns. 47. **Some shooting stars are traveling as fast as 162,000 miles per hour (260,000 kph) when they hit Earth's atmosphere.** 48. Over half the stars in the sky are actually binary—a combination of 2 stars. 49. The 6 *Star Wars* movies have raked in more than $4.4 billion worldwide. 50. **The entire Milky Way galaxy revolves around a giant black hole. It takes the sun 230 million years to complete one revolution around it.** 51. Besides the Milky Way, there are billions of other galaxies, each made up of billions of stars. 52. Meteor showers, like the Orionids and Geminids, get their names from the constellations they appear to start from. 53. **Black holes can swallow planets or even an entire star.** 54. Like the sun, all stars move across the sky on a regular schedule. 55. Two constellations are named after dogs: Canis Major (Big Dog) and Canis Minor (Little Dog). Both are said to be companions to Orion. 56. **The Milky Way is a spiral-shaped galaxy.** 57. The Leonids meteor storm, which occurs about every 33 years in November, showers Earth with thousands of shooting stars every minute. 58. The temperature of the sun's surface is 10,000°F (5,500°C). 59. **A baby star is bigger than an adult star.** 60. Scientists use the word "skeleton" to describe the structure of the Milky Way galaxy, with pieces and parts called "bones" and "arms." 61. A recently discovered "bone" of dust and gas within the Milky Way has as much material as 100,000 suns. 62. In ancient times, people believed that Earth spun around the North Star. 63. Before they had compasses, sailors used the North Star to help guide their ships in the right direction. 64. There is real gold in the sun. All the other metals found on Earth are there too. 65. In about 4 billion years, the Milky Way and the Andromeda galaxy—its closest neighbor—will collide. 66. The smallest stars are about 12 miles

(19 km) wide. **67.** Some galaxies "burp" huge blasts of very hot, high-speed gas. **68.** In a billion years, the sun will be about 10 percent warmer than it is now—hot enough to boil oceans. **69.** Over 2,400 brass stars engraved with names of celebrities make up the Hollywood Walk of Fame in Los Angeles, California, U.S.A. **70.** For about $20, you can buy and name your own star. **71. The Big Dipper is not a constellation. It's an asterism, or a group of stars located within a constellation—in this case, Ursa Major. 72.** Stars do not twinkle. It's just an optical illusion caused by the air surrounding Earth bending the light from the star. **73.** Upon its discovery in 1781, the planet Uranus was briefly called "George's Star" after Britain's King George III. **74. In southern France, the Big Dipper is called a saucepan. 75.** The Hubble Space Telescope, which has been taking images of space without interference from Earth's atmosphere since 1990, is the size of a school bus. **76.** The Hubble orbits Earth every 97 minutes and travels fast enough to cross the United States in just 10 minutes. **77. The sun contains more than 99.8 percent of the total mass of our solar system. 78.** The shortest-lived stars last about 50 million years. **79.** The Eskimo Nebula, a gigantic cloud of dust and gas that may eventually form a star, resembles a face surrounded by a fur parka. **80. Red giant stars are hundreds of times larger than the sun. 81.** Astrologers use the zodiac—12 constellations along the path the sun appears to travel during a year—to make predictions about people and events on Earth. **82.** The very first astrologers were considered to be highly intelligent philosophers who believed that stars were gods. **83. The famous 16th-century French astrologer Nostradamus is said to have predicted major future events like World War II. 84.** Starfish have 2 stomachs. **85.** The ancient Romans called the band of light across the night sky *via lactea,* meaning "milky road or way." **86. Scientists think that as many as 7 stars are born every year in the Milky Way galaxy. 87.** The heavier a star is, the faster it burns through its fuel and the faster it dies. **88.** Starlight is created by the nuclear explosions in a star's core as hydrogen is changed to helium. **89. The mass of a star determines how hot it is, what color it is, and how long it will live. 90.** Light from the Andromeda galaxy takes 2 million years to reach Earth, which means it left the galaxy when our earliest ancestors were just appearing on the planet. **91.** Neutron stars give off radio signals while rapidly spinning in space. **92.** LGM-1, meaning "Little Green Men-1", was the nickname given to the first pulsar discoveries. **93.** A nebula is like a nursery for stars. The easiest one to find without a telescope is midway along the sword in the Orion constellation. **94.** Scientists use scrambled letters of the alphabet—O, B, A, F, G, K, and M—to rank the temperatures of stars. O stars are the hottest; M stars are the coolest. **95. A white dwarf is the hot, dead core of a star that will cool down to become a cold, black dwarf. 96.** The calcium in our bones and the iron in our blood come from ancient explosions of giant stars. **97.** A gamma ray burst—like the energy that transformed Marvel Comic's Bruce Banner into the Hulk—is the most powerful kind of explosion in the universe. **98. In some countries, the center of Milky Way candy bars comes not only in standard nougat but in other flavors, like strawberry and banana. 99.** Over the next thousands of years, the stars in the Big Dipper will move so far apart that the dipper pattern will disappear. **100.** The term "astronaut" comes from Greek words that mean "star" and "sailor."

# 100 SPARKLING FACTS ABOUT STARS

**1**

A predator is something that **KILLS AND EATS** something else.

**2**

A cone snail is a deadly sea creature that hunts fish by firing a **TOXIC HARPOON** from the tip of its tongue.

**3**

The most poisonous species of cone snail has enough poison to **KILL 15 PEOPLE—** and there's no known antivenom.

**4**

The Goliath bird-eating tarantula has fangs the size of a **CHEETAH'S CLAWS.**

**5**

Saltwater crocodiles, or "salties," are Earth's **LARGEST REPTILES.** When prey comes close, they explode out of the water, grab it, and drag it underwater.

**6**

The Sydney funnel-web spider has fangs sharp enough to **PIERCE A HUMAN TOENAIL.**

**7**

Great white sharks can grow to be 20 feet (6 m) long and weigh 5,000 pounds (2,268 kg). They **ATTACK FROM BELOW,** making it hard for prey to escape.

**8**

The fastest insect-eating plant is the bladderwort. This small plant floats on the surface of ponds and **SUCKS IN MOSQUITO** larvae in just 20 milliseconds.

**9**

Man-eating leopards are legendary in local cultures. The Panar leopard of India reportedly **KILLED 400 PEOPLE** before being killed by a hired hunter in 1910.

**10**

Leopards often **DRAG THEIR PREY INTO A TREE** to eat. A male leopard can carry an animal 3 times its own weight.

**11**

Tigers have a special **REFLECTIVE LAYER** in their eyes. This means they can see much better at night than their prey does.

**12**

A sloth bear can gobble up as many as 10,000 termites **IN ONE MEAL.** A special flap in its nose helps keep the bugs out of its nostrils.

**13**

Leopards can kill and eat just about **ANYTHING—** even saltwater crocodiles.

**14**

Hyenas are thought of as scavengers—the cleanup crew—but they sometimes hunt. Their bite is **STRONGER THAN A LION'S.**

**15**

The **DEATH STALKER** scorpion can help save human lives. An ingredient in its venom binds to cancer cells and helps doctors detect tumors.

**16**

The only predator that hunts adult hippos is the lion. But it takes a pride to bring one down. **HIPPOS' JAWS** are powerful enough to bite a crocodile in half.

**17**

The golf ball–size blue-ringed octopus injects crabs and mollusks with a venom-and-saliva mix that is **10,000 TIMES MORE TOXIC** than cyanide.

**18**

The Nile crocodile can **HOLD ITS BREATH** underwater for up to 2 hours while waiting for prey.

# FACTS ABOUT
# 50 DEADLY PREDATORS

**Great hammerhead**

**19**
Polar bears have super noses. They can **SNIFF OUT** a seal on the ice from as far as 20 miles (32 km) away!

**20**
Bobcats are nighttime hunters that **SNEAK UP** on their prey, then deliver the fatal blow by pouncing on them—sometimes jumping up to 10 feet (3 m).

**21**
Wallace's flying frog searches for prey as it **GLIDES MORE THAN 50 FEET (15 M)** through the air. These amphibians use their webbed toes like a parachute for landing.

**22**
Peregrine falcons, the fastest-flying birds in the world, **SWOOP DOWN** at speeds of more than 200 miles per hour (320 kph) to grab their prey in midair.

**23**
Wide-spaced nostrils and eyes plus glands that sense electrical signals given off by other animals help make the hammerhead shark a **SKILLED HUNTER.**

**24**
Komodo dragons have 60 teeth, but they're for slicing and tearing—not chewing. These lizards **SWALLOW CHUNKS OF FOOD WHOLE.**

**25**
Komodos can **DEVOUR 5 POUNDS** (2 kg) of meat in less than a minute. Any extra fat they eat is stored in their tails.

**26**
Moray eels have **2 SETS OF JAWS** that they use to help pull prey down their throats.

**27**
Orcas get the nickname **KILLER WHALES** from the way they hunt—in packs of up to 40, using tactics similar to those of wolves.

**28**
The Siberian tiger—like all tigers—**HUNTS ALONE.** It will travel up to 37 miles (60 km) in a night to search for a meal.

**29**
Red-bellied piranhas, fish known for their feeding frenzies, hunt in schools and use their razor-sharp teeth to **STRIP THE FLESH** off their prey.

**30**
The highly aggressive bull shark has a **SPECIAL GLAND** that stores salt, which makes it possible for this saltwater shark to hunt in fresh water.

**31**
A Goliath bird-eating tarantula **PARALYZES PREY** with its venomous fangs and injects juices that turn the victim to mush, then slurps up its meal.

**32**
The Brazilian huntsman is the **MOST VENOMOUS** spider in the world. Just 0.00000021 ounces (0.006 mg) of its venom will kill a mouse.

**33**
Electric eels have 6,000 special cells on their bodies that **STORE POWER LIKE TINY BATTERIES** and stun predators when the fish is threatened.

**34**
Crocs have some serious chops! Scientists measured the **BITE FORCE** of modern crocodiles at a whopping 3,700 pounds per square inch (260 kg/cm²).

**35**
The Siberian tiger hunts where temperatures can drop to minus 40°F (-40°C). Their **POWERFUL MUSCLES** can launch them 20 feet (6 m) in one leap.

**36**
Snow leopards hunt blue sheep and ibex in the mountains of Central Asia. They've been spotted as high as **18,000 FEET** (5,486 m)—almost half the height of Mt. Everest.

**37**
A bear's **SENSE OF SMELL** is 7 times more powerful than a bloodhound's and thousands of times stronger than a human's.

**38**
Crocodiles have special sensor pits all over their bodies to **DETECT MOTION** in the water. Alligators have these sensors only near their jaws.

**39**
Japan's giant hornets rip apart insects and chew them into a paste. Just a few hornets can **WIPE OUT** a nest of 30,000 honeybees within hours.

**40**
One theory about the disappearance of Neanderthals—our prehistoric ancestors—is that early modern humans **ATTACKED AND ATE** them 30,000 years ago.

**41**
The name "jaguar" comes from the Native American word *yaguar*, which means "he who **KILLS WITH ONE LEAP."**

**42**
The **FEARLESS HONEY BADGER** will eat just about anything. More than 65 different creatures—mostly snakes and rodents—are on its menu.

**43**
Prehistoric saber-toothed cats, or *Smilodon fatalis*, had 7-inch (18-cm)-long teeth they used for **RIPPING OPEN** their prey's belly or throat.

**44**
Scientists used to think it was the deadly bacteria in the drool of Komodo dragons that killed their prey. Research now shows that Komodos kill with a **VENOMOUS BITE.**

**45**
The Portuguese man-of-war has venomous, barbed tentacles that can dangle 165 feet (50 m) below the water's surface to **PARALYZE** passing fish and other prey.

**46**
**HUMBOLDT SQUID** live up to 2,300 feet (701 m) below the ocean's surface, eating lanternfish, mollusks—even injured members of their own kind.

**47**
A harpy eagle diving at speeds of 50 miles per hour (80 kph) can **SNATCH-AND-CARRY** unsuspecting sloths and monkeys—prey that weigh almost what it does.

**48**
Carnivorous—or meat-eating—plants get more nutrition from the **FOOD THEY EAT** than from the soil they grow in.

**49**
The Venus flytrap, a kind of carnivorous plant, uses sugary nectar to lure insects into its **JAWLIKE TRAP.**

**50**
To trigger a Venus flytrap to **CLOSE ON ITS PREY,** an insect must touch 2 of the hairs on the plant within 20 seconds.

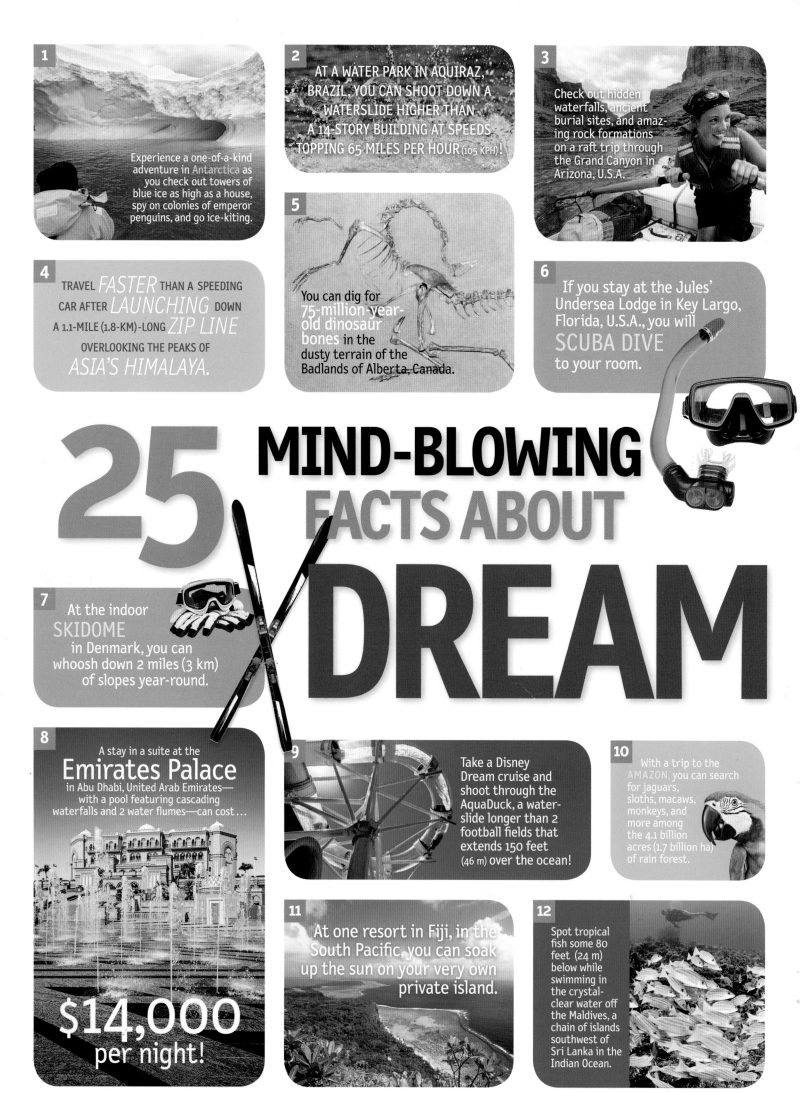

**1** Experience a one-of-a-kind adventure in Antarctica as you check out towers of blue ice as high as a house, spy on colonies of emperor penguins, and go ice-kiting.

**2** AT A WATER PARK IN AQUIRAZ, BRAZIL, YOU CAN SHOOT DOWN A WATERSLIDE HIGHER THAN A 14-STORY BUILDING AT SPEEDS TOPPING 65 MILES PER HOUR (105 KPH)!

**3** Check out hidden waterfalls, ancient burial sites, and amazing rock formations on a raft trip through the Grand Canyon in Arizona, U.S.A.

**4** TRAVEL *FASTER* THAN A SPEEDING CAR AFTER *LAUNCHING* DOWN A 1.1-MILE (1.8-KM)-LONG *ZIP LINE* OVERLOOKING THE PEAKS OF *ASIA'S HIMALAYA.*

**5** You can dig for 75-million-year-old dinosaur bones in the dusty terrain of the Badlands of Alberta, Canada.

**6** If you stay at the Jules' Undersea Lodge in Key Largo, Florida, U.S.A., you will SCUBA DIVE to your room.

# 25 MIND-BLOWING FACTS ABOUT DREAM

**7** At the indoor SKIDOME in Denmark, you can whoosh down 2 miles (3 km) of slopes year-round.

**8** A stay in a suite at the **Emirates Palace** in Abu Dhabi, United Arab Emirates—with a pool featuring cascading waterfalls and 2 water flumes—can cost ... $14,000 per night!

**9** Take a Disney Dream cruise and shoot through the AquaDuck, a waterslide longer than 2 football fields that extends 150 feet (46 m) over the ocean!

**10** With a trip to the AMAZON, you can search for jaguars, sloths, macaws, monkeys, and more among the 4.1 billion acres (1.7 billion ha) of rain forest.

**11** At one resort in Fiji, in the South Pacific, you can soak up the sun on your very own private island.

**12** Spot tropical fish some 80 feet (24 m) below while swimming in the crystal-clear water off the Maldives, a chain of islands southwest of Sri Lanka in the Indian Ocean.

**13** For around $50 MILLION, you can have an out-of-this-world vacation with a 12-day trip to the International Space Station.

**14** Run down the steep face of a quarter-mile (0.4-km)-high coastal dune, or check out the mysterious "fairy circles"—barren patches in grassy areas of Africa's Namib Desert.

**15** Get up-close-and-personal with southern Africa's Victoria Falls, THE WORLD'S TALLEST WATERFALL, in a micro-light airplane over the rushing water.

**16** You don't have to go far to see wildlife with a stay at CAMP JABULANI IN SOUTH AFRICA. A herd of elephants lives right on the property!

**17** Adrenaline lovers can bungee jump, paraglide, snow-board, and more in Queenstown, New Zealand—often called the Adventure Capital of the World.

**18** BRANCH OUT with a stay at a treetop hotel on Hainan Island, China, where you cross a sway-ing suspension bridge to get to a room that over-looks the blue waters of the South China Sea.

**19** Hitch a ride on the back of a dolphin or swim alongside stingrays in the warm, clear waters off Grand Cayman Island in the Caribbean.

# VACATIONS

**20** LOOKING FOR A REALLY HOT RIDE? PEDAL DOWN THE SIDE OF AN ACTIVE VOLCANO ON A MOUNTAIN BIKE IN HAWAI'I VOLCANOES NATIONAL PARK, U.S.A.

**21** Walk in the foot-steps of famous scientist Charles Darwin while snor-keling amid sea turtles, penguins, sea lions, and marine iguanas on the Galápagos Islands west of Ecuador.

**22** If you like butterflies, you won't want to miss the La Paz Waterfall Gardens in Costa Rica. It's home to more than 4,000 of the winged beauties.

**25** Cuddle with a real live koala at the Cleland Wildlife Park near Adelaide City, Australia.

**23** Channel your inner Batman by staying in a cave hotel in Cappadocia, Turkey. Some rooms were carved out by monks in the 12th century.

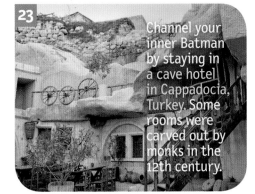

**24** Chill out in one of the geothermal pools in Reykjavík, Iceland's capital city. Many feature fountains and slides.

# (15) JIFFY FACTS

**1** LION'S MANE, the world's LARGEST KIND OF JELLYFISH, can be over **6 FEET (2 M) IN DIAMETER** with tentacles that can reach more than 49 FEET (15 M) IN LENGTH.

**2** Jellyfish, or jellies as scientists call them, ARE NOT FISH. They have **NO BRAIN, NO HEART,** and **NO BONES**.

**3** Jellyfish Fields, in *SPONGEBOB SQUAREPANTS*, is home to over **4 MILLION JELLYFISH.**

**4** A jellyfish is almost **100 PERCENT WATER** and is nearly WEIGHT-LESS in the ocean.

**5** A GIANT CROP CIRCLE in the shape of a jellyfish 820 feet (250 m) long and 197 feet (60 m) wide MYSTERIOUSLY APPEARED overnight in a barley field IN ENGLAND in 2009.

**6** A dead jelly can still have a POWERFUL STING. Even **A BROKEN TENTACLE** can zap you as long as it is **WET**.

**7** A NOMURA'S JELLY can weigh as much as **440 POUNDS** (200 kg). In 2009, **A NET FULL OF THEM SANK A JAPANESE FISHING SHIP** when its crew tried to haul them aboard.

**8** CEPHEA jellies are the size of PUNCH BOWLS, but they are harmless to humans.

# ABOUT JELLYFISH

**9** Jellyfish have been ON OUR PLANET LONG BEFORE—AND AFTER—DINOSAURS ROAMED EARTH. A rare fossil of a jellyfish found in Utah, U.S.A., dates back MORE THAN 500 MILLION YEARS.

**10** A tiny jelly called *TURRITOPSIS NUTRICULA* has more lives than a cat. Adults, by REGENERATING their cells, can seemingly LIVE FOREVER.

**11** More than **900 MILLION POUNDS** (408,240 MT) of jellyfish are HARVESTED EACH YEAR FOR FOOD. The CHINESE HAVE BEEN EATING CHEWY JELLYFISH for more than **1,700 YEARS.**

**12** JELLIES LIVE IN EVERY SEA ON OUR PLANET and even in some freshwater ponds.

**13** A group of jellyfish is not a **HERD,** or a **SCHOOL,** or a **FLOCK; IT'S CALLED A SMACK.**

**14** Some **TINY FISH** find shelter from bigger predators among the **TENTACLES OF A STINGING JELLYFISH.**

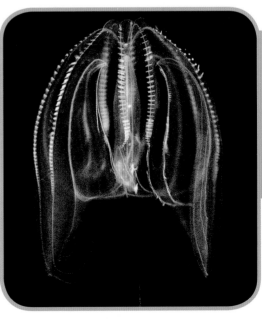

**15** Those NIGHT LIGHTS you sometimes see on the ocean's surface are **GLOWING COMB JELLIES.**

# 75 ROCKIN' WORLD RECORDS

**1** Earth's brightest and most colorful aurora borealis was seen as far south as Australia on September 2, 1859.

**2** Nanga Parbat, a mountain in the Himalaya, is believed to grow by 0.3 to 0.4 inches (8–10 mm) each year. That's more than any other mountain.

**3** Black swifts are considered North America's most mysterious bird because they nest on steep, wet cliffs and fly high while migrating, making them almost impossible to study.

**4** Krubera Cave in the country of Georgia is the deepest in the world. So far, people have descended 7,188 feet (2,191 m) but haven't hit bottom yet.

**5** The stinky rafflesia is the world's heaviest flower, weighing up to a whopping 22 pounds (10 kg).

**6** The springbok, a type of African antelope, wins the long jump medal in the animal world. It can leap as far as 50 feet (15 m).

**7 THE WORLD'S MOST LUMINOUS INSECT IS THE FIRE BEETLE, A TROPICAL RELATIVE OF THE FIREFLY IN YOUR BACKYARD.**

**8** The Rubik's Cube, with sales of over 350 million since 1980, is the best-selling toy of all time.

**9** Sloths are the world's slowest-moving animal. It can take them more than a day to move from one tree to another.

**10** Baseball's "Longest Game," played between the Rochester Red Wings and the Pawtucket Red Sox, lasted a record 33 innings and took more than 8 hours over 2 days to complete.

**11** The *coco de mer*, also known as the sea coconut, is the world's largest seed.

**12** Bamboo, a favorite food of pandas, is the fastest-growing plant. One species grows almost 4 feet (1.2 m) in a day.

**13** A giant sequoia named General Sherman is the world's largest tree by volume. Just its trunk measures 52,500 cubic feet (1,487 m³). That's equal to the amount of cement in 138 cement mixers.

**14** Look carefully the next time you swat at a fly. It just might be Robo-fly—the world's smallest robot—buzzing by.

**15** Blue whales are the largest animals on the planet—so large that 50 people could stand together on the tongue of one adult whale.

**16 DON'T DRIVE OVER THE WEIHE GRAND BRIDGE IN CHINA IF YOU'RE LOW ON GAS. AT JUST SHY OF 50 MILES (80 KM), IT'S THE LONGEST IN THE WORLD.**

**17** Worldwide land surface temperatures from June 2012 through August 2012 were the hottest ever recorded, with nearly 52 record-high temperature days.

**18** The world's smallest snake—the tiny Barbados thread snake—is as thin as spaghetti and averages only 4 inches (10 cm) in length.

**19** A banyan tree in Howrah, India, holds the record for the tree with the largest crown. Its top measures 270 acres (109 ha)—an area big enough to fit about 115 standard Walmarts.

**20** The world's tallest building, the Burj Khalifa in Dubai, United Arab Emirates, holds 100 world records, including the world's highest swimming pool. It is on Level 76, more than 853 feet (260 m) above the ground.

**21** The year 2012 was the warmest on record in the United States. The average temperature for the whole year for the lower 48 states was 55.3°F (13°C).

**22** The Great Wall of China, which once stretched for 13,170 miles (21,194 km), has held the record for the longest man-made structure in the world for over a thousand years.

**23** Cheetahs can run 70 miles per hour (113 kph)—faster than any other mammal on the planet.

**Rubik's Cube**

24 The Pacific Ocean, at over 65 million square miles (168 million km²), is the world's largest ocean.

25 Walt Disney holds the record for receiving the most Oscars: 22. Some of them were awarded after his death.

26 Korean pop singer Psy's YouTube video "Gangnam Style" has had over 1.5 trillion views, making it the most watched video.

27 *National Geographic Kids* set a record in 2011 for the most people doing jumping jacks: 300,265, including First Lady Michelle Obama.

28 The youngest person to act as president of a country is 5-year-old Razvan Gogan from Romania. During his day in office, he signed a Presidential Decree for children's rights.

29 Tokyo, Japan, with over 37 million people, holds the world record for the most populous metropolitan area.

30 Big Jake, a 9-year-old Belgian gelding, is the tallest living horse, measuring close to 7 feet (2 m) tall at the shoulder.

31 China's South China Mall, the largest in the world, has a theme park with land and water rides, a replica of France's Arc de Triomphe, and over 1,000 shops.

32 You'll need to crack open your piggy bank to pay for the world's most expensive ice-cream sundae. It sells for $1,000 at Serendipity 3 in New York City, U.S.A.

33 Serendipity 3 also has the world's most expensive burger. It's made with Wagyu beef, truffle butter, a gourmet salt known as salish, a gold-flaked bun, and Montgomery cheddar cheese and sells for $295.

34 **THE MOST EXPENSIVE CHOCOLATE IN THE WORLD, CHOCOPOLOGIE BY KNIPSCHILDT, WON'T END UP IN YOUR HALLOWEEN STASH. A DARK CHOCOLATE TRUFFLE COSTS $250.**

35 Indonesia is made up of more islands than any other country, with over 17,000.

36 The world's largest swimming pool, at the San Alfonso del Mar Resort in Chile, holds 66 million gallons (250 million L) of water, took 5 years to build, and is over 1,000 yards (914 m) long.

37 At over $80,000 a night, the Royal Penthouse Suite at the President Wilson Hotel in Geneva, Switzerland, is the world's most expensive hotel suite.

38 Royal Caribbean's *Oasis of the Seas* and its sister ship, *Allure of the Seas*, are the world's largest cruise ships. Both are 5 times the size of the *Titanic*!

39 **THE WORLD RECORD FOR THE LONGEST-LIVED PERSON IS HELD BY JEANNE CALMENT, A FRENCHWOMAN WHO DIED IN 1997 AT THE AGE OF 122.**

40 Vatican City is the world's smallest country at 0.2 square miles (0.5 km²) and a population of less than 1,000 people.

41 With more than 155 million items and 838 miles (1,349 km) of bookshelves, the Library of Congress in Washington, D.C., U.S.A., is the largest library in the world.

42 Australia's Great Barrier Reef is the world's largest coral reef. With almost 3,000 individual reefs and 900 islands, it covers an area larger than Italy.

43 Irv Gordon has set a record by driving his 1996 Volvo 3 *million* miles (4,827,900 km). That's like traveling to the moon and back 6 times!

44 The Dry Valleys in Antarctica are the driest cold place on the planet.

45 Is Paradise the snowiest place on Earth? Paradise Ranger Station on Washington State's Mount Rainier averages over 56 feet (17 m) of snow each year.

46 Italy's Mount Stromboli, known as the Lighthouse of the Mediterranean, has been blowing its top for at least 2,500 years, making it the world's longest continuously erupting volcano.

47 The oldest living woman in the world, 116-year-old Misao Okawa, lives in Japan.

48 Mr. Ashrita Furman holds 167 world records—more than any other person.

49 Rhinoceros beetles are the strongest animals relative to size. They can lift 850 times their own weight.

50 Wear comfy shoes when you visit the Smithsonian Institution in Washington, D.C. It's the world's largest research and museum complex, with more than 137 million objects.

51 *National Geographic Kids* magazine holds the record for the most people running 100 meters (328 ft) in a 24-hour period: 30,914 people.

52 Rob Roy Collins escaped from a straitjacket while hanging upside down in a record 1 minute, 53 seconds, beating Harry Houdini's record of 2 minutes, 37 seconds.

53 The Chinese giant salamander can grow to be 6 feet (1.8 m) long, making it the largest salamander in the world.

54 Because our planet is more egg-shaped than ball-shaped, the point closest to outer space is Ecuador's Mount Chimborazo, at over 20,000 feet (6,000 m) above sea level.

55 **THE WORLD'S MOST EXPENSIVE CAR IS A $3.9 MILLION LAMBORGHINI VENENO. ONLY 3 WERE EVER BUILT!**

56 At 70 miles per hour (113 kph), El Toro at Six Flags Great Adventure in New Jersey, U.S.A., is the fastest wooden roller coaster in the world.

57 The steepest wooden coaster in the world is Outlaw Run in Branson, Missouri, U.S.A., with an 81° maximum vertical angle.

58 The leggiest critter on record is a millipede that has 750 legs. It lives in California, U.S.A., and is smaller than your pinky finger.

59 The Dubai Eye, set to open in 2015 in the United Arab Emirates, will be the world's largest Ferris wheel, standing 689 feet (210 m) tall.

60 New Jersey's Six Flags Great Adventure is the largest outdoor theme park in the world.

61 Ferrari World in Dubai is the world's largest indoor theme park.

62 Australia is home to the largest herd of camels in the world—about 750,000 roam wild.

63 **MALARIA-CARRYING FEMALE ANOPHELES MOSQUITOES KILL OVER A MILLION PEOPLE EACH YEAR, MAKING THEM THE DEADLIEST CREATURE.**

64 The world's longest floating boardwalk, the 3,300-foot (1,006-m)-long Coeur D'Alene in Idaho, U.S.A., has pass-throughs for sail- and powerboats, a picnic area, and even a marine convenience store.

65 After 72 years (including 15 on radio), *Guiding Light*, the world's longest running scripted program in broadcasting history, was canceled in 2009.

66 *Meet the Press*, the longest running TV show of any kind, began broadcasting in 1947.

67 At 4-plus miles (6.4 km), the boardwalk in Atlantic City, New Jersey, U.S.A., is the world's longest.

68 Britain's *Blue Peter*, which began in 1958, is the world's longest running children's TV show.

69 In 2013, 9-year-old Quvenzhane Wallis became the youngest ever Academy Award nominee for Best Actress.

70 At 2,133 feet (650 m), the world's longest waterslide was constructed for a charity event in New Zealand. It was open for only 2 days.

71 Bumblebee bats, which weigh only about .07 ounces (2 g), hold the record as the smallest mammal.

72 Imagine the lunchroom crowds in the world's largest school. City Montessori School, in Lucknow, India, has close to 47,000 students.

73 The world's fastest train—China's bullet train—goes 302 miles per hour (486 kph). At that speed you could travel between New York City and Washington, D.C., U.S.A., in under an hour.

74 Russia is the biggest country in the world, covering 6,592,850 square miles (17,075,400 km²).

75 China, with a population of about 1,400,000,000, has more people than any other country in the world.

# 35 FACTS ABOUT TEETH

**1** About 1 in every 2,000 **BABIES** is **BORN WITH TEETH.**

**2** Over 7,000 years ago, Egyptians scrubbed their teeth with a powder that included **OX HOOVES** and **EGGSHELLS.**

**3** Some early toothbrushes were made from **COARSE PIG HAIRS** attached to a bamboo stick.

**4** Some people used to believe that **KISSING A DONKEY** could relieve a toothache.

**5** Only 1 percent of pet owners **BRUSH THEIR DOGS' TEETH DAILY,** but 77 percent purchase dental treats for their pooches.

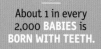

**6** Tooth enamel—the outer layer of your teeth—is **HARDER THAN BONE.**

**7** No cavities were found in **KING TUT'S TEETH.**

**8** Some Egyptian mummies have been found with **METAL BANDS** around their teeth—possibly an early form of **BRACES.**

**9** Dentists are experimenting with a device that uses electronic pulses to **STRAIGHTEN TEETH** up to 50 percent faster than braces do.

**10** Researchers are developing a **GUM THAT KILLS CAVITY-CAUSING BACTERIA** while you chew.

**11** Birds called Egyptian plovers **ACT LIKE DENTAL FLOSS** for crocodiles. They fly into the croc's mouth and pick out tiny bits of food stuck in its teeth.

**12** Right-handed people tend to **CHEW FOOD** on the right side of their mouth, while left-handed people tend to chew on the left side.

**13** Scientists can tell how old a dolphin is by **COUNTING THE GROWTH RINGS**—similar to the rings in trees—in its teeth.

**14** Each year, Americans make about **500 MILLION VISITS** to dentists.

**15** A store in Japan invented multicolored **LIGHT-UP BRACES** for an ad campaign.

**16** A company once sold toothpaste in **INDIAN CURRY** and **COLA** flavors.

**17** **COWS, SHEEP, AND GOATS** do not have top front teeth.

# TO CHEW ON

**18** ELEPHANT TUSKS are actually enlarged incisors. They can measure almost 11 feet (3 m), making them the longest teeth in the world.

**19** A man from Malaysia PULLED 2 COMMUTER TRAINS WITH HIS TEETH. That's a total weight of 287.5 tons (258.8 MT)!

**20** The record for SIMULTANEOUS TOOTH-BRUSHING is held by 13,380 PEOPLE gathered at a stadium in San Salvador, El Salvador.

**21** A study found that EATING CHEESE may help prevent tooth decay.

**22** Even though DOLPHINS have about 100 teeth, they DON'T CHEW. They swallow their food whole.

**23** PEOPLE REPORTEDLY PREFER BLUE toothbrushes over red ones.

**24** The plaque on your teeth contains more than 300 SPECIES OF BACTERIA.

**25** SHEEPSHEAD FISH LOOK LIKE THEY HAVE HUMAN TEETH, except they have 3 rows of molars on their upper jaw and 2 rows on the lower jaw.

**26** SKULLS OF VIKING WARRIORS show that some of them filed patterns into their front teeth, possibly to scare their enemies.

**27** Some SNAILS have thousands of TINY TEETH on hard, ribbonlike organs that look like tongues.

**28** Your teeth are AS UNIQUE AS YOUR FINGERPRINTS. Even the teeth of identical twins are not exactly the same.

**29** You can buy JEWELRY made from HUMAN TEETH.

**30** One famous pop star COLLECTS TEETH from her fans and uses them to make necklaces, earrings, a crown, and more.

**31** In parts of Ireland and Great Britain, kids BURY THEIR BABY TEETH when they fall out.

**32** The SHARPEST TEETH ever found on Earth belonged to a prehistoric fish that first appeared 500 million years ago.

**33** Some electronic tooth-brushes SYNC TO YOUR CELL PHONE so you can keep track of how often you brush, how long, and what spots you miss.

**34** PENGUINS have toothlike barbs on their tongues and on the roofs of their mouths to help them swallow slippery fish.

**35** There is a toothpaste that uses COCOA EXTRACT to strengthen and clean teeth.

1. Hurricane Sandy slammed the mid-Atlantic region of the United States in the fall of 2012, becoming the second largest Atlantic tropical cyclone on record. 2. The 1958 Lituya Bay Megatsunami generated the highest wave ever recorded—almost as tall as the new World Trade Center in New York City, U.S.A. 3. The 1815 Tambora volcano eruption in Indonesia was 52,000 times more powerful than the atomic bomb that destroyed Hiroshima, Japan, during World War II. 4. Kansas and Oklahoma, U.S.A., were hit by a total of 74 tornadoes in a single day—May 3, 1999. 5. The asteroid or comet that hit Siberia, Russia, on June 30, 1908, toppled 80 million trees but killed no one. 6. China's 1931 floods were the worst natural disaster in the country's history. 7. Help after 2005's Hurricane Katrina came to the U.S. from China, Bangladesh, India, and other countries that had suffered similar disasters. 8. For the first time since 1888, weather—in the form of Hurricane Sandy—shut down the New York Stock Exchange for 2 days . 9. At 9.5 on the Richter scale, Chile's 1960 earthquake is the strongest quake on record. 10. An 8.9 quake hit Japan in 2011, causing a tsunami powerful enough to reverse the directions of rivers. 11. The day became 1.8 microseconds shorter after Japan's 2011 disaster shifted the mass of the planet. 12. The greatest impact of the earthquake that struck Haiti in 2010 was felt by the almost 3 million people living in the capital city. 13. Haiti's 2010 earthquake measured 7 on the Richter scale—the country's strongest since 1770. 14. Nearly 80 percent of the schools in Haiti were either damaged or destroyed by the 2010 quake. 15. The disaster that struck Japan in 2011 released radioactivity from the Fukushima Daiichi nuclear power plant. 16. Japan's government called up 100,000-plus troops, the most since World War II, to aid in the 2011 relief effort. 17. The deadliest earthquake in recorded history occurred in 1156 in what is now China's Shaanxi Province. 18. In 2004, the deadliest tsunami on record occurred in the Indian Ocean, affecting 11 countries. 19. After the 1889 flood in Johnstown, Pennsylvania, U.S.A., Clara Barton's branch of the Red Cross set up "hotels" to provide shelter to those who lost their homes. 20. In 1975, 62 dams on China's Yangtze River failed, causing floods and famine across Henan Province. 21. Millions of dollars in aid were sent to Bangladesh in 1988 and in 1998 when floods covered as much as 75 percent of the country. 22. In 1910, the worst natural disaster in the history of Washington State, U.S.A, occurred when an avalanche slammed into 2 Great Northern trains traveling through the mountains. 23. Clear cut-

**100 FACTS ABOUT**

ting of timber above the tracks and forest fires caused by train sparks created the perfect environment for the avalanche. 24. A massive 2-mile (3-km)-high dust storm traveled 2,000 miles (3,218 km) across the United States from the Plains states to the East Coast during the 1930s Dust Bowl. 25. In addition to the dust storms and drought that ravaged the country during the Dust Bowl, plagues of jackrabbits and grasshoppers ate any surviving crops. 26. On Black Sunday—April 14, 1935—the amount of static electricity generated during one enormous Dust Bowl storm could have powered all of New York City. 27. In 2013, 1,000 rescue workers fought altitude sickness and bad weather to try to free gold miners trapped in a landslide in Tibet, China. 28. The largest wildfire in U.S. history burned close to 4 million acres (1.6 million ha) in Wisconsin and Michigan in 1871 and created a fire tornado. 29. Since 1996, the National Search Dog Foundation has aided in natural disaster recovery efforts in the United States and abroad. 30. One of the worst wildfires in California, U.S.A., occurred in 2003 when a firestorm, fueled by at least 14 major fires, burned over 740,000 acres (299,478 ha). 31. During the Great Idaho Fire of 1910, U.S. troops were ordered to set off dynamite for 60 hours, but the explosions didn't bring any rain. 32. The Black Friday Bushfire in Australia burned for more than a month in 1939, destroying an area about the size of El Salvador. 33. On average, more than 100,000 wildfires occur in the United States each year and burn an area larger than the state of Connecticut. 34. In 2013, an early start to the rainy monsoon season in India caused record amounts of rainfall, flooding, and landslides in the foothills of the Himalaya. 35. Each year, the world suffers on average 1 earthquake measuring 8 or higher on the Richter scale and 15 that measure a point lower. 36. The earthquake that caused the 2004 tsunami in the Indian Ocean was the third strongest on record, reaching a magnitude of 9.1 on the Richter scale. 37. Record flooding in Calgary, Canada, in June 2013 caused waters to rise as high as the 10th row in the city's hockey arena. 38. The pollution index reached a record 401 in Singapore in June 2013 when smoke and haze from forest fires in neighboring Indonesia reached the country. 39. In 1994, 90 percent of the drinking water in Florida, U.S.A., was contaminated when a 15-story-deep sinkhole opened up beneath a pile of toxic industrial waste. 40. The United States has an average of 1,000 tornadoes each year—more than any other country. Canada, which ranks number 2, averages 100. 41. Tornado Alley, a region named for its high number of tornadoes, encompasses several states in the central United States. 42. Dixie Alley is the nickname of a tornado-prone area along the U.S. Gulf Coast. 43. April 2011 holds the record for the most tornadoes in a single month: 753. 44. Tornadoes are classified by wind speeds. F0 is the weakest, and F5 is the strongest, with winds reaching at least 260 miles per hour (418 kph). 45. The highest wind speed recorded for a tornado was 302 miles per hour (486 kph) on May 3, 1999, in Oklahoma, U.S.A. 46. A series of severe thunderstorms—called a derecho—dropped damaging hail in Mississippi, U.S.A., in the spring of 2013. 47. Tornado Alley frequently produces huge, supercell thunderstorms, which create F2 or greater tornadoes. 48. Scientists and meteorologists risk their lives chasing tornadoes to increase knowledge of these dangerous storms. 49. Barry I, the most famous St. Bernard avalanche search dog, rescued almost 50 people between 1800 and 1812. 50. The Swiss Army began training dogs to search for victims buried by avalanches in the 1930s. 51. Each year, the American Red Cross responds to about 70,000 natural and man-made disasters around the world. 52. In February 2014, a sinkhole opened up under the National Corvette Museum in Bowling Green, Kentucky, U.S.A., swallowing eight expensive cars. 53. A monster, multivortex, F5 tornado—a large tornado with smaller ones inside it—ripped through Joplin, Missouri, U.S.A., in May 2011. 54. A single text message to a friend helped to locate and save a man trapped under rubble in Joplin. 55. The word "hurricane" comes from the Spanish huraca'n and from the Taino huraaca'n, which means "center of wind." 56. Hurricanes, rotating tropical storms with winds of at least 74 miles per hour (119 kph), form over the Atlantic Ocean and the eastern Pacific Ocean. 57. Names of hurricanes are reused every seventh year, except if the hurricane was particularly severe, in which case the name is retired. 58. Your chances of experiencing a hurricane are greatest if you live in Miami, Florida; Cape Hatteras, North Carolina; or San Juan, Puerto Rico. 59. Some 20,000 people lived out Hurricane Katrina in the Louisiana Superdome in New Orleans. 60. The Great Famine in Ireland in the mid-1800s was caused by a fungus that destroyed the potato crop. **61.** Most of the people who escaped Ireland during the famine emigrated to the United States. **62.** A severe drought in 1769 led to a famine in India. **63.** An outbreak of "Spanish flu" caused a pandemic that spread around the globe in 1918. **64.** One of the most famous pandemics was the Black Death that ravaged Europe from 1347 to 1351. **65.** Yellow fever was once thought to be caused by rotting vegetables rather than by a bite from an infected mosquito. **66.** Yellow fever spread through Philadelphia, Pennsylvania, U.S.A., in 1793, causing 17,000 people to flee the city. **67.** Lava flows from a volcanic eruption can reach temperatures up to 2,000°F (1,250°C), but deaths can also occur from mudflows, toxic gases, and showers of ash. **68.** The most famous eruption of Italy's Mount Vesuvius, the only active volcano on the mainland of Europe, occurred in A.D. 79. **69.** The disaster in A.D. 79 was the first volcanic eruption to be described in detail, thanks to the writing of Pliny the Younger. **70.** In Pompeii, Italy, you can see plaster casts of actual bodies of people killed instantly by the extreme heat from Vesuvius's 79 eruption. **71.** Dust from the April 1815 eruption of Indonesia's Mount Tambora blocked light from the sun, affecting climate well into 1816, which became known as the Year Without a Summer. **72.** The dark and gloomy weather of 1816 inspired Mary Shelley to write *Frankenstein.* **73.** The Year Without a Summer caused famines and food shortages as crops failed. **74.** A similar global darkness was created after the 1883 eruption of Krakatoa, a volcanic island in Indonesia. **75.** The eruption of Krakatoa blew apart the entire island, sending pieces of it to distant countries. **76.** Krakatoa's massive eruption could be heard 3,000 miles (4,828 km) away. That would be like hearing an explosion in New York across the United States in California. **77.** For the first time in history, telegraph machines were able to alert the world to Krakatoa's eruption immediately after it happened. **78.** The world experienced at least 6 billion-dollar natural disasters in 2013—all before hurricane season officially started! **79.** Hurricane Iniki, in 1992, was the most powerful hurricane to hit the Hawaiian Islands in their recorded history. **80.** In just 1 forceful minute of shaking, the 1906 earthquake in California, U.S.A., became the deadliest in the state's history. **81.** The 1906 San Francisco quake produced fires that burned for 3 days, destroying a total of 28,000 buildings in 500 blocks—one-quarter of the city. **82.** The 1906 earthquake and the fires that followed were the first natural disasters well documented by photography. **83.** More than 18 million people in 18 African countries are suffering starvation after a severe drought in 2012. **84.** Iran's strongest earthquake in 50 years—a magnitude 7.8—occurred in April 2013. Fortunately, it struck where few people lived. **85.** Mount St. Helens erupted in Washington State, U.S.A., in May 1980, wiping out 229 square miles (593 km²), an area about the size of Chicago, Illinois, U.S.A. **86.** The Mount St. Helens eruption destroyed several million dollars' worth of timber, making it the costliest volcanic disaster in U.S. history. **87.** A 4.2 earthquake in March 1980 reawakened Mount St. Helens, which had been dormant for 123 years. **88.** Ash and lava released by Mount St. Helens created such darkness that streetlights came on during daylight hours. **89.** Mount St. Helens's volcanic ash reached the U.S. East Coast 3 days after the eruption and encircled the planet in 15 days. **90.** Spiders and beetles were the first creatures to return to Mount St. Helens after the eruption. **91.** Hurricane Irene, which struck the U.S. East Coast in 2011, was so destructive that its name will never be used again. **92.** Over 4 million people lost power during Hurricane Irene. **93.** Hurricane Irene became the 10th billion-dollar disaster of 2011 in the United States. **94.** Irene broke flood records for 26 rivers in New York, New Jersey, and Vermont. **95.** Many historic covered bridges were damaged or destroyed by Irene. **96.** A record-breaking nor'easter hit New England, U.S.A., in October 2011, leaving 3 million customers without power. **97.** In 2012, Superstorm Sandy wiped out the famous boardwalk in Atlantic City, New Jersey. **98.** Hurricane Sandy, with its rain, wind, and snow, earned the nicknames Frankenstorm, Blizzacane, and Snoreastercane. **99.** Hurricane Olga in 2001 set the record for the largest Atlantic tropical cyclone. **100.** In August 1980, Hurricane Allen stayed a category 5 storm longer than any other hurricane.

# NATURAL DISASTERS
## THAT MAKE YOU GLAD YOU WEREN'T THERE

Hurricane Katrina

# 50 PRECISE FACTS ABOUT TIME

**1**
The famous **BIG BEN** clock tower and bell went dark and **SILENT** during World War II to prevent enemy aircraft from using it to pinpoint England's government buildings.

**2**
If the sun suddenly **STOPPED SHINING**, we on Earth wouldn't know for **8 MINUTES**. Mercury would know 5 minutes earlier.

**3**
An **ASTRONOMICAL CLOCK** in Prague, Czech Republic, shows the medieval view of the universe: Earth is at the center with the sun and moon traveling around it.

**4**
For nearly 90 years, the **COLGATE CLOCK**, 50 feet (15 m) in diameter, was a landmark along the shoreline of Jersey City, New Jersey, U.S.A.

**5**
While you're visiting North America's Niagara Falls, check out the time on the 40-foot (12-m)-wide **FLORAL CLOCK** in Niagara Park, created with over 16,000 plants.

**6**
India's 12th-century **BRIHAT SAMRAT YANTRA**——the world's largest sundial—is very accurate. The dial's shadow moves only .04 inches (1 mm) every second.

**7**
Experts say the best time to **READ SOMETHING** and **REMEMBER** it is at 8 a.m. or 10 p.m.

**8**
The gigantic **MAKKAH CLOCK ROYAL TOWER** in Mecca, Saudi Arabia, has the largest clockface in the world. It is a feature of one of the world's tallest buildings.

**9**
**JAMES BOND'S** wristwatches are equipped with an endless array of gadgets, including a laser beam for cutting and a telex for receiving messages from MI6.

**10**
Scientists say that the best time to **TAKE A NAP** is between 1 p.m. and 2:30 p.m. because that's when a dip in body temperature makes us feel sleepy.

**11**
The price for the first LED watch in 1972 was **$2,100**, the equivalent of about $11,000 today. **LED WATCHES** now sell for as little as **$10**.

**12**
**PLANCK TIME** is the smallest known unit of time. It's 0.00000000000 0000000000000000000 0000000000001 second.

**13**
**NUREMBERG EGGS**, egg-shaped watches worn around the neck in the 16th century, were the first portable timepieces.

**14**
If lightning appears in **LESS THAN 30 SECONDS** after you hear a clap of thunder, the storm is within **6 MILES** (10 km).

**15**
The Countess Koscowicz of Hungary sported the world's **FIRST WRISTWATCH** in 1876. Much chunkier than today's watches, hers required a key to wind it.

**16**
"I'll be ready in a **JIFFY**" actually means that you will be ready in **ONE-HUNDREDTH OF A SECOND**, so use it only when you know you can be very fast.

**17**
Milliseconds, microseconds, and nanoseconds are **MEASUREMENTS OF TIME** equal to 1/1,000, 1/1,000,000, and 1/1,000,000,000 of a second.

**18**
There are **31,536,000 SECONDS** in a 365-day year.

**19**

The Navajo reservation is the only place in Arizona, U.S.A., that observes **DAYLIGHT SAVING TIME,** but that's because it stretches into 2 other states that do observe it.

**20**

If you become an expert in making and repairing clocks and watches, you'd be known as a **HOROLOGIST.**

**21**

A **GIGAYEAR** is equal to 1,000,000,000,000 years!

**22**

**MICKEY MOUSE** first appeared on the face of a wristwatch in 1933. Reportedly more than 11,000 were sold in one day at Macy's in New York City, U.S.A.

**23**

The hourglass from *THE WIZARD OF OZ* film was part of collector Joe Maddalena's Oz memorabilia until he sold it in 1998 for $325,000.

**24**

Dr. Robert Langdon, the lead character in the *DA VINCI CODE* thriller, wears a Mickey Mouse watch.

**25**

**WATCHMAKING** began in Switzerland more than 400 years ago. Watches are still among its leading exports.

**26**

The world's **LARGEST CUCKOO CLOCK** is almost 2½ stories tall. Every 30 minutes, a wooden figure dances to polka music "played" by a 5-piece wooden band.

**27**

The U.S. Department of Energy claims that **3 MILLION FEWER BARRELS** of oil are used during daylight saving time thanks to a decrease in demand for electricity.

**28**

**THE FIRST WRIST-WATCH,** manufactured in 1868, was designed for a women and intended to be worn as jewelry.

**29**

An **EON**—the longest division of geologic time— is made up of **2 OR MORE ERAS.**

**30**

**MILITARY TIME** uses a 24-hour time scale and eliminates the need for the use of "a.m." and "p.m." One o'clock p.m. becomes 1300 hours.

**31**

The **JULIAN YEAR,** created by Julius Caesar, was 365.25 days long. To solve the problem of that extra quarter day each year, Leap Day was added every fourth year.

**32**

**KOEI'S SPACE PRINTER** in Osaka, Japan, arranges drops of water to display the time, as well as words, flowers, or other objects, until the next minute pops up.

**33**

Most scientists believe that **TIME BEGAN 13.77 BILLION YEARS** ago during the Big Bang that created the universe.

**34**

You'd never make your next appointment if you were relying on one of the **FIRST CLOCKS** made in 1344. It only had an hour hand and Roman numerals.

**35**

The ancient Romans, Egyptians, and Greeks divided the day into **TWO 12-HOUR PERIODS.** Hours varied in length as the amount of daylight changed.

**36**

The average time it takes for **1 HEARTBEAT** is 0.8 seconds. In 60 minutes you can have **4,500 HEART-BEATS.**

**37**

If the time for 1 game of soccer is 90 minutes, you could play **112 GAMES IN A WEEK**—if you didn't sleep, eat, or go to the bathroom.

**38**

China uses **1 TIME ZONE.** When it is 10 a.m. in Beijing, the sun might just be rising in faraway Tibet, but clocks there would still read 10 a.m.

**39**

A hummingbird's wings can beat **200 TIMES** every **SECOND.**

**40**

The time it takes for a **PAPER TOWEL** to decompose in the environment is **2 TO 4 WEEKS.** A disposable baby diaper takes **450 YEARS.**

**41**

Because the speed of Earth's rotation changes over time, a **DAY** in the age of **DINOSAURS** was just **23 HOURS** long.

**42**

An **ANCIENT WOODEN SUNDIAL** found in Greenland may unlock the mystery of how the Vikings navigated on their voyages.

**43**

The last cycle of the **MAYA CALENDAR** ended on December 21, 2012, but fortunately, the **WORLD DIDN'T END** as some predicted it would.

**44**

**RAMSES II'S TEMPLE** was engineered so that on the Egyptian ruler's birth and coronation dates the rising sun would shine on his golden statue.

**45**

To count seconds without a watch, you can say, **"ONE MISSISSIPPI,** two Mississippi." The British use, **"ONE PICCADILLY,** two Piccadilly."

**46**

Riverdance star **MICHAEL FLATLEY** holds the record for the most taps per second: **35.**

**47**

Since the TV show *60 MINUTES* first aired in 1968, it has used 3 different **STOPWATCHES** to tick away the minutes during the broadcast.

**48**

**COMMON ERA** (c.e.) and **BEFORE COMMON ERA** (b.c.e.) are other ways of saying the calendar terms a.d. and b.c.

**49**

If a day represented all events in Earth's history, the first humans would show up **40 SECONDS** before **MIDNIGHT.**

**50**

**BENJAMIN FRANKLIN** proposed daylight saving time in 1784 while he was an American delegate in Paris. He saw it as a way to save wax used in candlemaking.

**1** When building a waterslide, a construction crew follows the manufacturer's directions and puts the slide together piece by piece at the park. It's like assembling a **HUGE TOY RACETRACK!**

**2** Riders reach speeds of 65 miles an hour (105 kph) on the Insano waterslide at Beach Park in Fortaleza, Brazil.

**3** On the Conja waterslide at the Blue Bayou Water Park in Baton Rouge, Louisiana, U.S.A., riders sit one behind the other in a **RAFT THAT SPIRALS DOWN THE SLIDE.**

**4** Waterslides made out of *STAINLESS STEEL ARE FASTER* than those that are made out of fiberglass.

**5** THE 145,000-SQUARE-FOOT (13,471-M²) WAVE PALACE AT SIAM PARK IN SPAIN'S CANARY ISLANDS USES **185,000 gallons (700,301 L) of salt water** TO CREATE HUGE, OCEANLIKE WAVES FOR SURFERS.

**6** RIDERS ON THE DOLPHIN PLUNGE RIDE AT SEAWORLD FLORIDA, U.S.A., FEEL LIKE THEY ARE SWIMMING WITH **REAL DOLPHINS** AS THEY SLIDE THROUGH A CLEAR TUBE IN A DOLPHIN POOL.

# 25 SPLASHY FACTS ABOUT WATER

**7**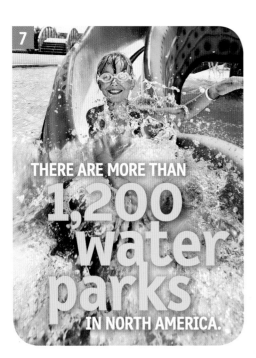
THERE ARE MORE THAN **1,200 water parks** IN NORTH AMERICA.

**8** HALF THE PEOPLE CHICKEN OUT WHEN THEY GET TO THE TOP OF THE BOMB BAY RIDE AT ORLANDO, FLORIDA'S WET 'N WILD PARK. **Dropping 76 feet (23 m)** STRAIGHT DOWN IS A SCARY THOUGHT.

**9**
You can wade in the water with STINGRAYS at SeaWorld Aquatica in San Antonio, Texas, U.S.A.

**10** A group raft ride in Wisconsin Dells, U.S.A., plunges riders into a 58-foot (18-m)-long tunnel with fake fog and lightning. **It's like riding into a hurricane.**

**11** In 2011, more than 2 million people visited Typhoon Lagoon in Orlando. That's more than the entire population of Slovenia, in eastern Europe.

**12** The **mile (1.6 km)-long** Raging River inner tube ride in Texas's Schlitterbahn (German for "slippery road") takes some **45 minutes** to complete.

**13** New water parks are designed to **CONSERVE WATER.** They generally use less water than people living in a neighborhood of about the same size.

**14** TEN OF THE TOP 20 WATER PARKS IN THE WORLD ARE IN ASIA; 6 ARE IN THE UNITED STATES, AND 4 OF THOSE ARE IN FLORIDA.

**15** The tight turns of the Constrictor ride at Wet 'N Wild in Phoenix, Arizona, U.S.A., make riders feel like they are traveling inside a giant snake.

**18** If you step on the wrong stones in the water maze at Hever Castle in England, you'll get soaked by a stream of water.

**16** PEOPLE LOVE WATER PARKS. IN 2011, THE TOP 20 IN THE WORLD ATTRACTED A TOTAL OF NEARLY **24 million visitors.**

**17** Riders inside a **CLEAR TUNNEL** pass through **A POOL OF SHARKS** on the Leap of Faith waterslide in the Bahamas.

**19** SEAWORLD SAN ANTONIO CONSERVES MORE THAN 25 MILLION GALLONS (95 MILLION L) OF WATER EACH YEAR. IT HAS EVEN WON A WATERSAVER PIONEER AWARD.

# PARKS

**20** SURFERS TRY TO GET AIR ON 9-FOOT (2.7-M)-HIGH WAVES IN THE WAVE POOL AT SUNWAY LAGOON IN MALAYSIA.

**21** Yas Waterworld in Abu Dhabi, in the United Arab Emirates, spreads across 37 acres (15 ha). That's more than 330 NBA-size basketball courts!

**22** In 24 hours, a man in Erding, Germany, covered 94.5 miles (152 km) riding one water-slide 427 times. That's about the distance between New York City and Philadelphia, U.S.A.!

**25** At 197 feet (60 m), the Divertical water ride in Italy's Mirabilandia theme park is **THE WORLD'S TALLEST—** taller than the U.S. Statue of Liberty from its base to the torch.

**23** Wisconsin Dells calls itself the "Waterpark Capital of the World." The town boasts more than 20 indoor and outdoor water parks.

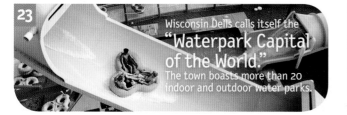

**24** On the Cannonball at Austria's Area 47 Water Park, riders are launched 33 feet (10 m) into the air and land with a huge splash in a lake.

# 15 SUPERCOOL FACTS

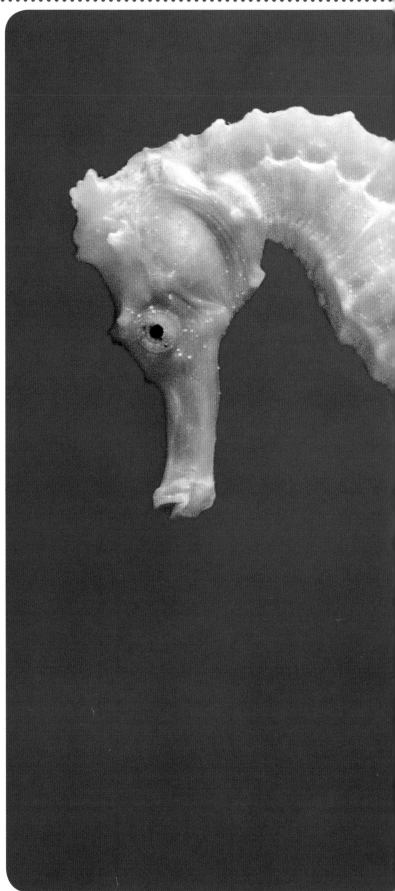

**1** SEAHORSE DADS, not moms, GIVE BIRTH TO THE BABIES.

**2** Male seahorses have a **FRONT POUCH** like a KANGAROO'S where they **CARRY THE EGGS UNTIL THEY HATCH.**

**3** Some species of seahorses **GIVE BIRTH** to up to **2,000 BABIES** at one time.

**4** A seahorse can **MOVE ITS EYES** in OPPOSITE DIRECTIONS—all the better to scan the water for food and predators.

**5** Seahorses are about the **SIZE OF AN M&M AT BIRTH.**

**6** From the start, **BABY SEAHORSES** are ON THEIR OWN TO FIND FOOD and hide from PREDATORS.

**7** Seahorses have NO **TEETH** and NO STOMACH. They use their **TUBELIKE SNOUTS** to suck in tiny animals like SHRIMP AND CRABS.

8 Most adult seahorses **WOULD FIT IN A TEACUP.** Only one species grows to be longer than a dinner plate is wide.

# ABOUT SEAHORSES

**9** Seahorses eat constantly and can CONSUME 3,000 or MORE TINY CRUSTACEANS a day.

**10** A group of seahorses is called a HERD.

**11** Seahorses use their CURLY TAILS to anchor themselves to coral, plants, and other things in the ocean SO THEY CAN FEED ON WHATEVER FLOATS BY.

**12** To stay hidden from predators, most seahorses CAN CHANGE COLOR TO BLEND IN WITH CORAL OR PLANTS.

**13** The DWARF SEAHORSE is a real SLOWPOKE. It travels only about 5 feet (1.5 m) in AN HOUR.

**14** Unlike most other fish, SEAHORSES stay with one mate their ENTIRE LIVES.

**15** Unlike most fish, seahorses are COVERED IN BONY PLATES rather than SCALES.

**Cliff diving in Kauai, Hawai'i**

**1** The blue whale eats 11,000 pounds (5,000 kg) of krill every day. That's almost 6 tons (5.5 MT) of food!

**2 HURRICANES CAN DROP 2.4 TRILLION GALLONS (9 TRILLION L) OF RAIN IN 24 HOURS.**

**3** Sections of the German autobahn, a high-speed expressway, have no speed limits. Although the recommended speed is 80 miles per hour (130 kph), the fastest recorded speed is 271.5 miles per hour (436.9 kph)!

**4** There is no land underneath the ice at the North Pole, but there is an entire continent beneath the South Pole.

**5** Skyaking is jumping out of a plane while sitting in a kayak and landing—with the help of a parachute—in a body of water.

**6** To stay cool out of water, hippos sweat what looks like red blood! This really thick, dark red mucus keeps their skin from getting sunburned.

**7** Able to survive at 21,325 feet (6,500 m), Himalayan jumping spiders live at a higher elevation than any other species. They eat frozen insects that winds blow up the slopes.

**8** The farthest known galaxy from Earth is 13.3 billion light-years away.

**9** Cliff diving has earned the nickname "tombstoning" because the sport has sent some jumpers to an early grave.

**10** Louis-Sebastien Lenormand survived a jump off an observation tower in France in 1783 using a wood-framed parachute that looked like an umbrella. He envisioned the device serving as a portable fire escape.

**11** While Death Valley, California, U.S.A., has the hottest air temperature—134°F (56.7°C)—Iran's Lut Desert recorded the hottest land surface temperature: 159.3°F (70.7°C).

**12 TO COOK AN EGG, A SIDEWALK NEEDS TO BE 158°F (70°C).**

**13** In 2012, skydiver Felix Baumgartner jumped out of a capsule that was carried more than 24 miles (39 km) above Earth by a balloon.

**14** Maryland, U.S.A., holds the record for the most rain to fall anyplace on Earth in 60 seconds: more than 1 inch (2.5 cm).

**15** The deepest part of the ocean, the Pacific's Mariana Trench, is nearly 7 miles (11 km) deep and 5 times longer than the Grand Canyon in Arizona, U.S.A.

**16** It would take 100 Earths, lined up end-to-end, to stretch across the face of the sun.

**17** Arica, Chile, once went 173 months without a drop of rain. That's more than 14 years!

**18** The longest mountain range on Earth is 90 percent underwater. The Mid-Ocean Ridge spans 40,389 miles (65,000 km) as it crisscrosses the globe.

**19** The platypus—one of only 2 kinds of mammals that lay eggs—is also the most venomous mammal. Its venom is powerful enough to kill a small animal.

**20** Venezuela's Angel Falls, the longest uninterrupted waterfall on Earth, has a 3,212-foot (979-m) drop. That's more than 17 times the height of North America's Niagara Falls.

**21** The fastest-ever Iditarod racer covered the 1,049-mile (1,688-km) course across the wilderness of Alaska, U.S.A., with his team of sled dogs in 8 days, 18 hours, and 46 minutes.

**22** The Dead Sea is 10 times saltier than the ocean.

# 75 FACTS THAT GO TO THE EXTREME

**23** The Badwater Ultramarathon is a 135-mile (217-km) run from the lowest point in California, U.S.A. (Death Valley) to the trailhead of its highest peak (Mount Whitney).

**24** A howler monkey's howls can be heard 3 miles (4.8 km) away.

**25** The Great Barrier Reef is the only living organism visible from space.

**26** Madagascar, which is about the size of Texas, U.S.A., is home to 5 percent of the world's plant and animal species.

**27** Less than half of 1 percent of Antarctica is ice-free.

**28** Frederic Weill accomplished a spectacular feat when he made an 86-foot (26-m) dive from a helicopter into an Italian lake.

**29** Maxwell Montes, the tallest mountain on Venus, is almost 7,000 feet (2,150 m) higher than Mt. Everest and may contain large quantities of fool's gold (iron pyrite).

**30** American Alex Honnold used no ropes or safety devices to climb the 2,130-foot (649-m)-high granite face of Half Dome in Yosemite National Park, California, in 2 hours and 45 minutes.

**31** Evel Knievel's attempt to jump a 1,600-foot (488-m)-wide canyon in Idaho, U.S.A., on a superpowered motorcycle failed when his parachute opened early and carried him to the canyon floor—without injury.

**32** The meteor that struck Earth 65 million years ago and is believed to have wiped out the dinosaurs was the size of San Francisco, California.

**33** Because a flea jumps so high—about 38 times its body length—it has adapted to withstand 100 Gs, or 100 times the force of gravity. (Fighter pilots can withstand only 8 or 9 Gs without special suits.)

**34** **A MAN ONCE BLEW A BUBBLE-GUM BUBBLE 20 INCHES (50.8 CM) IN DIAMETER. THAT'S MORE THAN TWICE AS BIG AS A BASKETBALL!**

**35** The bar-headed goose—the world's highest flying bird—migrates over the Himalaya, the world's highest mountain range.

**36** **AT ANY SINGLE MOMENT, THERE ARE ABOUT 20 VOLCANOES ERUPTING WORLD-WIDE—NOT COUNTING THE SEAFLOOR.**

**37** Vatican City, an independent country, is located entirely within the city of Rome, Italy.

**38** Remote Tristan da Cunha Island is 1,740 miles (2,800 km) from South Africa and has fewer than 300 people, but it has Internet access.

**39** The bulldog ant is considered the most dangerous kind of ant. It bites with sharp mandibles and has a sting that is lethal enough to kill a human.

**40** A saguaro cactus can store up to 200 gallons (757 L) of water in order to survive in the desert.

**41** Ski kiting—sometimes called snow kiting—is skiing or snowboarding while harnessed to a giant kite. Wind power can send you downhill at speeds of 62 miles per hour (100 kph).

**42** Researchers must wear ice-cooled suits while studying Mexico's Cave of Crystals. Temperatures exceed 112°F (44°C) because the cave lies above a cauldron of pressurized molten rock.

**43** More than 1.5 million wildebeests migrate in a 1,200-mile (1,931-km) loop through Africa's Serengeti every year in search of food and water.

**44** On the straightaways, NASCAR drivers travel almost the length of a football field in 1 second.

**45** The wingspan of the largest species of albatross is as wide as 3 baseball bats lined up end-to-end.

**46** There are about 332,519,000 cubic miles (1,386,000,000 km³) of water on the planet. That's the equivalent of over 36 sextillion (that's 36 with 21 zeros) gallons (136 sextillion L) of milk.

**47** When the Texas horned lizard is frightened, it can squirt a third of the volume of blood in its body out through a pore in its eye!

**48** An electric eel has 5 times the voltage of a household electrical outlet.

**49** The world's smallest movie was recently made by moving atoms to create images that show a boy playing with a ball and bouncing on a trampoline. The images had to be magnified 100 million times to be visible to the human eye.

**50** The weight of all the ants in the world is equal to that of all the humans in the world.

**51** **THE "INFINITY CHILLI SAUCE" IS 235 TIMES HOTTER THAN TABASCO SAUCE.**

**52** The Luther Burger, named after singer Luther Vandross, is a bacon cheeseburger sandwiched between 2 glazed doughnuts.

**53** A sailfish can swim 13 times faster than the fastest Olympic swimmer.

**54** The highest wave ever surfed was as tall as a 10-story building.

**55** Tibet's Yarlung Tsangpo is considered the "Everest" of rivers. At 13,000 feet (4,000 m), it has the highest average elevation of any major river in the world and is 3 times deeper than Arizona's Grand Canyon.

**56** Volcano surfers slide down active volcanoes on specially designed boards at speeds up to 50 miles per hour (80 kph).

**57** The world's largest tire, located in Allen Park, Michigan, U.S.A., was once a Ferris wheel at the 1964–65 New York World's Fair.

**58** The root system of a type of Christmas tree that grows in Sweden is as old as the last ice age!

**59** Tony Hawk got his first skateboard when he was 9 years old. He turned pro at 14.

**60** A 1920 baseball game ended in a 1-to-1 tie after 26 innings—the most innings ever played in a game. The umpire had to end the game because of darkness.

**61** The world's tallest tree—a coast redwood in California, U.S.A.—is about twice as high as the Statue of Liberty.

**62** The world's largest jack-o'-lantern weighed 1,810 pounds (821 kg)—that's as much as 4 African lions.

**63** In summer, the temperature on Mars can range from 70°F (21°C) at noon at the Equator, to a low of -225°F (-143°C) at the North or South Poles.

**64** Thrill seekers bungee jump from a 764-foot (233-m)-high platform on Macau Tower, in Macau, China. After a 4- to 5-second free fall, jumpers ultimately land on an air bag.

**65** The oldest Aldabra giant tortoise on record lived 255 years.

**66** Humans can survive only a few days without water. Camels can go at least a week without drinking and more than a month without eating!

**67** The world's largest cookie, made by a bakery in North Carolina, U.S.A., weighed over 40,000 pounds (18,144 kg). That's as much as at least 80 mountain gorillas!

**68** Zeus, a Great Dane, is the world's tallest dog. From paw to shoulder, he is 44 inches (112 cm) high and eats 15 pounds (6.8 kg) of dog food per week.

**69** Krubera Cave is at least 7,000 feet (2,134 m) deep—room enough to fit at least 5 of New York City's Empire State Buildings!

**70** In 1974, Philippe Petit walked back and forth on a high wire between New York City's two World Trade Center Towers for an hour while police waited on each side to arrest him.

**71** **THE AUSTRALIAN PELICAN'S BILL CAN STRETCH TO HOLD 3 GALLONS (11.4 L) OF WATER.**

**72** Winter Olympics luge athletes travel as fast as 86 miles per hour (138 kph). Street lugers have reached speeds of almost 100 miles per hour (161 kph)!

**73** *Argentinosaurus*, the largest known dinosaur, was the length of 3 school buses.

**74** *Tinkerbella nana*, a wasp named after Peter Pan's fairy friend, is a little bigger than the diameter of a human hair.

**75** Kids as young as 4 used to race on camels as jockeys in some Middle East countries, but they've been replaced by remote-control robots dressed as jockeys.

**1**

**ST. EDWARD'S CROWN** was made for England's King Charles II in 1661. The solid gold crown is covered in jewels, like amethysts, rubies, topazes, and sapphires.

**2**

**KING BHUMIBOL** of Thailand is the **RICHEST** royal in the world. His fortune is estimated at over $30 billion.

**3**

**QUEEN ELIZABETH II** of the United Kingdom and Northern Ireland loves corgis. She's owned over 30 of the fluffy pups.

**4**

In **THAILAND**, it is **ILLEGAL TO INSULT** any member of the royal family.

**5**

**QUEEN AMIDALA'S** regal and elaborate costumes in the movie *STAR WARS EPISODE I* were inspired by clothing from Tibet and Mongolia.

**6**

**PRINCESS DIANA** and Prince Charles of Wales reportedly brought 7,000 pounds (3,175 kg) of **LUGGAGE** on their first visit to the United States in 1985.

**7**

**THE NETHERLANDS** loves the color **ORANGE!** The Dutch royal family line is known as the House of Orange-Nassau, and the national color is orange.

**8**

**ELVIS PRESLEY**, also known as **THE KING**, once sang his famous song "Hound Dog" to a basset hound on TV.

**9**

An artist created a 16.5 ton (15 MT) sand sculpture of **BRITAIN'S PRINCE WILLIAM** and his wife, **KATE**, holding baby **PRINCE GEORGE**.

**10**

Almost overnight, Peggielene Bartels, a secretary in Washington, D.C., U.S.A., became the new king of Otuam, a village in Ghana. "**KING PEGGY**" replaced her uncle, who had died.

**11**

**BURGER KING**—the fast-food chain—had TV commercials in 1976 that featured characters like The King, Sir Shakes a Lot, the Duke of Doubt, and the Wizard of Fries.

**12**

Chinese emperor Qin Shi Huang Di's tomb was a **HUGE UNDERGROUND CITY**, complete with a terra-cotta (clay) army of more than 7,000 warriors, horse-drawn chariots, and weapons.

**13**

**QUEEN VICTORIA** of England started the tradition of **BRIDES** wearing **WHITE WEDDING DRESSES**.

**King Peggy of Otuam**

**14** In a **CONSTITUTIONAL MONARCHY**, laws are made by an elected government, as in Great Britain, Japan, and Denmark, not the king or queen.

**15** An **ABSOLUTE MONARCH** is one who makes all decisions and has ultimate authority. Most of the few remaining, such as in Oman and Saudi Arabia, are in the Middle East.

**16** **HADRIAN**, whose rule began in A.D. 117, was the first Roman emperor to have a **BEARD** during his reign.

**17** **HATSHEPSUT** was one of the few women Egyptian pharaohs. Among the monuments she built are two 10-story, 450-ton (408-MT) obelisks that were towed down the Nile by 27 ships.

**18** In 1922, India's **NAWAB OF JUNAGADH** invited thousands of guests to a **LAVISH ROYAL WEDDING** for his dog Roshanara and Bobby, a golden retriever.

**19** The **HEART** of England's King Richard I (Richard the Lionheart) was **MUMMIFIED** after his death in 1199 and placed in a **LEAD BOX** in a church in France.

**20** Archaeologists believe King Arthur's **CAMELOT** was an old **ROMAN AMPHITHEATER** in Chester, England. The "round table" where he met with his knights was the circle in the middle.

**21** In 2010, the **ROYAL CANADIAN MINT** issued a ferocious-looking, special-edition 50-cent coin. One side features an animated *DASPLETOSAURUS*—one of *T. rex*'s relatives!

# 35 REGAL FACTS ABOUT ROYALTY

**22** Queen Elizabeth II has visited over 116 **COUNTRIES** during her 60-year reign, but she **DOESN'T HAVE A PASSPORT.**

**23** **TOPKAPI PALACE**, built in Istanbul by Sultan Mehmed II in what is now Turkey, still houses its prize piece: an 86-carat diamond called the Spoonmaker's Diamond.

**24** **ENGLAND'S WILLIAM THE CONQUEROR** had a gruesome burial. When his obese body was stuffed into his small coffin, his abdomen is said to have **EXPLODED.**

**25** What is now the U.S. state of **HAWAII** was once a kingdom. **QUEEN LILIUOKALANI**, its last monarch, was overthrown in 1893.

**26** The **SKELETON** of England's **KING RICHARD III** was found beneath a **PARKING LOT** in Leicester, England, more than 500 years after his death.

**27** **MARIE ANTOINETTE** loved being royal and rich. She once made a model farm at the palace so she and her handmaidens could play milkmaids and shepherdesses.

**28** On the way to the **GUILLOTINE** where she was beheaded, Marie Antoinette **APOLOGIZED TO THE EXECUTIONER** for accidentally stepping on his foot.

**29** In 1736, before her marriage to Frederick, Prince of Wales, the nervous Augusta of Saxe-Gotha **THREW UP** all over her wedding dress and her **MOTHER-IN-LAW**-to-be.

**30** One queen of **ENGLAND** never even went there! Berengaria of Navarre in northern Spain married King Richard the Lionheart in 1191, but she **NEVER SET FOOT** in his homeland.

**31** **GRACE KELLY** quit her successful acting career to marry Prince Rainier of Monaco in 1956. To become princess, she had to pay a **$2 MILLION DOWRY.**

**32** In 1252, King Haakon of Norway gave what may have been a **POLAR BEAR** to England's Henry III. The white bear sometimes swam in the River Thames.

**33** Attila, the brutal **KING OF THE HUNS**—barbarian invaders from central Asia—called himself *flagellum Dei*, "the scourge of God."

**34** According to legend, **KING SOLOMON** was given a magical ring called the Seal of Solomon. Today, Jewish people know the symbol on the ring as the **STAR OF DAVID.**

**35** Even ancient royalty loved **ICE CREAM!** Alexander the Great was said to enjoy snow and ice flavored with honey or nectar.

**1.** The world's largest reproduction of the "Mona Lisa" is a paint-by-number that is 50 times the size of the original. **2.** Using only clothes hangers, a Scottish artist made a 7-foot (2.1-m) sculpture of a gorilla beating its chest. **3.** The Museum of Bad Art in Massachusetts, U.S.A., collects and exhibits what its curators consider bad art. Admission is free. **4.** The Matchstick Marvels Tourist Center in Iowa, U.S.A., has on display an 8-foot (2.4-m)-long replica of Notre Dame Cathedral made from 400,000 matchsticks. **5.** For 47 days no one noticed that a painting by Henri Matisse was hung upside down at the Museum of Modern Art in New York City, U.S.A. **6.** Some people thought Auguste Rodin's bronze sculptures were so realistic that he was accused of forming the molds around live bodies. **7.** Sixteenth-century Italian painter Giuseppe Arcimboldo painted fruits, vegetables, and bits of nature that, when put together, looked like a humorous human portrait. **8.** Sometimes Jackson Pollock, an abstract expressionist, signed his paintings with his handprint. **9.** Leonardo da Vinci kept the "Mona Lisa" with him until he died. **10.** Op artists create works that are optical illusions. A series of wavy lines or rows of dots can appear to move if you stare at them long enough! **11.** During the American Civil War, newspapers hired sketch artists to draw the battles they saw for publication. **12.** The painting "American Gothic" appears to show a farmer with a pitchfork standing next to his daughter. The real people who posed for the painting were the artist's sister and his dentist. **13.** Before he painted a scene of a boat on the rough sea, J. M. W. Turner tied himself to the mast of a ship to experience what violent wind and thrashing waves felt like. **14.** Van Gogh, a post-impressionist painter, signed his work with only his first name, Vincent. **15.** Did van Gogh really cut off part of his own ear? No one knows for sure, but he did paint a portrait of himself with his ear bandaged. **16.** Some of the most famous pieces by pop artist Andy Warhol are of canned soup. One painting of 4 stacked soup cans recently sold for nearly $10 million. **17.** American artist Jeff Koons has created 10-foot (3-m)-tall colored, stainless-steel sculptures of dogs shaped like twisted balloons. **18.** Jackson Pollock laid huge canvases on the floor and used a brush or even just a stick to splatter paint on them—straight from a can. **19.** A 4-story stainless-steel sculpture of a West Highland terrier puppy was covered with more than 70,000 flowering plants and put on display at the Guggenheim Museum in Bilbao, Spain. **20.** The first known paintings were of stenciled hands. They were made on cave walls in Spain more than 40,000 years ago. **21.** Cave painters crushed colored rock into a powder and mixed it with animal fat or plant sap to make paint. **22.** When ancient Egyptian artists drew humans, the eyes faced the viewer—even in profile—but the feet always faced sideways. **23.** To paint the ceiling of the Sistine Chapel in what is now Vatican City, Michelangelo had to stand on a platform with his neck bent back. This caused terrible headaches. **24.** To better understand the human body, Michelangelo dissected bodies he dug up at a graveyard. **25.** The statue of Nike of Samothrace, the winged goddess of victory, stands at the Louvre, a museum in Paris, France, just as she was found—headless, footless, and armless. **26.** A drought in the southwestern United States during the 1930s inspired artist Georgia O'Keeffe to paint her famous cow skulls.

# 100

## FACTS ABOUT

## MASTERPIECE ART

**27.** The Bayeux Tapestry, an embroidered piece of linen longer than an Olympic-size swimming pool, shows more than 70 scenes that represent the Norman conquest of England in 1066. **28.** Pierre-Auguste Renoir, who suffered from a disease that caused pain in his hands, eventually had to paint by strapping a brush to his arm. **29.** Steve Jobs, co-founder of Apple, studied calligraphy in college and later used his skills when designing the typography for Apple's Macintosh computer. **30.** A café at the Museum of Modern Art in San Francisco, California, U.S.A., serves up desserts that mimic pieces of modern art. **31.** Famed artist Marcel Duchamp once bought a urinal, wrote the name R. Mutt on it, and entered it in an art show. **32.** A man once paid some $12 million for a dead tiger shark suspended in a tank of formaldehyde. **33.** M. C. Escher was known for drawing pictures that morphed into other pictures. "Drawing Hands" shows a hand drawing another hand, which is drawing the first hand. **34.** A woman in Russia created colorful designs on the outside of her home using 30,000 plastic bottle caps. **35.** "Cupid's Span" is a 6-story, stainless-steel-and-fiberglass bow and arrow on the waterfront in San Francisco, California. **36.** Some of the paintings and sculptures that come to life in the movie *Night at the Museum 2: Battle of the Smithsonian* aren't even in the Smithsonian's collection! **37.** A piece from Claude Monet's "Water Lilies" series was recently auctioned for over $43 million. The money was given to a school. **38.** Over the past 100 years, the 17th-century painting "The Night Watch" by Rembrandt van Rijn has been attacked twice with a knife and had acid thrown on it once. **39.** A woman fell into a Pablo Picasso painting on display at a gallery, causing a 6-inch (15-cm) tear. The painting is still valued at $130 million. **40.** Two different versions of Edvard Munch's painting "The Scream," which shows a distressed figure against a blood-red sky, have been stolen from museums. Both were recovered. **41.** Nothing is known about the person in Johannes Vermeer's painting "Girl With a Pearl Earring," but that didn't stop a woman from writing a popular novel about her. **42.** A painting of 2 men playing cards by Paul Cézanne was bought for a quarter of a billion dollars—the most ever paid for any piece of art. **43.** The glass pyramid at the entrance to the Louvre museum in Paris is made up of 673 diamond- and triangular-shaped glass panels. **44.** A California "sand artist" drags garden tools and rolls of fence behind a car across the desert to make geometric shapes that can be seen from flying aircraft. **45.** A mobile by sculptor Alexander Calder that hangs in the National Gallery of Art in Washington, D.C., U.S.A., weighs as much as 2 mountain gorillas. **46.** France's Lascaux Cave, site of some of the world's oldest and most famous cave art, was discovered in 1940 by 4 boys looking for their dog. **47.** A group of artists knitted a 200-foot (61-m)-long pink rabbit that can be seen from space! **48.** People who had their photographs taken in the 19th century had to sit perfectly still for up to 8 seconds, or the picture would be blurry. **49.** U.S. astronaut Alan Bean became an artist after he retired. His paintings re-create his space explorations. **50.** A man in London, England, paints pictures on wads of chewing gum that people spit out on city sidewalks. **51.** The oldest known body art is on the 5,300-year-old mummy known as Iceman. His tattoos were made by rubbing charcoal into tiny cuts in his skin. **52.** Reportedly, Pablo Picasso's first spoken word was *piz*, short for *lápiz*, which means "pencil" in Spanish. **53.** Famed Spanish surrealist Salvador Dalí created the logo for Chupa Chups lollipops. **54.** Mexican artist Diego Rivera created 2.5 miles (4 km) of murals in his lifetime. All show the struggle between rich and poor people. **55.** "The Night Watch" wasn't titled for about 150 years after Rembrandt painted it. By then, it had darkened with age, making it look like a night scene. **56.** To warm up his fingers, French painter and sculptor Henri Matisse would play the violin before he started working. **57.** Marcel Duchamp collected dust on a pane of glass for a year, then covered it with thin cement. The work now hangs in the Philadelphia Museum of Art in Pennsylvania, U.S.A. **58.** French artist Edgar Degas painted more than 1,500 paintings of dancers—many from a behind-the-scenes perspective. **59.** Most oil brushes are made from hog bristle—the hair on a pig's back. **60.** After Michelangelo's sculpture "David" was completed, it took 40 men 4 days to move it a half mile (0.8 km) from his workshop in Florence, Italy, to the city plaza. **61.** William Wegman made a successful career out of dressing up, then photographing or making videos of, his Weimaraner dogs. **62.** Christo's "Running Fence," a 24.5-mile (39.4-km)-long, 18-foot (5.5-m)-tall piece of nylon fabric held up with steel poles, stood on hillsides in northern California for 2 weeks. **63.** The special Google logos that change on the home page with holidays and events are made by illustrators called doodlers. **64.** During his lifetime, Pablo Picasso created over 20,000 drawings, sculptures, and paintings. **65.** Porcupine quills are used in Native American embroidery. **66.** Tossing a coin in the Trevi Fountain in Rome, Italy, is said to ensure a quick return to the city. **67.** A Japanese artist creates fog sculptures by releasing water vapor from tiny nozzles. **68.** X-ray-style rock art created by Australian Aborigines 4,000 years ago shows an animal's bones and organs inside an outline of its body. **69.** The farmer who found "Venus de Milo," the famous armless statue of the Greek goddess, also found part of the hand from her missing left arm. It holds an apple. **70.** Egyptian tomb paintings showed scenes of daily life to ensure the dead person's happiness in the afterlife. **71.** Some zoo animals get art supplies to help keep their minds sharp. **72.** Giraffes carved into stone nearly 8,000 years ago are evidence that Niger's Tenere Desert was once a lush landscape. **73.** The annual Nail Olympics determine who can create the best fingernail art. **74.** Scans of the "Mona Lisa" show that she might once have had eyebrows, but they have faded with time. **75.** Japanese artist Katsushika Hokusai signed one of his last paintings The Art-Crazy Old-Man. **76.** In his old age, when he could no longer stand or see well, Henri Matisse turned to cutting shapes out of paper and arranging them into collages. **77.** Some of the plants in Henri Rousseau's famous jungle scenes were inspired by houseplants. He never traveled to the tropics. **78.** A 27-foot (8.2-m)-tall harp plays music that is strummed by the wind on a pier in San Francisco. **79.** Artist Keith Haring drew his early chalk drawings on blank advertising spaces while riding the subway in New York City. **80.** As a tribute to his love of jelly beans, a portrait of President Ronald Reagan was made out of 10,000 Jelly Belly–brand jelly beans. **81.** A British street artist known as Banksy keeps his real identity a secret, but his work pops up on walls, bridges, and roadways around the world. **82.** Enough Crayola crayons are made every year to circle the globe 6 times! **83.** Swiss sculptor Alberto Giacometti stayed up all night making his "Man Pointing" figure. It was still wet when he sold it the next day! **84.** The ancient Nasca lines in the desert of Peru take the shapes of gigantic geometrical figures and animals when seen from the air. **85.** The wingspan of the "Angel of the North," a steel sculpture in England, almost equals that of a 747 jet! **86.** The fingers and thumb of a hand coming out of the Atacama Desert in Chile are as tall as 5 stacked camels! **87.** Artist Damien Hirst used real teeth in his platinum-and-diamond-covered cast of a human skull! **88.** George Vlosich spends up to 80 hours on an Etch A Sketch, creating art that has sold for $10,000. **89.** Lascaux Cave has been closed to the public for more than 50 years because the carbon monoxide exhaled by crowds of tourists was destroying the paintings on the walls. **90.** The Trash Museum in New York City is a collection of tossed items salvaged by a city garbage worker. **91.** It took a college student more than 330 hours and 65,000 rubber bands to make a chair strong enough to support an adult! **92.** A man spent 2 summers building a sand-castle replica of Minas Tirith, the castle in *The Lord of the Rings*. **93.** A British artist transforms used cardboard into life-size bicycles and pianos. **94.** There's a sculpture of a giraffe covered in bottle caps at the Smithsonian American Art Museum in Washington, D.C. **95.** To create replicas of famous paintings on bananas, an artist pricks the skin with a pushpin to make "lines" of brown spots. **96.** Ice sculptors compete to turn 300-pound (136-kg) blocks of frozen water into art. **97.** A Taiwanese artist paints portraits on grains of rice! **98.** Liu Bolin makes "invisible art" by camouflaging his body to blend in to his surroundings, then taking a photo. **99.** Researchers found that doodling in class can help students pay better attention. **100.** An American artist creates sculptures by covering spiderwebs with colorful spray paint.

**1** Ancient Greeks and Romans believed in many mythical gods and goddesses who looked like people, but had **SUPERHUMAN POWERS.**

**2** According to myths, the gods and goddesses **CONTROLLED EVERYTHING** from the weather to the outcome of wars.

**3** The word "myth" comes from the **GREEK WORD** *MYTHOS,* referring to stories about the supernatural.

**4** A Greek poet wrote the first myth about **3,000 YEARS AGO.**

**5** Twelve Greek gods and goddesses—known as the Olympians—ruled the universe from **MOUNT OLYMPUS,** an enormous mountain that soared above the clouds.

**6** The ancient Romans **ADOPTED THE GREEK GODS** and goddesses but gave them new names.

**7** In Roman mythology, Zeus was called **JUPITER.**

**8** The Greek name for the 12 Olympians is *DODEKATHEON.*

**9** Zeus, the most powerful of all the Greek gods, was **RELATED** to every member of the *Dodekatheon.*

**10** The **TALLEST PEAK** in Greece is Mount Olympus, named for the mythical mountain.

**11** The ancient Greeks believed that natural disasters, like floods and thunderstorms, were Zeus's way of **PUNISHING EVIL MEN.**

**12** Cyclopes—giants with a **SINGLE EYE** in the middle of their foreheads—gave Zeus the gifts of thunder and lightning for freeing them from the underworld.

**13** Zeus had a **WINGED HORSE** named **PEGASUS** that carried his lightning bolts and an **EAGLE** that retrieved them.

**14** The ancient Greeks built **TEMPLES,** usually out of stone, to honor their gods and goddesses.

**15** People brought food, flowers, and money to the temples, or they sacrificed an animal as an **OFFERING TO THE GODS.**

**16** The Colossus of Rhodes, a **GIANT BRONZE SCULPTURE** of the sun god Helios, was an inspiration for the Statue of Liberty in the United States.

**17** The Romans turned to people called **SOOTHSAYERS** to tell them what the gods wanted and to predict the future by looking at the insides of dead animals.

**18** The still-standing Temple of Olympian Zeus in Athens, Greece, took almost **700 YEARS** to complete.

# 50 MYSTIFYING FACTS ABOUT GREEK&ROMAN MYTHOLOGY

**A statue of Poseidon**

**The Parthenon on the Acropolis, Athens**

**19**
The website Amazon.com is named for the Amazons, a nation of **ALL-FEMALE WARRIORS** in Greek mythology.

**20**
The *Titanic* got its name from **THE TITANS**, the gigantic, powerful beings often mentioned in Greek myths.

**21**
Neptune, the Roman god of the sea, had a son called Triton, who was **HALF-MAN, HALF-FISH.**

**22**
Hermes, the Greek name for the **MESSENGER OF THE GODS**, was said to have invented boxing and gymnastics.

**23**
The Olympic Games were named for their location at **OLYMPIA** in Greece.

**24**
**POSEIDON**, the Greek god of the sea, lived in a coral palace and drove a chariot pulled by horses on the ocean floor. In art, he's usually shown with dolphins.

**25**
Poseidon had the power to **SHAPE-SHIFT** and sometimes appeared as a horse.

**26**
Nike sneakers are named after the Greek **GODDESS OF VICTORY.**

**27**
To punish the mortal Medusa for being too vain, Athena, the Greek goddess of wisdom and war, turned her into a monster with **VENOMOUS SNAKES FOR HAIR.**

**28**
Many **CONSTELLATIONS**, like Heracles—or Hercules—**GET THEIR NAMES** from Greek and Roman mythology.

**29**
It's said that Ares, the Greek god of war, murder, and bloodshed, had a throne on Mount Olympus that was covered in **HUMAN SKIN.**

**30**
The Apollo spacecraft, which landed American astronauts on the moon, was named for the Greek god Apollo, who rode through the skies on a **GOLDEN CHARIOT.**

**31**
Director George Lucas got many of his ideas for the **STAR WARS** movies from Greek mythology.

**32**
After Zeus married his sister Hera, they took a 300-year-long **HONEYMOON.**

**33**
The origins of modern Mother's Day are linked to the spring celebrations in ancient Greece in honor of Rhea, known as the **MOTHER OF THE GODS.**

**34**
The month of January is named for Janus, the Roman **GOD OF BEGINNINGS.**

**35**
Pluto, the Roman god of the **UNDERWORLD** (known as Hades in Greek mythology), wore a helmet that made him invisible and drove a chariot pulled by 4 black horses.

**36**
Hermes, known as **MERCURY** in Roman mythology, appears in more myths than any other god.

**37**
Zeus's daughter Athena was said to have **SPRUNG FROM HIS HEAD.**

**38**
Cerberus, a vicious **3-HEADED DOG**, guarded the gates to the underworld. Mourners at funerals would leave honey cakes to please him.

**39**
Athens, the capital of Greece, is named for the goddess **ATHENA.**

**40**
Aphrodite, the Greek **GODDESS OF LOVE**, is said to have been born from the foam of the sea.

**41**
**PLUTO**, a dark and distant dwarf planet, was named for the Roman god of the underworld.

**42**
The famous statue of **VENUS DE MILO**, believed to depict the goddess of love, is over 2,000 years old.

**43**
Eros, or Cupid—the god of love—could over-power the minds of gods and men by **SHOOTING THEM** with his arrows. Although very old, he looked like a little boy.

**44**
Hercules, a half-god, half-human son of Jupiter, was so strong that he **KILLED A LION** with his bare hands.

**45**
Mars, the Roman **GOD OF WAR**, was the father of Romulus and Remus, the legendary founders of Rome.

**46**
The **GOLD-AND-IVORY** statue of Athena that stood in the Parthenon in Athens was taller than a 3-story building and con-tained more than 2,500 pounds (1,144 kg) of gold.

**47**
The word "museum" stems from the Greek *museion*, meaning "HOUSE OF THE MUSES"—goddesses of the arts.

**48**
Pan, the **GOD OF MUSIC**, was famous for playing his flute. People still play the instrument—called a panpipe—today.

**49**
The word "lunar" comes from Luna, the Roman **GODDESS OF THE MOON.**

**50**
There's a 5,000-year-old altar on a mountaintop in Greece that's believed to be the mythical **BIRTHPLACE OF ZEUS.**

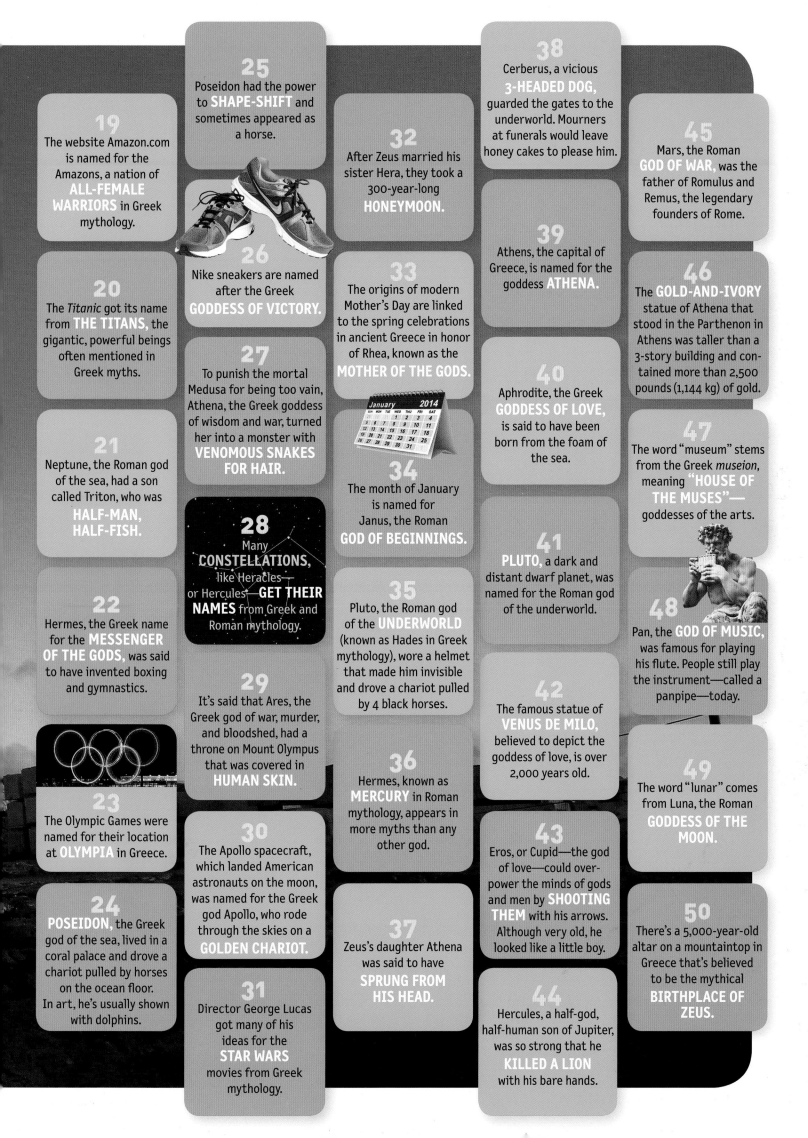

**1** Bilbo, a 7-year-old Newfoundland, is credited with saving at least 3 lives as Britain's only canine lifeguard.

**2** A black Lab named Tucker is helping researchers find out why the killer whale population off Washington State, U.S.A., is dwindling by SNIFFING OUT THEIR POOP in the ocean.

**3** Giant African rats have helped clear more than 7 million square yards (6 million m²) of land mines in Mozambique, where over 800 people are killed by mines each month.

**4** DANIEL GREENE HAS AN UNUSUAL SERVICE ANIMAL. IT'S A 5-FOOT (1.5-M) BOA CONSTRICTOR THAT ALERTS HIM WHEN HE'S ABOUT TO HAVE A SEIZURE.

**5** Historic Human Remains Detection dogs, working with archaeologists, can sniff the difference between a human bone and one from an animal.

# 25 HELPFUL FACTS ABOUT ANIMALS

**6** Cats not only offer sailors companionship at sea, they also help KEEP SHIPS FREE FROM RATS that would spread disease and raid the kitchen.

**7** Honk! Honk! GUARD GEESE WILL ALERT YOU RIGHT AWAY IF AN INTRUDER COMES NEAR YOUR PROPERTY. EVEN THE U.S. MILITARY HAS STARTED USING THEM.

**8** Roselle, a Seeing Eye dog, guided her master down 78 floors when the World Trade Center was attacked in 2001.

**9** The American Kennel Club estimates that there are 50,000 registered therapy animals in the United States, including potbellied pigs and llamas.

**10** Move over, sheepdogs. Donkeys can be just as helpful at protecting sheep from coyotes.

**11** Jim Egger's parrot Sadie helps calm his bipolar behavior. When he starts to get upset or agitated, Sadie tells him to calm down.

**12** LILA HAS A SEVERE PEANUT ALLERGY, BUT PIXIE, HER ALLERGY-ALERT DOG, KEEPS HER SAFE BY SNIFFING OUT ANYTHING THAT MIGHT TRIGGER A REACTION.

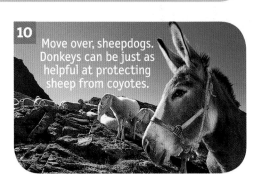

**13**

## Cats can

relieve stress, calm your nerves, and lower your blood pressure. That's why there's a growing demand for them in nursing homes.

**14**

LLAMAS MAKE GREAT PACK ANIMALS. THEY DON'T EAT MUCH, AND THEIR HOOVES LEAVE NO TRACE.

**15**

## SGT. STUBBY

was the first United States war dog. He received many medals for his bravery and met 3 presidents— Wilson, Harding, and Coolidge.

**16**

BEAGLES AS FEDERAL AGENTS? The Beagle Brigade, used in 21 international airports in the U.S., keeps a yearly average of 75,000 illegal items out of the country.

**17**

MINIATURE HORSES make terrific guide animals for the blind and live on average 25 to 35 years. That's much longer than a Seeing Eye dog.

# ON THE JOB

**18**

Minnie, a Helping Hands Capuchin monkey, can pick up the phone, turn on the computer, and do lots of other tasks for her paralyzed owner.

**19**

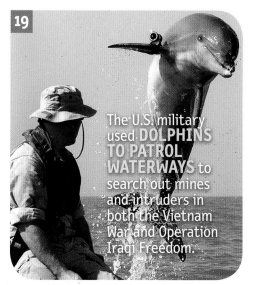

The U.S. military used **DOLPHINS TO PATROL WATERWAYS** to search out mines and intruders in both the Vietnam War and Operation Iraqi Freedom.

**20**

All the dogs that played Lassie on TV had **DOG COMPANIONS,** including a pair of poodles named Buttons and Bows, to play with on the set.

**21**

MORE THAN 250,000 CARRIER PIGEONS WERE USED DURING WWII TO TRANSPORT CODED MESSAGES.

**22**

MIDGE, AN 8-POUND (3.6-KG) CHIHUAHUA-TERRIER MIX, IS THE TINIEST POLICE DOG IN THE WORLD.

**23**

You might think of horses as being only on farms or racetracks, but there are about 60 serving with the mounted police in New York City, U.S.A.

**24**

Pigs can help sniff out expensive, tasty truffles from as deep as 3 feet (1 m) underground.

**25**

It's no wonder **DALMATIANS BECAME BELOVED FIREHOUSE MASCOTS.** They once ran beside the horses that pulled fire carriages, protecting them from nipping neighborhood dogs.

# 15 FACTS ABOUT

**1** A house outside of Denver, Colorado, U.S.A., is **OUT OF THIS WORLD.** When viewed from **FAR AWAY,** it looks like a **UFO HOVERING OVER A MOUNTAIN.**

**2** A businessman in Mumbai, India, spent $1 billion to build a **40-STORY HOUSE,** complete with **3 HELICOPTER PADS** and a **50-SEAT MOVIE THEATER.**

**3** A renovated **MISSILE SILO** left over from the COLD WAR turns into the perfect UNDERGROUND HIDEOUT home in upstate New York, U.S.A. An aboveground house **CAMOUFLAGES THE ENTRANCE** to the subterranean silo.

**4** Ever wonder what it would be like to live in a **TOPSY-TURVY** house? People who visit the **UPSIDE-DOWN HOUSE** in **POLAND** say it makes them feel **DIZZY.**

**5** The HOBBIT HOUSE in Switzerland is sunk into a mountain, and you enter through a **SECRET ENTRANCE** in a neighboring barn.

**6** In the 1930s, famed architect FRANK LLOYD WRIGHT built a house over a **WATERFALL** in western Pennsylvania, U.S.A. He named it **FALLINGWATER.**

**7** If you're afraid of heights, you won't like the **MINISTER'S TREE HOUSE** in Crossville, Tennessee, U.S.A. It's **10 STORIES TALL** and takes up 10,000 square feet (929 m²). That's nearly a quarter of an acre (1 ha).

**8** There's a company that sells a house measuring only 7 x 11 FEET (2 x 3.4 m) that includes a **BEDROOM,** BATHROOM, **KITCHEN,** and **LIVING ROOM.**

# FUNKY HOUSES

**9** J.K. ROWLING, author of the Harry Potter books, got **SPECIAL PERMISSION** to build two HOGWARTS-STYLE PLAY-HOUSES for her kids, complete with **SECRET TUNNELS** and a rope bridge.

**10** An APARTMENT in New York City, U.S.A., just might make you **SEASICK.** The master bedroom looks like the INSIDE OF A SHIP.

**11** If the owners of **"SAFE HOUSE" IN POLAND** get **SPOOKED,** they can CLOSE UP ALL THE WINDOWS and doors, pull up the **DRAWBRIDGE,** and turn the house into a **SOLID CUBE.**

12 A house in Pittsford, New York, looks just like a **GIANT MUSHROOM** nestled in the **WOODS.**

**13** The view from the windows of an **OLYMPIC AIRWAYS 727 JET** is of trees, not clouds. A man living near PORTLAND, OREGON, U.S.A., REFURBISHED the OLD PLANE and now calls it **HOME.**

**14** The **MOUNTAIN RETREAT** of a Portuguese family is wedged between **2 HUGE BOULDERS** that make the stone house look like something out of a **FLINTSTONES** cartoon.

**15** An **EARTHSHIP HOUSE** is the ultimate in living **"GREEN."** One family built theirs out of ALUMINUM CANS and used **TIRES** packed with—**EARTH.**

# 75 JUICY FACTS ABOUT FRUITS & VEGGIES

1. There are over 500 different kinds of bananas.

2. Holding a slice of cucumber between your tongue and the roof of your mouth for about 90 seconds can help fight bad breath.

3. **THE LARGEST FRUIT SALAD EVER MADE WEIGHED MORE THAN AN ELEPHANT AND WAS BIG ENOUGH TO FILL A LARGE, INFLATABLE SWIMMING POOL.**

4. Many fruits, including apples, peaches, and plums, are members of the rose family.

5. Every strawberry has about 200 seeds.

6. Pumpkins and avocados are fruits, not vegetables.

7. Orange carrots weren't produced until the 16th century. Before that, people ate red, purple, and yellow varieties.

8. For the Night of the Radishes festival in Oaxaca, Mexico, artists create elaborate carvings of people and animals out of giant radishes.

9. Peppers are known as capsicums in Australia.

10. Watermelon seeds were found in King Tut's tomb.

11. Some pear trees can produce fruit for more than 100 years.

12. In 1893, the United States Supreme Court ruled the tomato was a vegetable, not a fruit, to protect farmers from a hefty import tax.

13. Some carrots grow longer than an SUV.

14. During the U.S. Civil War, soldiers used soybeans to brew "coffee" because coffee beans were scarce.

15. It's believed that grapefruit got its name because the fruit grows in bunches, like grapes.

16. The average person in the United States eats 20 pounds (9 kg) of onions each year.

17. It takes only 1 ounce (28 g) of celery seeds to grow more than 30,000 plants.

18. Green peppers are actually unripe red or yellow peppers.

19. Only 5 percent of peas sold around the world are bought fresh—the rest are frozen or canned.

20. **STUDIES SHOW THAT SMELLING AN ORANGE CAN MAKE YOU FEEL LESS STRESSED.**

21. The Egyptians who built the pyramids were paid with radishes, onions, and garlic.

22. A man once peeled and ate 3 kiwifruits in 21.1 seconds.

23. By grafting (implanting) buds from different trees, a man in Chile created a tree that grows apricots, cherries, nectarines, plums, and peaches.

24. **IT TAKES AT LEAST 4 WEEKS FOR A BANANA PEEL TO DECOMPOSE.**

25. Some apples can weigh about as much as a half gallon (2 L) of milk.

26. Humans have been growing onions since 3500 B.C.

27. Chewing crunchy veggies, like carrots and celery, helps remove plaque from your teeth.

28. Bell peppers become sweeter as they ripen.

29. Cantaloupes are named for Cantalupo, Italy, where they were first grown.

30. One jicama, a member of the potato family, can weigh up to 50 pounds (23 kg)—as much as a 7-year-old child.

31. Lettuce belongs to the sunflower family.

32. Raspberries aren't just red. They can also be black, purple, or golden.

33. The ancient Greeks made golden replicas of radishes as an offering to the gods.

**34** Florida, U.S.A., produces around 2 million tons (1.8 million MT) of grapefruit every year.

**35** Tomatoes were once called love apples.

**36** Spanish explorers called pineapples *piñas* because they thought the fruit resembled pinecones.

**37** Madame Tallien, a French socialite who lived at the turn of the 19th century, was famous for taking baths in strawberry juice.

**38** The state vegetable of Oklahoma, U.S.A., is the watermelon.

**39** Kiwis grow on vines, like grapes.

**40** Native Americans used cranberry juice to dye clothing, rugs, and blankets.

**41** In the 15th century, women in Europe wore lacy carrot flowers in their hair.

**42 CORN IS GROWN ON EVERY CONTINENT EXCEPT ANTARCTICA.**

**43** Papaya seeds taste like black pepper.

**44** Wild banana plants can grow to be 30 feet (9 m) tall. That's as high as a 3-story building.

**45** Blueberries are the only blue fruit found in nature.

**46** One sweet potato contains the same amount of vitamin A as 23 cups (5,216 g) of broccoli.

**47** The "belly buttons" on navel oranges are actually another orange starting to grow.

**48** Rubbing the inside of a banana peel on a mosquito bite can reduce swelling and redness.

**49 IF ALL OF THE STRAWBERRIES GROWN EACH YEAR WERE LAID END-TO-END, THEY WOULD WRAP AROUND EARTH 15 TIMES.**

**50** There are about 600 kernels on every ear of corn.

**51** One-third of the world's pineapples are grown in Hawaii, U.S.A.

**52** Pattypan squash looks like a miniature flying saucer.

**53** An Israeli artist uses vegetables to re-create famous paintings, like the "Mona Lisa" by Leonardo da Vinci.

**54 APPLES ARE 25 PERCENT AIR AND FLOAT IN WATER.**

**55** When cranberries are ripe, they will bounce off the ground like a rubber ball. That's why they're sometimes called bounce berries.

**56** Native Caribbeans placed pineapples outside their homes to symbolize friendship.

**57** There's an orchestra in Vienna, Austria, that plays instruments made entirely from vegetables.

**58** People eat over 900 percent more broccoli today than they did 25 years ago.

**59** Kiwi is sometimes used as a natural meat tenderizer.

**60** Cucumbers are 96 percent water.

**61** You can polish your shoes with the slippery side of a banana peel.

**62** President Thomas Jefferson is credited with introducing eggplant to North America in the early 1800s.

**63** Breaking pomegranates on the ground during a Greek wedding is thought to bring many future children.

**64** Artichokes are flower buds from a kind of thistle plant.

**65** People have been cooking with spicy chili peppers for more than 6,000 years.

**66** Kiwis are native to China, where they are known as gooseberries.

**67** A cucamelon—found in Mexico and Central America—is the size of a grape, looks like a watermelon, and tastes like a cucumber with a hint of lime.

**68** Scientists in England have created a low-fat chocolate made with fruit juice instead of cocoa butter and milk.

**69** The amount of Brussels sprouts sold in England in 2009 almost equaled the weight of the *Titanic*.

**70** The world's heaviest pumpkin weighed more than a Smart Car.

**71** The durian fruit has such an offensive stench that it has been banned from subways and buses in Singapore.

**72** Avocados are sometimes called alligator pears because of their leather-like green skin and pear shape.

**73** A rare type of pineapple grown in Britain in horse manure is believed to be worth around $16,000.

**74 NEITHER BLACKBERRIES NOR RASPBERRIES ARE BERRIES. BOTH ARE ACTUALLY A CLUSTER OF TINY DRUPES— FRUIT WITH PITS INSTEAD OF SEEDS.**

**75** The world's smallest fruit—a utricle—is the size of a small ant.

# 35 HAIR-

**1** You have as many as **150,000 HAIRS** on your head.

**2** Every strand of hair grows about 0.4 inches (1 cm) per month. All combined, that's **10 MILES (16 KM) OF HAIR GROWTH** each year!

**3** You lose about **50 TO 100** hairs a day.

**4** Human hair is a very strong fiber—the combined hair on your head could support **THE WEIGHT OF 2 ELEPHANTS!**

**5** Your hair contains **TRACES OF GOLD.**

**6** Hair grows **FASTER IN SUMMER** than in winter.

**7** The word "shampoo" comes from a **HINDI WORD** that means "to massage."

**8** Hair is the **FASTEST GROWING TISSUE** in the human body after bone marrow.

**9** Hair can stretch as much as **55 PERCENT OF ITS LENGTH** before it snaps.

**10** Blondes typically **HAVE MORE HAIR THAN BRUNETTES,** and redheads have less than brunettes.

**11** **THE ROOT IS THE ONLY PART OF HAIR THAT IS ALIVE.** The part you brush is dead cells.

**12** Hair **GROWS ALL OVER YOUR BODY** except on the palms of your hands, the soles of your feet, and your lips.

**13** Tests run on a single **STRAND OF HAIR FOUND AT A CRIME SCENE** can help detectives prove the guilt or innocence of a suspect.

**14** At any one time, about **90 PERCENT OF THE HAIR ON YOUR SCALP IS GROWING.** The other 10 percent is at "rest" for 2 to 3 months before falling out.

**15** Your hair doesn't grow in sync! Each hair **HAS ITS OWN GROWTH CYCLE,** which is why we don't molt, like some other animals do.

**16** Hair taken from **FROZEN WOOLLY MAMMOTHS** found in Siberia may make it possible for scientists to clone this extinct species.

**17** A study shows that straight hair gets nearly **TWICE AS TANGLED** as curly hair.

**18** Snippets of **JUSTIN BIEBER'S** hair sold on eBay for $40,668.

**19** In 1698, Russian tsar Peter the Great imposed a **BEARD TAX** on all men except peasants and clergy. He thought Russian nobles should be clean-shaven.

**20** Only **1 PERSON IN 200** has red hair.

**21** Every summer in the Netherlands, several thousand people gather for Roodharigen, or Redhead Days, in **CELEBRATION OF HAVING RED HAIR.**

**22** Devices that resemble **CURLING IRONS** have been found in ancient Egyptian tombs.

# RAISING FACTS

**23** Phoenicians, an ancient Mediterranean culture, **SPRINKLED GOLD DUST IN THEIR HAIR** to give it a blond look.

**24** To cover up their gray hair, Romans used a dye that was a mixture of **ASHES, BOILED WALNUT SHELLS, AND EARTHWORMS.**

**25** By age 30, half of **ALL MEN START TO GO BALD.**

**26** **SOME VIKINGS WANTED BLOND BEARDS,** so they used lye to bleach the hair.

**27** In 19th-century England, people **WORE RINGS AND BRACELETS MADE OF HUMAN HAIR.**

**28** Some people in ancient Greece wore **FAKE EYEBROWS** made from goat hair. They used tree resin to attach the hair to their skin.

**29** Most men and women in ancient Egypt had **SHORT HAIR BECAUSE OF THE HEAT,** but on special occasions they wore long-haired wigs.

**30** Thousands of years ago, some cultures believed **SPIRITS ENTERED THE BODY THROUGH HAIR.** Since cutting it had to be handled carefully, barbers became spiritual leaders.

**31** **TALL HAIRDOS** were popular in the 17th century. Some reached **5 FEET (1.5 M) HIGH!**

**32** The record for the **WORLD'S TALLEST HAIRDO WAS SET IN 2009.** Several hairdressers used real and fake hair to create a style that was 8.7 feet (2.7 m) high.

**33** It was fashionable in the 18th century for women **TO WEAR OBJECTS IN THEIR HAIR,** including jewels, ostrich feathers, and even **BIRDCAGES!**

**34** About **75 PERCENT OF WOMEN** in America dye their hair.

**35** Human hair is a great source for an **INGREDIENT THAT CAN IMPROVE THE TEXTURE OR TASTE OF PIZZA** and bagel dough.

**1**
When vultures go on the defense, they PUKE ROTTEN FLESH that smells so bad an attacker will steer clear.

**2**
If PLAYING DEAD isn't enough to make predators move on, OPOSSUMS will make themselves even more undesirable by pooping a green, smelly mucus.

**3**
When threatened, the sluglike SEA HARE covers itself with a purple inky substance that tastes terrible to lobsters, its main predator.

**4**
When Australian frilled lizards feel threatened, they spread the skin around their necks to look FIERCE and bigger.

**5**
When threatened or sleeping, the SPINY HEDGEHOG curls up into a prickly ball that would make any predator think twice before attacking.

**6**
A type of SQUID WILL DETACH part of one of its own arms to distract an attacking predator.

**7**
Like X-Men's Wolverine, the AFRICAN HAIRY FROG can break its own toe bones and push out the jagged pieces to make fierce claws.

**8**
Some types of birds in New Guinea have developed a killer defense: TOXIC FEATHERS and skin. The poison may come from beetles the birds eat.

**9**
"Soldiers" in some termite colonies in French Guiana have POISON SACS THAT EXPLODE when the colony is attacked, covering the enemy with paralyzing venom.

**10**
When sharks or other predators attack a HAGFISH, it releases slime that clogs the predator's gills.

**11**
It takes a hagfish only 0.4 seconds to release 17 pints (8 L) of SNOTTY SLIME.

**12**
Foxes often prey on the NORTHERN FULMAR. To combat their predators, the birds will projectile vomit a smelly, oily liquid at them.

**13**
DWARF SPERM WHALES release a reddish brown cloud of poop into the water to hide their escape route from predators.

**14**
Australia's bird-dropping spiders disguise themselves to look like PILES OF BIRD POOP. No predator wants to eat that!

**15**
Beware of caterpillars with spines, hair, or spikes. Many RELEASE POISON or other irritants when touched.

**16**
To make itself look unappetizing, the NOLID CATERPILLAR can grow the front part of its body into a green ball that looks like an unripe berry.

**17**
If you can't beat 'em, join 'em. METALMARK MOTHS have developed wing markings and movements that mimic the jumping spider, their chief predator.

**18**
SKUNKS can spray their FOUL ODOR at predators up to 10 feet (3 m) away, and the smell can last for days.

**19**
Some skunks do a handstand and wave their tail as a warning before they SPRAY.

**20**
TORTOISE BEETLE LARVAE protect themselves with a toxic "fecal shield"—poop that covers their backs.

**21**
Cryptic locomotion is a special kind of defense where an animal—like a loris—MOVES SO SLOWLY that predators don't notice it.

**22**
The POTTO, a primate found in African rain forests, has a "scapular shield"—spikes on its spine covered by thick skin and fur.

**23**
The PANGOLIN, a scaly mammal that eats ants and termites, has valves to close off its ears and nostrils to keep the insects out when it is raiding their nests.

**24**
ECHIDNAS, one of the few egg-laying mammals, have 2-inch (5-cm)-long spines, and their tan-and-black color blends in with the forest floor.

**25**
The echidna can quickly dig a hole to hide from predators, leaving only its SPINY BUTT visible.

**26**
Brightly colored JUNGLE FROGS are known as "jewels of the rain forest," but the colors are a warning to predators that the frogs are poisonous.

**27**
Some kinds of octopuses always have A PLACE TO HIDE. They carry around coconut shell halves so they can duck inside to escape danger.

**28**
The CAPYBARA—the world's largest rodent—can hide underwater from predators for 5 minutes before it has to come up for air.

**29**
"ARMADILLO" is a Spanish word meaning "little armored one."

**30**
Not all armadillos can CURL INTO A BALL for protection. The 3-banded armadillo is the only species that can.

**31**
AFRICAN CAPE BUFFALO are tasty targets for lions. But thick, leathery skin around the neck makes it tough for lion teeth to penetrate.

**32**
AMAZON HORNED FROGS are so fierce that some villagers wear high leather shoes as protection against the frog's sharp-toothed bite.

**33**
Colonies of thrushlike birds called FIELDFARES weigh down the wings of predatory birds by bombing them with poop.

**34**
A PORCUPINE has about 30,000 QUILLS with microscopic barbs that make removing the quills difficult and painful for a predator that's been attacked.

**35**
To escape a sea star or other predator, a SCALLOP will shoot off through the water by rapidly opening and closing its shell.

**36**
While they sleep, PARROT FISH cover themselves in a MUCOUS BUBBLE to mask their scent from parasites and other predators.

**37**
Inside their burrows, PRAIRIE DOGS build listening posts—places where they can keep an ear out for predators.

**38**
VENEZUELAN PEBBLE TOADS curl themselves into a ball and use their muscles to bounce themselves down a hill, away from predators.

**39**
CARIBBEAN REEF SQUID hide from danger by changing their texture and color to match their surroundings.

**40**
LOBSTER MOTH CATERPILLARS shoot attackers with an acid that causes blisters and has a terrible smell!

**41**
PEACOCK BUTTERFLIES can hiss like a snake to scare predators away. If that doesn't work, they flash their wings, which have spots that look like owl eyes.

**42**
BOXER CRABS can pack quite a punch! They hold stinging anemones in their front claws like pom-poms.

**43**
DRACO LIZARDS avoid predators by taking to the air! Using their tails like rudders and skin flaps like wings, they can glide for 30 feet (9 m).

**44**
The TOMATO FROG'S red color warns predators to keep away. The frog can also slime its enemies with a sticky, irritating mucus.

**45**
The edible dormouse, also known as the FAT DORMOUSE, is able to lose its tail when a predator grabs on.

**46**
When food becomes scarce, the KARAKUL—a type of sheep—can live off the fat stored in its tail.

**47**
DIVING BELL SPIDERS keep away from flying predators by living underwater in a bubble of oxygen!

**48**
The INDONESIAN MIMIC OCTOPUS can imitate at least 10 different types of animals, including jellyfish and lionfish.

**49**
A scorpion's sting is usually its best defense, but the grasshopper mouse has the ability to BLOCK THE PAIN so it can eat the scorpion.

**50**
BABY EURASIAN ROLLER BIRDS throw up on themselves to make predators think twice about eating them.

Draco lizard

# ON GUARD!

# 50 FACTS ABOUT ANIMAL DEFENSES

**1.** There are 156,001 miles (251,060 km) of country borders—counting shared borders only once—throughout the world. Forty countries are islands that don't border any other country. **2.** There are 45 countries in the world that are landlocked—meaning they don't have a coastline on an ocean. **3.** The question "What makes a country?" is tough to answer. Some countries, like the Czech Republic and Liechtenstein, don't recognize each other. More than 30 countries don't recognize Israel. **4.** McDonald's—the fast-food restaurant—can be found in at least 119 countries and on every continent except Antarctica. **5.** Buzkashi, the national sport of Afghanistan, is played on horseback. It means "goat-grabbing." **6.** The national hero of Albania is known as Skanderbeg. In the 15th century, he became commander in chief of the army, defending the country against 13 Turkish invasions. **7.** Algiers, Algeria's capital city, was a center for piracy in the Mediterranean Sea for almost 300 years, beginning in the early 1500s. **8.** Andorra sits between France and Spain and is only two and a half times bigger than Washington, D.C., U.S.A. **9.** Africa's giant sable antelope is a critically endangered animal found only in Angola. **10.** Antigua and Barbuda takes its name from the country's 2 main islands. There are actually 3 islands in the country, but Redonda is uninhabited. **11.** Argentina means "land of silver." **12.** Armenians refer to themselves as "Hye" after Hayk Nahapet, the name used for the ancestor of the Armenian people. **13.** Australia's temperatures have gotten so hot that meteorologists have added 2 new colors—deep purple and pink—to its temperature range. **14.** Every spring, snowmelt from surrounding peaks floods Austria's Green Lake, turning the hiking trails, picnic benches, and trees along its banks into an underwater park. **15.** Azerbaijan's Oil Rocks is a huge oil rig 75 miles (120 km) from shore with 256 oil wells connected by 186 miles (300 km) of roads. **16.** The Bahamas is made up of 700 islands and 2,400 cays—

# 100 COOL FACTS ABOUT COUNTRIES

small islands atop coral reefs. **17.** The Tree of Life in Bahrain has definitely earned its name. It has been growing for 400 years in a nearly rainless desert! **18.** The Bengal tiger—a big cat that loves water—is the national animal of Bangladesh. **19.** Grapefruit was first grown in Barbados in the 18th century and was called "forbidden fruit." **20.** Belarus has the world's largest population of European bison. **21.** Belgium hosts the world's largest sand sculpture festival. **22.** The world's second largest coral reef lies off the coast of Belize. **23.** There's a village in Benin where thousands of people live in the middle of a lake in stilt houses. **24.** Bhutan means "land of the thunder dragon" because of the extreme storms that come from the Himalayan peaks. **25.** La Paz, Bolivia, is the world's highest national capital city. **26.** Tuzla, Bosnia and Herzegovina's third largest city, is famous for its salt production. Its name comes from the Turkish word *tuz*, which means "salt." **27.** Tourists flock to Botswana to go on safari. Its baobab trees can be over 2,000 years old, and its elephants are the largest in the world. **28.** Although as many as 20 million people live and work in Brazil's Amazon rain forest, there are some indigenous groups that have never had contact with the "outside" world. **29.** The country of Brunei pays for all of its citizens' medical care and education, including college. It helps that fewer than 420,000 people live there. **30.** In Bulgaria, people give each other *martenitsas*—red-and-white ornaments—on March 1 to bring good health. **31.** Burkina Faso means "land of the honest people." Its earlier name, Upper Volta, came from the Volta River, which has its source there. **32.** Some people who live on the Irrawaddy River in Myanmar use freshwater dolphins to help them catch fish. **33.** Track and field is popular in Burundi. In 1996, the country won its first Olympic gold medal when Venuste Niyongabo won the 5,000-meter race. **34.** Angkor Wat, a temple in Cambodia, is the largest religious monument in the world. **35.** The Dja River, by almost surrounding the Dja Faunal Reserve in Cameroon, helps protect lowland gorillas, chimpanzees, and other endangered species that live there. **36.** Canada has 20 percent of all of Earth's fresh water. **37.** When the Portuguese first discovered the Cape Verde islands off the west coast of Africa in the 15th century, they were uninhabited. Now, over 500,000 people live there. **38.** One of the main industries in the Central African Republic is gold and diamond mining. **39.** Nile crocodiles became stranded thousands of years ago in Guelta Archei, an ancient water pool in the middle of the Sahara in northern Chad, when the once wet and lush area dried up. **40.** Rain has never been recorded in parts of the Atacama Desert in Chile, yet more than a million people live there—mostly along the coast. **41.** Ketchup, which originated in China over 500 years ago, was first made with anchovies—a sardine-like fish—not tomatoes. The word means "fish sauce" in a Chinese dialect. **42.** There's a cathedral carved into salt deposits inside an old mine in Zipaquirá Mountain in Colombia. It took more than 100 miners and sculptors 4 years to build. **43.** The country of Comoros is called the perfume islands because it is the main supplier of ilang-ilang essence—a main ingredient in high-end perfumes. **44.** More than 700 languages are spoken by people living in the Democratic Republic of the Congo. **45.** The Congo River separates the capital cities of the Republic of the Congo (Brazzaville) and the Democratic Republic of the Congo (Kinshasa). **46.** People from Costa Rica call themselves *ticos* (men) and *ticas* (women). **47.** Chocolate lover alert: Côte d'Ivoire, on the west coast of Africa, is the world's leading producer of cocoa beans. **48.** Neckties originated in Croatia. **49.** Eighty percent of the reptiles and amphibians in Cuba are found nowhere else on Earth. **50.** The bones of what may be the oldest pet cat were discovered on Cyprus. At 9,500 years old, it's older than cats found in Egypt. **51.** The Czech Republic was once part of Czechoslovakia until the "velvet divorce" divided the country in 1992. The other part is called Slovakia. **52.** Legos were created in Denmark. The country's Legoland is the first theme park of its kind and took over 60 million Lego bricks to build all its models! **53.** Djibouti has many travertine chimneys—tall rock formations created by minerals from hot springs. Some of the chimneys reach as high as 165 feet (50 m)! **54.** Boiling Lake on Dominica, a volcanic island in the Caribbean, is actually a flooded fumarole—an opening in Earth's crust where molten rock is close to the surface. **55.** The palmchat is the national bird of the Dominican Republic. That's also the name of an instant messaging app. **56.** The finches, marine iguanas, giant tortoises, and other unique wildlife on the Galápagos Islands, which belong to Ecuador, inspired biologist Charles Darwin's famous theory of evolution. **57.** It took 20,000 to 30,000 people to build the massive Great Pyramid at Giza, Egypt. **58.** The San Miguel volcano, one of the most active in El Salvador, has erupted at least 29 times since 1699. **59.** Spanish is still the official language of Equatorial Guinea, which was a Spanish colony for 190 years. **60.** A bowling alley in Asmara, Eritrea, is one of the last of its kind in the world. Likely built in the mid-1900s for U.S. servicemen, the pins are reset manually. **61.** Today, Estonia is an independent nation, but from the 12th to the early 20th century, it was occupied by different groups, including Teutonic knights and Russian tsars. **62.** Ethiopian wolves are found in the wild only in Ethiopia. Their population numbers only about 500. **63.** The Pacific island country of Fiji has over 4,000 square miles (10,000 km²) of coral reefs. **64.** Hevisaurus is a heavy metal band from Finland whose members dress up in dinosaur costumes and rock about homework, monsters, and exploration. **65.** The Eiffel Tower in Paris, France, was built for the 1889 World's Fair. Most people thought the iron structure was ugly. **66.** Gabon is home to indigenous hunter-gatherers called Pygmies, also known as "people of the forest." **67.** Gambia's main export is peanuts. **68.** Georgia's capital, Tbilisi, comes from the Georgian word for "warm" because of the city's natural hot springs. **69.** Germany has the largest population of any country located entirely in Europe. **70.** When Ghana was a British colony, its name was Gold Coast. **71.** Meteora, Greece, has monasteries atop high sandstone cliffs. Years ago, monks and pilgrims either used ladders to climb up to them or were lifted up in baskets. **72.** The national flower of Grenada is the bougainvillea. It grows in many colors, including pink, purple, red, and orange. **73.** More than half of the population of Guatemala is descended from the Maya. **74.** Guinea, a country about the size of the U.S. state of Oregon, has about half the world's supply of bauxite, an ore used to make aluminum. **75.** Portuguese is the official language of Guinea-Bissau, but few people outside the capital city speak it. **76.** Eighty percent of Guyana is covered by the Amazon rain forest. **77.** Voodoo is one of the main religions of Haiti. **78.** The ruins of Copán—one of the most famous examples of Maya civilization—are a major tourist attraction in Honduras. **79.** The Rubik's Cube was invented by a professor of interior design from Hungary. **80.** Iceland is rewriting its constitution, incorporating comments posted on Facebook and Twitter. **81.** Darjeeling tea is grown in tea gardens high in the Himalaya in Darjeeling, India. Legend says that the tea gets its unique flavor from the breath of God. **82.** Indonesia is made up of 17,000 islands. Jakarta, the capital city, is on the island of Java, which has more than 3 dozen volcanoes! **83.** Forty-three percent of Iran's population is under the age of 25. **84.** Baghdad's House of Wisdom, in what is now Iraq, was a center of learning. In the 9th century, scholars from around the world came to study math, astronomy, zoology, and more. **85.** Ireland's nickname is the Emerald Isle because of its lush, green landscape. **86.** The first instant messaging system—ICQ, short for "I seek you"—was developed by a company in Israel. **87.** Vibrations caused by all the tourists walking around Michelangelo's famous statue of David in Florence, Italy, could cause it to crack or even collapse. **88.** To describe the mountainous terrain of Jamaica, Christopher Columbus crumpled up a piece of paper and threw it on a table. **89.** In Japan, macaques, or snow monkeys, sometimes treat themselves to a dip in natural hot springs in areas that have cold winters. **90.** Parts of the movie *Indiana Jones and the Last Crusade* were filmed in the ancient city of Petra, Jordan. **91.** The Baikonur Cosmodrome in Kazakhstan is where the first satellite into space was launched. It is still a major launch site for Russian space missions. **92.** Nairobi, the capital of Kenya, used to be a water hole used by railroad workers. The name means "cool water." **93.** Kiribati was originally named the Gilbert Islands in 1820 after British explorer Thomas Gilbert. **94.** In North Korea, the government controls nearly everything about how people live. There are even 28 government-approved haircuts. **95.** The elaborate ceremony that traditionally surrounded drinking green tea in South Korea is making a comeback. **96.** Kosovo—a country that is smaller than the U.S. state of Connecticut—has 4 medieval monuments. All are world heritage sites. **97.** The name Kuwait is from an Arabic word meaning "fortress built near water." **98.** Mountains cover 75 percent of Kyrgyzstan. **99.** Watching rhinoceros beetles wrestle is a popular sport in Laos. **100.** The epic hero of Latvia is Lacplesis, the Bear Slayer. In the poem, he's half man, half bear and can kill a bear with just his hands.

**1**
The ROCKET that boosted the first humans to the moon was built in Huntsville, Alabama.

**2**
Denali, meaning "THE HIGH ONE," is the Athabascan name for 20,320-foot (6,194-m)-tall Mount McKinley in Alaska.

**3**
The bola tie is the OFFICIAL NECKWEAR of Arizona. It's a cord or strip of braided leather with an ornamental clasp.

**4**
The world championship of DUCK CALLING takes place in Stuttgart, Arkansas.

**5**
If California were a country, it would have the NINTH LARGEST economy in the world.

**6**
So far, Colorado is the only U.S. state to TURN DOWN hosting the Olympics.

**7**
The state animal of Connecticut is the SPERM WHALE, which played an important role in the state's historic whaling industry.

**8**
Delaware hosts the National PUNKIN CHUNKIN World Championship every year in Bridgeville.

**9**
Florida wouldn't be the top U.S. producer of oranges and grapefruit if COLUMBUS hadn't brought citrus fruit to the New World.

**10**
The Girl Scouts of the U.S.A. started in Georgia in 1912 with just 18 GIRLS. Today, the organization has 2.3 million members.

**11**
Hawaii is the only state composed only of ISLANDS. It was also the last state to join the Union.

**12**
Around 60 percent of all the POTATOES grown in Idaho are used to make french fries.

**13**
The first AIR-CONDITIONED theater opened in Chicago, Illinois, more than 100 years ago—in 1889.

**14**
The first professional BASKETBALL GAME was held in Fort Wayne, Indiana, in 1871.

**15**
Iowa is the only state with a name that starts with TWO VOWELS.

**16**
The town of Liberal, Kansas, has a replica of DOROTHY'S HOUSE as it appeared in the movie *The Wizard of Oz*.

**17**
The first burgers to be called CHEESEBURGERS were served in 1934 in Louisville, Kentucky, at Kaelin's Restaurant.

**18**
The city of New Orleans, Louisiana, is about 6 feet (2 m) BELOW SEA LEVEL on average.

**19**
The official state cat of Maine—the Maine COON CAT—is one of the oldest breeds of domestic cat native to North America.

**20**
The state sport of Maryland is JOUSTING, and its state team sport is lacrosse.

**21**
FIG NEWTONS were named after the town of Newton, Massachusetts.

**22**
The shoreline of Michigan on the GREAT LAKES is longer than the distance between New York City and Los Angeles.

**23**
Minnesota has more than 200 lakes that are named MUD LAKE.

**24**
Coke was FIRST BOTTLED in Vicksburg, Mississippi, in 1894.

**25**
The name Missouri comes from an Algonquin word meaning "town of the LARGE CANOES."

**26**
The governor of Montana wore a GRIZZLY BEAR hat when he signed the law making that bear the state animal.

**27**
Chimney Rock in Nebraska was a NATURAL SIGNPOST for settlers traveling west on the Oregon-California Trail.

**28**
Nevada has a total of at least 314 mountain ranges and peaks, making it the most MOUNTAINOUS of all the states.

**29**
New Hampshire was the first American colony to DECLARE INDEPENDENCE from Britain.

**30**
New Jersey has the world's highest concentration of SHOPPING MALLS.

**31**
Six sovereign nations, including Spain, Mexico, and the Republic of Texas, have governed NEW MEXICO.

**32**
The official baked good of New York is the APPLE MUFFIN.

**33**
North Carolina produces around $15 million worth of honey every year. No wonder the HONEYBEE is the state insect.

# 50 DANDY FACTS ABOUT THE 50 STATES

Mount McKinley (aka Denali), Alaska

**34**
If you play golf at a course in Portal, North Dakota, you'll be hitting most of your balls IN CANADA!

**35**
The WRIGHT BROTHERS built an early version of their flying machine in their bicycle shop in Dayton, Ohio.

**36**
The SHOPPING CART was invented in Oklahoma City, Oklahoma, in 1936. Before then, shoppers used baskets.

**37**
Oregon is the only U.S. state that has a flag with a DIFFERENT DESIGN on each side.

**38**
In 1920, KDKA, the first permanent U.S. commercial RADIO STATION, began broadcasting in Pittsburgh, Pennsylvania.

**39**
In 1904, Rhode Island became the first state to send a person to jail for SPEEDING in a car.

**40**
More Revolutionary War skirmishes and battles were fought in SOUTH CAROLINA than in any other state.

**41**
Murals made of different colors of corn decorate the CORN PALACE in Mitchell, South Dakota.

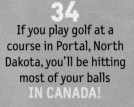

**42**
Tennessee has the largest underground lake in the United States—THE LOST SEA in Craighead Caverns.

**43**
The Texas version of Bigfoot is known as WOOLY BOOGER.

**44**
Utah's state fossil is the ALLOSAURUS, a meat-eating dinosaur that stood 17 feet (5 m) tall.

**45**
Ben & Jerry's in Vermont gives its ice-cream waste products to local farmers. PIGS will eat any flavor except mint.

**46**
Virginia is the site of JAMESTOWN. Founded in 1607, it was the first permanent English colony in North America.

**47**
Washington is the only state NAMED FOR A PRESIDENT.

**48**
Until the Civil War broke out in 1861, West Virginia was part of Virginia. It became the 35TH STATE in 1863.

**49**
More than 600 KINDS OF CHEESE are produced in Wisconsin at more than 125 factories.

**50**
DEVILS TOWER National Monument in Wyoming was featured in the film *Close Encounters of the Third Kind*.

**1**

The Harry Potter books have been translated into at least 70 different languages, including Luxembourgish and Mongolian.

**2**

The discoverers of a 66-million-year-old dinosaur named it *Dracorex hogwartsia* in honor of the series.

**3**

If you mail a postcard from the Owl Post at the Wizarding World of Harry Potter theme park in Orlando, Florida, U.S.A., it can be stamped with the Hogsmeade postmark.

**4**

The British version of the first Harry Potter book is titled *Harry Potter and the Philosopher's Stone*, rather than the *Sorcerer's Stone*.

**5**

J.K. Rowling first thought of the name of the 4 Hogwarts houses while on an airplane—and WROTE THEM DOWN ON THE BACK OF A SICK BAG!

**6**

DURING THE MAKING OF THE 8 FILMS, DANIEL RADCLIFFE, THE ACTOR WHO PLAYED HARRY POTTER, WENT THROUGH 160 PAIRS OF GLASSES AND ABOUT 60 WANDS.

# 25 SPELLBINDING FACTS ABOUT HARRY

**7**

Harry Potter author J.K. ROWLING HAS THE SAME BIRTHDAY as Harry—July 31.

**8**

A hotel in Edinburgh, Scotland, has a statue signed by J.K. Rowling that says she finished writing *The Deathly Hallows* there on January 11, 2007.

**9**

A Seattle, U.S.A., mom spent a year building a replica of Hogwarts out of some **400,000 LEGO PIECES.** She even created scenes in the inside rooms, including a feast in the Great Hall and a potions class.

**10**

In the movies, HAGRID'S DOG FANG was played by several different Neapolitan mastiffs. In the books, Fang was a boarhound.

**11**

Emma Watson, the actress who plays Hermione, had to **audition eight times** for the part.

**12**

Makeup artists glued GOAT HAIR to the face, arms, and legs of the actor who played GREYBACK to give him his werewolf look.

**13**

J.K. ROWLING IS THE FIRST AUTHOR TO EARN **$1 BILLION.**

**14** Students at more than 300 colleges and high schools worldwide **PLAY QUIDDITCH.** Players run with broomsticks and throw quaffles through goal hoops.

**15** Scientists are working toward making **a real invisibility cloak.** So far, they have succeeded in making one that can conceal objects less than 1/10 of an inch (2 mm) tall.

**16** YOU CAN BUY **BERTIE BOTT'S EVERY FLAVOUR BEANS.** FLAVORS INCLUDE EARTHWORM AND EARWAX.

**17** The actor who played Hagrid once got a **FRUIT BAT** stuck in his beard while filming!

**18** In the *Prisoner of Azkaban* film, the snowballs Harry throws at Draco Malfoy from under his invisibility cloak are made of a coconut mixture similar to cake batter.

**19** J.K. Rowling once said that **Professor Dumbledore** was 150 years old, explaining that wizards live much longer than Muggles (nonmagic folk).

**20** THE LAST NAME OF NEARLY HEADLESS NICK, THE GHOST OF GRYFFINDOR HOUSE, IS De Mimsy-Porpington.

# POTTER

**21** An estimated **450 million copies** of the books have been sold worldwide. That's about 1 book for every 16 people on Earth.

**22** "DRACO" MEANS "**DRAGON**" IN LATIN.

**23** Aragog, Hagrid's spider that dies in *The Half-Blood Prince*, was nearly the size of a polar bear in the film.

**24** THOSE AREN'T REAL OWL DROPPINGS IN THE OWLERY AT HOGWARTS IN THE FILMS. THEY'RE MADE FROM FOAM AND PUTTY.

**25** J.K. Rowling hid puns in some of her place-names. DIAGON ALLEY read quickly is "diagonally"; KNOCKTURN ALLEY is "nocturnally." Sirius Black's family home was on GRIMMAULD PLACE, or "Grim Old Place"!

**1** Historians believe that **CLEOPATRA,** one of ancient Egypt's most powerful rulers, REALLY WASN'T BEAUTIFUL. It was her personality, intelligence, and extreme wealth that eventually gave her that reputation.

**2** In Greek mythology, **HELEN OF TROY'S** beauty caused the **10-YEAR-LONG TROJAN WAR.**

**3** **AGNI IS THE HINDU GOD OF FIRE.** He has been described as having a red body, **2 FACES COVERED IN BUTTER,** 7 fiery tongues, and GOLD TEETH.

**4** In Greek mythology, **NARCISSUS** was a DROP-DEAD-GORGEOUS MAN who turned down all his admirers. The goddess **NEMESIS** cursed him into FALLING IN LOVE WITH HIS OWN REFLECTION.

**5** Tales of the **QUEEN OF SHEBA** say she was so beautiful that **KING SOLOMON** of Jerusalem told her SHE COULD HAVE ANYTHING SHE DESIRED IN HIS KINGDOM.

**6** Sixteenth-century **FRENCH BEAUTY DIANE DE POITIERS** consumed a drink that **CONTAINED GOLD TO HELP KEEP HER YOUNG.** Problem is, she drank so much that it was the likely cause of her death.

**7** FREYA, the goddess of love in Norse mythology, was so beautiful that **HUMANS, GIANTS, AND DWARVES ALL FELL IN LOVE WITH HER.**

**8** Even WOMEN WHO HAD NEVER SEEN the famous outlaw JESSE JAMES swooned over him. HE LOVED THE ATTENTION he got from newspapers so much that sometimes he would **LEAVE BEHIND PRESS RELEASES** after robbing a bank.

# HOTTiES OF HiSTORY

**9** The Greek goddess **APHRODITE** is best known for **HELPING PEOPLE FALL IN LOVE,** but she could also be cruel. **ANYONE WHO SCORNED HER RISKED BEING CURSED** or turned from human to a different form.

**10** Santiago Ramón y Cajal, **WINNER OF A 1906 NOBEL PRIZE** for his work in neuroscience, was into bodybuilding. **HE SPENT MONTHS WORKING ON HIS MUSCLES AT THE GYM.**

**11** **HARRY HOUDINI** was a famous magician in the early 1900s who loved to **SHOW OFF HIS MUSCULAR BODY.** In one act, police locked him naked in a jail cell, but he magically escaped and **RETRIEVED HIS CLOTHES** from the cell next door.

**12** Two of the most famous lovers of all time are **ROMEO AND JULIET.** Pop star Taylor Swift even wrote about them in her smash hit "Love Story."

**13** Mata Hari was the stage name of a dancer who gained fame as a spy during World War I. Accused by the French of **REVEALING SECRETS ABOUT A NEW WEAPON—THE TANK**—to the Germans, **SHE WAS EXECUTED BY FIRING SQUAD IN 1917.**

**14** Britain's **KING HENRY VIII** was known for his good looks and fine clothes. With age, **HIS WAISTLINE GREW, BUT AT THE TIME THIS WAS VIEWED AS EVIDENCE OF HIS GREAT WEALTH.** Poor men could not afford to eat so well.

**15** **IN THE BIBLE, THE TEMPTRESS DELILAH** tricks Samson into telling her the **SECRET OF HIS STRENGTH,** then watches as he becomes powerless when his enemies cut off his hair.

# 75 STRIKING FACTS ABOUT SNAKES

Jungle carpet python

**9** The world's largest snake species—including pythons, anacondas, and boas—all belong to the Boidae family.

**10** INDIA HAS 50-PLUS SPECIES OF VENOMOUS SNAKES THAT BITE MORE THAN 200,000 PEOPLE AND KILL AT LEAST 50,000 YEARLY.

**11** The prize for the snake with the longest fangs goes to a Gaboon viper: 2 inches (5 cm).

**12** There's an app that translates your speech into Parseltongue, the language of snakes in the Harry Potter series.

**13** Russell's viper keeps the mice population in rice paddies in check, but humans working in the fields are also at risk from its venomous bite.

**14** On cold nights, the venomous common krait often crawls into bed with sleeping people. Often they don't even feel the bite.

**15** Africa has over 400 kinds of snakes; 90 are venomous.

**16** Every year, more people in Africa are killed by the Cape Cobra than by any other kind of snake.

**17** The bright green scales of Africa's eastern green mamba snake give it perfect camouflage for hunting birds and rodents in treetops.

**18** Sounds cause a snake's skull and jaws to vibrate, alerting the snake to its prey's movement.

**19** To get into trees, the black mamba raises half of its 14-foot (4.2-m)-long body onto low branches.

**1** Unlike its namesake, the deadly tiger snake doesn't always have stripes. Even when it does, the colors vary from snake to snake.

**2** A death adder will lie still and camouflaged for days or even weeks waiting to ambush its prey.

**3** The taipan is a deadly snake from Australia. In China, its name means "big boss."

**4** Venom from 1 taipan bite reportedly can kill 250,000 mice.

**5** The eastern brown snake twists its body into an S-shape when threatened.

**6** A KING COBRA DELIVERS BETWEEN .007 AND .017 OUNCES (198 TO 482 MG) OF VENOM IN 1 BITE— MORE THAN ENOUGH TO KILL A HUMAN BEING.

**7** A king cobra can grow up to 18 feet (5 m) long and use its muscles to raise one-third of its body high enough to look an adult human in the eye.

**8** Pythons can hunt on land and in water and kill by coiling around their prey and suffocating it.

**20** Black mambas actually have brown scales. They get their name from the black-blue color of the inside of their mouths.

**21 SOME KINDS OF PYTHONS CAN GO FOR A YEAR OR LONGER BETWEEN MEALS.**

**22** Pit vipers have 2 heat-seeking organs on their faces that help them find warm-blooded prey, like birds and rodents. This heat "vision" is especially useful for nighttime hunting.

**23** Snakes smell with their tongues, not their nostrils.

**24** The southern Indonesian spitting cobra can spit venom up to 7 feet (2 m) that can cause blindness.

**25** In the movie *Aladdin*, the evil sorcerer, Jafar, turns into a giant cobra after Aladdin calls him a "cowardly snake."

**26** The banded sea krait lives in coral reefs and is one of the few snakes that hunt in packs.

**27** The bushmaster is the largest member of the viper family.

**28** The biggest snake on Earth is the green, or giant, anaconda. These constrictor snakes can grow almost 30 feet (9 m) long, weigh more than 550 pounds (250 kg), and measure more than 12 inches (30 cm) around.

**29** The green anaconda can eat 300-pound (136-kg) caimans—a kind of alligator—and even jaguars.

**30** Japan's yamakagashi snakes eat poisonous toads, store their toxins in special neck glands, then release the poison when threatened.

**31** There are nearly 3,000 different species of snakes on Earth.

**32** Most garter, or garden, snakes are black or brown. But in Florida, U.S.A., garter snakes can be bright blue.

**33** Rattlesnakes return to the same den to hibernate year after year. Scientists have found active dens that are over 100 years old.

**34** Yellow-bellied sea snakes have skin that absorbs oxygen right from the water.

**35** The eyelash palm pit viper has upturned scales above its eyes that look like eyelashes.

**36** A tentacled snake tricks fish by faking where it will strike. The fish flees in the opposite direction—often right into the snake's mouth.

**37** Young jararaca snakes that haven't learned how to control the amount of venom in their bites are more dangerous than adult jararacas.

**38** Most pit vipers are ovoviviparous, which means the eggs are produced and hatch inside the mother.

**39 AT INDONESIA'S SEA SNAKE SPA, PYTHONS ARE USED IN MASSAGE TREATMENTS!**

**40** There are two types of snake scales: smooth and keeled. Smooth scales are shiny and soft; keeled scales have a raised edge.

**41** By flattening their bodies and forming an S-shape, some snakes can make turns in midair while gliding.

**42** The paradise tree snake is an expert glider, traveling up to 330 feet (100 m) through the air.

**43** Freshwater-dwelling rainbow snakes love to make meals of eels. They are sometimes called eel moccasins.

**44** According to Chinese astrology, people born in the year of the snake are intelligent, organized, and charming—but also deceitful and show-offs.

**45** Titanoboa, a 48-foot (15-m)-long prehistoric snake, weighed 2,500 pounds (1,134 kg)—about as much as 20 people!

**46** Venomous coral snakes will curl their tails to confuse predators about which end is the head.

**47** A basilisk appears as a giant snake in *Harry Potter and the Chamber of Secrets*. But according to medieval lore, it could also be a rooster with a snake's tail.

**48 CATS MAY HAVE LEARNED TO HISS BY IMITATING SNAKES.**

**49** A woman in China awoke to a scratching noise and found a snake with a clawed foot coming out of its body crawling across her bedroom wall!

**50** The "Party Python" is a 26-pound (12-kg), 36,000-calorie gummy snake.

**51** In the movie *Monster's Inc.*, Celia Mae has 5 snakes on her head—Ophelia, Cordelia, Amelia, Bobelia, and Madge—that reflect her mood.

**52** Sterling Holloway, who was the voice of Kaa, the rock python, in Disney's *Jungle Book* movie, was also the voice of Disney's Cheshire Cat and Winnie-the-Pooh.

**53** In 2011, after a young Egyptian cobra escaped from the Bronx Zoo in New York City, U.S.A., more than 200,000 people followed its imaginary exploits on Twitter!

**54** Someone who studies amphibians and reptiles—including snakes—is called a herpetologist.

**55** Snakes that look like they're dancing for a snake charmer are really responding to the movement and shape of the charmer's flute, not the music. Snakes are deaf!

**56** All snakes grow by shedding their skin, a few times a year.

**57** The Snake River in the United States may get its name from the S-shaped hand signal the Shoshone Indians made to imitate the salmon swimming in the river.

**58 THE LARGEST CONSTELLATION IN THE NIGHT SKY IS CALLED HYDRA, WHICH MEANS "WATER SNAKE" IN LATIN.**

**59** A serpent is a curvy bass instrument, invented in 1590, that looks like a snake.

**60** Ophidiophobia is a fear of snakes.

**61** Shawnee National Forest in Illinois, U.S.A., closes down "Snake Road" to cars to make way for the spring and fall snake migration between lowland swamps and upland cliffs. People are welcome to walk it, though.

**62** Decapitated snakes can bite and even deliver venom up to an hour after their death.

**63** A Cambodian village once held a wedding ceremony for 2 pythons.

**64** A rat snake with 2 heads named "We" lived at the World Aquarium in St. Louis, Missouri, U.S.A. The aquarium bought her for $15,000.

**65** Most 2-headed snakes live short lives because the heads will fight with each other over prey and want to travel in different directions.

**66** Snakes are powerful symbols in Hinduism, the main religion of India. The god Shiva is often shown with a cobra around his neck.

**67** Viper, from the movie *Kung-Fu Panda*, never developed poison fangs and took up ribbon dancing, which is what gives her the unique moves.

**68** The game Chutes and Ladders originated in India, where it was called Snakes and Ladders. The ladders represented good deeds and the snakes represented evil.

**69 IN THE HARRY POTTER SERIES, VOLDEMORT HAS A HUGE PET SNAKE NAMED NAGINI. HER NAME COMES FROM THE SANSKRIT WORD *NAGA*, MEANING "SERPENT."**

**70** The reticulated python is the world's longest snake, measuring more than 30 feet (9 m). That's longer than 2 sedan-size cars!

**71** Most baby snakes are born with 1 tooth—called the egg tooth—that helps them break out of their shells.

**72** The spectacled cobra is known for the eyeglass shape on the back of its hood.

**73** Inclusion body disease is an illness that affects snakes, causing them to stare off into space, twist into knots, and lose their appetites.

**74** When a python eats after going a long time without food, its heart and other organs will double in size to help it digest the food faster.

**75** Some scientists think that some kinds of snake venom may slow the growth of certain cancers in people.

# 35 OUT-OF-

**1**
Moons, also called **NATURAL SATELLITES**, come in all sizes. There are at least 146 in our solar system.

**2**
We see only **ONE SIDE OF THE MOON** because it orbits Earth in about the same time it takes to spin once on its own axis.

**3**
Saturn, with **53 NAMED MOONS**, boasts the most natural satellites in our solar system—at least for now.

**4**
You don't need to worry about taking **GOLF BALLS** to the moon. Astronaut Alan Shepard **LEFT 2 BEHIND** on his last mission.

**5**
Temperatures on Earth's moon can rise as high as **260°F (127°C)** where the sun is shining and dip as low as **MINUS 280°F (-173°C)** on the dark side. Now that's extreme!

**6**
Tasty **MOONCAKES** filled with bean paste are eaten by Asian families during the popular Moon Festival, celebrating autumn's large, full moon.

**7**
**MARS** is named after the Roman god of war, but its 2 moons—**PHOBOS**, meaning "fear," and **DEIMOS**, meaning "flight"—are named for sons of the Greek god of war. Confusing, right?

**8**
Pluto's moon **CHARON** is half the size of Pluto. It is so large that the 2 are sometimes considered a **DOUBLE DWARF PLANET** system.

**9**
True to its name, the **MOONFLOWER** blooms in the evening and stays open until the sun rises in the morning.

**10**
*A Trip to the Moon*, one of the first science-fiction films, featured a **SPACE-SHIP** landing in the "**EYE" OF THE MOON**.

**11**
Jupiter's **GANYMEDE** is the largest moon in our solar system. It is even larger than the planet Mercury.

**12** Whether you call **PLUTO** a planet, a dwarf planet, or a plutoid, it still has 5 moons to call its own. The last was discovered in 2012.

**13** A **BLUE MOON** isn't really blue, but in 1883 the moon did appear blue when ash from a volcano in Indonesia covered the sky.

**14** In Japan, instead of a "man in the moon," people see a "**RABBIT IN THE MOON.**"

**15** **TRITON**, unlike Neptune's other moons, has a retrograde orbit, meaning it orbits **OPPOSITE** to the way the planet spins.

**16** U.S. astronaut **EUGENE CERNAN** scratched his daughter's initials (TDC) into the surface of the moon. Since the moon has no weather, they could last forever.

**17** Not all moons are dry and dusty like ours. Jupiter's **EUROPA** has a **LIQUID OCEAN** under an icy crust.

**18** The Chattanooga Bakery in Tennessee, U.S.A., created the **MOONPIE** in 1917. Pat Bertoletti set a record by eating 60 in 8 minutes in 2011.

**19** **MOON TREES** have sprouted from seeds carried to the moon and back by astronaut and former U.S. Forest Service smoke jumper Stuart Roosa.

**20** The moon doesn't glow on its own. It actually acts as a mirror, **REFLECTING THE SUN'S LIGHT.**

**21** Since the moon's **GRAVITY** is only one-sixth of Earth's, a 100-pound (45-kg) person on Earth would **TIP THE SCALES** at just under 17 pounds (7 kg).

# THIS-WORLD
## FACTS ABOUT MOONS

**22** **GOODNIGHT MOON**, by Margaret Wise Brown, has been helping kids fall asleep for over 60 years. You can read it in many languages—even American Sign Language.

**23** The tiny **RUFA RED KNOT BIRD**, tagged by scientists as B95, is known as the **MOONBIRD**, because it has flown the distance to the moon and halfway back.

**24** **TITAN**, Saturn's largest moon, is the only moon in the solar system that has clouds.

**25** Earth's full moons have many different names depending on the season. March's full moon is sometimes called the **FULL SAP MOON** because it's when maple trees are tapped.

**26** It's a bird! It's a plane! No, it's a "**SUPERMOON**"! The full moon appears larger and brighter than usual when its path brings it closest to Earth.

**27** **NEPTUNE'S 14TH MOON**, discovered in 2013, needs a name, but to be accepted, the name must have a link to the **UNDERWORLD.**

**28** There are **THOUSANDS OF CRATERS ON THE MOON.** Three near the Apollo 11 landing site are named after U.S. astronaut buddies Neil Armstrong, Buzz Aldrin, and Michael Collins.

**29** After disappearing during a fire some 40 years ago, the **MOON ROCKS** given to the U.S. state of Alaska in 1969 by President Nixon are back on display.

**30** The **SHARK-EYE MOON SNAIL** feeds on highly prized New England clams by drilling a hole in the shell and sucking out the clam.

**31** U.S. astronaut Neil Armstrong claims his first words from the moon in 1969 were, "**ONE SMALL STEP FOR A MAN, ONE GIANT LEAP FOR MANKIND.**" Most people didn't hear the "a."

**32** You don't need a telescope to see some of **JUPITER'S MOONS.** Four of the largest can be seen with a pair of ordinary **BINOCULARS.**

**33** According to NASA, volcanic activity on Jupiter's moon IO looks "like a **GIANT PIZZA** covered with melted cheese and splotches of tomato and ripe olives."

**34** William Shakespeare would be excited to know that most of Uranus's moons, including **JULIET, PUCK**, and **OPHELIA**, are named after characters from his plays.

**35** You'd have dark, **MOONLESS NIGHTS** if you lived on Mercury or Venus. Both planets lack natural satellites.

**1.** Spinning tops have been around so long that no one knows for sure where they came from. **2.** By some accounts, Akbar the Great, a ruler in India nearly 500 years ago, kept a stable of more than 9,000 cheetahs so that he could watch them chase prey. **3.** It's believed that in ancient times Asia's Hmong people hid words in the embroidery on their clothes. **4.** Istanbul, in Turkey, is the most recent name of a city that dates back some 2,600 years and has been known as Byzantium and Constantinople. **5.** About 2,000 years ago, Romans read about daily events and government actions in the *Acta diurna,* an early newspaper. **6.** People in the Sahara used axes and arrows to hunt antelope and turtles some 12,000 years ago when the region was not the desert it is today. **7.** South of Egypt, the kingdom of Kush thrived on the Nile River from 2000 to 1500 B.C. Their source of wealth? Gold. **8.** The name *Olmec,* which means "rubber people," comes from the fact that this ancient civilization in what is now Mexico took latex from rubber trees and added juice from a vine to make rubber. **9.** Neanderthals ate about 5,000 calories a day—about the same number as an NBA basketball player does today. **10.** In 2350 B.C., the first indoor toilet was built in a palace in what is now Iraq. **11.** Built for foot travel, the Inca road system included long stone stairways for climbing over the mountains. **12.** During the late Stone Age, people in what is now southern Turkey entered their homes through a trapdoor in the roof. **13.** One of the rulers of India's first empire had Buddhist sayings carved on rocks and in caves. One 3-story-high pillar had a seated lion on the top. **14.** Thanks to a coin, we know what Kushan Empire ruler Vima Kadphises looked like right down to the wart on his cheek. **15.** In 4000 B.C., about as many people lived in the world as now live in just the U.S. state of Washington: 7 million. **16.** A peasant named Liu Bang led a revolt 2,200 years ago

# 100 BLASTS FROM PAST CIVILIZATIONS

Front and back of a coin depicting Kushan Empire ruler Vima Kadphises

that made him the first ruler of China's Han Empire . **17.** The ancient Han Empire included about the same area where most of China's current population lives. **18.** The ancient Sumerians called themselves *sag giga* or "the black-headed ones." **19.** According to legend, a mythical hero named Gilgamesh built the 6 miles (10 km) of brick walls that surrounded the ancient Sumerian city of Uruk. **20.** Pyramids in ancient Mesopotamia (now Iraq) were square or rectangular in shape. **21.** It was a Viking tradition to leave a dead cow above the entrance to a house as an offering to the gods. **22.** Around 10,000 years ago, people in Scandinavia used combs made from antlers to remove fleas and lice. **23.** The world's first molded bricks were made around 6000 B.C. in Mesopotamia. **24.** Dogs are the oldest domesticated animal. They have been living with us for at least 14,000 years. **25.** Ancient Egyptians used bronze pins to hold their robes together. **26.** The African kingdom of Aksum created the world's largest obelisk—a 4-sided column—made from a single stone. It weighed 500 tons (454 MT) and stood 100 feet (30 m) tall. **27.** Almost 5,000 years ago, the Chinese emperor Shen Nung used herbal medicine and acupuncture to relieve tooth- aches. **28.** The ancient Egyptians mixed the gummy bark of the acacia tree with soot to make the first ink. **29.** A battle helmet covered with dozens of male pig tusks protected the head of a king of Mycenae, a city in ancient Greece. **30.** The name "Neanderthal" comes from the location where the first bones of this prehistoric relative were found—a limestone quarry in Germany's Neander Valley. **31.** A stone slab believed to be part of a shower dating from 1350 B.C. in Tell el-Amarna, Egypt, may be evidence that ancient Egyptians took more than baths. **32.** Bells made in 1350 B.C. during the Shang dynasty in China used bronze-casting techniques that were 1,000 years ahead of those used by any other civilization. **33.** The ancient Hopewell people of North America were connected by a network of trade routes that stretched from the southern United States into Canada. **34.** Scandinavians crafted ice skates out of iron at least 1,800 years ago. Earlier skates used bone blades. **35.** Warriors in ancient Sumer (now southern Iraq) braided their beards and knotted their long hair at the back of their heads. **36.** Pueblo Bonita, built by ancestral Puebloan people between 850 and 1150 in Chaco Canyon, New Mexico, U.S.A., had more than 800 rooms. **37.** Ancient Egyptians used a cream made from oil, lime, and perfume to smell fresh. **38.** For 2,000 years the Phoenicians were the chief merchants of the Mediterranean world. **39.** British officers stationed in India found murals dating to the 2nd century B.C. in the Ajanta Caves that reveal the life of the Buddha. **40.** The Assyrians put collars with scarlet feathers around the necks of their horses before battle. **41.** While excavating the ancient Mesopotamian city of Ur, archaeologists discov- ered a tomb that held the remains of Queen Puabi and the skeletons of 10 handmaidens and 5 soldiers. **42.** Paintings in ancient Egyptian tombs show ball games and acrobatics. **43.** The Indus Valley civilization covered an area of South Asia about the size of Texas, U.S.A.—making it the largest civilization of its time. **44.** The Chavin people of the Americas started making collars and ornaments out of gold 3,500 years ago. **45.** Early Chinese rulers colored their nails with gold and silver. **46.** In 1234, Koreans used movable type to print books by hand, some 200 years before Johannes Gutenberg developed his mechanical printing press in what is now Germany. **47.** The first book entirely about children's medicine was written in the 9th century by a Muslim doctor. **48.** The Maya used a number system in the 4th century that was ahead of that used in Europe by a thousand years. **49.** The large stones found in the Nabta Playa in southern Egypt are the world's oldest known astronomical devices. **50.** The largest ancient structure in southern Africa is the Great Enclosure, in Zimbabwe—a stone wall nearly 4 stories tall built by the Shona people. **51.** Al-Razi, a Muslim doctor born in 864, was the first to write about how to diagnose and treat smallpox and measles. **52.** The Ganges civilization that ruled most of northern India 2,500 years ago developed Sanskrit, India's first written language. **53.** The founder of China's Han dynasty, who wasn't a fan of education, once urinated into the hat of a court scholar. **54.** Ancient Egyptians often went barefoot, but nobles sometimes wore leather sandals, while the poor wore sandals made of grass or papyrus. **55.** The Jomon, the earliest known people to live in Japan, were skilled potters. **56.** Almost 700 years ago, the Arab explorer Ibn Battuta traveled some 75,000 miles (120,700 km). That's like walking around the Equator 3 times. **57.** The Sumerians were probably the first to keep track of time by using a calendar based on the phases of the moon. **58.** The fighting skills of people in Japan's Yamato Clan gave them control over all other Japanese clans around A.D. 300. **59.** Archaeologists have found evidence that the Chinese began making silk at least 6,000 years ago. **60.** A group of nomadic people called Scythians controlled part of the Silk Road that linked Asia and Europe. They would allow travelers to pass along the trade route for a fee. **61.** First built in the mid-1200s, the Great Mosque in Djenné, Mali, is the largest mud-brick building in the world. **62.** A ruler of Nubia in northern Africa restarted the practice of building pyramids 1,400 years after the ancient Egyptians stopped building them. **63.** Between 1405 and 1433, Zheng He sailed trading vessels from China to Africa and brought back lions, zebras, and "camel birds" (ostriches). **64.** Some 4,600 years ago, Caral, the earliest civilization in the Americas, began in what is now Peru. **65.** Jenne-jeno, in Mali, is the oldest known inhabited city in western Africa. People have lived there for almost 1,600 years. **66.** The ancient Sumerians used pictures and symbols to create the world's first written language more than 5,000 years ago. **67.** North America's native Inuit men in North America wore decorated sealskin gloves with quills and bird beaks to make them rattle during ceremonial dances. **68.** Tattoos of horses, eagles, and stags have been found on the 2,500-year-old mummified bodies of Scythian chiefs. **69.** We know from writings found on tablets that Sargon of Akkad ruled in Mesopotamia 4,300 years ago, but archaeologists are still searching for his capital city. **70.** A Roman found in a grave in Egypt must have wanted straight teeth. His were fitted with a gold wire. **71.** The Dance of the Flyers is an ancient tradition still practiced in Mexico and Guatemala. Four dancers spin around a 100-foot (30-m)-high pole upside down. **72.** The *Rigveda*, Hinduism's oldest known sacred text, dates to around 1500 B.C. and has 1,028 poems. **73.** Phoenician women wore elaborate jewelry, including small beads made to look like lotus flowers, animal heads, pomegranates, and acorns. **74.** Archaeologists uncovered a small casket in Gujarat, India, with writing that identified the contents as the ashes of the Buddha. **75.** The ancient Chinese believed a solar eclipse was caused by a dragon eating the sun. **76.** Sudan has more pyramids than Egypt. **77.** Not all Roman slaves were owned by a family or individual—some belonged to an entire town. **78.** The Code of Hammurabi contained 282 laws covering everything from marriage to stealing and prices. It was the first time a king (Hammurabi) had given his people a set of laws to live by. **79.** A scholar in ancient China invented the first known mechanical device to accurately tell where an earthquake would happen. **80.** Some 3,500 years ago, the Lapita people set out into the unknown waters of the South Pacific in long canoes with sails, settling on many remote islands. **81.** In 1994, a group of French archaeologists found artifacts from the ancient city of Alexandria, Egypt, under 33 feet (10 m) of water in the current city's harbor. **82.** St. Brendan was a 6th-century Irish monk who, according to legend, sailed to America almost 1,000 years before Columbus. **83.** The Alhambra, built more than 650 years ago when Muslims ruled Spain, was a menacing fortress on the outside, but a beautiful palace inside. **84.** Salt was so precious in the ancient world that cakes of it were used as money in places like Ethiopia and Tibet. **85.** Battle swords collected from one enemy might be repaired and used to fight another enemy. That may be how a Turkish sword came to have a grip from the Mughal Empire and a blade from the Ottoman Empire. **86.** The name of Carthage, a suburb in Tunisia, means "new town" even though the city was founded by Phoenicians in 814 B.C. **87.** Excavations at Knossus on the Mediterranean island of Crete in 1900 proved that a place long thought to exist only in Greek mythology was real. **88.** One side of the Maya House of the Governor in Uxmal, Mexico, is decorated with 15,000 carved pieces of stone. **89.** Betelgeuse, Vega, and Rigel are examples of Arabic names given to some stars by Muslim astronomers. **90.** The Inca used *quipus*—colored cords with knots tied in them—to record information. **91.** Potatoes were first cultivated in South America some 1,800 years ago. **92.** The ancient Shona people of what is now Zimbabwe believed eagles were messengers of the gods. Today, the country's flag includes an eagle. **93.** Masks—often representing animal spirits—have been an important part of Inuit culture for at least 2,500 years. **94.** Archaeologists have discovered 24 horses buried standing up in a Nubian grave in what is now Sudan. **95.** Farmers in Mesopotamia were spinning wool to make clothes some 10,000 years ago. **96.** Islamic cultures experienced a "golden age" of learning from the 7th to the 17th centuries. **97.** Alexandria, Egypt, was founded by Alexander the Great in 332 B.C. **98.** Doctors in ancient Greece believed that blood caused some illnesses. The cure? Remove some blood. **99.** In traditional Navajo culture, girls wore pendants in their ears until they got married. Then they took them out, attached them to necklaces, and saved them to give to their daughters. **100.** Some Viking chiefs were buried inside their ships.

**1**
DYNAMITE was used to carve 90 percent of the heads of the 4 U.S. presidents on MOUNT RUSHMORE in South Dakota, U.S.A.

**2**
TOWER BRIDGE, across the River Thames in London, is raised more than 1,000 times a year to let tall ships and other watercraft through.

**3**
The record for RACING UP the 1,576 steps to reach the 86th floor of the EMPIRE STATE BUILDING in New York City, U.S.A., is 9 minutes, 33 seconds.

**4**
Each minute hand on the Great Clock at the top of the BIG BEN tower weighs about as much as a GIANT PANDA.

**5**
The length of STEEL WIRE used to hold up San Francisco's Golden Gate Bridge in California, U.S.A., could CIRCLE EARTH 3 times.

**6**
The bottom of HOOVER DAM, on the Nevada-Arizona, U.S.A., border is as thick as the length of 2 FOOTBALL FIELDS measured end-to-end.

**7**
There are 2 staircases leading to the top of Italy's LEANING TOWER OF PISA—but one has 2 EXTRA STEPS to make up for the lean.

**8**
If the seated statue of Abraham Lincoln in the LINCOLN MEMORIAL in Washington, D.C., U.S.A., could stand up, it would be nearly 3 STORIES TALL.

**9**
Up until the end of the U.S. Civil War, the WHITE HOUSE, in Washington, D.C., was the LARGEST HOUSE in the United States.

**10**
BUCKINGHAM PALACE, Queen Elizabeth II's official residence in London, England, has 775 ROOMS, including 78 BATHROOMS.

**11**
The STATUE OF LIBERTY in New York Harbor, U.S.A., has a 35-foot (10.7-m) WAISTLINE.

**12**
Michelangelo REFUSED TO BE PAID for his work on St. Peter's Basilica in what is now Vatican City.

**13**
The DOME of the U.S. Capitol in Washington, D.C., was made with almost 9 million pounds of iron. That's nearly as much as 600 AFRICAN ELEPHANTS weigh!

**14**
Moscow's ST. BASIL'S CATHEDRAL has 9 chapels, each with its own colorful "onion" dome.

**15**
ANGKOR WAT, a shrine located in what is now Cambodia, is more than 15 miles (24 km) wide, making it the world's LARGEST RELIGIOUS STRUCTURE.

**16**
The COLOSSEUM in Rome, which was built in the first century A.D., fell to ruin over hundreds of years due to damage from lightning, earthquakes, and vandalism.

**17**
At least 6 RAVENS always live at England's TOWER OF LONDON because, according to legend, the tower would crumble if they left.

**18**
The WASHINGTON MONUMENT in Washington, D.C., is as tall as the length of 794 PENCILS standing end-to-end.

# 50 MONUMENTAL
## FACTS ABOUT LANDMARKS

**19**
The GREAT PYRAMID of Giza, in Egypt, is the only one of the Seven Wonders of the Ancient World that is STILL STANDING.

**20**
Researchers think that the ENTIRE FACE of the Great Sphinx of Giza in Egypt was once painted red.

**21**
The exterior of India's TAJ MAHAL was built of marble and inlaid with semiprecious and rare stones—like onyx, jade, and goldstone.

**22**
Archaeologists are trying to figure out exactly how BLUESTONES, weighing up to 4 tons (3.6 MT), were moved 160 miles (257 km) from Wales to build Stonehenge, in England.

**23**
In Nashville, Tennessee, U.S.A., there is a full-scale replica of the PARTHENON, an ancient Greek temple. Nashville's columns are concrete; the real ones are marble.

**24**
The Potala Palace in Lhasa, Tibet, has been the WINTER PALACE of the Dalai Lama since the 7th century. Inside there are 698 murals and nearly 10,000 painted scrolls.

**25**
THE LOUVRE museum in Paris, France, is the world's most visited museum. Almost 10 million people view the exhibits every year.

**26**
To celebrate the end of World War I, a French pilot made a daring pass under the ARC DE TRIOMPHE in Paris in a biplane.

**27**
EACH LETTER of the 91-year-old Hollywood sign perched on a hillside above Los Angeles, California, U.S.A., is 4 stories tall.

**28**
HENDERSON WAVES, the highest pedestrian bridge in Singapore, looks like a GIANT, GOLDEN SNAKE moving along the skyline.

**29**
The National Stadium in Beijing, China, is nicknamed the "BIRD'S NEST" because of its delicate, crisscross steel design.

**30**
The National Aquatics Center in Beijing—nicknamed the "WATER CUBE" during the 2008 Olympics—now has a 40-foot (12.2-m)-high, free-fall waterslide.

**31**
A RED SEAT in the bleachers at Fenway Park in Boston, Massachusetts, U.S.A., marks where the stadium's longest home-run ball landed: 502 feet (153 m) from home plate.

**32**
At 2,716.5 feet (828 m), Dubai's BURJ KHALIFA is more than twice as tall as France's Eiffel Tower.

**33**
The walls and roof of BEIJING'S NATIONAL AQUATICS CENTER contain more than 3,000 air-filled "cushions" that look like bubbles.

**34**
LIQUID MERCURY inspired the artist who created the stainless-steel Cloud Gate at Chicago's Millennium Park in Illinois, U.S.A.

**35**
There are over 90 POPES buried in St. Peter's Basilica in Vatican City.

**36**
The roof of the 605-foot (184-m)-high Space Needle in Seattle, Washington, U.S.A., has 25 LIGHTNING RODS.

**37**
The original nickname for Seattle's SPACE NEEDLE was "The Space Cage."

**38**
Arizona's GRAND CANYON SKYWALK lets you look straight down through the glass floor to the Colorado River 4,000 feet (1,219 m) below.

**39**
The architect of the OPERA HOUSE in Sydney, Australia, got his inspiration for the design while peeling an ORANGE.

**40**
MACHU PICCHU, an ancient Inca citadel in the Andes, sat abandoned and hidden from view by vegetation for hundreds of years. Now, 2,500 people visit each day.

**41**
The EIFFEL TOWER in Paris, France, is made up of 18,038 pieces of iron and held together with 2.5 million rivets.

**42**
Some of the GROTESQUE GARGOYLES on Notre-Dame Cathedral in Paris are used as waterspouts to drain rainwater off the roof.

**43**
The National September 11 Memorial in New York City has the LARGEST MAN-MADE WATERFALLS in North America. Altogether they are about 5 city blocks long.

**44**
Germany's 19th-century Neuschwanstein castle served as the inspiration for SLEEPING BEAUTY'S CASTLE in Disneyland, California.

**45**
CHICHÉN ITZÁ, a Maya temple on Mexico's Yucatán Peninsula, has 365 steps—one for each day of the calendar year.

**46**
The GREAT WALL OF CHINA is more than twice as LONG as the distance between the U.S. cities of New York and Los Angeles.

**47**
CENTRAL PARK in New York City has more than 9,000 BENCHES.

**48**
There are more than 17.5 miles (28 km) of hallways in the PENTAGON, headquarters of the U.S. Department of Defense, in Virginia, U.S.A.

**49**
Masjid al-Haram in Mecca, Saudi Arabia—also known as the HOLY MOSQUE—can hold as many as 820,000 worshippers.

**50**
MOAI, huge, humanlike statues on EASTER ISLAND in the Pacific Ocean, weigh on average 20 tons (18,144 kg)—that's as much as 4 large pickup trucks.

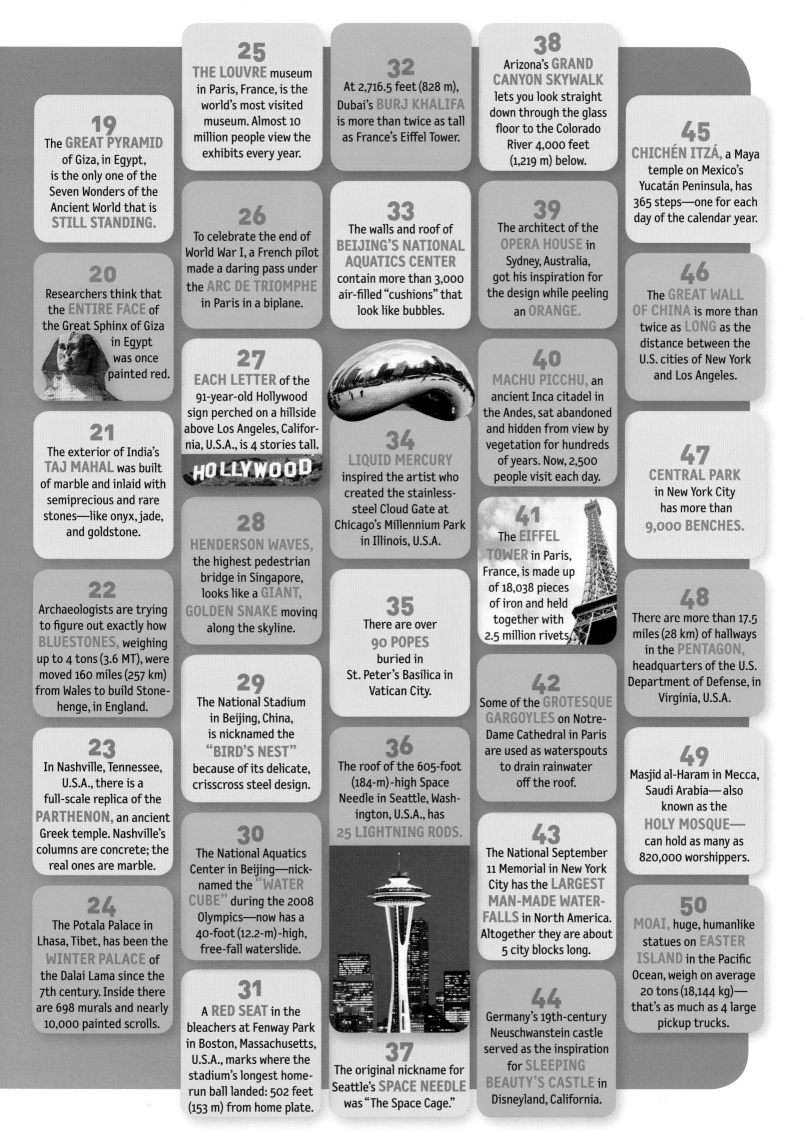

**1** A female German cockroach can have **35,000** offspring a year.

**2** There are about **4,000** species of cockroaches.

**3** **COCKROACHES WILL EAT** glue, leather, and even flakes of human skin.

**4** **COCKROACHES WERE AROUND FOR millions of years BEFORE THE DINOSAURS.**

**5** You can name one of the Madagascar hissing cockroaches at the Bronx Zoo in New York City, U.S.A., for your Valentine.

**6** SOME ADULT FEMALE COCKROACHES ARE **PREGNANT** FOR THEIR WHOLE LIVES.

An egg case!

**7** Only adult female cockroaches can have colored blood. **SOMETIMES IT'S ORANGE.**

**8** **A WHITE COCKROACH** is a roach that has just shed its skin.

**25**

**9** **A million cockroaches** were found living in a house in Schenectady, New York, in 1979. They were streaming out of the windows and had plastered the walls.

**10** Cockroaches can survive a small **NUCLEAR EXPLOSION.**

**11** **COCKROACHES ARE social animals** AND SUFFER POOR HEALTH IF **isolated.**

**12** "Cockroach" was first written in English as "cacaroch," after the Spanish word *cucaracha*.

**13** THE MEXICAN FOLK SONG "LA CUCARACHA" IS ABOUT A COCKROACH THAT HAS LOST 1 OF ITS 6 LEGS.

**14** IT ONLY TAKES **A DAY** FOR A SMALL GROUP OF MADAGASCAR HISSING COCKROACHES TO **EAT A LARGE CARROT.**

**15** A bus traveling from Atlantic City, New Jersey, to New York City, U.S.A., had to pull over when cockroaches started **CRAWLING OUT OF ITS AIR VENTS.**

**16** Wall-E, the robot from the Disney-Pixar movie, had a pet cockroach. The roach had no name in the movie, but the film's artists nicknamed it Hal after a silent film producer named Hal Roach.

**17** Male and female common wood cockroaches look so different that **SCIENTISTS THOUGHT AT ONE TIME THEY WERE DIFFERENT SPECIES.**

**18** If you could move as fast as a cockroach, you could run a 100-yard (91-m) dash in 1 second.

**19** Cockroaches use **sticky pads** between the claws on their feet to walk upside down on smooth surfaces.

**20** You can buy gummy cockroach treats with lime-, orange-, or cherry-flavored legs.

# CREEPY FACTS ABOUT COCKROACHES

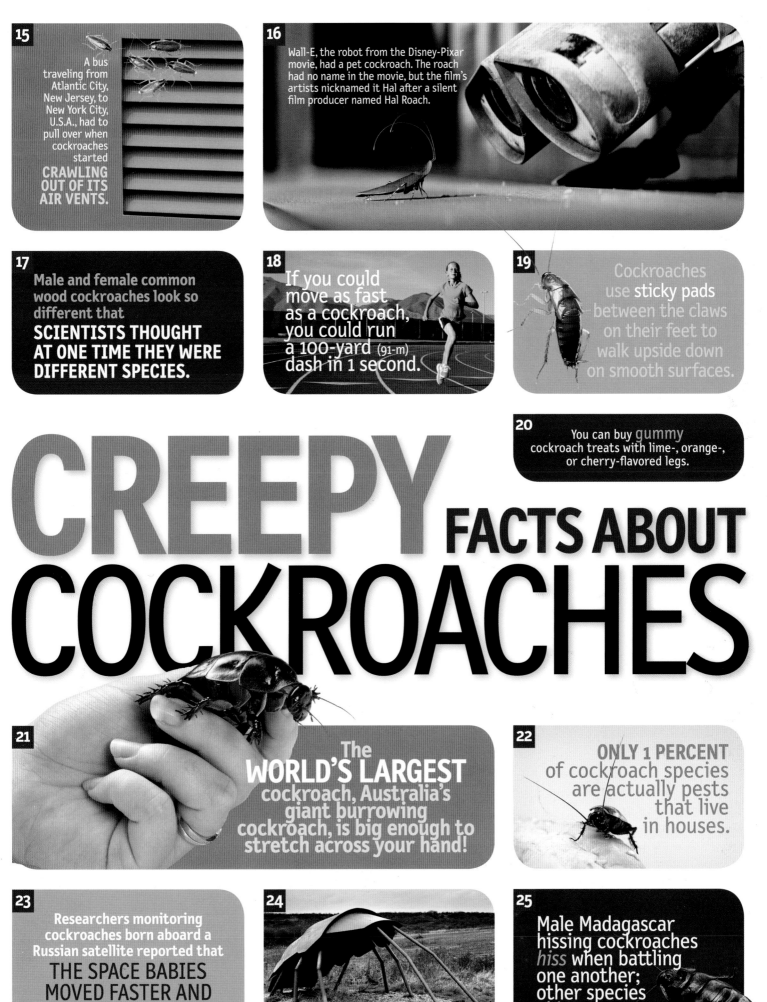

**21** The **WORLD'S LARGEST** cockroach, Australia's giant burrowing cockroach, is big enough to stretch across your hand!

**22** **ONLY 1 PERCENT** of cockroach species are actually pests that live in houses.

**23** Researchers monitoring cockroaches born aboard a Russian satellite reported that **THE SPACE BABIES MOVED FASTER AND HAD MORE ENERGY** than cockroaches born on Earth.

**24** A giant steel cockroach towers 8 feet (2.4 m) above the ground at a sculpture park in the United Kingdom.

**25** Male Madagascar hissing cockroaches *hiss* when battling one another; other species *chirp*.

**1** **SAUCER-SHAPED** lenticular clouds have been mistaken for **UFOs.**

**2** A single cloud may hold **BILLIONS OF POUNDS OF WATER,** but not all clouds bring rain.

**3** Fog is actually **CLOUDS THAT TOUCH THE GROUND.**

**4** The highest clouds are at 50,000 feet (15,240 m). That's taller than 33 EMPIRE STATE BUILDINGS stacked on top of each other!

**5** A **MASSIVE HURRICANE** swirling above **SATURN** produced clouds the SIZE OF TEXAS, U.S.A.

**6** A volcanic eruption in Iceland once produced an **ASH CLOUD** that rose 3 MILES (5 km) into the atmosphere, **STALLING AIR TRAFFIC** in the area for an entire week.

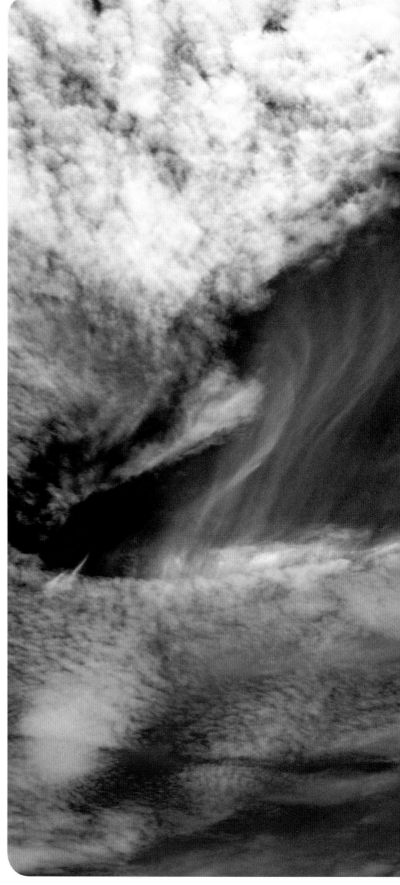

**7** Unlike a tornado, A FUNNEL CLOUD NEVER TOUCHES THE GROUND.

# ABOUT CLOUDS

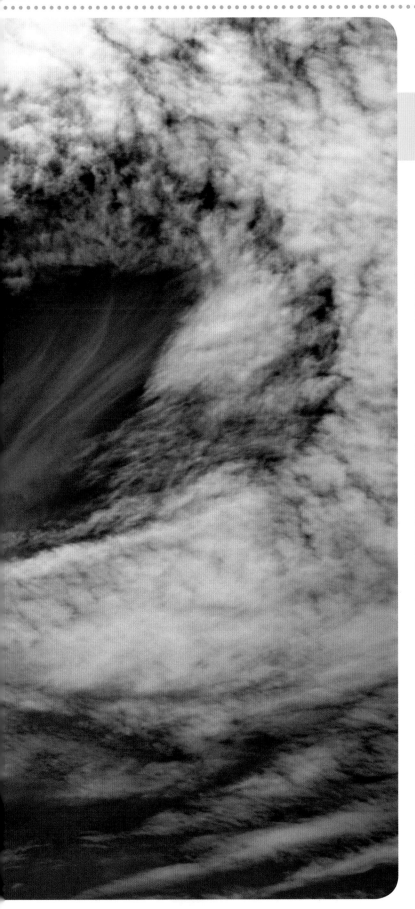

**8** Depending on the speed of the wind, some clouds TRAVEL UP TO 100 MILES PER HOUR (160 kph) across the sky.

**9** FIRE RAINBOW—clouds that look like colorful flames—are a rare result of LIGHT PASSING THROUGH WISPY, HIGH-ALTITUDE, CIRRUS CLOUDS.

**10** At any moment, CLOUDS COVER ABOUT 60 PERCENT OF EARTH.

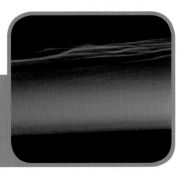

**11** Clouds that GLOW ELECTRIC BLUE may have been formed by water vapor from METEOR SMOKE.

**12** The YELLOW-ORANGE CLOUDS above Venus, which are so thick that they hide the planet from our view, are made of SULFURIC ACID.

**13** MUSHROOM CLOUDS form when dense, hot gas from a NUCLEAR EXPLOSION OR OTHER MASSIVE BLAST hits cool air in the atmosphere. These gigantic clouds can be SEEN MORE THAN 50 MILES (80KM) AWAY.

**14** Some of Earth's clouds can SPAN MORE THAN 600 MILES (965 KM) OF SKY—that's about the DISTANCE BETWEEN WASHINGTON, D.C., AND CHICAGO, ILLINOIS, U.S.A.

**15** People have reported seeing clouds SHAPED EXACTLY LIKE THE BATMAN SIGNAL, PINOCCHIO, HORSES, and more.

**1** African wild dogs aren't homebodies. They rarely stay in one place for more than a day.

**2** A GIRAFFE'S EYE IS THE SIZE OF A PING-PONG BALL.

**3** Male spiral-horned antelope use their wavy horns to lock horns with other bulls in fights.

**4** Hippos have a clear membrane that covers their eyes so they can see underwater.

**5** Domesticated African wild asses brought to the southwestern United States by Spaniards in the 1500s came to be known as burros.

**6** With ears that are more than 5 inches (13 cm) long, it's no wonder the African bat-eared fox has a good sense of hearing. The ears not only help it zero in on insect prey, they also keep the bat's body cool.

**7** An African python can eat an entire wildebeest calf—whole!

**8** Bonobos, a type of ape, have been seen using pieces of moss like sponges to soak up water out of tree trunks.

**9** One of an elephant's closest living relatives is the African hyrax, which looks like a guinea pig but has teeth, toes, and a skull similar to its pachyderm cousin.

**10** If threatened, some African cobras will play dead by flailing around and then lying perfectly still.

**11** Even though they look like dogs, hyenas are more closely related to cats.

**12** Cheetahs, found in eastern and southern Africa, are the only cats that can turn in midair to follow prey.

**13** Sitatungas, a type of central African antelope, jump in water when they feel threatened and hide with only their noses sticking out.

**14** Chimps are one of the few animals with the intelligence to use tools. They use long blades of grass to fish termites out of mounds.

**15** Crocodiles store fat in their tails as a food reserve in case there is a long wait until the next meal.

**16** An African elephant's skull weighs as much as 115 pounds (52 kg). It would weigh more, but air spaces in the bone make the skull lighter.

**17** During the annual migrations across the Serengeti Plain in Tanzania, zebras usually go first, followed by wildebeests and gazelles.

**18** In East Africa, more than a million lesser flamingos gather into one gigantic nesting flock each year.

**19** The fossa, found only on Madagascar, has claws like a cat and a tail like a monkey, but its close relative is the mongoose.

**20** THE NECK OF AN ADULT GIRAFFE IS LONGER THAN AN AVERAGE MAN IS TALL AND WEIGHS MORE THAN A MOUNTAIN GORILLA!

**21** Just like human fingerprints, gorilla noses are unique. Scientists take pictures of them to keep track of individuals they are studying.

**22** Guenons, a type of African monkey, use pouches in their cheeks to stock up on food. They can store almost as much as it takes to fill their stomachs.

**23** Royal antelope, which live in West Africa's lowland rain forest, are the world's smallest antelope. A calf could sit in the palm of an adult human's hand!

**24** Hedgehogs that live in the deserts of Africa eat scorpions and small snakes.

**25** One of the hippopotamus's closest living relatives is the dolphin.

**26** Male impalas stick out their tongues to tell other males to back off.

**27** The hump on Arabian camels, which live in northern Africa, can store up to 80 pounds (36 kg) of fat.

**28** Pygmy hippos, found in forests of West Africa, are 10 times smaller than regular hippos.

**29** Honey badgers, which live throughout sub-Saharan Africa, aren't bothered by bee stings or snake venom.

**30** The southern ground hornbill, a bird that likes to eat meat, makes a sound like a roaring lion.

**31** Fossils of hyenas have been found in North America, Europe, and Asia, but today these animals live only in Africa.

**32** Impalas are able to leap almost the length of a school bus.

**33** Spotted hyenas can digest skin and bone.

**34** Just like bees, giraffes are pollinators! They transfer tree pollen that gets stuck to their noses as they eat.

**35** A hyrax, a small East African hoofed animal that looks like a rodent, is inactive 95 percent of the day.

**36** More than a million mummies of a bird called the African sacred ibis have been found in a group of tombs in Egypt.

**37** Mandrills, the world's largest monkey species, live in African forests. The ridges along the male's nose are purplish blue, the nose is red, and the beard is blond.

**38** A meerkat is not a cat. It's a member of the mongoose family that uses its stiff tail for balance so it can stand upright.

**39** COLOBUS MONKEYS ARE BIG BURPERS! DIGESTING THEIR LEAFY DIET PRODUCES A LOT OF GAS AND RESULTS IN FREQUENT BELCHING.

**40** Cheetahs have black "tear marks" on their face, which researchers think might act as sun protection.

**41** It's hard to run backward, but naked mole rats can run in both directions in their underground burrows in the African desert.

**42** What looks and sounds like a sneeze coming from a guenon monkey is actually a call of alarm.

**43** Male Nile lechwes, a type of antelope that lives in the Nile River Valley, use their horns as back scratchers as well as for fighting.

**44** Like its cousin the giraffe, the okapi has a long tongue—so long, it can use it to clean its ears!

**45** An oryx, a kind of antelope that lives in eastern and southern Africa, has such a good sense of smell that it can sniff out rainfall from 50 miles (80 km) away.

**46** Ostriches, which live in the African savanna and desert, lay huge eggs. Each one weighs about as much as 24 chicken eggs.

**47** Hippos can hold their breath for as long as 30 minutes underwater.

**48** Chimpanzees sometimes munch on medicinal plants when they are sick or injured.

**49** Ostriches can't fly, but they can use their wings as rudders to change direction while running.

**50** THE QUILLS ON AFRICAN PORCUPINES ARE AS LONG AS 3 PENCILS.

**51** The African rock python, Africa's largest snake, is over twice as long as a regulation basketball hoop is high.

**52** The black rhino's 2 horns grow as much as 3 inches (8 cm) each year.

**53** A giraffe's heart is 2 feet (0.6 m) long, and its lungs can hold 12 gallons (45 L) of air.

**54** Adult emperor scorpions, which live in western Africa, don't sting their prey to kill them—they tear them apart with their pincers.

**55** A warthog's "warts" are actually bumps of fat that help protect the animal's face in a fight.

**56** The greater kudu, a type of woodland antelope found in eastern and southern Africa, can jump 6 feet (1.8 m) without a running start.

**57** African buffaloes are territorial and known for their mean temper. They work together in herds to defend each other and are capable of killing leopards, hyenas, and even lions.

**58** A zebra's night vision is thought to be as good as an owl's.

**59** Nile crocodiles eat fish, porcupines, small hippos, other crocodiles, and even people!

# FACTS ABOUT
# 75 AFRICAN ANIMALS TO MAKE YOU ROAR

**60** A hyena's bite pressure can reach 800 pounds per square inch (56 kg/cm²)—about 7 times as powerful as a human's.

**61** The horn of a bongo, an African forest antelope, can grow as long as an average 4-year-old child is tall!

**62** Thick-tailed greater bush babies, a kind of nocturnal primate, make a call that sounds like a crying human baby.

**63 ALL APES LAUGH WHEN THEY ARE TICKLED.**

**64** Naked mole rats are sometimes called sand puppies.

**65** East African vervet monkeys live in mountain rain forests at elevations as high as 13,000 feet (3,962 m).

**66** Camels move both legs on the same side of their body at the same time.

**67** The dik-dik, a dwarf antelope found in East Africa, stands 14 inches (36 cm) tall—about the size of a small dog.

**68** Penguins live in Africa! Coastal areas of South Africa are home to the African penguin, which makes a donkey-like bray.

**69** The African gray parrot is able to mimic over 700 words.

**70** Some desert antelope, like Dama gazelles, never need to drink water. They get all their moisture from the plants they eat.

**71** An okapi's ears move independently so it can hear a predator coming from any direction.

**72** Hippos act like rafts for other animals in African rivers. Birds perch atop their backs while looking for fish, and baby crocodiles climb aboard to sun themselves.

**73** Giraffes sometimes moo and whistle.

**74** In 1895, there were fewer than 100 southern white rhinos in Africa. Thanks to conservation efforts, there are more than 20,000 today.

**75** Every May or June, about 1.5 million wildebeests migrate about 2,000 miles (3,219 km) to greener pastures in southeastern Africa.

Lion

# 35 FACTS TO

**1** Over time, "etiquette" has come to mean ALL THE DOS AND DON'TS of how to behave WHEN and WHERE.

**2** The Egyptian PTAH-HOTEP wrote the first known guide to GOOD BEHAVIOR about 5,000 years ago.

**3** The word "etiquette" comes from a French word meaning "LITTLE TICKET." It refers to signs King Louis XIV posted in his palace gardens telling guests to KEEP OFF the flowers.

**4** During the Renaissance in Europe, displaying GOOD MANNERS—especially at the dinner table—became a way to identify the PRIVILEGED CLASS.

**5** CHEWING GUM in public is a big no-no for kids in France.

**6** Experts believe people have been saying "THANK YOU" to show gratitude for thousands of years.

**7** People of the Renaissance era were expected to THROW THE BONES from their meat ON THE FLOOR, not place them on their plates.

**8** In the 12th century, KING DAVID I of Scotland offered TAX REBATES to any subject who was willing to learn to eat more elegantly.

**9** It's considered rude to write in RED INK in PORTUGAL.

**10** CHARLESTON, South Carolina, is considered the most MANNERLY city in the United States.

**11** Greeting with a HANDSHAKE has been practiced at least as far back as the 5TH CENTURY B.C.

**12** A governor of New Mexico, U.S.A., once shook more than 13,000 HANDS in 8 HOURS—a world record.

**13** "THANK YOU" is believed to come from the German word *danken*, meaning "to thank."

**14** In many Asian countries, it's proper etiquette to use 2 HANDS when offering a gift.

**15** In Europe, it's considered rude to place your HANDS IN YOUR LAP while you eat. You are supposed to always keep your wrists on the dinner table.

**16** The world's LONGEST HANDSHAKE lasted 42 HOURS, 35 MINUTES.

**17** During the Middle Ages, it was considered RUDE to put your FINGERS IN YOUR EARS, your hands on your head, or to blow your nose with your hands during a meal.

**18** If you DROP YOUR BREAD on the ground in most Middle Eastern countries, you should pick it up, kiss it, and RAISE IT to your forehead to show RESPECT for your food.

**19** At dinnertime in Japan and China, it's polite to SLURP YOUR NOODLES or soup.

**20** A SMALL BURP at the end of your meal shows respect among the indigenous INUIT PEOPLE of Canada.

**21** BLOWING YOUR NOSE in public in Japan is considered CRUDE.

**22** In INDIA, it's rude to open a GIFT in front of the person who gave it. Gifts are OPENED IN PRIVATE.

**23** People were expected to eat with 1 HAND, not 2, during the Middle Ages, when FORKS WERE RARE.

**24** People in Egypt are taught to keep BOTH FEET ON THE GROUND when sitting. Showing the bottoms of their shoes to others sends the message "YOU ARE BENEATH ME."

**25** When dining with the QUEEN OF ENGLAND, you must STOP EATING as soon as she does.

**26** The "OK" hand symbol in America is considered rude in BRAZIL and GERMANY.

# MIND ABOUT MANNERS

**27**
Many table manners that came out of the Renaissance—like keeping your **ELBOWS OFF THE TABLE** and your mouth closed while chewing—are still practiced today.

**28**
In Thailand, it is **DISRESPECTFUL TO LICK** a postage stamp that has the **KING'S PICTURE** on the front.

**29**
Saying *gesundheit* (German for "health") when someone sneezes became popular in the United States with the rise in **GERMAN IMMIGRATION** in the early 20th century.

**30**
In the United States, people are expected to **MAKE EYE CONTACT** during a conversation. In other countries, it's rude to stare someone in the eye while speaking to them.

**31**
The tradition of **REMOVING YOUR HAT** as a sign of respect dates to **MEDIEVAL** times when **KNIGHTS** had to take off their helmets to identify themselves.

**32**
**LEAVING A BIT** of food in the bottom of your bowl shows that you've **HAD ENOUGH** to eat in Mongolia.

**33**
In Bangladesh, women **DO NOT SHAKE HANDS.** Instead, they greet others with a **POLITE NOD.**

**34**
It's totally acceptable for people in **SHANGHAI**, China, to go **SHOPPING IN THEIR PAJAMAS.**

**35**
Cutting your **POTATOES WITH A KNIFE** in Germany is insulting to the host. It suggests the food isn't cooked enough.

**1.** People worldwide spend 3 billion hours a week playing computer games. **2.** Fifty-eight percent of the U.S. population plays video games. **3.** In 1969, Ralph Baer designed the first multiplayer video game system. On his Brown Box, you could play Ping-Pong, checkers, and tennis. **4.** In 1972, Magnavox Odyssey became the first home video game console. It included accessories like dice, cards, and fake money. **5.** Pong, the first video game to reach mainstream popularity, was created by Atari founder Norman Bushnell and released in 1975. **6.** The Atari founder also created Chuck E. Cheese—a chain of family entertainment centers—in 1977. **7.** In 2013, a man used 1,514 LED lights to set up a 29-story-tall Pong video game on the side of a Philadelphia, Pennsylvania, U.S.A., office building. **8.** Sega, which makes games like Sonic the Hedgehog, was originally known as Service Games. It made and sold jukeboxes and slot machines to the U.S. military. **9.** Service Games moved to Tokyo, Japan, and changed its name to Sega, using the first 2 letters of "Service" and "Games." **10.** One out of 3 U.S. households has purchased the PlayStation 2 console, which came out in 2000. **11.** The company that makes Nintendo video games started out by making Japanese playing cards 125 years ago! **12.** The Konami code is a popular cheat code that has become a symbol of geek culture and involves pressing up, up, down, down, left, right, left, right, B, A. **13.** In the movie *Wreck-It Ralph*, the Konami code is used to open a secret door. **14.** Starting in 2000, China banned all foreign video game consoles—even Xbox and Wii. The ban was lifted in January 2014. **15.** Minoru Arakawa, the founder of Nintendo, is an owner of the Seattle Mariners, a U.S. baseball team. **16.** So many people complained of getting blisters from using the joystick to play Mario Party that Nintendo offered free gloves with the game. **17.** A woman in California, U.S.A., played Dance Central 2 for over 24 hours, clinching a world record. **18.** *Lord of the Rings*, *Harry Potter*, and *Pirates of the Caribbean* are movies that have been turned into video games starring Lego characters. **19.** When Mario Bros. was created, Nintendo wanted Mario to ride Yoshi the dinosaur. But it took years for the company to develop the technology so he could do it. **20.** EVE game players held a huge space battle with some 4,000 players—one of the largest online game battles ever. **21.** One of the worst selling video games was based on the movie *E.T.: The Extra-Terrestrial*. Rumors say that millions of copies were buried in a landfill. **22.** The 1978 arcade-style game Space Invaders was the first to save players' scores so gamers could attempt to reach the top spot. **23.** Space Invaders inspired a street artist to paste game-themed mosaics on historic sites in Paris and on the Hollywood sign in California in 2010. **24.** The fictional games that appear in the movie *Wreck-It Ralph*—Fix-It Felix Jr., Hero's Duty, and Sugar Rush—are all inspired by real-life games. **25.** The inventor of Nintendo's handheld Game Boy started as a janitor at the company. **26.** Guitar Hero: Aerosmith earned the band more money than any one of its albums. **27.** More than 800 million Game Boy games have been sold. That's more than 2 games for every person living in the United States! **28.** Mario's original name was Jumpman. **29.** Mario's nemesis Wario gets his name from the Japanese word *warui*, meaning "evil." **30.** Some U.S. universities have orchestras that play only music from video games. **31.** In Portal, players are promised cake. But it only appears as a recipe in binary code—a computer language—that calls for ingredients like dirt and solid waste. **32.** Pokémon started as a video game in 1998 with 151 different animal-like Pokémon. Now there are over 700. **33.** Pokémon characters never actually die—they faint.

# 100 HIGH-SCORING

**34.** Pokémon creator Tajiri Kojiro wanted to make a game that pushed children to connect with nature. He got the idea from his love of collecting beetles as a child. **35.** Pikachu, the star of Pokémon, is a small, yellow mouse with electric cheek pouches. **36.** One scientific study showed that players of Super Mario Sunshine—a game where players have to help one another—were more likely to be helpful in real life. **37.** Sonic the Hedgehog's shoes, which he uses while running at lightning speeds, were inspired by the singer Michael Jackson's *Bad* album cover. **38.** Sonic the Hedgehog can't swim in the video games because the developer thought real hedgehogs couldn't swim—but they can. **39.** Scientists named a protein that controls where limbs and organs grow in the human body "sonic hedgehog." **40.** Actors Tom Hanks and Arnold Schwarzenegger turned down leading roles in the 1993 *Super Mario Bros.* movie. **41.** Atari's 1980s game Battlezone was considered so lifelike that a U.S. Army training center asked the company to create an edition to use as a combat simulator. **42.** In some versions of The Sims game series, the cheat code "rosebud" will earn you 1,000 Simoleons each time you enter it. **43.** Nintendo's Star Fox, a space shooting game starring a fox, was inspired by Japanese mythology and a shrine to foxes near the company's offices in Japan. **44.** Microsoft tested the buttons on the controllers for Xbox One by pressing each button 2 million times. **45.** Pac-Man eats 240 dots and 4 energizers on each level. **46.** The original name of Pac-Man was Puck-Man. **47.** The name "Donkey Kong" came from the fact that the game's gorilla is stubborn like a donkey and because the Japanese word *kong* translates to "gorilla." **48.** Not all of today's games are super high-tech. Minecraft is built in 16-bits, which makes the graphics look blocky to match the game's building theme. **49.** A teacher in Australia built a world in Minecraft to allow students to explore and learn about ancient civilizations. **50.** Ms. Pac-Man, designed to get girls into gaming, debuted in 1981 with a character that looked just like Pac-Man, but with yellow lipstick, a freckle, and a red bow. **51.** One name idea for the classic Q*bert was Snots and Boogers because the small orange character was originally supposed to shoot from his oversized nose. **52.** The video game hero Mega Man is called Rockman in Japan. **53.** Disney's Infinity combines toys with digital technology. Players buy action figures, power-ups, and more to place on a special mat that launches the game when connected to the console. **54.** Researchers have successfully shared brain signals using a video game. **55.** EyeWire is an online game that helps scientists map brain cells called neurons in a game-like format. **56.** A Japanese man became a worldwide sensation after he developed the ability to vibrate his fingers so he could press a controller button 16 times per second. **57.** Studies show that surgeons who play video games perform surgery better than those who don't. **58.** A cat food company created a game app especially for cats. One features fish swimming around on the screen. **59.** In Mister Mosquito, players become a mosquito that has to suck up as much blood as possible to prepare for winter. **60.** Gamers worldwide spend a total of over 300 million minutes per day playing Angry Birds. **61.** The theme song from Tetris is based on a Russian folk song and music by German composer Johann Sebastian Bach. **62.** In 2012, the Smithsonian Institution in Washington, D.C., U.S.A., featured an exhibit called "The Art of Video Games." **63.** Disney's first mobile app—called Where's My Water?—features Swampy the Alligator, who knows the word "soap" in 10 languages. **64.** Swampy probably needs to take shorter showers! Every day, he uses 440 million digital gallons (1.7 million digital L) of water. **65.** In the 1982 version of the Disney film *Tron*, the Pac-Man game makes an appearance on the villain's control screen. **66.** Kingdom Hearts held a contest where players could get their names in the game. The winner, Kurt Zisa of New York, U.S.A., was turned into a 6-armed creature. **67.** In World of Warcraft, a spell called "Corrupted Blood" infected players throughout the game and spread like a real-life virus. Initially, the creators couldn't stop it. **68.** Some scientists used the virus incident in World of Warcraft to study people's reactions to real-life disease outbreaks. **69.** Studies have found that certain types of video games improve vision. **70.** Dance Dance Revolution is an official sport in Norway. **71.** Some gamers hire "gold farmers" to earn loot and win points for them. **72.** Nintendogs + Cats lets you play with a virtual dog or cat that can recognize your face and your voice! **73.** People who play strategy-based video games have better cognitive flexibility—the ability to think "outside the box." **74.** *Video Game High School (VGHS)* is an online web TV show that takes place in a world where video gamers are celebrities. **75.** At VGHS, students are ranked by their video game scores. If their score falls below zero, they're automatically expelled. **76.** The Legend of Zelda, released in 1986, was the first console game that allowed players to save their progress without having to start over. **77.** The Prince of Persia, released in 1989, was the first console game to display lifelike movements. **78.** Wondering what cards to play next in Windows's Solitaire? Holding down H will give you hints. **79.** Bowser, the turtle-like villain in the Mario Bros. games, was originally sketched to look like an ox. **80.** In the 25th anniversary Street Fighter arcade game tournament, the winner walked away with a Street Fighter–themed sports car and half a million dollars. **81.** If you're up late playing Animal Crossing: New Leaf at 3:33 a.m. on Sundays and Mondays, you'll see an alien deliver a strange message. **82.** One of the characters in Mass Effect 3 was designed to look like actor Clint Eastwood. **83.** The building-block game Tetris was designed by a mathematician. **84.** The planet Koppai, the home of the main characters in Nintendo's Pikmin 3, is a reference to the company's original name: Nintendo Koppai. **85.** Joysticks were first used in early aircraft and elevators. **86.** Instead of a controller, Xbox can use a Kinect, which recognizes players' hand movements, verbal commands, dance moves—even their faces. **87.** Kinectimals recognizes your mood by analyzing voice tone and body movement. The animals in the game reflect whatever mood Xbox's Kinect picks up. **88.** A psychologist is developing a video game designed to help people with mental health issues like anxiety and stress. **89.** The fork controller in the game Pixelate recognizes what you pick up. You win if you eat the right foods in the right order in under a minute. **90.** The popular app Candy Crush Saga has celebrity fans like race car driver Danica Patrick. **91.** Singer Lady Gaga has used fashion accessories featuring art from the app Doodle Jump in her shows. **92.** Video gaming is a multibillion-dollar industry. In 2012, people spent over $20 billion on video games. **93.** At Digipen Institute of Technology in Washington, U.S.A., students can major in video game design, music, and more. **94.** Classes at Digipen Tech include Artificial Intelligence for Games and Character Animation. **95.** By making you constantly strive to reach new levels, playing video games may increase your confidence. **96.** Competitive video gaming is called eSports. **97.** Twitch is a website that streams video games and hosts tournaments with professional video game players. **98.** Pro gamers practice with their team for 8 hours a day—up to 14 if a tournament is coming up. **99.** Pro players on the Evil Geniuses team sign contracts to play, much like in the sports world. Some get paid a 6-figure salary. **100.** Pro gamers are known by their usernames. Evil Geniuses team members include iNcontroL, Froggen, and Yellowpete.

## FACTS ABOUT VIDEO GAMES

**Angry Birds plush toys**

**1**

In 2004, 4-year-old cancer patient ALEXANDRA SCOTT sold lemonade to raise money to help cure childhood cancer. So far, her foundation has raised more than $60 million.

**2**

FAKE BRACES are a fashion fad in some Asian countries. They are seen as a STATUS SYMBOL because orthodontics are so expensive.

**3**

Before the Renaissance, artists portrayed kids by drawing ADULT HEADS ON SMALL BODIES.

**4**

In 1994, an 11-year-old girl flew a single-engine CESSNA AIRPLANE across the United States from Maine to California.

**5**

SNOWY OWLS don't have white feathers when they're born. First they grow gray, downy feathers, then after about 2 months the down is replaced by white feathers.

**6**

If you grew like a POLAR BEAR, by the time you were a few months old you'd weigh over 100 pounds (45 kg).

**7**

The story of PIPPI LONGSTOCKING, a spunky Swedish girl, seems to appeal to kids everywhere. It has been translated into at least 64 languages.

**8**

Fifty years ago, Mattel introduced a little sis for Barbie to babysit: SKIPPER.

**9**

A baby goat is called a kid.

**10**

In SPARTA, a city in ancient Greece, stealing food was part of WARRIOR TRAINING for boys. Getting caught meant you needed to run faster.

**11**

Kids born since 2000 are the first to live in a COMPLETELY DIGITAL AGE. That's why their generation is being called names like Net Generation or iGen.

**12**

During World War II, kids in the United Kingdom were NOT ALLOWED TO FLY KITES, because it might have confused pilots flying overhead.

**13**

Teenage *T. rex* dinosaurs packed on as much as 3,950 POUNDS (1,792 kg) in 1 YEAR.

**14**

The light brown spots on young male giraffes TURN BLACK, not gray, AS THEY AGE.

**15**

In 1959, the United Nations established INTERNATIONAL CHILDREN'S DAY. Today, over 100 countries celebrate kids with a special day.

**16**

A 9-year-old boy is India's YOUNGEST PATENT HOLDER. He invented a circular game board so that 6 people can play chess at one time.

**17**

Boys as young as 5 on the Pacific island of Pentecost JUMP OFF A TALL PLATFORM with 2 vines tied to their ankles—sort of like bungee jumping.

**18**

ELEPHANTS NEVER STOP GROWING, but the bulk of it happens by the time they are 20. They live to be about 70 years old.

**19**

By the time he was 16, a young Boston entrepreneur named JONATHAN MANZI made his first million dollars by changing the way some Internet ads work.

**20**

On his first night in the WHITE HOUSE, President Gerald Ford's son, Steve, and a friend listened to MUSIC UP ON THE ROOF.

**21**

For special occasions, girls and women in parts of Asia and the Middle East use HENNA to paint their hands—sort of like a temporary tattoo.

**22**

In 1994, MICHAEL KEARNEY, a Japanese-American boy from Hawaii, earned his COLLEGE DEGREE when he was just 10 years old.

**23**

A Latina girl celebrates her 15th birthday with a huge party, called la fiesta QUINCEAÑERA, to mark becoming an adult. She also receives *la última muñeca*—her last doll.

**24**

In North Korea, boys as young as 11 years old practice MARTIAL ARTS not just for fun but also to get READY TO BE SOLDIERS.

**25**

AMY CARTER sold sandwiches and lemonade to reporters when her dad—Jimmy Carter—was running for president of the United States.

**26**

Kids need as much as 4 MORE HOURS OF SLEEP a night than adults.

**27**

Young ATLANTIC SALMON live in fresh-water streams, but when they mature they migrate to the open ocean.

**28**

The Secret Service code names for President Obama's daughters are "ROSEBUD" for Sasha and "RADIANCE" for Malia.

**29**

It takes 2 YEARS for bullfrog tadpoles to become FROGS. Other tadpoles take only 8 days to make the switch.

**30**

Young RADIATED TORTOISES have white or off-white markings that turn bright yellow as they get older.

**31**

A brother-sister team that started making CHOCOLATE CANDIES at ages 13 and 10 ended up managing 50 employees in their Chocolate Farm company.

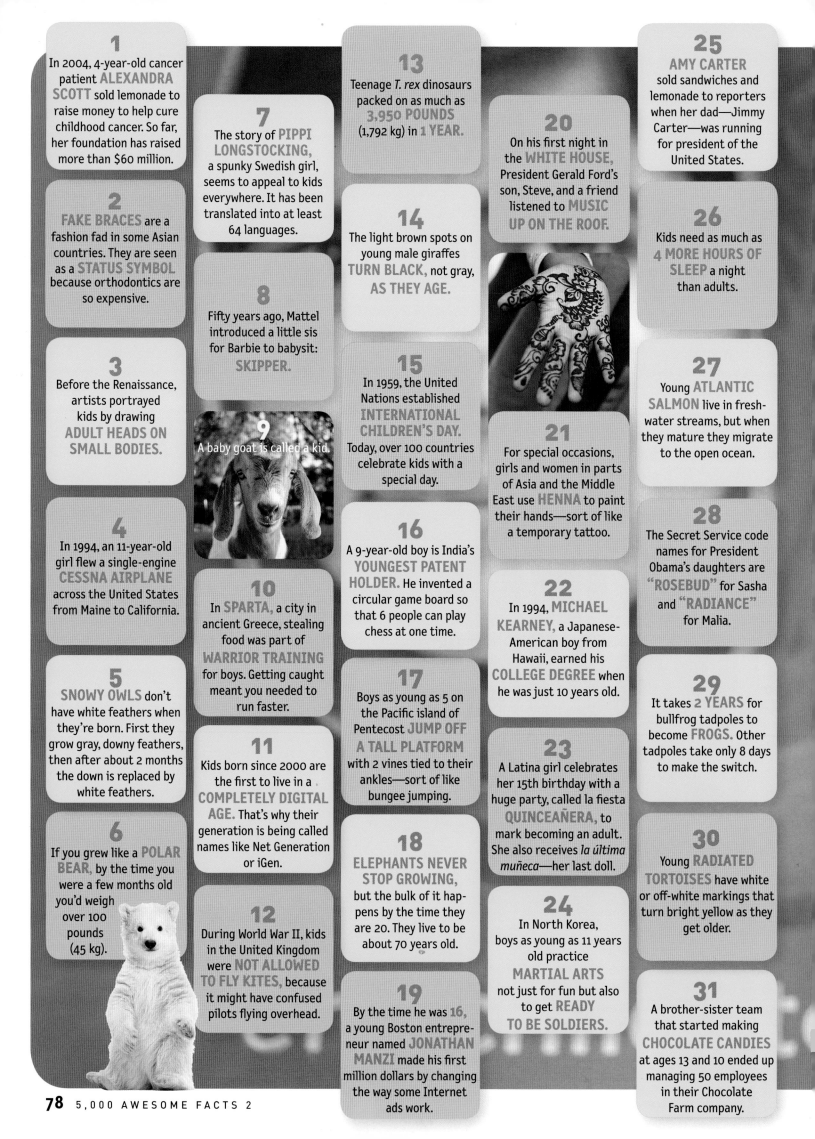

**32**
You can expect to LOSE ABOUT A HALF INCH (1.3 cm) in height each decade you live past the age of 40.

**33**
Unlike adults, JUVENILE BARBARY MACAQUES, a kind of monkey, don't seem to be able to recognize members of their own group.

**34**
Kids in ancient Greece played a game with nuts that was similar to TIDDLYWINKS.

**35**
In South Dakota, U.S.A., you can DRIVE without supervision when you are 14 YEARS AND 3 MONTHS OLD; in New Jersey, you have to wait until you are 17.

**36**
Young GORILLAS stay with their mom for only about 3 years.

**37**
CHIMPANZEES don't start walking until they are about 4 YEARS OLD. Humans usually walk around age 1.

**38**
Malala Yousafzai, a Pakistani teen attacked by the Taliban for encouraging girls to go to school, is the youngest person ever nominated for the NOBEL PEACE PRIZE.

Malala Yousafzai

**39**
In 2008, a 15-year-old girl in Michigan, U.S.A., sold 17,328 BOXES of Girl Scout cookies.

**40**
A young bird that has its flight feathers and is ready to leave the nest is called a FLEDGLING.

**41**
STORES LOVE TWEENS. According to sales figures, U.S. kids between the ages of 9 and 13 spend at least $40 *billion* a year of their own money!

**42**
Kids and adults have the same number of TASTE BUDS, but since kids' tongues are smaller, sugary candies taste MORE INTENSE.

**43**
MICHAEL JACKSON released his first singles (as part of the Jackson 5) when he was just 11 years old. One of them, "I Want You Back," went to number 1 on the charts.

**44**
VIKING KIDS learned from stories and songs instead of by going to school. By age 15, they were considered adults and had to work.

**45**
Do you know what you want to be WHEN YOU GROW UP? The top picks among kids in Europe include veterinarian, teacher, and soccer player.

**46**
During the AMERICAN CIVIL WAR boys as YOUNG AS 10 went off to fight. Some were drummer boys who signaled units when it was time to march or flee.

**47**
HOOLOCK GIBBONS, apes that live in parts of Asia, don't leave their parents until they have gone through adolescence—sort of like human kids.

**48**
In their quest to find the next SUPERSTAR, some professional soccer teams are signing kids as YOUNG AS 7 to their training academies.

**49**
As part of a coming-of-age ritual, boys and girls in Kenya's Okiek tribe use WHITE CLAY and charcoal to make themselves look like WILD CREATURES.

**50**
LION CUBS are always the last to eat after mom—or sometimes dad—has made a kill.

# 50 FACTS TO GROW ON

**1**  SCIENTISTS BELIEVE THAT PEOPLE WHO DREAM ABOUT AN ACTIVITY WILL **ACTUALLY GET BETTER AT IT IN REAL LIFE.**

**2** 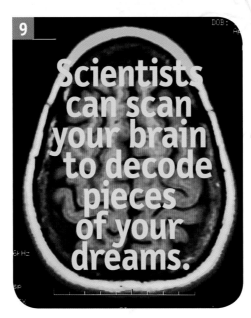 **Nightmares can be caused by a fever or an illness.**

**3** People who **SOMNAMBULATE,** or sleepwalk, claim to do some strange stuff. In 1919 a man named Dr. John D. Quackenbos said he **WROTE AN ENTIRE ESSAY IN HIS SLEEP.**

**4** Some people who grew up without color TV **DREAM IN BLACK-AND-WHITE.**

# 25 FACTS ABOUT DREAMS

**5** People who experience more of a type of brain wave called a theta wave while they are sleeping are

**MORE LIKELY TO REMEMBER THEIR DREAMS.**

**6** **DreamWorks,** the film company behind movies like *Kung Fu Panda* and *Madagascar*, has its headquarters in California, U.S.A. It's designed like a Mediterranean town, complete with gardens and a lagoon.

**7** FRED AND GEORGE WEASLEY, FROM THE HARRY POTTER SERIES, CREATED A DAYDREAM CHARM THAT WOULD PUT STUDENTS IN A DREAM LONG ENOUGH TO GET THROUGH A BORING CLASS AT HOGWARTS.

**8** MANY BLIND PEOPLE HAVE **AUDITORY DREAMS—** ONLY SOUNDS, NO PICTURES.

**9** **Scientists can scan your brain to decode pieces of your dreams.**

**10** MOST PEOPLE HAVE ONE OR MORE **recurring dreams** —A DREAM THAT REPEATS ITSELF AT DIFFERENT TIMES OF YOUR LIFE.

**11**  Paul McCartney, from the famous band The Beatles, says he wrote the song "Yesterday" from **a melody in one of his dreams.**

**12** REM Sleep Disorder causes your body to physically "act out" dreams because it does not go into **TEMPORARY PARALYSIS** as it does in normal REM sleep.

**13**  President Abraham Lincoln had a **recurring dream** that told him something important was going to happen. He had the dream before Bull Run, Gettysburg, and other major U.S. Civil War battles.

**14** IN ANCIENT GREECE, THE SICK WOULD TRAVEL TO AN **ORACLE'S TEMPLE** WHERE THEY BELIEVED THE MEDICINE GOD WOULD APPEAR IN THEIR DREAMS TO HEAL THEM.

**15**  Humans dream the most during REM (Rapid Eye Movement) sleep. That's when the brain is very active, the eyes move back and forth, and body muscles are relaxed.

**16** *Dreams may make you* **SMARTER** *and more* **CREATIVE.**

THAT WON'T PUT YOU TO SLEEP

**17** WE **daydream** FOR ONE-THIRD OF THE TIME WE'RE AWAKE. IF YOU GET 8 HOURS OF SLEEP, THAT MEANS YOU DAYDREAM FOR MORE THAN **5 HOURS!**

**18** 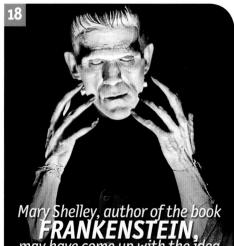 *Mary Shelley, author of the book* **FRANKENSTEIN,** *may have come up with the idea for her scary monster in a dream.*

**19**  Scientists believe astronauts have more dreams in space than on Earth.

**21** As a kid, **Walt Disney** loved to hang out under a big cottonwood tree that grew on his family's farm. He called it his **"dreaming tree."**

**20**  Most people dream at least **4 to 6 times** a night.

**22**  Scientists believe we dream about some of the same things our prehistoric ancestors probably did—like being chased by something scary.

**23** Morpheus is the Greek god of dreams. In the book *The Last Olympians,* featuring hero Percy Jackson, **Morpheus puts the entire city of New York, U.S.A., to sleep.**

**24**  Martin Luther King, Jr.'s "I Have a Dream" speech didn't actually have those words in the draft he prepared.

**25** A JAPANESE TOY MAKER MAKES A **dream machine** THAT LETS YOU **design your own dreams** USING DIFFERENT SOUNDS, SMELLS, AND LIGHTS.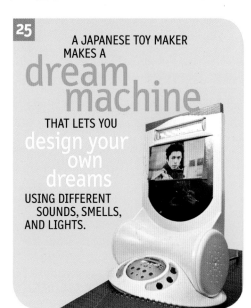

# 15 CUDDLY FACTS

**1** A cartoon showing **U.S. PRESIDENT TEDDY ROOSEVELT REFUSING TO SHOOT A BEAR** while he was on a hunting trip inspired Morris Michtom, a candy shop owner in Brooklyn, New York, U.S.A., to create a stuffed toy he called **"TEDDY'S BEAR."**

**2** Morris Michtom's bears became so popular that the candy store owner founded the **IDEAL NOVELTY AND TOY COMPANY** in 1907.

**3** Steiff's limited edition **125-CARAT TEDDY BEAR** had a **GOLD MOUTH** and **EYES MADE OF SAPPHIRES** surrounded by **DIAMONDS.**

**4** **CHRISTOPHER ROBIN MILNE** named his toy Edward Bear but later changed it to **WINNIE-THE-POOH,** after a bear named Winnie at the London Zoo and a storybook swan named Pooh.

**5** Jackie Miley never owned a teddy bear growing up, but she now has a **COLLECTION OF NEARLY 8,000** that are housed in Teddy Bear Town, in South Dakota, U.S.A. Admission is free!

**6** **A LOUIS VUITTON TEDDY BEAR,** made by the German toy company Steiff, sold at auction for **$2.1 MILLION** in 2000.

**7** The **OLINGUITO,** a fuzzy animal with a **TEDDY BEAR FACE,** is the **FIRST NEW CARNIVORE SPECIES TO BE IDENTIFIED** in the Western Hemisphere in over **3 DECADES.**

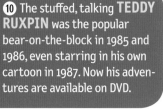

**8** The first exclusive TY BEANIE BABY—Maple, the Canadian bear—was released in 1996 only in Canada. It started a frenzy among collectors.

**9** Before they were called teddy bears, **STUFFED TOY BEARS WERE CALLED "BRUINS"** after the bear in the medieval European tale about Reynard the Fox.

**10** The stuffed, talking **TEDDY RUXPIN** was the popular bear-on-the-block in 1985 and 1986, even starring in his own cartoon in 1987. Now his adventures are available on DVD.

**11** PRESIDENT TEDDY ROOSEVELT used the teddy bear as the **SYMBOL OF THE REPUBLICAN PARTY** in the 1904 election.

**12** **TEDDY BEAR FESTIVALS** have been held in Germany, Japan, the United States, Canada, Great Britain, and Australia.

**13** The real **WINNIE-THE-POOH**—the one A.A. Milne gave to his son in 1921—**RESIDES AT THE NEW YORK PUBLIC LIBRARY** with his friends Tigger, Piglet, Kanga, and Eeyore.

**14** The not-so-lovable **LOTS-O'-HUGGIN' BEAR** made a cameo in the movie *Up* before appearing in *Toy Story 3*. **IF YOU MISSED HIM** in the movie, he is on the floor next to the girl's bed in the scene where the balloons lift the house past her window.

**15** July 10th is **TEDDY BEAR PICNIC DAY**—the perfect day to share your lunchtime with your favorite bear.

1. The musical *Cats* was based on a book of poems by T.S. Eliot titled *Old Possum's Book of Practical Cats*.

2. There is a series of stained glass windows called the Lewis Carroll windows in a church in Daresbury, England, that feature *Alice in Wonderland* characters in biblical scenes!

3. **NANCY DREW WAS ALMOST NAMED STELLA STRONG.**

4. Mary Pope Osborne, author of the Magic Tree House series, considered an enchanted cellar and artist's studio before she decided on a tree house to transport Jack and Annie on adventures.

5. Norman Bridwell, author of *Clifford the Big Red Dog*, considered naming the canine Tiny, but his wife thought it was boring.

6. J.M. Barrie, author of *Peter Pan*, gave the rights to the book to a children's hospital in London, England.

7. It took Dr. Seuss a year and a half to write *The Cat in the Hat*.

8. Author Kate DiCamillo wrote *The Tale of Despereaux* after a friend's son asked her to write a story in which the hero had big ears. She chose a mouse.

9. **OF THE 50 WORDS USED IN THE BOOK *GREEN EGGS AND HAM*, 49 HAVE 1 SYLLABLE.**

10. Before Maurice Sendak's *Where the Wild Things Are* was turned into a movie, it was an opera.

11. When author Ann M. Martin first started writing the Baby-Sitters Club series, she wrote one book a month—in longhand!

12. Before he wrote *The Wonderful Wizard of Oz*, L. Frank Baum wrote a book on how to raise chickens.

13. Roald Dahl, author of *Charlie and the Chocolate Factory*, was a World War II flying ace in Britain's Royal Air Force.

14. "Carolyn Keene" gets credit for writing the Nancy Drew books, but that is just a made-up name. Different authors write the books, but don't get the credit.

15. Dr. Seuss's *If I Ran the Zoo*, published in 1950, was the first printed use of the word "nerd."

16. There are 169 pop-ups in a 348-foot (106-m)-long pop-up book made by kids in Taiwan about sites to see in their city.

17. A book containing 1,000 life-size drawings of birds by famed naturalist John James Audubon sold at auction for $11.4 million.

18. *War and Peace* was originally going to be titled *All's Well That Ends Well*.

19. Judy Blume thought of the title for her book *Freckle Juice* before she had a story to go with it.

20. *Pat the Bunny,* published over 70 years ago, was one of the first "touch and feel books." Author Dorothy Kunhardt was trying to come up with a fun way to interact with her daughter.

21. In Boston Public Garden, you can visit bronze statues of Mrs. Mallard and her ducklings from *Make Way for Ducklings*.

22. Author Cornelia Funke researched fire-eaters, book thieves, and martens for 6 months before she wrote the first word of *Inkheart*.

23. Reverend Awdry carved his son a wooden train that the boy named Thomas. That's how the starring character in the Thomas the Tank Engine books and TV show was born.

24. One of the first people to buy a copy of Beatrix Potter's *Tales of Peter Rabbit* was Arthur Conan Doyle, creator of the Sherlock Holmes detective series.

25. **ERIC CARLE WAS INSPIRED TO WRITE *THE VERY HUNGRY CATERPILLAR* AFTER PLAYING WITH A HOLE-PUNCHER.**

26. *Alice's Adventures in Wonderland* was once banned in parts of China because it was considered an insult to humanity to show bears and lions talking.

27. Jeff Kinney, author of the Diary of a Wimpy Kid series, also designs online games.

28. The ending line from the Madeline books, "That's all there is; there isn't any more," was inspired by an actress who spoke the same line during her curtain call at a play.

29. Curious George's name was changed to Zozo in the United Kingdom when the book *Curious George* was first published in 1941 so as not to be disrespectful to King George VI.

# 75 PAGE-TURNING FACTS ABOUT BOOKS

**30** Author Kay Thompson lived at the Plaza Hotel in New York City, U.S.A., when she wrote the first Eloise book.

**31** Author Rick Riordan got the idea for *The Lightning Thief* after telling his 8-year-old son Greek mythology bedtime stories.

**32** YOU CAN CHECK OUT A FISHING POLE AT THE HONEOYE PUBLIC LIBRARY IN NEW YORK STATE!

**33** Old Man's Cave, a popular setting in the graphic novel series Bone, is a real place in Hocking Hills State Park in Ohio, U.S.A.

**34** Dr. Seuss's *Oh the Places You'll Go!* sells about 300,000 copies each year because it is a popular graduation present.

**35** Before he wrote *Don't Let the Pigeon Drive the Bus*, author Mo Willems was an animator for *Sesame Street*.

**36** Richard Atwater began writing *Mr. Popper's Penguins* after watching a documentary about Richard E. Byrd's explorations in Antarctica.

**37** Graphic novelist Raina Telgemeier knocked out her front 2 teeth in sixth grade while chasing friends, an event that eventually led to the plot of her book *Smile*.

**38** E.B. White got his inspiration for *Charlotte's Web* after feeding a pig on his farm and feeling bad that it was doomed to die.

**39** The names of Marc Brown's children are hidden in the illustrations of the Arthur books.

**40** Before he was a famous author, Maurice Sendak worked on window displays at F.A.O. Schwarz toy store.

**41** The Library of Congress has some 838 miles (1,349 km) of bookshelves.

**42** WILSON RAWLS, AUTHOR OF *WHERE THE RED FERN GROWS*, DIDN'T READ A BOOK UNTIL HIGH SCHOOL.

**43** A Barnes & Noble in New York City, U.S.A., has 12.87 miles (20.71 km) of shelving, making it the world's largest bookstore.

**44** When Beverly Cleary—author of the Ramona Quimby series—was a young girl, a school librarian suggested she become a children's author when she grew up.

**45** Author Kate DiCamillo said she got the idea for *Because of Winn-Dixie* after wanting to have a dog, but not being able to get one because she lived in an apartment building that wouldn't allow it.

**46** Henry Winkler, the Fonz on *Happy Days*, is also the co-author of a series of books about a fourth grader—Hank Zipzer—who has learning difficulties.

**47** Just like her character Sheila Tubman from *Otherwise Known as Sheila the Great*, author Judy Blume was afraid of dogs and thunderstorms.

**48** Brothers Jacob and Wilhelm Grimm didn't make up their own fairy tales. They collected stories that had been passed on for generations, including *Hansel and Gretel*, *Rapunzel*, and *Cinderella*.

**49** Boris Karloff, the actor who played the monster in the 1931 *Frankenstein* movie, was the voice of the Grinch in *How the Grinch Stole Christmas*, based on the Dr. Seuss book.

**50** At the end of Hans Christian Andersen's *The Little Mermaid*, the mermaid turns into sea foam instead of marrying a prince as she does in the Disney movie.

**51** The author of *Lemony Snicket's A Series of Unfortunate Events* is Daniel Handler, but his name doesn't appear on the book. Handler often pretends to be Lemony Snicket at author readings.

**52** What's called the "world's smallest library" is a bright yellow structure that sits on a sidewalk in New York City and holds 40 books.

**53** *Cloudy With a Chance of Meatballs*—a picture book with only 32 pages—was made into a full-length movie *plus* a sequel!

**54** E.B. White said he got the idea for *Stuart Little* after having a dream about a little mouse that acted like a boy.

**55** In East Belfast, Northern Ireland, there is a statue of the professor opening the wardrobe from *The Lion, the Witch, and the Wardrobe*.

**56** Chris Van Allsburg, author of *The Polar Express* and *Jumanji*, draws a picture of a bull terrier dog—or at least part of one—in all of his books.

**57** Laura Ingalls Wilder didn't begin writing about her childhood in the Little House series until she was in her sixties.

**58** The Eric Carle Museum of Picture Book Art in Amherst, Massachusetts, U.S.A., collects and presents picture books from around the world. Chairs in the auditorium all have holes in them, like Carle's famous caterpillar book.

**59** After losing his trumpet on a subway, Don Freeman—author of *Corduroy*—decided to give up being a musician and start focusing on becoming an illustrator.

**60** A BOOK VERSION OF THE NURSERY RHYME "OLD KING COLE" IS SO SMALL IT CAN ONLY BE READ WITH A MICROSCOPE.

**61** R.L. Stine's Goosebumps series has sold more than 300 million copies!

**62** Peggy Rathmann, author and illustrator of *Goodnight, Gorilla*, considered a profession in teaching sign language to gorillas, but decided instead to draw pictures of them.

**63** Ludwig Bemelmans got his inspiration for his Madeline books from a little girl who was in the hospital room next to his. She was having her appendix out; he was recuperating from a bicycle accident.

**64** Brian Selznick said much of his book *The Invention of Hugo Cabret* is told with illustrations—not words—because he wanted it to feel like a silent movie.

**65** Dr. Seuss's real name was Theodor Seuss Geisel.

**66** James Kelly Benton, the author of the Dear Dumb Diary series, named Jamie Kelly, the female character who writes the diary entries, after himself.

**67** The main character in *Holes* is Stanley Yelnats. Yelnats is Stanley spelled backward.

**68** Before R.L. Stine wrote the spooky Goosebumps series, he wrote joke books!

**69** JULES FEIFFER, ILLUSTRATOR OF *THE PHANTOM TOLLBOOTH*, USED THE AUTHOR, NORTON JUSTER, AS A MODEL FOR "THE WHETHER MAN."

**70** In addition to writing *The Hobbit*, J.R.R. Tolkien illustrated the book and made maps to go with it. Tolkien wanted to use invisible ink for some of the maps, but the publisher said it was too expensive.

**71** Author Laura Numeroff thought up *If You Give a Mouse a Cookie* while trying to entertain a friend on a boring car trip.

**72** Before he got a book for himself, the BFG (Big Friendly Giant) appeared in Roald Dahl's *Danny, the Champion of the World*.

**73** In the book *Flat Stanley*, Stanley is so flat that his parents can put him in an envelope and mail him to see a friend. Many schools make their own paper Stanleys and mail them to faraway schools as a pen-pal project.

**74** The inspiration for the slobbery dog Mudge in the Henry and Mudge series was a Great Dane that belonged to the illustrator's brother.

**75** The Man With the Yellow Hat isn't named in the Curious George series, but he's called Ted in the movies.

**1** A planet TWICE THE SIZE OF EARTH and 40 light-years away is made up largely of DIAMOND.

**2** Ancient Egyptians wore GEMSTONE NECKLACES as PROTECTION from an EARLY DEATH.

**3** A "WATERMELON" tourmaline, a semiprecious gemstone, has a kind of PINK CORE surrounded by a green rind.

**4** The Heart of the Kingdom, a HEART-SHAPED RUBY valued at $14 million, is considered the world's MOST VALUABLE cut ruby.

**5** ORGANIC GEMSTONES are made by living things—like pearls formed inside OYSTERS.

**6** The SAPPHIRE in Catherine, Duchess of Cambridge's ENGAGEMENT RING is said to be worth $300,000.

**7** Gemstone hunters are heading for GREENLAND, where RUBIES have been popping up in areas in which the ice has melted.

**8** GROUND TURQUOISE has been used as an ANTIDOTE TO POISON by some cultures.

**9** According to tradition, wearing your BIRTHSTONE will bring you GOOD LUCK.

**10** There is a superstition that if you wear a RUBY THAT BLACKENS, you will soon FACE DISASTER.

**11** Some Australian Aborigine stories say OPAL is formed by a RAINBOW SERPENT.

**12** OPAL has been discovered on MARS.

**13** JADEITE is one of the RAREST and MOST EXPENSIVE gemstones. One carat of this green stone can cost over $3 million!

**14** The word "DIAMOND" is from the Greek word *adamastos*, which means "INVINCIBLE."

# 35 GLITTERING

**15** The HOPE DIAMOND, a 45.52-carat blue diamond, has been owned by King Louis XIV of France, England's King George IV, and French jeweler Pierre Cartier.

**16** The finest-quality EMERALDS are MORE VALUABLE THAN DIAMONDS.

**17** The 75-carat HOOKER EMERALD BROOCH is believed to have been worn as a buckle by a TURKISH SULTAN.

**18** EMERALDS were one of CLEOPATRA'S favorite gemstones.

**19** In the book *The Wonderful Wizard of Oz*, Oz gives all the people green glasses to wear in the EMERALD CITY so that the ordinary city will look emerald green.

**20** Less than 20 PERCENT of the DIAMONDS mined each year are suitable for use as GEMS.

**21** DIAMONDS are made of CARBON—like the soot in a fireplace.

**22** PINK-COLORED DIAMONDS occur naturally in only 1 of every 100,000 diamonds.

**23**
RUBIES and SAPPHIRES are variations of the same mineral.

**24**
In its pure state, QUARTZ is COLORLESS.

**25**
AMETHYST was once considered a precious gem, but when large amounts were found in Brazil, it dropped in value and was degraded to SEMI-PRECIOUS.

**26**
GRAPHITE, used in pencils, is one of the SOFTEST MINERALS. It is made of the same carbon atoms as diamond, but in a different arrangement.

**27**
Twenty-five hundred years ago, NATIVE AMERICANS adorned their TEETH with JADE.

**28**
For Britain's Queen Elizabeth II's DIAMOND JUBILEE—the celebration of 60 years on the throne—10,000 people were treated to a picnic in the Buckingham Palace garden.

# FACTS ABOUT GEMSTONES

**29**
BLACK, or CARBONADO, DIAMONDS may have come to Earth embedded in an asteroid billions of years ago.

**30**
THE IMPERIAL CROWN OF INDIA, made for King George V's visit to the country, contains more than 6,000 diamonds and other precious gems.

**31**
U.S. swimmer RYAN LOCHTE wore a stars-and-stripes DENTAL "GRILL" made with diamonds and rubies when he accepted his gold medal at the 2012 London Olympics.

**32**
Scientists are studying the opal-like shell of a kind of beetle called the AUSTRALIAN WEEVIL to try to make a synthetic version of the gem.

**33**
"SPACE GEMS" are olive green crystals embedded in some meteorites that hit Earth.

**34**
New TECHNOLOGY makes it possible to cut gemstones into all sorts of CLEVER SHAPES—hearts, 4-leaf clovers, stars, and more.

**35**
In the late 17th century, a man dressed as a priest tried to STEAL the BRITISH CROWN JEWELS from the Tower of London. He was caught at the gate.

# 100 ILLUMINATING FACTS ABOUT LIGHT

**1.** It's impossible to travel faster than light does through space—186,000 miles (300,000 km) a second. **2.** Light travels at different speeds through different materials. It travels through glass at about 124,000 miles (200,000 km) a second. **3.** There is a special bicycle wheel attachment that makes the spokes light up with colorful animations when the rider goes 10 miles per hour (16 kph). **4.** A deep-sea lantern fish has 2 "headlights" that it uses to send out a beam of white light 12 inches (30 cm) long. **5.** Fiber optics, also known as optical fibers, are thin strands of glass that can carry light signals over long distances. **6.** Some gummy worms are sold in packages with LED tongs, which make the candy glow when you pick them up. **7.** Our eyes take in the light that is reflected off objects and then send electrical signals to our brains so that we see them. **8.** A black light produces ultraviolet light, making anything that has fluorescent material glow when exposed to the light. **9.** In the United States, more than one-fifth of electric power is used for lights. **10.** Some special lightbulbs can change color when you tap settings on your smartphone or tablet. **11.** Since nesting turtles are bothered by bright city lights, amber-colored "turtle lights" illuminate the beaches without disturbing the nesting turtles. **12.** Gravity bends light, but the effect is too small to be seen on Earth. **13.** A light-year measures distance, not time. In space, light can travel 5.9 trillion miles (9.5 trillion km) in a year. This is called a light-year. **14.** It takes light nearly 100,000 years to travel from one side of the Milky Way galaxy to the other. **15.** Ancient Romans used oil lamps to light up some of their streets at night. **16.** On January 1, the first place the sun rises in North America is Cape Race, Newfoundland, Canada. **17.** Visible light makes up the smallest part of the electromagnetic spectrum, which also includes radio waves, x-rays, and gamma rays. **18.** The largest solar power plant is located in the United Arab Emirates, in Asia. It produces enough power for 200,000 homes. **19.** Stars twinkle because their light is refracted, or bent, by Earth's atmosphere. **20.** Engineers use laser beams to mark straight lines when constructing underground tunnels and other projects. **21.** Spectacular light displays illuminate famous German buildings and monuments each year during Berlin's Festival of Lights. **22.** Each night, 2 light beams, reaching 50 miles (80 kilometers) into the sky, shine from the top of the Eiffel Tower in Paris, France. **23.** Light therapy helps patients who suffer from a type of depression caused by living in regions that don't receive enough sunlight during fall and winter months. **24.** The Marine Tower in Yokohama, Japan—the tallest lighthouse in the world—is almost as tall as a 35-story building. **25.** The remote control for your TV uses infrared light pulses to change the channel. **26.** The filament in an incandescent lightbulb must be heated to a temperature of 4,000°F (2,200°C) to shine white light. **27.** Humans cannot see infrared light, but some species of snakes, insects, and bats can. **28.** The gravitational pull of a black hole is so strong that nothing in space—not even light—can escape from it. **29.** If the sun suddenly stopped shining, we wouldn't know for about 8 minutes. That's the time it takes sunlight to reach Earth. **30.** The light from large wildfires can be seen from space. **31.** The color of an object is a result of how it absorbs and reflects light. **32.** Rainbows form when tiny water droplets in the air separate light into colors. **33.** Lighthouses use mirrors and lenses to reflect and bend light from a large bulb into a superstrong beam. **34.** The pupils in your eyes get smaller in bright light and bigger in dim light. **35.** The inside of a fluorescent light tube is coated with a substance that glows when the gas inside the tube is heated up. **36.** Lasers produce a concentrated beam of light that can be used for eye surgery and for cutting metal. **37.** Light from a laser is always a single color, unlike white light, which is a mixture of all the colors in the visible spectrum. **38.** In 2002, students at the University of Montana, U.S.A., created an art exhibit using bacteria that glowed in the dark. **39.** The moon glows because it reflects light from the sun. **40.** Pilots turn on a plane's landing lights about 10 miles (16 km) from an airport to make the plane more visible. **41.** Strobe lights can trigger seizures in people who suffer from epilepsy, a kind of brain disorder. **42.** Although auto companies are still experimenting with producing solar cars—vehicles that use sunlight for fuel—people have been making their own since the 1970s. **43.** Light pollution occurs when outdoor lights shine into the night sky, making it difficult to see the stars. **44.** Because of light pollution, people in a typical suburban area can see only 200 to 300 of the 2,500 stars that are visible to the naked eye. **45.** The Las Vegas strip in Nevada, U.S.A., is the brightest place on Earth at night. **46.** The Chinese New Year celebration lasts for 15 days and ends with the Lantern Festival, which showcases legendary stories. **47.** Sharky, an electric eel at the Living Planet Aquarium in Utah, U.S.A., lights up a small Christmas tree with the electric currents he gives off. **48.** The Centennial Light Bulb at Fire Station No. 6 in Livermore, California, U.S.A., has been burning ever since it was installed in 1901. **49.** In 1930, the Cleveland Municipal Airport in Ohio, U.S.A., became the first airport to install runway lights. **50.** All Chicago Cub baseball games at the team's Wrigley Field stadium in Illinois, U.S.A., were played during the day until the stadium installed lights in 1988. **51.** The Empire State Building in New York City, U.S.A., is designed to be a lightning rod for the area. **52.** In Great Britain, the "ancient lights" law makes it illegal to build anything that blocks light from entering a home owner's windows. **53.** Countries on the Equator receive roughly the same amount of daylight year-round. **54.** Sundials use shadows cast by the sun to tell the time. The oldest ones are from 3,500 years ago. **55.** Sunlight typically reaches a depth of some 656 feet (200 m) in the ocean—a zone known as the euphotic, or sunlight, zone. **56.** Early humans used primitive lamps made out of shells or rocks filled with grease. **57.** It takes just a little over 1 second for light to travel 238,900 miles (384,400 km) from Earth to the moon. **58.** Light waves can travel through space, but sound waves can't. Sound needs to travel through an atmosphere. **59.** Animals and plants that can produce their own light through chemical reactions are bioluminescent. Corals, mushrooms, and squid all have species that glow. **60.** White light is a mixture of colors that when separated into a spectrum always appear in the same order: red, orange, yellow, green, blue, indigo, and violet. **61.** Different chemical compounds added to fireworks create the various colors. Blue is the most difficult color to make. **62.** An artist in Chicago, Illinois, U.S.A., created a live bunny that glowed green when under a blue light. **63.** Unlike other bioluminescent animals, the Jamaican click beetle can produce a range of colors from yellow to orange and green. **64.** The lights on an airplane's wingtips—red on one side, green on the other—signal the plane's direction to other pilots. **65.** In 2012, California had 11 solar power plants turning sunlight into other forms of energy. That's more than any other U.S. state. **66.** Of the electricity used by an incandescent lightbulb, only 10 percent is used to produce white light. The other 90 percent is given off as heat. **67.** The colorful, shimmering lights of an aurora are created when a gas cloud emitted from the sun interacts with Earth's magnetic field. **68.** Glowworms aren't worms at all; most are beetles. **69.** In 1957, Sony was among the first companies in Japan to use neon signs to advertise its business. Now, neon lights up all major Japanese cities at night. **70.** NASA's Hubble telescope can detect ultraviolet and infrared light, types of light that humans are unable to see. **71.** People who have a photic reflex sneeze when they see bright lights. **72.** The light that is reaching Earth now was created in the sun's core more than 100,000 years ago. **73.** The first red-yellow-and-green traffic lights in the United States were used in Detroit, Michigan. **74.** Two brothers, Joe and Bob Switzer, invented Day-Glo, a paint that glows in daylight. **75.** The sun will continue to provide Earth with light for 5 billion more years. **76.** People have been using candles for at least 1,600 years. **77.** It took Thomas Edison over 6,000 tries to figure out how to keep an electric lightbulb shining for a long period of time. **78.** When you bend a plastic light stick, 2 chemical solutions inside mix together and start to glow. **79.** Ripe bananas glow blue under ultraviolet light. **80.** On a bright summer day, the sunlight on Earth's surface is as bright as if 10,000 candles were burning a foot (30.5 cm) away from you. **81.** Scientists have created algae in the lab that can grow without sunlight. **82.** Explorer Scouts in the United Kingdom created a chain of 4,500 glow sticks that stretched for nearly a half mile (0.8 km). **83.** The coal we burn for fuel is stored solar energy that has been trapped in plants buried underground for millions of years. **84.** The first populated place to see the sun rise on New Year's Day is Kahuitara Point in the Chatham Islands in the South Pacific Ocean. **85.** When fireflies flash at night, they are sending messages to potential mates. **86.** In the middle of June, Miami, Florida, U.S.A., gets 13 hours and 45 minutes of sunlight a day. **87.** Barrow, Alaska, U.S.A., located above the Arctic Circle in the "Land of the Midnight Sun," gets 24 hours of sunlight for 85 days from mid-May to early August. **88.** Dragonfish are the only fish able to produce red light. They have 2 red "headlights" under each eye. **89.** The Very Large Telescope, located on a mountaintop in Chile, can detect objects in space about 4 billion times fainter than we can see with our eyes. **90.** In 2010, a Christmas tree in Belgium shone bright with 194,672 lights. **91.** The light produced by most bioluminescent sea life is bluish green. **92.** The U.S. government has successfully tested a defense system that uses high-powered lasers mounted on an airplane to bring down a missile. **93.** A flashlight invented by Canadian high school student Ann Makosinski is powered by body heat. **94.** In the Star Wars movies, the lightsabers are personalized for specific Jedi. **95.** The Lite-Brite toy, which makes colorful designs, comes in a supersize version that is 6 feet (1.8 m) tall and 8 feet (2.4 m) wide. **96.** A family in Lagrangeville, New York, U.S.A., lit up their house for the holidays with 346,283 lights. **97.** "Photophobia" is the word for being sensitive to bright light. **98.** The Olympic torch traveled to the International Space Station and was even taken on a space walk. **99.** A sparkler firework burns at more than 15 times the boiling point of water (212°F/100°C). **100.** To celebrate the 50th anniversary of its constitution in 2012, the country of Kuwait set off a huge fireworks display that lasted for more than an hour.

**1**
Every U.S. president has a favorite food. **GEORGE WASHINGTON'S WAS ICE CREAM.**

**2**
President Andrew Johnson **WAS A TAILOR** before he took office.

**3**
Abraham Lincoln was the first president to **HAVE A BEARD.**

**4**
Martin Van Buren was called Old Kinderhook after his birthplace in New York. During his campaign, the **INITIALS O.K.** became an expression of support and approval.

**5**
James Polk was the first president to **HAVE HIS PHOTOGRAPH TAKEN** while in office.

**6**
Theodore "Teddy" Roosevelt was the first president to **RIDE IN A CAR** during his time in office.

**7**
James Garfield was the first **LEFT-HANDED PRESIDENT.** As a teen, he drove the horses that pulled boats along the Ohio & Erie Canal.

**8**
William Henry Harrison, who studied to be a doctor, **DIED OF PNEUMONIA** a month after giving his inaugural address in the rain!

**9**
Franklin Delano Roosevelt was the first president to **TAKE TO THE SKIES** in an airplane.

**10**
Theodore Roosevelt named the president's residence **THE WHITE HOUSE.**

**11**
John Adams and Thomas Jefferson both **DIED ON JULY 4, 1826,** the 50th anniversary of the signing of the Declaration of Independence.

**12**
President George H.W. Bush **HATED BROCCOLI** and banned it from the White House.

**13**
President William Henry Harrison's grandson, Benjamin Harrison, became the **23RD PRESIDENT.**

**14**
Rutherford B. Hayes was the first commander in chief to make a visit to **THE WEST COAST** while president.

**15**
James Monroe was the first president to **RIDE ON A STEAMBOAT.**

**16**
President Ulysses S. Grant once received a **TICKET FOR SPEEDING** while driving his horse-drawn carriage through the streets of Washington, D.C.

**17**
James Buchanan was the first president to receive a **TELEGRAM** from overseas.

TELEGRAM

**18**
John F. Kennedy was the first (and so far, only) **ROMAN CATHOLIC** to be elected president.

**19**
The only president elected to 2 **NONCONSECUTIVE TERMS** was Grover Cleveland.

**20**
Zachary Taylor was the first president who hadn't served in any **POLITICAL OFFICE** before he was elected.

**21**
President John Quincy Adams used to go **SKINNY-DIPPING** every morning in the Potomac River.

**22**
Franklin Pierce was the first president to put a **CHRISTMAS TREE** in the White House.

**23**
To honor their environmental efforts, Presidents Obama, Clinton, Carter, and Teddy Roosevelt each had a species of **DARTER FISH** named after him in 2012.

**24**
President Woodrow Wilson, nicknamed **THE PROFESSOR,** was the first president with a Ph.D.

**25**
During his lifetime, President John Tyler had **15 CHILDREN,** more than any other president.

**26**
Ronald Reagan, who died at **AGE 93,** lived longer than any other elected president.

**27**
President Dwight Eisenhower carried **THREE LUCKY COINS** in his pocket.

**28**
Martin Van Buren, whose birth date was December 5, 1782, was the first president to be born as a **CITIZEN OF THE UNITED STATES.**

**29**
Calvin Coolidge is the only president born on **INDEPENDENCE DAY.**

**30**
The S in the middle of President Harry S. Truman's name is **SIMPLY AN INITIAL** with no name behind it.

**31**
Lyndon Baines Johnson, known as LBJ, enjoyed riding visitors around his Texas ranch at **90 MILES PER HOUR** (145 kph) in his Lincoln Continental.

**32**
Out of 44 presidents, only 11 **DID NOT SERVE** in a branch of the U.S. military.

**33**
Theodore Roosevelt is the only president to receive the **MEDAL OF HONOR.** It was presented to his great-grandson in 2001 by President Clinton.

**34**
Thomas Jefferson was the first president to take the **OATH OF OFFICE** in Washington, D.C., and the first to walk to the ceremony instead of riding in a carriage.

**35**
James Madison was the **PRIMARY AUTHOR** of the U.S. Constitution.

**36**
Andrew Jackson's pet parrot, Poll, **CURSED AT HIS FUNERAL** and had to be removed from the service.

**37**
President Bill Clinton's cat, Socks, was the first presidential pet to **HOST A WEBSITE.**

**38**
Barack Hussein Obama **WAS RAISED** in Indonesia and Hawaii.

**39**
Presidents George W. Bush and John Quincy Adams were both the **SONS OF PRESIDENTS.**

**40**
When George W. Bush moved into the White House, the *W*s **WERE MISSING** from computer keyboards. It cost the government close to $5,000 to replace them.

**41**
President Rutherford B. Hayes's wife, Lucy, loved pets. The couple owned the **FIRST SIAMESE CAT** in the country.

**42**
Many people believed Chester Arthur was **BORN IN CANADA,** not Vermont, and challenged his citizenship while he was in office.

**43**
George Washington loved exploring **CAVES.**

**44**
William McKinley **WAS SHOT** while greeting the public after giving a speech in Buffalo, New York.

**45**
James Garfield was the first president to speak both English **AND SPANISH** during his campaign in 1880.

**46**
When President Herbert Hoover and his wife wanted to speak privately to each other, they **SPOKE CHINESE.**

**47**
Warren Harding enjoyed **PLAYING POKER** twice a week.

**48**
As president, George Washington refused to **TAKE A SALARY.**

**49**
William Taft— the **HEAVIEST PRESIDENT,** at 332 pounds (151 kg)—once got stuck in a White House bathtub.

**50**
Thomas Jefferson, the only president who **FOUNDED A UNIVERSITY,** could read English, French, Latin, and Greek.

The White House, Washington, D.C., U.S.A.

# 50
## COMMANDING FACTS ABOUT
# U.S. PRESIDENTS

**1** CAROL VAUGHN OF BIRMINGHAM, ENGLAND, MAY BE THE CLEANEST PERSON ON THE PLANET. SHE HAS A COLLECTION OF **MORE THAN 5,000 BARS OF SOAP.**

**2** The Reverend Paul Johnson owns 3,400 pencil sharpeners, including one that is more than 100 years old. They're on display at the Hocking Hills Regional Welcome Center in Ohio, U.S.A.

**3** Julie Boaler's **ENGAGEMENT RING** proved just right for an English magpie's collection. It was found in the **BIRD'S NEST** outside her house a few years after it disappeared.

**4** To get Tom Hanks to appear on his podcast, Nerdist host Chris Hardwick sent the famous actor a vintage typewriter to **add to his collection.**

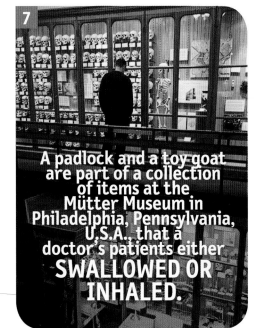

# 25 WACKY
## FACTS ABOUT WEIRD

**5** Want to be grossed out? Check out the **world's largest tapeworm** and other parasites at the Meguro Parasitological Museum in Tokyo, Japan.

**6** Dr. Michael Zuk, a dentist from Alberta, Canada, paid a record $31,000 to add **THE MOLAR OF BEATLE JOHN LENNON** to his celebrity tooth collection.

**7** A padlock and a toy goat are part of a collection of items at the Mütter Museum in Philadelphia, Pennsylvania, U.S.A., that a doctor's patients either **SWALLOWED OR INHALED.**

**8** AFTER SHARON REYNOLDS OF CALIFORNIA, U.S.A., FILLED EVERY ROOM IN HER HOUSE WITH **PIG CURIOS,** SHE ADDED A REAL LIVE PIG TO HER COLLECTION.

**9** PETER THE GREAT'S CHAMBER OF CURIOSITIES in St. Petersburg, Russia, is filled with oddities that he collected, including Siamese twins, teeth that he pulled, and a lamb with 8 legs.

**10** Before you trash that pan of burnt brownies, you might want to contact the **BURNT FOOD MUSEUM.** It has an entire collection of charred goodies.

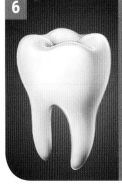

**11** The National Museum of Health and Medicine, near Washington, D.C., U.S.A., celebrated National Hairball Awareness Day by displaying

# HAIRBALLS
from 10 animals, including a horse, a cow, and a chicken.

**12** Ye Olde Curiosity Shop in Seattle, Washington, U.S.A., exhibits a unique collection of oddities that includes shrunken heads, mummies, origami money, and even a 2-headed lamb.

**13** THE GALILEO MUSEUM IN FLORENCE, ITALY, INCLUDES A DISPLAY OF

## 3 FINGERS AND A TOOTH
FROM THE MUSEUM'S NAMESAKE, 16TH-CENTURY ASTRONOMER/SCIENTIST GALILEO GALILEI.

**14** Can airplane barf bags be considered art? Steven Silberberg thinks so. His collection numbers **2,216.**

**15** Peter Scanlon spent so much of his life collecting memorabilia about former U.S. President Teddy Roosevelt that he started to look like his idol.

**16** John Reznikoff holds a world record for collecting the most **celebrity hair,** including snips from Abraham Lincoln and Marilyn Monroe.

**17** Wood rats collect toys, garbage, jewelry, pet waste, and anything else they find interesting for their nests. That's why they're often called pack rats.

**18** EACH AUGUST, TRASH-AND-TREASURE SEEKERS FLOCK TO THE WORLD'S LARGEST YARD SALE. IT STRETCHES ALONG HIGHWAY 127 ALL THE WAY FROM MICHIGAN TO ALABAMA, U.S.A.

**19** Rebecca Chulew thinks about her **$80,000** BARBIE DOLL COLLECTION every minute of the day. Once a week she has her hair styled to match one of them.

# COLLECTIONS

**20** Johnny Depp—also known as **CAPTAIN JACK SPARROW**—collects just about everything from bugs and pigeon skeletons to pictures of clowns.

**21** The largest collection of human hair is in a cave in Avanos, Turkey. The Chez Galip Hair Museum has samples from more than 16,000 women.

**22** Want history you can taste? Visit the **GELATO MUSEUM** outside of Bologna, Italy.

**23** Zanadu's Museum of Curiosities & Gift Shop in Lake George, New York, U.S.A., includes debris from a UFO crash site and the world's largest Popsicle stick structure.

**24** THE **ASPHALT MUSEUM** IN SACRAMENTO, CALIFORNIA, U.S.A., HOUSES THE WORLD'S LARGEST COLLECTION OF—YOU GUESSED IT—ASPHALT.

**25** When Imelda Marcos, former First Lady of the Philippines, fled the country in 1986, she left almost half of her famous collection of 3,000-plus pairs of shoes behind. Termites and floods have since ruined many of them.

**1** At the 1968 Olympics, 2 black sprinters—TOMMIE SMITH AND JOHN CARLOS—dared to stand up against racial discrimination in the United States **BY RAISING A BLACK-GLOVED FIST DURING THEIR MEDAL PRESENTATION CEREMONY.** They were sent home for using the games to make a political statement.

**2** Mexican-American activist CÉSAR CHÁVEZ used nonviolent methods in the 1960s, '70s, and '80s to win FAIR WAGES, SAFE WORKING CONDITIONS, and other rights for U.S. FARMWORKERS. He once fasted for 36 days—drinking only water—to bring attention to the danger of pesticide poisoning for grape workers and consumers.

**3** As leader of India's independence movement, MAHATMA GANDHI introduced the concept of *satyagraha*—THE DETERMINED PURSUIT OF ONE'S GOALS WITHOUT VIOLENCE—in the early 20th century to fight against BRITISH RULE.

**4** NELSON MANDELA spent 27 years in prison for trying to end apartheid—RACIAL DISCRIMINATION—in South Africa. Four years after his release, he saw his efforts fulfilled when he was elected the country's first black president in 1994.

**5** In the mid-1800s, reformer AMELIA BLOOMER campaigned for the right of WOMEN TO DRESS COMFORTABLY. She urged women to wear knee-length dresses with pants underneath—which became known as "bloomers."

**6** In 1960 when she was 6 years old, **RUBY BRIDGES BECAME THE YOUNGEST AFRICAN AMERICAN TO GO TO AN ALL-WHITE SCHOOL.** For almost a year, she was the only student in her first-grade class in New Orleans, Louisiana, U.S.A., because the parents of her white classmates kept their children home.

# PEOPLE WHO TOOK A STAND

**7** An 8-year-old California, U.S.A., GIRL HAS RAISED OVER $300,000 TO HELP FIGHT CHILD SLAVERY AROUND THE WORLD by selling lemonade.

**8** Actor MARLON BRANDO refused his best actor Oscar for his work in *The Godfather* as a way of PROTESTING POOR TREATMENT OF NATIVE AMERICANS by the film industry.

**9** In 1947, JACKIE ROBINSON became the first African American to PLAY ON A MAJOR LEAGUE BASEBALL TEAM. By standing up to racist attitudes, he was an inspiration to the civil rights movement.

**10** In the 17th century, astronomer GALILEO GALILEI wrote a book confirming NICOLAUS COPERNICUS'S THEORY that the sun—not Earth—was the center of the universe. The Catholic Church disapproved, and he spent the rest of his life under house arrest.

**11** On May 3, 2013, MILLIONS OF STUDENTS across the United States stood up for 5 minutes as part of a nationwide ANTI-BULLYING PROGRAM called Stand4Change.

**12** RAOUL WALLENBERG, a Swedish diplomat in German-occupied Hungary during World War II, HELPED SAVE ALMOST 100,000 HUNGARIAN JEWS from the Holocaust by issuing them Swedish passports and renting safe houses where they could seek refuge.

**13** In 1973, Wimbledon tennis champ BILLIE JEAN KING accepted the challenge to COMPETE AGAINST MALE TENNIS PRO BOBBY RIGGS, and won—proving that women could play at the same competitive level as men.

**14** From 1955 until his assassination in 1968, MARTIN LUTHER KING, JR., leader of the U.S. civil rights movement, never gave up on his belief that ALL PEOPLE ARE CREATED EQUAL.

**15** In the 1960s, EUNICE KENNEDY SHRIVER wanted to give kids with intellectual disabilities the opportunity to participate in the same physical activities other kids enjoy, so she started a summer day camp in her backyard. Eventually, this led her to found the SPECIAL OLYMPICS.

**1** Germs are microscopic organisms (microorganisms) such as bacteria, viruses, and fungi that eat, poop, reproduce, and die. Many are essential to our survival.

**2** A company has created a screen for touch screen cell phones that keeps them 99.9 percent germ free.

**3** A BACTERIUM FOUND ONLY IN SOIL FROM JAPAN TURNED UP IN ONE MAN'S BELLY BUTTON, AND HE HAD NEVER EVEN BEEN TO JAPAN!

**4** In the workplace, men's offices have up to 20 percent more germs than women's offices. Chairs and telephones are the most germ-covered.

**5** Hate washing your jeans? A student who wore a pair for 15 months proved they had no more germs on them than on day 13.

**6** Scientists found that kids who grow up with dogs as pets are healthier! Exposure to their dog's germs strengthens their immune systems.

**7** People in China and Greece used the penicillin mold to treat infections thousands of years before it was "discovered" as an antibiotic.

**8** Alexander Fleming, who discovered the antibiotic penicillin, "painted" with bacteria by growing different colored germs into shapes such as ballerinas, houses, stick figures, and more.

**9** The petri dish that grew the penicillin mold found by Alexander Fleming is in the Smithsonian's American History Museum, in Washington, D.C., U.S.A.

**10** When they signed the Outer Space Treaty in 1967, the United States, United Kingdom, and Soviet Union (now Russia) agreed to avoid contaminating space with Earth's microbial life.

**11** In keeping with the 1967 treaty, NASA got rid of all but about 300,000 bacterial spores in the Mars rover Curiosity before launching it in 2011.

**12** Inside an adult human there can be as many as 200 trillion organisms and microorganisms, including bacteria, fungi, and viruses.

**13** Every adult human is home to 1,000 species of microorganisms.

**14** The secret to getting rid of germs is how long you scrub your hands, not whether you use soap and water or just water.

**15** The oldest thing ever brought back to life may be a germ—a 250-million-year-old bacterium discovered in a salt crystal in 2000.

**16** Some germs are even worse when they grow in space. Salmonella bacteria were found to be 3 times more deadly in mice when grown on the space shuttle Atlantis.

**17** Vuvuzelas, favorite horns to blow at soccer games, spit out 4 million germs every second. That's 4 times more than from a sneeze.

**18** Scientists have found that babies whose pacifiers are cleaned with mom or dad's spit are less likely to develop eczema, allergies, and other conditions.

**19** Getting a little dirty is a good thing. Without exposure to germs, our bodies have a tough time distinguishing what's harmful and what's not.

**20** There are more than 1 billion cases of the common cold in the United States every year, and more than 200 different kinds of cold viruses.

**21** GERMS THAT CAUSE THE COMMON COLD, OR RHINOVIRUSES, CAN SURVIVE FOR UP TO 2 DAYS OUTSIDE THE BODY.

**22** Get ready to run when someone sneezes! The greatest distance germs from a sneeze travel is 6 feet (2 m).

**23** Bacteria—possibly from a comet or meteor—may have started life as we know it on Earth.

**24** Some scientists think the dinosaurs became extinct because they had no immunity to deadly germs that appeared about 65 million years ago.

**25** One company invented an "infection resistant" keyboard that warns the user when it is dirty.

**26** A computer keyboard can harbor 5 times more bacteria than a toilet seat.

**27** The Handheld Germ Eliminating Light uses nanotechnology and ultraviolet light to kill germs in as little as 10 seconds. Now that's killer light!

**28** Most vaccines contain dead or weak germs that make your body build antibodies—proteins that help fight off a disease.

**29** Germs "talk" to each other by pumping chemicals through their cell walls to the same and different species nearby.

**30** You should think twice before you share food with your dog. It's possible for disease-causing oral bacteria to pass between pooches and their humans.

**31** Forget the subway—germs can travel by hurricane! Microbes can survive and even thrive in the stratosphere, over 6 miles (10 km) above Earth's surface.

**32** Bacteria and germs that hitch a ride on leafy greens and vegetables are the cause of more than half of all food-borne illnesses.

**33** In an effort to stop the spread of germs in Australia, kids aren't allowed to blow out birthday candles at school.

**34** At a North Carolina, U.S.A., hospital, robots called RD-D2s kill 99 percent of germs in hospital rooms by using ultraviolet light.

**35** Athletic equipment can be home to some nasty germs. Some athletes' mouth guards have been found with traces of animal poop.

**36** Can you imagine blowing your nose with a tissue that's nearly 20 feet (6 m) wide? That's how big the largest box of tissues ever made is.

**37** The average cell phone has more than 25,000 germs per square inch (6 cm²).

**38** THE TV REMOTE IS THE DIRTIEST ITEM IN A TYPICAL HOUSEHOLD, HOSPITAL, OR HOTEL ROOM.

**39** Talk about thinking with your gut! Intestinal microbes may make people more adventurous and even reduce stress.

**40** For a fee, the American Gut project will analyze your poop, mouth, or skin sample and tell you how your microbes compare with those of other Americans.

**41** A baby is nearly germfree while in its mother's womb.

**42** Gut bacteria that babies get from their mothers can affect the way their brains develop and even how they will behave as adults.

**43** THERE ARE 10 TIMES MORE BACTERIA IN OUR INTESTINES THAN THERE ARE CELLS IN OUR ENTIRE BODIES.

**44** The intestines of Japanese people have special bacteria that can break down all the seaweed they eat as a source of nutrition.

**45** Best not to use your cell phone in the bathroom! A study showed that 16 percent of phones in the United Kingdom are tainted with poop germs.

**46** There is a high-tech bracelet that allows employers to monitor their employees' hand-washing habits. It vibrates when the wearer is done at the sink.

**47** Four kinds of bacteria survive only by eating caffeine that they get from dirt around caffeine-producing plants.

**48** Is that floating snot in the water? Nope, just mucilage—a mass of living and dead stuff that carries millions of bacteria and viruses. Some blobs can be 124 miles (200 km) long.

**49** Our noses are our dirtiest organs because their mucus, or snot, filters out germs, dirt, and whatever else tries to get up our nostrils.

**50** Snot is actually filled with special proteins that kill bacteria and viruses.

**51** Even if an object spends only a millisecond on the floor, it's contaminated. So much for the 5-second rule.

**52** Pasteurization is a method of preventing perishable liquids like milk from spoiling by heating them to a temperature that slows the growth of microbes.

**53** Viruses are the smallest kind of germ. They can be up to 10,000 times smaller than bacteria.

**54** Viruses come in all different shapes. Some are multisided—like cut diamonds—and others look like lunar landing pods.

# 75 GROSS FACTS ABOUT GERMS

**63** "SUPERBUGS" ARE FAST-SPREADING, QUICK-CHANGING, DRUG-RESISTANT GERMS THAT CAN BE VERY DEADLY.

**64** A group of scientists in Singapore has created a coating that acts like a magnet to attract germs. It destroys 99 percent of bacteria—even superbugs.

**65** Vitamin B3 could be the key in the war on superbugs. It has been shown to boost good immune cells that kill and eat harmful germs in the body.

**66** One-third of Americans skip washing their hands after using the bathroom.

**67** One 4-million-year-old New Mexico, U.S.A., cave is home to hundreds of bacteria that are resistant to known antibiotics.

**68** Polio, a virus that causes paralysis, has been wiped out in the United States thanks to a vaccine developed by Jonas Salk in 1953.

**69** *Osmosis Jones* is a cartoon movie that stars a white blood cell police officer who kills germs living inside a man's body.

**70** Bacteria on our skin affects how we smell, since each type emits a different scent. Without bacteria, those sweaty gym clothes wouldn't stink.

**71** Mosquitoes are attracted by certain types of bacteria. One species prefers people with lots of *Staphylococcus* or *Variovorax* bacteria.

**72** Hippopotamuses secrete an oily red substance that may protect their skin from germs.

**73** Yeti crabs have big, fuzzy claws to trap bacteria. Besides providing food for the crab, the bacteria filter out toxins and germs in the water.

**74** The germs that live on the outside of our noses feed on lipids—fat, oil, or wax—and produce a moisturizer that helps prevents dry skin.

**75** One type of bacteria poops gold. *Cupriavidus metallidurans* eats gold chloride—a toxin—and turns it into 24-carat-gold nuggets in about a week.

**55** Archaeans are microbes that look and act like bacteria but are structured differently. Drugs that kill bacteria do nothing to Archaeans.

**56** ARCHAEANS AND BACTERIA EVOLVED FROM ONE COMMON ANCESTOR OVER 4 BILLION YEARS AGO.

**57** There are between 10,000 and 10 million germs on each of your hands. Each human hand has its own bacterial fingerprint—no 2 hands are the same.

**58** During the 1897 U.S. yellow fever epidemic, people believed mail spread the disease. In Alabama, postal workers punched holes in the mail, then treated it with germ-killing fumes.

**59** Double dipping isn't as unhealthy as it sounds. The number of germs you add to the salsa or dip is small compared with how many are already in it.

**60** Some ships are equipped with poop burners—giant incinerators that turn human waste into germ-free ashes.

**61** To kill germs, Levi Strauss, the blue jeans company, recommends that people freeze their jeans instead of washing them. Microbiologists say this won't kill the "bugs."

**62** Most germs growing on your clothes are feeding on your dead skin cells, not the clothing. Washing your clothes removes the food source.

Illustration of a virus

**1**
There are more **SPECIES OF BEETLES ON EARTH** than any other kind of creature.

**2**
Beetles have lived on Earth for about **300 MILLION YEARS.**

**3**
The **BOMBARDIER BEETLE** can shoot **BOILING-HOT POISON** from its rear end at predators.

**4**
The horns of some male **RHINOCEROS BEETLES** can be longer than their bodies.

**5**
**SIBERIAN BEETLES** can survive temperatures as low as minus 40°F (-40°C).

**6**
Researchers named a handful of **NEWLY DISCOVERED** beetles in Papua New Guinea by **RANDOMLY SELECTING** family names from a local phone book.

**7**
The **HERCULES BEETLE** can grow big enough to cover an adult human hand.

**8**
**BEETLES** are not picky. They'll eat plants, other insects, carcasses, dung, and **EVEN SLIME LEFT BY SNAILS.**

Colorado beetle

# 35 BUGGY FACTS ABOUT BEETLES

**9**
DIVING BEETLES can breathe underwater.

**10**
Many beetles COMMUNICATE by making SQUEAKING NOISES by rubbing parts of their bodies together.

**11**
The FEATHER-WINGED BEETLE, the world's smallest insect, can fit on the head of a pin.

**12**
Beetles and their larvae are a POPULAR SNACK for people in parts of Asia, Africa, and Australia.

**13**
Some species of beetles are named after CELEBRITIES, like BEYONCÉ and the U.S. president THEODORE ROOSEVELT.

**14**
WHIRLIGIG BEETLES, which swim on the surface of ponds, have divided eyes: one-half for vision underwater, the other half for seeing above the water.

**15**
DUNG BEETLES, which feed and grow their eggs in animal waste, CAN MOVE A BALL of dung that's 50 TIMES their own weight.

**16**
LEAF BEETLE larvae are so POISONOUS that hunters have used their juices on the tips of their ARROWS.

**17**
FIREFLIES and LADYBUGS are part of the beetle family.

**18**
The JEWEL BEETLE, which lays its eggs in burnt wood, can SNIFF OUT A FIRE from 50 miles (80 km) away—10,000 times the distance of most home fire detectors.

**19**
A CLICK BEETLE can flip from its back to its front by snapping its head and abdomen together.

**20**
DUNG BEETLES will fly up to 10 miles (16 km) in search of JUST THE RIGHT DUNG for laying their eggs.

**21**
CARNIVOROUS BEETLES can devour more than 8 pounds (4 kg) of ANIMAL FLESH in one week.

**22**
Beetles have STRONG JAWS. In fact, the word "beetle" is derived from the Anglo-Saxon *bitan*, meaning "TO BITE."

**23**
Special receptors in the American BURYING BEETLES' antennae help it to detect DEAD MEAT within an hour after an animal dies.

**24**
LADYBUGS beat their wings about 85 TIMES PER SECOND while in flight.

**25**
To keep enemies away, ladybugs release a FOUL-SMELLING CHEMICAL from their "KNEES."

**26**
Adult beetles have 2 pairs of WINGS.

**27**
Most beetles LIVE for only 1 YEAR.

**28**
The SACRED SCARAB beetle was worshipped as a sun god by the ancient Egyptians.

**29**
Some BEETLE species RELEASE POISON when crushed.

**30**
The GOLIATH BEETLE weighs as much as a quarter-pound hamburger.

**31**
The TIGER BEETLE hunts and kills other insects by slamming them against the ground.

**32**
It can take up to 5 YEARS for some types of beetles to GROW from an egg to an ADULT.

**33**
The ELEPHANT BEETLE has horns on its head that look like tusks.

**34**
Beetles are found everywhere EXCEPT in the OCEAN and on ANTARCTICA.

**35**
One man from Germany has a collection of 30,000 BEETLES that represent more than 6,000 species from 22 countries.

**1.** Buddhists believe that a strand of the Buddha's hair balances the Golden Rock on the edge of a cliff in Myanmar. **2. About 1 out of every 3 people in the world is Christian. 3. More than a billion Christians are Roman Catholic. 4.** Worldwide, 300 million people go on faith pilgrimages each year. **5. The Dome of the Rock, a Muslim shrine in Jerusalem, is built over the stone where the Prophet Muhammad is believed to have ascended into heaven. 6. At least once in their lives, Muslims are expected to make a pilgrimage to Islam's holiest site—the Grand Mosque in Mecca, Saudi Arabia. 7.** In India, Hindus make an offering of lamps to the sacred Ganges River. They believe the river can wash away sins. **8. Indonesia is home to over 200 million Muslims—more than live in any other country. 9. Ethiopia's Bet Medhane Alem church was carved from a single block of volcanic rock over 800 years ago. 10.** In North Korea, 71 percent of the people call themselves atheists, meaning they don't believe in any deity. **11. The population of Vatican City is 100 percent Roman Catholic. 12. The almost 1,500-year-old Hagia Sophia, which means "Holy Wisdom," was once the world's largest Christian church. It is now a museum in Istanbul, Turkey. 13.** There are over 50,000 Catholic priests in Italy—more than in any other country. **14. About 13 percent of the world's Jews live in New York City, U.S.A. 15. Australia's Aborigines believe that Uluru, a massive sandstone rock also known as Ayers Rock, was formed by their ancestors during creation time. 16.** According to Polynesian tradition, Mauna Kea in Hawaii, U.S.A., is home to several deities, including a snow goddess who stopped the volcano from erupting with a mantle of ice. **17. Islam is the world's largest religion after Christianity. 18. Hinduism, which dates back to at least 2000 B.C., is the world's oldest major religion and has nearly 1 billion followers. 19.** There are 330,000 Hindu deities. **20. Tens of millions of Hindu pilgrims attend Kumbh Mela in India, making it Earth's largest human gathering. 21. According to local tradition, the Holy Thorn tree in Glastonbury, England, sprang to life after Jesus' great-uncle touched the ground there with his staff in the first century A.D. 22.** Six thousand Buddhist sites in Tibet have been

# 100 FACTS ABOUT RELIGION TO INSPIRE YOU

Mudra, a Buddhist hand symbol

destroyed since 1949, when China began enforcing its claim over the region. **23. Chinese policies have forced the Dalai Lama, the spiritual leader of Tibetan Buddhists, to live in exile since 1959. 24. Some believe Stonehenge, a cluster of massive stone pillars on England's Salisbury Plain, was a temple for sun worship or for healing. 25.** Most archaeologists believe that the Inca built Machu Picchu high in the Andes of Peru as a religious center dedicated to the sun god. **26. Taoism promotes finding your way in the natural order of things and learning to harness the yin and the yang—complementary energies that hold the universe in balance. 27. Taoism is practiced mainly in East Asia, especially China. 28.** Unlike many other religions, Shinto, the traditional religion of Japan, does not have a known founder or a sacred scripture. **29. Followers of Shinto perform rituals that help them communicate with** *kami*—spirits that help bring good health and success. **30.** Many Japanese make offerings of flowers and say prayers at shrines in their homes. **31.** The word "religion" comes from the Latin *religio,* meaning "duty." **32. Jerusalem's Western Wall, a remnant of Solomon's Second Temple complex, is the site most revered by Jews and a place of pilgrimage. 33. Ancient Greeks believed that lightning was a sign that their god Zeus was angry. 34.** Hindus believe in karma—the idea that a person's actions and thoughts influence how his or her life will turn out. **35. Hindus believe that a person can be reborn in many forms—even as an insect. 36. Holi is a Hindu celebration of spring where people mimic the mischievous tricks of the god Krishna by throwing powdered dyes at each other. 37.** Pope Francis, leader of the Roman Catholic Church, has been known to randomly call people who have written him letters to offer them guidance or support. **38. Copies of the Torah—the first part of the Jewish Bible that contains all the laws of the religion—are handwritten in Hebrew on scrolls. 39. Jewish Orthodox men cover the top of their head with a** *kippah,* also called a *yarmulke,* as a sign of respect for God. **40.** Jewish synagogues—places of study and worship—are usually rectangular with seats on 3 sides. The fourth side faces Jerusalem. **41. Orthodox Jews eat food that is prepared according to strict kosher guidelines. For example, meat and milk are prepared separately and with different utensils; pork and shellfish are never eaten. 42.** When a Jewish boy turns 13, he becomes a *bar mitzvah,* meaning "a son of the Covenant," and is expected to behave as an adult according to Jewish law. **43.** A traditional Jewish wedding is held under a *chuppah*, a special piece of cloth held up by 4 poles that symbolizes the new home the couple is making. **44. Hanukkah, or the Jewish Festival of Lights, is held every November or December for 8 days and celebrates the Jews' ancient struggle for religious freedom. 45.** Buddhist monks shave their heads and wear a simple robe as symbols that they are turning away from everyday wealth and possessions. **46.** Buddhist prayers are sometimes written on flags and flown outside. When the flags wave, it is believed the prayers are blown across Earth. **47. Buddhist prayer wheels have been used for over 1,000 years. Spinning one, which makes a noise, is a form of saying prayers. 48.** China's Spring Temple Buddha is over 100 feet (30 m) taller than the Statue of Liberty in the United States. **49.** The basilisk lizard is also known as the Jesus lizard for its ability to move across the surface of ponds and streams. **50. The motto "In God We Trust" first appeared on U.S. money in 1864. In 1956, Congress passed a law making it the national motto. 51.** Muslims believe the word of Allah (God) was revealed to Muhammad through an angel and then written as the Koran, the central text of Islam. **52.** A Turkish businessman has a collection of prayer beads valued at $100 million. Some are made with rare black diamonds, others with gold and ivory. **53. Muslims gather and pray at mosques. Most mosques have at least 1 tower—called a minaret—where a call to prayer is recited 5 times a day. 54.** In keeping with the Koran's teaching about modesty, women in some Muslim countries wear a burka, a robe that conceals the whole body except for an opening around the eyes. **55.** To Hindu people, cows are sacred. You can be sent to jail for killing or injuring one in India or Nepal. **56. Celts, who lived in Europe more than 2,000 years ago, threw precious items into rivers and ponds as gifts to some of their gods. 57.** When traveling in Argentina, Charles Darwin met native people who believed that making an offering to a kind of thorn tree would keep their horses from tiring. **58.** The Bible is the world's best-selling book. **59. There are 6 billion copies of the Bible in circulation. 60.** The percentage of people who follow Islam is higher in Afghanistan than in any other country: 98.7 percent. **61.** Aztecs believed red poinsettias symbolized purity and used them in religious ceremonies long before the plants became popular at Christmastime. **62. A former bus stop in Forestville, California, U.S.A., has been converted into an "independent spiritual church" that has seers on-site to tell your fortune. 63.** Known as the world's smallest church, the Cross Island Chapel sits on a platform in the middle of a pond in Oneida, New York. It seats 2 people. **64.** The medieval steeple on Germany's Suurhusen Church is the most tilted tower in the world. It even beats Italy's Leaning Tower of Pisa. **65. The architect of Iceland's Hallgrimskirkja Church used cooled lava flows as his inspiration for the design of the concrete church. 66.** The Metropolitan Cathedral of Rio de Janeiro in Brazil can hold 20,000 worshippers. **67.** In the Catholic and Orthodox Christian churches, holy water is water that has been blessed by a priest or bishop. **68. It took a New York man 4 years to hand copy all 788,000 words of the King James Bible. 69.** The praying mantis is named for the position of its front legs, which are bent and held together. **70.** Vatican City issues its own coins and stamps and has its own radio station. **71. ATMs in Vatican City include Latin as one of the languages that users can choose! 72.** A U.S. federal court ruled that veganism can be considered a religion if a person practices it with great sincerity. **73.** Over 176,000 people in Wales and England consider themselves part of the Jedi Faith, which is based on the philosophy and spiritual ideas presented in the *Star Wars* movies. **74. Christianity and Judaism share the same roots. The Jewish Torah has the same content as the first 5 books of the Christian Old Testament. 75.** A fish is a symbol of the Christian religion partly because of the Bible story that tells how Jesus fed 5,000 people with 2 fish and 5 loaves of bread. **76.** Sikhism, which was founded in South Asia in the 16th century, has over 20 million followers. Sikhs—male and female—do not cut their hair. **77. The world's tallest pagoda—a kind of Buddhist temple—is in Changzhou, China. It stands nearly 505 feet (154 m) high—taller than Egypt's Great Pyramid at Giza. 78.** The symbol of the Baha'i Faith, founded in what is now Iran in the 19th century, is a 9-point star, representing completeness. **79.** Some of the people in the Bible and the Torah, such as Abraham and Moses, are also in the Koran. **80. When Catholic cardinals gather to vote on a new pope, black smoke from the chimney of the Sistine Chapel indicates they are undecided; white means they have made a decision. 81.** Pope Francis chose his name in honor of St. Francis of Assisi, who gave up wealth to work with the poor. **82.** The Holy Grail—the cup Jesus drank from at the Last Supper—was the subject of a hunt for eternal life in an Indiana Jones movie. **83. Some people believe the Shroud of Turin, a yellowed piece of linen, is Jesus' burial cloth, but carbon dating says it was made almost 1,500 years after his death. 84.** Each year, people in Naples, Italy, wait to see if the dried blood of their patron saint turns to liquid. Some believe that if the change doesn't happen, disaster will strike the city as it has in the past. **85.** What are said to be pieces of the Prophet Muhammad's beard are displayed in the Topkapi Palace Museum in Istanbul, Turkey. **86. The Temple of the Tooth in Kandy, Sri Lanka, holds what is said to be the Buddha's tooth. 87.** Chartres Cathedral, in France, houses what is traditionally said to be a tunic worn by the Virgin Mary during the birth of Jesus. **88.** According to tradition, the Prophet Muhammad left imprints of his footsteps on some stones now on display at mosques and museums. **89. Some 5 million people a year visit the Sistine Chapel in Vatican City. 90.** Twice as many people visit the Golden Temple, a Sikh shrine in Amritsar, India, as visit the Sistine Chapel. **91.** The Hebrew letters on each side of a dreidel stand for the saying "A great miracle occurred here." The miracle was the Jews' defeat of the Greeks in 165 B.C. **92. The Bodhi Tree in Bodh Gaya, India, is said to be the tree that the Buddha sat under while reaching enlightenment (supreme wisdom). 93.** To Buddhists, the lotus, which grows in muddy waters, represents rising to achieve enlightenment. **94.** Some people seeking forgiveness crawl on their knees for miles to pray at Our Lady of Guadalupe Basilica in Mexico City. **95. A 98-foot (30-m)-tall statue of Jesus stands atop Corcovado Mountain in Brazil, the world's largest Catholic country. 96.** Mormons, members of the Church of Jesus Christ of Latter-day Saints, go without food or drink for 2 consecutive meals on the first Sunday of each month. **97.** Mormons believe that God has a physical body, is married, and can have children. **98. Rastafarianism is a religion that developed in 1930s Jamaica after the coronation of Haile Selassie I as King of Ethiopia. Followers believe Selassie was an incarnation of God. 99.** Protestant churches attended by at least 2,000 people each week are called megachurches. **100.** Every Sunday, almost 150,000 people attend 1 of 7 services at the Pentecostal Yoido Full Gospel Church in Seoul, South Korea. Several hundred thousand more watch on TV.

**1**

Animals in **TORPOR**—a short-term state of hibernation—become inactive and lower their body temperature to adapt to cold temperatures or a lack of food.

**2**

Some species of mice, bats, and birds enter a state of **TORPOR** almost **EVERY DAY**.

**3**

**TRUE HIBERNATION** is an extended state of torpor that can last for **MONTHS** or longer.

**4**

While **HIBERNATING**, arctic ground squirrels drop their body temperature below 32°F (0°C), with their hearts beating fewer than **5 TIMES** each minute.

**5**

Hibernating **SNAILS** cover their bodies with mucus to keep from drying out.

**6**

Mammals in true hibernation **WAKE UP EVERY WEEK** or so to warm up for a while before going back to sleep.

**7**

During dark winter months when prey can be hard to see, the **ANTARCTIC COD** reduces its need for food by hibernating in a burrow on the seafloor.

**8**

Bears are sometimes thought of as **SUPER HIBERNATORS** because they can last all winter without eating, drinking, exercising, or going to the bathroom.

**9**

Of the 9 species of bears, **ONLY 4 HIBERNATE**: the American black bear, Asiatic black bear, brown bear, and polar bear.

Chipmunk

**10**

When food is scarce, **ECHIDNAS**— small, spiny, egg-laying mammals found in Australia and New Guinea—can go to sleep for weeks to conserve energy, no matter the season.

**11**

**MALE POLAR BEARS** often don't hibernate. But females may hunker down for more than **240 DAYS** without nourishment.

**12**

Although **CHIPMUNKS** hibernate, they do not live off fat stored in their bodies. Instead, they stash food in their burrows and eat it throughout the winter.

**13**

**MARMOTS**, which hibernate for up to 8 months each year, take only 2 or 3 breaths per minute as they sleep.

**14**

While **HUMANS** don't naturally hibernate, people in **DEEP MEDITATION** can decrease their oxygen use to the point of entering a hibernation-like state.

**15**

During hibernation, a black bear's **HEART RATE** can drop from 40 to 50 beats per minute to just **8 BEATS** per minute.

**16**

The only species of bird known to hibernate is the common **POORWILL**. It will rest under rocks or in rotten logs for up to 5 months.

**17**

One **BROWN BAT** in captivity hibernated for **344 DAYS**. Normal time in the wild is only around 60 days.

**18**

Madagascar's **FAT-TAIL DWARF LEMURS** gain nearly half their body weight in preparation for a 7-month stint inside a tree during the dry season.

# 50
## REJUVENATING FACTS ABOUT
# HIBERNATION

**19**
If **BOX TURTLES** wake up too early from hibernation, they likely will not survive.

**20**
When box turtles hibernate, they do not breathe through their nostrils. They take in **OXYGEN** through their **SKIN**.

**21**
Male and worker bees die at the end of every summer, but **THE QUEEN HIBERNATES** in rotten trees, in the ground, or under leaves through the winter.

**22**
**GARTER SNAKES** hibernate in groups. One den in Canada had 8,000 snoozing snakes.

**23**
To stay safe during hibernation, **SNAILS** close up any holes in their shells with skin made of chalk and slime that keeps the moisture in.

**24**
Some **HEDGEHOGS** sleep through the whole winter, breathing so little that they appear to be dead.

**25**
**RACCOONS** that live in colder climates hibernate and can lose as much as half their weight during their deep winter sleep.

**26**
Black bears lose only about **25 PERCENT** of their muscle strength while in their winter dens. A human in a similar situation would lose around 90 percent.

**27**
Early German settlers in Pennsylvania, U.S.A., introduced the idea of a link between the shadows of hibernating animals and the length of winter that led to **GROUNDHOG DAY.**

**28**
Hibernation is triggered by the presence of **ADENOSINE**, a molecule produced by all animals—including humans—that **CAUSES SLEEPINESS** when it travels to the brain.

**29**
In the 19th century, it was common for people in France and Russia to spend much of the **WINTERS IN BED**, sometimes getting up just once a day.

**30**
Some animals, like desert tortoises, salamanders, and crocodiles, enter a hibernation-like state called **ESTIVATION** to stay cool in summer and survive droughts.

**31**
Animals usually know when it's time to hibernate based on the **NUMBER OF HOURS** of daylight and the temperature.

**32**
While getting ready to hibernate, bears can **GAIN** as much as **30 POUNDS** (14 kg) **PER WEEK.**

**33**
Some bears and other species enter a state of **"WALKING HIBERNATION."** They're awake, but their heart rate slows, body temperature drops, and they eat less.

**34**
Even though a hibernating bear **DRINKS NO WATER**, it does not become dehydrated because stored fat breaks down to provide water.

**35**
NASA has conducted research on putting **HUMANS** in a state of hibernation for long-distance **SPACE TRAVEL.**

**36**
While hibernating, a **PREGNANT BLACK BEAR** wakes up long enough to give birth in the den. She even stays asleep while her cubs nurse.

**37**
A woodchuck's **FRONT TEETH GROW CONTINUOUSLY** except during hibernation.

**38**
When bats are ready to hibernate, they gather in **CAVES CALLED HIBERNACULA** where the temperature stays above freezing.

**39**
Aquatic turtles **BURY THEMSELVES** in the **MUD** at the bottom of streams and ponds to stay warm in winter. They get oxygen from air trapped in the dirt.

**40**
**WATCH OUT!** If you come within 50 feet (15 m) of a hibernating mama bear's den, it will cause her **HEART RATE TO SPIKE**, and she will wake up.

**41**
The amount of **OXYGEN** flowing to the brain of a hibernating animal can be as little as 2 percent of the normal rate, producing a **COMA-LIKE STATE.**

**42**
While many butterfly species migrate south in winter, others spend it **TUCKED INTO CREVICES** in logs, underneath loose bark on trees, and even in people's homes.

**43**
Some small mammals like **VOLES** that can't grow long winter coats stay warm by burrowing under the snow, which acts as an **INSULATING BLANKET.**

**44**
During hibernation, a hedgehog's **BODY TEMPERATURE** dips from 95°F to 50°F (35°C to 10°C), a drop that would kill most other mammals.

**45**
**LADYBUGS** hibernate for up to 9 months in colonies that may contain thousands of the **SPOTTED INSECTS.**

**46**
Bears can take **3 WEEKS TO FULLY WAKE UP** from hibernation.

**47**
Black bears sometimes hibernate in the tops of **TREES.**

**48**
Bears normally remain in hibernation until **APRIL OR MAY**, but they will emerge earlier if the weather is warm.

**49**
In winter, wood frogs stop breathing, their heart stops beating, and they produce a **SPECIAL ANTIFREEZE** that keeps their cells from freezing.

**50**
For about $30,000, anyone can be cryogenically frozen—have their body **PRESERVED IN LIQUID NITROGEN—** with the hope of being brought back to life in the future.

**1** A fossil IS THE REMAINS OF AN ANCIENT ANIMAL OR PLANT THAT HAS BEEN PRESERVED.

**2** A LIVING FOSSIL is an animal or plant that hasn't changed much from its prehistoric ancestors.

**3** HORSESHOE CRABS, which are living fossils, are not crabs at all. They're actually in the spider family.

**4** BODY FOSSILS contain the remains of creatures that were once alive. Trace fossils are signs of prehistoric creatures, like footprints.

# 25 AGE-OLD FACTS ABOUT

**5** Amber, FOSSILIZED TREE RESIN FROM AS LONG AS 70 MILLION YEARS AGO, SOMETIMES CONTAINS INSECTS THAT WERE TRAPPED IN THE STICKY STUFF.

**6** The skull of a 246-million-year-old marine animal called a placodont was discovered in the Netherlands in 2013.

**7** THE LA BREA TAR PITS, the most famous Ice Age fossil excavation site in the world, is in downtown Los Angeles, California, U.S.A.

**8** THE PURPLE FROG, A LIVING FOSSIL FOUND IN INDIA, HAS BEEN DESCRIBED AS LOOKING LIKE A "BLOATED DOUGHNUT." IT EVOLVED FROM A CREATURE THAT LIVED ABOUT 130 MILLION YEARS AGO.

**9** A fossil of an elephant bird egg sold at auction for over $100,000. It's so large, 120 chicken eggs could fit inside it.

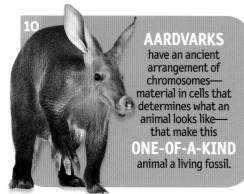

**10** AARDVARKS have an ancient arrangement of chromosomes—material in cells that determines what an animal looks like—that make this ONE-OF-A-KIND animal a living fossil.

**11** FOSSILS SHOW THAT EEL-LIKE HAGFISH HAVE BEEN LIVING ON EARTH FOR 330 MILLION YEARS.

**12** LA BREA'S PAGE MUSEUM HOUSES over 1 million Ice Age fossils FROM 650 SPECIES OF ANIMALS FOUND IN THE TAR PITS, INCLUDING THE BONES FROM 2 SPECIES OF PREHISTORIC CAMELS.

**13**

Horsetails, a kind of living fossil plant, have been on Earth since the Mesozoic period, more than 100 million years ago.

**14**

Australia's famous koalas are living fossils that have been around for at least 20 million years.

**15**

Endangered tuataras—lizard-like living fossils found only in New Zealand—may live to be **200 YEARS OLD.** They look very much like ancestors that lived 200 million years ago.

**17**

In 1938, a museum curator discovered a coelacanth among the day's catch from the Indian Ocean. This primitive-looking fish was thought to have gone extinct 65 million years ago.

**16**

Most of America's 50 states have an official state fossil. Alaska, Nebraska, and Washington gave this honor to the **MAMMOTH.**

**18**

The first discovery of fossilized tree stumps in the United States was made in 1850 by an amateur naturalist in the town of Gilboa, New York.

# FOSSILS

**19**

A population of living fossils, 8-inch (20-cm)-long, fluorescent pink slugs, has been isolated for millions of years atop Mount Kapator in Australia.

**20**

A fossil brought to the Natural History After School Club at England's Oxford University by 10-year-old Bruno Debattista turned out to be fossilized tracks left by a horseshoe crab some 320 million years ago.

**21**

ONE OF THE MOST BEAUTIFUL SEASHELLS IS HOME TO A KIND OF CEPHALOPOD CALLED A NAUTILUS. THIS LIVING FOSSIL HAS BEEN AROUND FOR AT LEAST **500 million years.**

**23**

An 11-year-old Russian boy made the discovery of a lifetime by finding a nearly intact 30,000-year-old mammoth fossil.

Known officially as Sopkarga Mammoth, it was nicknamed Zhenya after the boy.

**22**

Fossils found in the jungles of Colombia reveal **a giant Anaconda-like snake** the length of a bus that slithered through the rain forest 60 million years ago.

**24**

THE BIGGEST FOSSIL OF A SPIDER— MEASURING 1 INCH (2.5 CM) IN LENGTH—WAS FOUND IN CHINA AND IS 165 MILLION YEARS OLD.

**25**

In 1823, Mary Anning, one of the greatest fossil hunters of all time, discovered the complete skeleton of a long-necked *Plesiosaurus* known as the sea dragon.

**1** In 1950, it took a group of masked robbers **ABOUT 30 MINUTES TO FILL 14 CANVAS BAGS** with $2.7 million worth of money from the Brinks Truck Depot in Boston, Massachusetts, U.S.A. The total weight of the bags was more than half a ton (.45 MT).

**2** One of the first oil paintings from the Renaissance period—the "Ghent Altarpiece" by Dutch artist Jan van Eyck—**HAS BEEN STOLEN NUMEROUS TIMES.** For now, it's back on display in the Saint Bavo Cathedral in Ghent, Belgium.

**3** During an attempted **ROBBERY OF ENGLAND'S CROWN JEWELS** from the Tower of London in 1671, the thief tried to **FLEE WITH ONE OF THE CROWNS AFTER FLATTENING IT WITH A MALLET.** King Charles II was so impressed with his boldness that instead of punishing the crook, he pardoned him!

**4** A man using the name Dan Cooper **HIJACKED A PLANE** in 1971. When the plane landed, he released the passengers after receiving $200,000 in ransom, but made the pilot take off again. Then he **PARACHUTED OUT OF THE PLANE FROM 10,000 FEET** (3,048 m) in the air—**NEVER TO BE SEEN AGAIN.**

**5** In 2012, **$1.5 MILLION WORTH OF IPAD MINIS** were stolen from a cargo building at New York's John F. Kennedy airport. **THE THIEVES USED A FORKLIFT TO SCOOP UP THE GOODS.**

**6** Two thieves dressed as police officers stole **13 WORKS OF ART VALUED AT OVER $500 MILLION** from a museum in Boston, Massachusetts, in 1990. After so many years, the FBI's main focus now is finding the art, rather than capturing the thieves.

**7** In the biggest global cyber heist yet, thieves in over 24 countries were able to withdraw a total of **45 MILLION DOLLARS IN CASH FROM ATM MACHINES** in 2013—all in just a little over 10 hours.

**8** Historians still don't know if a real person inspired the legend of **ROBIN HOOD,** the outlaw who lived in England's Sherwood Forest and stole from the rich to give to the poor in the 12th or 13th century.

# FAMOUS HEISTS

**9** In 1911, 3 men **STOLE LEONARDO DA VINCI'S "MONA LISA"** from the Louvre—a museum in Paris, France—in broad daylight. For more than 2 years, it lay hidden in the false bottom of a trunk. The mastermind was arrested when he tried to sell it to an art dealer.

**10** For almost 2 years, robbers stole money from several banks in the San Gabriel Valley, California, U.S.A., by **CUTTING HOLES IN THE CEILINGS OF THE BANKS WITH POWER SAWS,** then leaving with the cash. The spree ended in 2013 when they were caught.

**11** Between 1995 and 2002, Stephane Breitwieser **STOLE OVER 172 PIECES OF ART WORTH $1.4 BILLION** from museums around Europe and stored them at his mother's house. When Stephane was arrested, his mother destroyed the art—even putting some in her garbage disposal!

**12** A **HALF-EATEN SALAMI SANDWICH** and some shredded documents helped police **CAPTURE THE THIEVES** who stole an estimated $100 million in diamonds from the Diamond Center in Antwerp, Belgium, in 2003.

**13** A group of burglars rented a building in 2005 near the central bank in Fortaleza, Brazil, **DUG A 256-FOOT (78-M)-LONG TUNNEL TO THE BANK'S VAULT,** and stole almost $70 million. The case is still being investigated.

**14** A **MONOPOLY GAME GAVE AWAY THE THIEVES** who stole millions of British pounds in the **GREAT TRAIN ROBBERY OF 1963.** Police matched fingerprints found on the board game at the robbers' safe house to those found at the crime scene.

**15** In 2012, a man convicted for stealing historical documents valued at more than $1 million from museums and libraries across the United States said he did it out of greed. His take included a **LAND GRANT SIGNED BY ABRAHAM LINCOLN** worth an estimated $100,000.

**1** The first organized baseball game was played in Hoboken, New Jersey, U.S.A., in 1846.

**2** In 1885, 2 German inventors added an engine to a wooden bicycle frame to build the first gasoline-powered motorcycle.

**3** Amelia Earhart was the first woman to cross the Atlantic Ocean in an airplane. She was a passenger on a flight from Newfoundland, Canada, to Wales, U.K., in 1928.

**4** In 2001, Erik Weihenmayer of Colorado, U.S.A., became the first blind person to summit Mount Everest. He followed the sound of bells tied to the jackets of his guides.

**5** In 1954, Roger Bannister, a 25-year-old British medical student, wowed a crowd of 3,000 spectators by becoming the first man to run a mile (1.6 km) in less than 4 minutes.

**6 THE FIRST TV COMMERCIAL—A 10-SECOND AD FOR WATCHES—AIRED IN 1941.**

**7** In 2013, Diana Nyad, at age 64, became the first person to swim from Cuba to Florida without a shark cage.

**8** In 1981, Sandra Day O'Connor became the first woman justice on the U.S. Supreme Court.

**9** In 2012, a man from the Czech Republic survived for 6 months after doctors replaced his heart with 2 mechanical pumps, making him the first person to live that long with an artificial heart.

**10** In 1910, Teddy Roosevelt became the first U.S. president to fly in an airplane. The flight lasted 4 minutes.

**11** When Manon Rheaume of Canada took to the ice for the Tampa Bay Lightning in 1992, she became the first woman to play in a National Hockey League (NHL) game.

**12** In 1972, African-American Shirley Chisholm became the first female candidate for president of the United States.

**13** The world's first 3-D talking feature film was released in Italy in 1936.

**14** A tailless alligator that has been living in captivity in Phoenix, Arizona, U.S.A., since it was found was fitted with a prosthetic tail in 2013—a first for its species.

**15** The world's first digital camera—invented in 1975—was the size of a toaster and created tiny black-and-white picture files.

**16** In 1963, a cat named Felix became the first feline in space.

**17** The very first text message was sent in 1992. It read simply "Merry Christmas."

**18** In 1892, Benjamin Harrison became the first U.S. president to attend a baseball game.

**19** In 1967, South African surgeon Christiaan Barnard performed the world's first whole-heart transplant from one person to another.

**20** The first Internet emoticon—the smiley—was created in 1982.

**21** In 2012, a British man became the first person to visit every country in the world without using an airplane.

**22** In 1845, Macon Bolling Allen became the first African American to practice law in the United States.

**23** The world's first flying car—built in 1946—could transition to a plane in just 10 minutes and fly at an elevation of 12,000 feet (3,658 m).

**24** In 2009, actor Ashton Kutcher became the first person to have over 1 million Twitter followers.

**25 SALLY RIDE, THE FIRST AMERICAN WOMAN IN SPACE, BECAME AN ASTRONAUT AFTER ANSWERING A NASA AD IN THE NEWSPAPER.**

**26** The first YouTube video—a 19-second clip called "Me at the Zoo"—was posted in April 2005.

**27** The world's first computer was as long as a tennis court.

**28** The world's first parking meters were installed in Oklahoma City, U.S.A., in 1935. The cost to park? Five cents for up to an hour.

Sally Ride

# '74
# FASCINATING

**29** The first Wiffle ball bats were made from broomsticks.

**30** The world's first Ferris wheel—built for the 1893 World's Fair in Chicago, Illinois, U.S.A., by an engineer named George Ferris—cost 50 cents to ride.

**31** THOMAS JEFFERSON WAS THE FIRST U.S. PRESIDENT TO SERVE FRENCH FRIES IN THE WHITE HOUSE.

**32** In 1985, Symbolics.com became the first ever domain name to be registered on the Web.

**33** In 1911, it took pilot Cal Rodgers 49 days and 69 stops to make the first airplane flight from New York to California, U.S.A.

**34** The world's first handheld cell phone, which hit stores in 1983, weighed over 2 pounds (1 kg) and cost $3,995!

**35** The first person arrested for speeding in the United States was driving 12 miles per hour (19 kph) in 1899.

**36** A sheep, a duck, and a rooster were all passengers on the world's first hot-air balloon flight in 1783.

**37** "HAPPY BIRTHDAY" WAS THE FIRST SONG TRANSMITTED FROM SPACE TO EARTH.

**38** In 1903, Bud the dog became the first pooch to travel across the United States in a car.

**39** Some of the first soles on Nike shoes were made by pouring rubber into a waffle iron.

**40** Groundhog Day began on February 2, 1887, in Punxsutawney, Pennsylvania, U.S.A., when a groundhog popped out of its hole.

**41** A woman in Binghamton, New York, became the world's oldest first-time grandmother at the age of 95 with the birth of twins to her son and his wife in 2008.

**42** At the 1992 Olympics, ice-skater Kristi Yamaguchi became the first Asian-American woman to nab a gold medal for the United States.

**43** In 2001, actress Halle Berry became the first African-American woman to win an Academy Award for best actress.

**44** In 2010, a man from England became the first person to walk the entire length of the Amazon River. It took him 28 months and 8 days.

**45** Edurne Pasaban, from Spain, is the first woman to climb all 14 of Earth's mountains that are over 26,000 feet (8,000 m) high.

**46** It took just under 15 days in 2002 for pilot Steve Fossett to complete the first solo circumnavigation of the globe in a hot-air balloon.

**47** A runner from Belgium finished 365 marathons in one year—the first person ever to accomplish that feat.

**48** Scientists think that a recently discovered 350-million-year-old scorpion was one of the first creatures to roam Earth.

**49** In 2012, British adventurer Felicity Aston became the first woman to ski alone across Antarctica.

**50** THE FIRST GIRL SCOUT COOKIES WERE CREATED IN A HOME KITCHEN IN 1917 AS PART OF A BADGE-EARNING PROJECT.

**51** In 2011, a Canadian woman earned the first ever master's degree in the Beatles and their music.

**52** In 2007, tiny invertebrates called tardigrades—or water bears—became the first animals to survive the extreme conditions of space unprotected.

**53** In 1931, 19-year-old golfer Ralph Guldahl became the first teenager to win on the Professional Golf Association (PGA) Tour.

**54** Known as America's first female professional artist, Henrietta Johnston painted portraits of prominent people in Charleston, South Carolina, U.S.A., in the early 18th century.

**55** AFTER HIS DEATH IN 2009, MICHAEL JACKSON BECAME THE FIRST ARTIST TO SELL OVER 1 MILLION SONG DOWNLOADS IN A SINGLE WEEK.

**56** In 2013, Tiger Woods became the first person to hit a golf ball from Europe into Asia. He teed off from a bridge in Turkey that links the 2 continents.

**57** Baseball great Lou Gehrig was the first athlete to be featured on a Wheaties cereal box.

**58** Over 100 years ago, a team of Norwegian explorers led by Roald Amundsen became the first people to reach the South Pole.

**59** The first athlete to say "I'm Going to Disney World!" after winning the Super Bowl was quarterback Phil Simms, in 1987.

**60** In 1621, lobsters, seals, and swans all may have been on the menu at the Pilgrims' first thanksgiving in what is now Massachusetts, U.S.A.

**61** The first TV remote, invented in 1950, was called Lazy Bones.

**62** Russian cosmonaut Alexei Leonov performed the first ever space walk in 1965.

**63** In 1840, Great Britain's Queen Victoria became the first person to appear on an adhesive postage stamp.

**64** It took until 1964 for the first nonroyal—William Shakespeare—to appear on a British stamp.

**65** Barack Obama became the first U.S. president to use Twitter when he posted a message in 2009.

**66** In 1919, Sir Barton won all 3 Triple Crown races—the Kentucky Derby, the Preakness, and the Belmont Stakes—the first of only 11 horses to accomplish this feat.

**67** In 2007, race car trailblazer Janet Guthrie became the first woman to earn a spot at both the Indianapolis 500 and the Daytona 500.

**68** In 1909, Wilbur Wright became the first person to fly around the Statue of Liberty. He did it as a publicity stunt.

**69** Passenger trains made the first crossing through the Channel Tunnel—or Chunnel—between England and France in 1994.

**70** RUTH WAKEFIELD, WHO RAN THE TOLL HOUSE INN IN WHITMAN, MASS-ACHUSETTS, IS CREDITED WITH BAKING THE FIRST CHOCOLATE CHIP COOKIES. THE YEAR WAS 1930.

**71** The world's first crossword puzzle, the creation of a British journalist, ran in the Sunday edition of the *New York World* newspaper on December 21, 1913.

**72** In 2006, Diana Taurasi became the first player in the Women's National Basketball Association to hit 800 points in one season. Her total for the season was 860.

**73** John D. Rockefeller, Sr., an American oil tycoon born in 1836, is considered to be the world's first billionaire.

**74** For her role in the 1963 film *Cleopatra*, Elizabeth Taylor became the first actress to be paid $1 million for a movie.

# FACTS ABOUT
# FAMOUS FIRSTS

**1**

By age 18, actor Matthew McConaughey had **WATCHED ONLY 2 MOVIES.**

**2**

Comedian and actor Jim Carrey **WORE HIS TAP SHOES TO BED** when he was young just in case his parents needed cheering up in the middle of the night.

**3**

When he was 4 years old, Bruno Mars earned attention **DOING ELVIS IMPERSONATIONS** in Hawaii as part of his dad's variety show.

**4**

Although Natalie Portman was reported to have played both Queen Amidala roles in *Star Wars: Episode 1*, **KEIRA KNIGHTLEY** actually played Queen Amidala's decoy.

**5**

**TAYLOR SWIFT** and Michael Jordan are among the many celebrities you can **"HANG OUT" WITH** at a Madame Tussauds wax museum.

**6**

Selena Gomez learned about acting working with a big **PURPLE DINOSAUR** on *Barney & Friends* when she was 7 years old.

**7**

Caryn Johnson changed her name to Whoopi Goldberg when **HER PROBLEM WITH GAS** made her friends nickname her after the whoopee cushion.

**8**

**THE MICKEY MOUSE CLUB** has launched many celebrity careers, including those of Britney Spears, Christina Aguilera, Justin Timberlake, and Ryan Gosling.

**9**

Although Elvis Presley first rocked the world in the 1950s, he is still ranked among the **TOP TEEN IDOLS** by *Rolling Stone*.

**10**

Celine Dion's mansion in Florida, U.S.A., comes with its **OWN WATER PARK**—just in case the private beach isn't enough!

**11**

That woman in the iconic **LITTLE BLACK DRESS** splashed across T-shirts, purses, and posters in malls is Audrey Hepburn as she appeared in the movie *Breakfast at Tiffany's*.

**12**

Daniel Radcliffe was **IN THE BATHTUB** when he received the phone call that he'd landed the role of Harry Potter.

**13**

Shakira **WROTE HER FIRST SONG** when she was 8 years old and signed her first record deal at 13.

**14**

**DR. MARTIN LUTHER KING, JR.,** was a huge *Star Trek* fan.

**15**

According to genealogists, **PRINCESS DIANA,** mother of Britain's Princes William and Harry, was the tenth cousin of 2008 U.S. vice presidential candidate **SARAH PALIN.**

Taylor Swift

**16** Nicole Kidman is **SCARED OF BUTTERFLIES.**

**17** Emma Stone convinced her parents to let her try acting by putting together a **POWERPOINT PRESENTATION.**

**18** James Bond actor Pierce Brosnan worked for years as a **FIRE-EATER** in a circus.

**19** Videos of Justin Bieber **SINGING ON YOUTUBE** when he was 12 years old launched his career.

**20** Sarah Jessica Parker's tenth great-grandmother was **ACCUSED OF WITCHCRAFT** during the Salem witch trials in the 1600s.

**21** According to the *Oxford English Dictionary*, the **FIRST PRINTED USE** of the word "celebrity" for a person was in 1849.

**22** Supermodel Heidi Klum presented her DOGNY sculpture "Dog With Butterflies" in tribute to America's **SEARCH AND RESCUE DOGS** on the anniversary of the 9/11 tragedies.

**23** Singer Alicia Keyes **APPEARED ON** *THE COSBY SHOW* in 1985 as one of Rudy's slumber party guests.

**24** Walt Disney, the creator of Mickey Mouse, was said to be **AFRAID OF MICE.**

**25** Grand Slam–winning tennis sensation Serena Williams began playing tennis **WHEN SHE WAS 4 YEARS OLD.**

**26** Rapper Ludacris started life with the name **CHRISTOPHER BRIAN BRIDGES.**

**27** Kunal Nayyar, who plays Raj on TV's *Big Bang Theory*, married **FORMER MISS INDIA** Neha Kapur in a traditional Indian wedding ceremony.

# 35 HOT-OFF-THE-PRESS FACTS ABOUT CELEBRITIES

**28** In 1867, British writer Charles Dickens traveled to America to promote his work in one of the world's first **CELEBRITY AUTHOR BOOK TOURS.**

**29** Pop star Carly Rae Jepsen **PLACED THIRD** when she was a contestant on *Canadian Idol.*

**30** Taylor Lautner is a former **JUNIOR WORLD KARATE CHAMPION.**

**31** Tom Hanks is a third cousin—4 generations removed—of U.S. President **ABRAHAM LINCOLN.**

**32** Accountant or rock star? That was Mick Jagger's choice as a graduate of the London School of Economics. **HE CHOSE ROCK STAR.**

**33** Drew Barrymore hosted *Saturday Night Live* at the ripe old age of 7 in 1982, making her the **YOUNGEST** *SNL* HOST.

**34** When Rebel Wilson was a teenager, she had malaria and **HALLUCINATED THAT SHE WON AN OSCAR.** That's when she decided she wanted to be an actress.

**35** Actor Leonardo DiCaprio has a Dutch song named after him. Titled **"I'M IN LOVE WITH LEONARDO DICAPRIO,"** it's sung by Flemish band K3.

**1.** The study of electricity goes back more than 2,000 years. **2. The word "electricity" comes from *elektron,* the Greek word for amber, a yellow, transparent substance that emits electricity when rubbed. 3.** The ancient Greeks discovered that rubbing fur on amber caused an electrical attraction between the two. **4. It was not until the 19th century that electricity was used to make light and provide power. 5.** In 1752, Benjamin Franklin used a kite to prove that electricity and lightning are the same thing. **6. China and the United States are the world's top producers of electricity. 7.** Thomas Edison, who made the first useful incandescent lightbulb in 1879, has been called the Father of the Electrical Age. **8. Edison used thin strips of bamboo to make the filaments in his early lightbulbs. 9.** By 1880, Edison was making lightbulbs with bamboo filaments that burned for 1,500 hours—more than 2 months! **10. The world's first power plant was built in Germany, in 1878. 11.** In 1882, Edison opened a power plant in New York City, U.S.A., that provided electricity to some 50 customers. Within a year, he had more than 500. **12. A 2000-year-old pottery jar with a copper tube and an iron rod found near Baghdad, Iraq, may be the earliest known electric battery. 13.** In 1800, Alessandro Volta used metal plates and acid to create the first battery that could store electricity. **14. In 1888, Charles Brush used a backyard windmill to generate electricity to power batteries in his cellar. 15.** When people first started using electricity, they paid about 40 times the current cost. **16. The abbreviation "kWh" stands for "kilowatt hour," the measurement used to calculate the cost of electricity. The W refers to James Watt, a Scottish inventor. 17.** Although most urban Americans had electricity by 1930, only 10 percent of people in rural areas had electric power. **18. In 1920, only about 2 percent of the energy in the United States was used to make electricity. Today, that figure is about 40 percent. 19.** There are nearly 7,000 power plants in the United States. **20. Electrons—tiny, negatively charged particles of an atom—stream through wires and circuits to create currents of electricity. 21.** There are 2 types of electricity: static (a buildup of electrons that can cause a spark) and current (the steady flow of electrons through a wire or other conductor). **22. Electricity is a secondary source of energy, meaning that coal, water, and other primary energy sources are needed to make electricity. 23.** Lightning bolts, giant discharges of static electricity, can reach over 5 miles (8 km) in length. **24. In 1844, Samuel Morse sent the first message by telegraph, a machine that uses electric signals to transmit words over wire. 25.** In 2025, 31 percent of the world's electricity is expected to come from coal—down from 34 percent in 2001. **26. Electricity travels at the speed of light—about 186,000 miles (299,330 km) per second. 27.** It takes only a fraction of a second for electricity to travel from a power plant to your home. **28. If you traveled as fast as electricity, you could**

**go around the world 8 times in the time it takes to turn on a light switch. 29.** One gigawatt is equal to 1 million kilowatts, which are equal to 1,000 watts. **30. There are 2.7 million miles (4.3 million km) of power lines in the United States. 31.** One spark of static electricity can be over 2,000 times as powerful as a flashlight bulb. **32. Temperatures in a lightning bolt can hit 50,000°F (27,760°C). 33.** Electric taxis cruised the streets of New York City over 100 years ago. **34. An electric eel can produce a charge strong enough to knock a horse off its feet. 35.** The annual amount of electricity used by the hotels on the Las Vegas Strip in Nevada, U.S.A., could power 160,000 homes for a year. **36. A developer is planning to build a community in Florida, U.S.A., that will run exclusively on energy harnessed from the sun. 37.** The amount of sunlight reaching Earth in 1 hour is enough to supply the world with electricity for 1 year. **38. Some dance floors have tiles with small generators inside them that let you create electricity as you boogie. 39.** There are 1.3 billion people around the world living without access to electricity. **40. All living things emit an electric field created by a beating heart, muscle movement, or the brain. 41.** Sharks and other fish can sense electricity generated by other animals underwater, which helps them hunt for prey. **42. On average, 100 bolts of lightning strike Earth every second. 43.** In July 2012, over 600 million people in India were left without power for several hours in the worst blackout in modern history. **44. Electricity plays a role in the way your heart beats by causing muscle cells in the heart to contract. 45.** Hydroelectric power, which uses moving water to generate energy, provides almost one-fifth of the world's electricity. **46. The first ever use of hydroelectric power occurred in 1882 in Appleton, Wisconsin, U.S.A. 47.** The Grand Coulee Dam on the Columbia River produces 70 percent of the electricity in Washington State, U.S.A. **48. You can be struck by lightning even when the center of a thunderstorm is 10 miles (16 km) away. 49.** Bees and other insects can generate up to 200 volts of electricity by rapidly flapping their wings. **50. The fastest electric car can travel over 300 miles per hour (482 kph). 51.** You can create electricity out of cow manure and elephant dung. **52. Methane gas from the waste of 60,000 cows on a Chinese dairy farm is used to produce electricity for at least 3,500 homes. 53.** A special kind of soccer ball called a SOCCKET creates enough energy when kicked around for 30 minutes to light an LED lamp for about 3 hours. **54. The chance of being struck**

by lightning in your lifetime is 1 in 3,000. **55.** Volcanic eruptions, forest fires, and snowstorms can all generate lightning. **56. Iceland generates 100 percent of its electricity with renewable energy—energy that comes from resources like water, wind, and animal waste that can be replenished by nature. 57.** Platypuses use electrical impulses to locate objects underwater. **58. A lightning storm on Saturn that began in 2010 lasted 267 Earth days! 59.** Digital devices—like smartphones and computers—use up about a tenth of the world's electricity. **60. Taking a hot shower uses more than 100 times more electricity than blow-drying your hair. 61.** A battery powered by electricity from the glucose (sugar) in a snail's bloodstream can produce steady power for months. **62. A waste-to-energy incinerator in Oslo, Norway, converts trash into heat and electricity. 63.** The biggest wind turbines generate enough electricity to supply about 600 U.S. homes. **64. By harnessing the electric current produced by microscopic organisms living in soil, scientists have found a way to bring electricity to remote areas. 65.** More than 30,000 Americans suffer from nonfatal electric shocks each year. **66. Bumblebees use the electric field around a flower to determine its shape or if it has been visited by other bees. 67.** Each year in the United States, wind energy produces the same amount of electricity as burning 320 million barrels of oil. **68. The electricity it takes to power the world's Internet costs about $4.5 billion a year. 69.** The world's first electric train went into service in 1879 in Berlin, Germany. **70. The third rail of the New York City subway is charged with 625 volts of electricity—about 6 times the voltage in a household electrical outlet. 71.** Scientists have attempted to harness electricity from the air by gathering charges from tiny droplets of water. **72. Tokelau, a group of remote islands in the Pacific Ocean, receives 100 percent of its electricity from solar energy. 73.** Sprites—reddish, ultrafast bursts of electricity ejected from the tops of thunderclouds—are often mistaken for UFOs. **74.** In 2013, a plane powered only by some 11,000 solar cells on its wings flew from California to New York. **75. A 2.2-mile (3.6-km)-long solar-paneled tunnel in Europe generates enough electricity to provide power to 4,000 trains a year. 76.** A tower designed to help provide

# SHOCKING FACTS
## ABOUT ELECTRICITY

electricity to a city in China is almost as tall as New York City's Empire State Building. **77. It would take the light of 25,000 fireflies to equal the brightness of one 60-watt incandescent lightbulb. 78. Because the human body is 70 percent water—and electricity moves quickly through water—you are a good conductor of electricity. 79.** Worldwide, the Internet uses about the same amount of electricity as is generated by 30 nuclear power plants. **80. Your brain gives off electric waves even when you're sleeping. 81.** The oriental hornet can generate electricity from sunlight. **82. A blackout during the 2013 Super Bowl left fans and players in the dark for 35 minutes. 83.** There is a dog leash that generates electricity to power an LED light every time you wind and unwind the leash's reel. **84. The violent dust storms that plagued the U.S. Midwest in the 1930s generated so much static electricity that blue flames leaped from barbed wire fences. 85.** You can generate up to 25,000 volts of electricity by dragging your feet across a carpet. **86. The Hoover Dam in Arizona and Nevada, U.S.A., supplies electricity to more than 20 million people. 87.** The White House in Washington, D.C., U.S.A., was wired for electricity in 1891. **88. In 1876, Alexander Graham Bell invented a machine that used electricity to transmit sound—the telephone. 89.** Huge electric currents are generated deep inside Earth. **90. These electric currents create a magnetic field that extends more than 40,000 miles (64,000 km) into space and helps protect Earth from harmful radiation. 91.** Earth's magnetic field also enables compasses to tell direction. **92. Competitors in the Tough Mudder obstacle race run through a field of wires charged with up to 10,000 volts of electricity. 93.** By 2015, worldwide there may be over 100,000 hybrid (half-gas, half-electric) trucks and buses—more than 10 times the current number. **94. Electricity can make a flame go out. 95.** Future firefighters may be able to tame flames by zapping them with electric current. **96. A "green" hotel in Copenhagen, Denmark, once offered a free meal to any guest who could generate 10 watts of electricity by pedaling an exercise bike. 97.** A 30-minute workout on an elliptical machine generates about 50 watts—enough to run a laptop for an hour. **98. Energy harnessed from ocean waves and tides along U.S. coasts could provide about 9 percent of the nation's electricity by 2030. 99.** Scientists revived a dying coral reef in Indonesia by shocking it with low-voltage electricity.

**1**
Ancient Egyptians believed that RE, the SUN GOD, was the creator of the universe and that humans were made from his tears.

**2**
Some 2,000 GODS AND GODDESSES were worshipped by ancient Egyptians.

**3**
ANUBIS, the god who cared for the deceased, was depicted as a man with the head of a JACKAL. His job was to guide the dead to the underworld.

**4**
THOTH, the moon god, lorded over the Egyptian CALENDAR, which was similar to ours but was based on phases of the moon.

**5**
Many Egyptians believed that the SKY was actually a FALCON, and the falcon's eyes were the sun and the moon.

**6**
BASTET, the cat deity, was said to have SAVED RE, the sun god, every night from the "serpent of chaos." Bastet was depicted as a woman with a cat's head.

**7**
All CATS were considered sacred in ancient Egypt. If you killed a cat, you could be sentenced to death.

**8**
In Egyptian mythology, right before the death of a PHOENIX—a long-lived, eagle-size bird—it made a nest, lit it on fire, and a new phoenix was born.

**9**
The GOD SHU and the GODDESS TEFNUT, deities of air and moisture, were said to be created when the sun god SNEEZED AND SPIT.

**10**
SEKHMET, a lion-headed goddess, was a symbol of POWER. Researchers think this may have been because in the wild, female—not male—lions are the strong hunters.

**11**
Ancient Egyptians began PREPARING for life in the NEXT WORLD as soon as they could, buying coffins and statues and stashing them in their houses.

**12**
Ancient Egyptian beliefs about the AFTERLIFE and how to prepare for it lasted for more than 3,000 years.

**13**
Ancient Egyptians thought that GOLD was the FLESH of the gods.

**14**
The GRIFFIN, a winged monster with a lion's body and a bird's head, was a MESSENGER for the SUN GOD.

**15**
TOMBS were filled with what would be needed in the afterlife, including food, drinks, mirrors, games—even makeup!

**16**
Egyptians imagined the afterlife to be MORE PERFECT than life on Earth. There, they expected to be stronger, work to be easier, and everything to be more plentiful.

**17**
The mythical mother to all Egyptian kings was the vulture goddess NEKHBET.

**18**
Tombs were filled with *ushebtis*, statues that represented SERVANTS to lend a hand in the AFTERLIFE.

**19**
Egyptian tombs were sealed, but there were ABOVEGROUND CHAPELS where mourners could come to say prayers and bring food for the dead.

**20**
At a time when the Nile River was filled with crocodiles, SOBEK, the crocodile god, was worshipped in the hope that the man-eating reptiles would not attack humans.

**21**
People paid to have CATS MUMMIFIED and placed in temples that honored the cat gods Sakhmet and Bastet.

**22**
RE was believed to die every night and be reborn every morning.

**23**
When mortals died, they joined RE on his nightly journey through the underworld. If all went well, they would be IMMORTAL BY DAWN.

**24**
Egyptians believed the journey after death through the night to REBIRTH could take SEVERAL EARTHLY LIFETIMES.

**25**
The MAKEUP worn by Egyptian kings was believed to have HEALING POWERS. Lead in the makeup helped prevent common infections.

**26**
In ancient Egypt, jackals and vultures were often seen SCAVENGING CORPSES at cemeteries. Both animals represented death.

**27**
Ruling Egyptian PHARAOHS were considered YOUNG GODS who connected ordinary people with the all-powerful gods.

**28**
BEADS were wrapped around mummies' necks to RESTORE BREATH in the afterlife.

**29**
Ancient Egyptians left FLOWERS at the tombs of their loved ones, just as flowers are left at graves today.

**30**
The BOOK OF THE DEAD was a collection of about 200 SPELLS designed to help the dead deal with dangers on their journey to eternal life.

**31**
The Book of the Dead was written on a PAPYRUS ROLL, then put inside a statue, wrapped with the mummy, or placed with belongings needed in the afterlife.

**32**
The UNDERWORLD was the place dead people traveled through before REACHING ETERNAL LIFE.

**33**
Some of the spells in the Book of the Dead allowed the dead person to TRANSFORM into different ANIMALS; others gave protection against creatures.

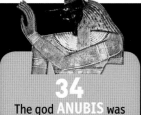

**34**
The god **ANUBIS** was said to weigh a person's heart against a feather. If the weights balanced, the person was allowed into the afterlife.

**35**
**SETH**, god of **THUNDERSTORMS**, was admired for his strength, but feared for his ability to do harm.

**36**
**THOTH**, a **MOON GOD**, was said to have a book that contained all the wisdom of the world!

**37**
Because ancient Egyptians believed cats protected homes and children from danger, nearly **ALL HOUSE-HOLDS** had a **CAT**.

**38**
Ancient Egyptians feared hippopotamuses, which sometimes attacked boats on the Nile River, but they worshipped **TAURET**, a goddess represented as a standing hippopotamus.

**39**
It was believed a **CHEETAH** would quickly carry the soul of a dead pharaoh to the underworld.

**40**
Ancient Egyptians associated the **DUNG BEETLE** with Re. They imagined that the insect rolled the sun across the sky, just like it rolls dung into balls for its eggs.

**41**
**AMULETS**, or charms, depicting dung beetles were worn by people in ancient Egypt to **KEEP EVIL AWAY.**

**42**
**COBRAS** were feared by Egyptians and became a **SYMBOL OF PROTECTION** for kings. One of these venomous snakes is at the top of King Tut's funeral mask.

**43**
Some researchers think the **NEMES CROWN,** or striped head cloth, on King Tut's funeral mask is meant to look like a lion's mane—a symbol of strength.

**44**
Figures of pharaohs painted on walls of their tombs often are holding a **CROOK**—a tool used by shepherds—to show how the pharaoh provided food for his people.

**45**
Ancient Egyptians put the **NAMES OF ENEMIES** on clay pots or tablets, then broke or buried them, believing this would destroy their rivals.

**46**
Boats possibly built to help the pharaoh Khufu **BATTLE BEASTS** as he sailed through the **AFTERLIFE** have been unearthed near Giza's Great Pyramid.

Statue of Ramses II, Abu Simbel Temple, Nubia, Egypt

**47**
It is believed that Egyptians chose **PYRAMID-SHAPED** burial chambers because Re was born on a pyramid-shaped piece of land.

**48**
**BES**, the god of music and laughter, was usually shown **BUG-EYED** and with his tongue sticking out!

**49**
**LOTUS FLOWERS,** which were seen as a symbol of eternal life for their ability to survive droughts, were sacred in ancient Egypt.

**50**
Ancient Egyptians believed that when **GEB**, the Earth deity, laughed, it caused **EARTHQUAKES.**

# 50
# TIMELESS FACTS ABOUT EGYPTIAN MYTHOLOGY

**1** Before joining a crew, pirates had to agree to the *SHIP'S ARTICLES* —a code that detailed how they were to *BEHAVE, BE PAID,* and *BE PUNISHED.*

**2** PIRATES HAD BEDTIMES TOO! ON CAPTAIN BART ROBERTS'S SHIP, "lights-out" was 8 p.m.

**3** The Golden Age of Piracy happened between 1660 and 1730. Pirates would attack ships carrying treasure from the Americas to Europe.

**4** When **Sam Bellamy's** pirate ship the *Whydah* sank off the coast of Cape Cod, North America, in 1717, it was carrying about **4.5 tons** (4 MT) **of treasure.**

**5** **BLACKBEARD** put **BURNING FUSES** on the ends of his beard to scare his enemies.

# ARRRGH!
# 25 FACTS ABOUT

**6** PIRATES IN THE GREEK ISLANDS ONCE CAPTURED THE ROMAN EMPEROR-TO-BE JULIUS CAESAR. HE WAS HELD HOSTAGE FOR MORE THAN A MONTH UNTIL A RANSOM WAS PAID.

**7** If a captain had a signed letter of marque— permission from a government to raid enemy ships—he was considered a privateer, not a pirate.

**8** Some of the first flags on pirate ships were **RED,** not black.

**9** There is no documented record of pirates having to "**walk the plank**" to their deaths.

**10** Two women pirates—*ANNE BONNY AND MARY READ*—sailed with Captain John "Calico Jack" Rackham in the early 1700s. Dressed like men, they fought alongside the rest of the crew.

**11** To a pirate, a ship's medicine cabinet was just as valuable as money or jewels. Disease, injuries, food poisoning, and flea or rat bites were common.

**12** The city of **Port Royal, Jamaica,** was a thriving town for pirates until 1692 when it was **destroyed** by a combination *EARTHQUAKE AND TSUNAMI.*

**13** The short, sharp swords pirates used to fight with were called *cutlasses.*

**14** Captain Hook in J.M. Barrie's play *Peter Pan* is loosely based on Blackbeard.

**15** The Welshman **BARTHOLOMEW ROBERTS** was captured by pirates who forced him to join them. As the pirate **BLACK BART**, he captured more than 400 ships.

**17** One of the most powerful female pirates was Madame Cheng. After her husband died in 1807, she took over his command and built it into 1,800 boats and 80,000 pirates.

**18** Cannons and gold dust are among the artifacts recovered from Blackbeard's ship, *Queen Anne's Revenge,* which was discovered by divers in the waters off North Carolina, U.S.A., in 1996.

**16** PIRATES DRANK GROG, a mixture of rum, lime juice, and water. Vitamin C from the lime helped prevent scurvy, a disease that can cause swelling, bleeding, and tooth loss.

**19** In battles, pirates used *pistols* that fired *only 1 shot* before they had to be reloaded.

# PIRATES

**20** THE PRIVATEER **Francis Drake** BROUGHT MUCH WEALTH TO ENGLAND'S QUEEN ELIZABETH I BY RAIDING SPANISH SHIPS. THE QUEEN KNIGHTED HIM IN 1581, CALLING HIM "MY PIRATE."

**21** The nickname "Jolly Roger" for pirate flags likely comes from the French words *jolie rouge,* which mean "pretty red."

**22** The skull and crossbones on many pirate flags was a **SYMBOL OF DEATH.** Today, it is used to warn of poison or danger.

**23** Pirates who broke ship rules were **OFTEN LEFT ON DESERTED ISLANDS** with no food or water. Sometimes they were given a **PISTOL WITH 1 BULLET.**

**24** HARDTACK BISCUITS were a staple on pirate ships, but pirates had to be careful when taking a bite. The biscuits were often infested with GRUBBY MAGGOTS.

**25** "Barbarossa," which means "red beard," was the name of 2 fearsome pirate brothers who operated along **North Africa's Barbary Coast** in the 16th century.

HORUSCE und HAREADEN BARBAROSSA
*Konige von Tunis und Algiers und ober See Admiralen*

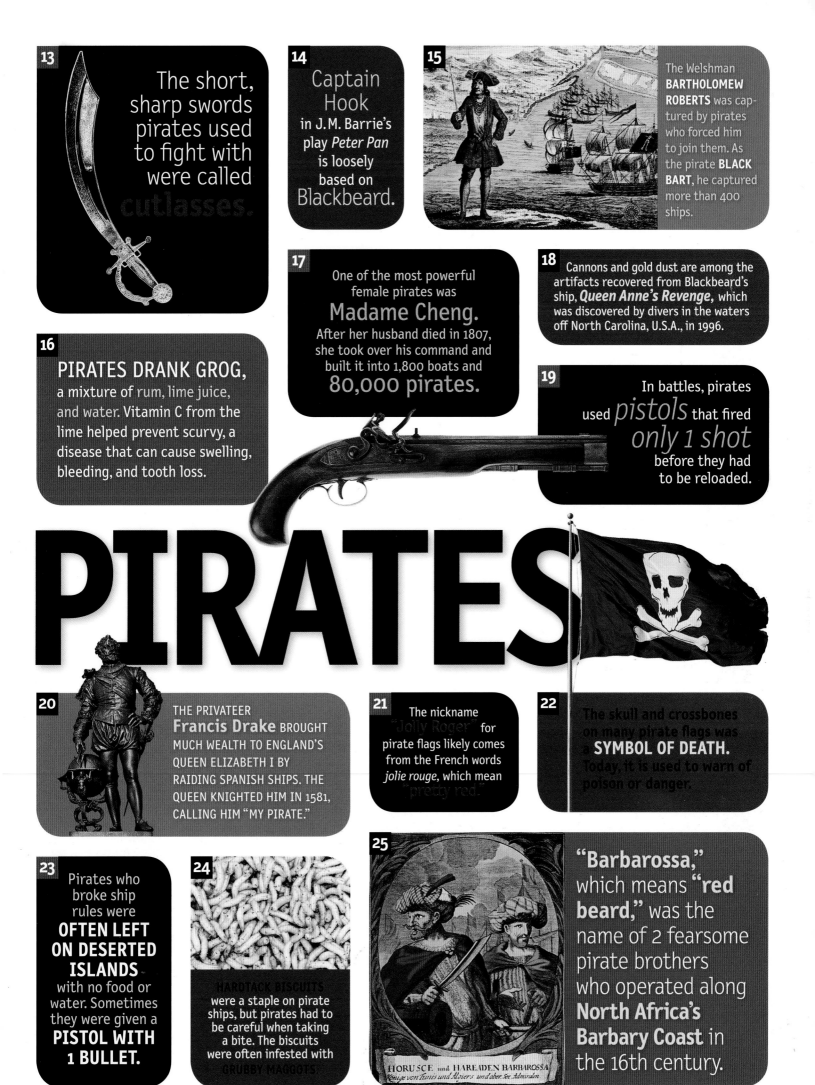

**1** A woman in Lincolnshire, England, claims to have the **WORLD'S OLDEST HOT CROSS BUN.** Baked in a shop where her great-great-great grandfather worked, the now hard-as-a-rock, **192-YEAR-OLD BUN** has been passed down through **5 GENERATIONS.**

**2** A family in Florida, U.S.A., has passed down an **ENORMOUS PICKLE** to family members **SINCE 1876.** The grower kept the pickle because she **COULDN'T REMOVE IT** without breaking the pickling jar.

**3** The 35.56 carat **WITTELSBACH BLUE DIAMOND** was passed down through **AUSTRIAN AND BAVARIAN ROYALTY** for centuries. The sparkly gem was sold in 2008 for over **$24 MILLION.**

**4** An Australian man plans on leaving his 10-foot (3-m)-long **SALTWATER CROCODILE**—one of the **MOST DANGEROUS** kinds of predators on the planet—to his kids. Charlene, the croc, has been in the family for **48 YEARS,** even after "accidentally" **BITING OFF A FAMILY MEMBER'S HAND.**

**5** When Scottish immigrant Dr. Robert Bruce Honeyman died in 1824 in Virginia, U.S.A., he willed his son a **BIZARRE HEIRLOOM**—a rib bone reportedly belonging to **SCOTLAND'S KING JAMES V,** who died in 1542. No one knows **HOW HE GOT THE BONE** or where it is today.

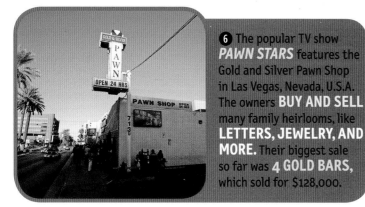

**6** The popular TV show **PAWN STARS** features the Gold and Silver Pawn Shop in Las Vegas, Nevada, U.S.A. The owners **BUY AND SELL** many family heirlooms, like **LETTERS, JEWELRY, AND MORE.** Their biggest sale so far was **4 GOLD BARS,** which sold for $128,000.

**7** Terry O'Kelly keeps a **115-YEAR-OLD BREAD ROLL** in a glass case. It was given to his grandfather while he was **IMPRISONED** in London for **REFUSING** to have his daughters **VACCINATED AGAINST SMALLPOX.**

CROSS BUN
aked in 1821.

# HEIRLOOMS TO PASS ALONG

**8** The ***TITANIC* DIAMOND** really exists, though it's not "The Heart of the Ocean" as seen in the movie. Passenger Walter Chamberlain Porter was WEARING A DIAMOND STICKPIN when the ship went down. That diamond—along with his body—was RECOVERED and has been a Porter family heirloom ever since.

**9** Heirloom flowers and vegetables are plants grown from seeds that have been **GROWN FOR GENERATIONS.** One of the oldest known varieties of roses has been cultivated since knights brought them home from the Crusades in the **12TH OR 13TH CENTURY.**

**10** Heirloom tomatoes are prized for their COLORS AND SHAPES. Some have STRANGE NAMES like Green Zebra and Aunt Gerdie's Gold.

**11** An Ohio, U.S.A., man put a **BOX OF BASEBALL CARDS** in the attic and **FORGOT ABOUT IT.** When his grandson discovered them more than 100 years later, the MINT-CONDITION cards—featuring players like TY COBB AND CY YOUNG—were worth over $3 million.

**12** Some lucky people are **REUNITED WITH THEIR TREASURES** long after they're lost. Metal detector hobbyists found a British man's 1700s-ERA GOLD RING in a field 25 YEARS AFTER he lost it while cutting hay.

**13** A family in the United Kingdom had a living heirloom—a **TORTOISE NAMED THOMAS**—that lived through 2 world wars and the reigns of 5 MONARCHS, only to die from a rat bite AT AGE 130.

**14** Space Farms Zoo and Museum in New Jersey, U.S.A., started as a repair and supplies shop. But during the Great Depression, LOCAL FARMERS WOULD PAY for items with family heirlooms, and soon a museum of antique dolls, cars, DEAD ANIMALS FLOATING IN GLASS JARS, skulls, and more was born.

**15** The huge 76.02-carat **ARCHDUKE JOSEPH DIAMOND** was an heirloom of an Austrian family whose origins go back to FRENCH ROYALTY. In 2012, the diamond was sold at auction for just OVER $21 MILLION.

✳ YOU HAVE LEARNED **2,764** FACTS

5,000 AWESOME FACTS 2  **119**

**1** Basketball player **MICHAEL JORDAN** was fined $5,000 every time he played an NBA game wearing Air Jordans because the shoes didn't exactly match the Chicago Bulls' uniform.

**2** Three-quarters of teenagers in the United States would prefer to get a **NEW PAIR OF SHOES** than to download 50 mp3s.

**3** Fashion goes to the dogs when they don hats and color-coordinated outfits to strut their stuff on the catwalk during the annual **PET FASHION SHOW** in New York City, U.S.A.

**4** In the mid-1700s, it was fashionable for European women to wear skirts that were so wide they had to **WALK SIDEWAYS TO GET THROUGH DOORWAYS.**

**5** You don't have to take your **GLOVES OFF** during cold weather to use a touch screen if you have a special pair of **TEXTING GLOVES.**

**6** **SIXTY-FOUR MILLION PAIRS OF NYLON STOCKINGS WERE SOLD IN 1940**—the first year they became available to the public. They cost $1.35 ($21 in today's money).

**7** **SKINNY JEANS** are not all that new. The tight style was first worn by **PUNK ROCKERS IN THE 1970S.**

**8** European women in the 15th century **PLUCKED THEIR EYEBROWS AND HAIRLINES** to make their foreheads look higher.

**9** **SIXTY PERCENT** of Americans have owned at least one pair of **CONVERSE ALL-STAR CHUCK TAYLOR** basketball shoes in their lifetime.

# 35 FASHION FACTS THAT WILL NEVER

**10** There are more than **80 DIFFERENT WAYS TO WEAR A SARI,** a long piece of cloth draped around the body. Saris are traditional clothing for women from southern Asia.

**11** In the 15th century, it was fashionable for men to wear poulaines, **LONG POINTED SHOES THAT WERE STUFFED WITH MOSS** or other material to keep their shape.

**12** A HENIN was a tall **CONICAL HAT THAT MANY WEALTHY EUROPEAN WOMEN WORE** in medieval times.

**13** American households spend an average of **$1,700 EACH YEAR** on clothes, shoes, and related products.

**14** The word "MACARONI" in the song "Yankee Doodle Dandy" refers to a nickname given to men in mid-18th-century England who dressed elaborately.

**15** During the 18th century, a Chinese emperor **DICTATED THE COLOR OF CLOTHES MEMBERS OF THE ROYAL COURT COULD WEAR.** The emperor and empress wore bright yellow.

**16** The **LACOSTE GREEN CROCODILE** emblem was the first designer logo on a shirt.

**17** In 16th-century Venice, Italy, women **WALKED ON TALL PLATFORM SHOES**—sometimes more than **20 INCHES (50 CM) HIGH**—to keep their feet from getting muddy.

**18** The **BIKINI WAS NAMED** after BIKINI ATOLL, and the swimsuit's small size shocked the world just as the nuclear bombs tested on that Pacific island did.

**19** The most **COMMON GIFT** on Father's Day is a **NECKTIE.**

**20** JAY-Z started his clothing line, Rocawear, with his friend Damon Dash in 1999. In 2007, the company was **SOLD FOR $204 MILLION.**

**21** In China, **BRIDES** typically wear a **RED DRESS** when they get married.

**22** A PAIR OF JEANS typically travels **20,000 MILES** (32,187 km) from manufacturer to retail store before the buyer wears them for the first time.

**23**
Nearly **5,000 PEOPLE** worked as fashion designers in California, U.S.A., in 2010—more than in any other state in the country.

**24**
In 1982, Calvin Klein designed the FIRST PAIR OF NAME-BRAND UNDERWEAR.

**25**
Barbie has over 1,000 DIFFERENT STYLES OF SHOES in her closet.

**26**
Roger "Buckey" Legried from Frost, Minnesota, U.S.A., collected over **109,000 DIFFERENT HATS** from around the world during his lifetime.

**27**
In the song "GANGNAM STYLE," Korean pop star Psy mimics the EXPENSIVE, FASHION-CONSCIOUS LIFESTYLE of the Gangnam District in Seoul, South Korea.

# GO OUT OF STYLE

**28**
The most **EXPENSIVE HANDBAG EVER SOLD** at an auction was a crocodile skin Hermès Diamond Birkin bag. It sold for $203,150 in 2011.

**29**
In COLONIAL AMERICA, it was fashionable to wear wigs. In addition to human hair, they were MADE OF HORSE, GOAT, AND EVEN YAK HAIR.

**30**
People who wear a British designer's M-dress can ANSWER A CELL PHONE call by HOLDING A SLEEVE UP to their ear.

**31**
WINKLEPICKERS were leather bootlike shoes with EXTREMELY POINTED TOES that were popular in the 1950s and '60s.

**32**
A JAPANESE KIMONO can take years to make depending on how ornate it is.

**33**
The Earl Spencer, a British nobleman, started a new style of short coat when he BURNED THE TAILS OFF HIS COAT while sitting too close to a fire.

**34**
Mercury (which is poisonous) was used in making hats in the 1800s. It made WORKERS GO INSANE, which some say is how the phrase "mad as a hatter" came about.

**35**
After WWII, France wanted to retain its role as fashion leader, so it hosted a TRAVELING FASHION SHOW with miniature mannequins to raise money for a relief fund.

**1.** Many cartoon characters are drawn with 4—not 5—fingers, partly because fewer fingers are easier for the artist to draw. **2.** The first full-length episode of *The Simpsons* was a Christmas special. **3.** The only time Mickey Mouse and Bugs Bunny appeared on screen together was in the film *Who Framed Roger Rabbit.* **4.** Before he was an animator, the creator of *SpongeBob SquarePants* was a marine biology teacher. **5.** The character Scooby-Doo was originally named Too Much. **6.** Members of the band One Direction bought a van that looks like the Scooby-Doo Mystery Machine. **7.** The real name of Peppermint Patty in "Peanuts" is Patricia Reichardt. **8.** The real name of the Penguin—from "Batman"—is Oswald Cobblepot. The Riddler's is Edward Nigma. **9.** The Hulk is said to stand 7 feet (2.1 m) tall and weigh 1,040 pounds (472 kg). **10.** A study found kids think breakfast cereal with a cartoon character on the box tastes better than the same cereal without a character. **11.** Virgin America and Aer Lingus airlines use funny cartoon characters in preflight safety videos. **12.** Dennis the Menace was based on cartoonist Hank Ketcham's mischievous son, Dennis. **13.** Original promotional material for *The Jetsons* said the show, which first aired in 1962, was set in the year 2062. **14.** *The Flintstones* was

# 100 CRAZY FACTS ABOUT CARTOONS

originally going to be called *The Flagstones.* **15.** Smurfs were once described as being 3 apples tall. **16.** U.S. President Barack Obama has watched *SpongeBob SquarePants* with his daughters. **17.** Smurfette was originally created by the evil wizard Gargamel as a way to capture the other Smurfs. (It didn't work.) **18.** In the comic book series, Ash's original starter Pokémon was Clefairy, but in the TV series it was replaced with Pinkachu. **19.** There are over 70 Yogi Bear's Jellystone Park campgrounds across the United States. **20.** The creator of *The Simpsons* chose the name Bart for Homer's son because it is an anagram for "Brat." (The same letters in "brat" spell "Bart.") **21.** Tweety Bird was originally pink. **22.** The Looney Tunes theme song is called "The Merry-Go-Round Broke Down." **23.** Bugs Bunny was the first cartoon character to be put on a U.S. postage stamp. **24.** Walt Disney was the original voice of Mickey Mouse. **25.** In 2011, a mushroom species that is shaped like a sea sponge was named *Spongiforma squarepantsii* after the yellow cartoon character. **26.** *Steamboat Willie,* featuring Mickey Mouse, was the first animated film to feature synchronized music and sound effects. **27.** Before he started drawing "Peanuts," Charles Schulz created a comic called "Li'l Folks," which featured Charlie Brown. **28.** Wonder Woman comes from the island of Themyscira, created by the Olympian gods in the middle of the Bermuda Triangle. **29.** The real name of the character Shaggy from *Scooby-Doo, Where Are You!* is Norville Rogers. **30.** The Apollo 10 command module was named Charlie Brown; the lunar module was named Snoopy. **31.** Scientists have identified a real mineral—jadarite—that has the same chemical makeup as the fictional kryptonite. **32.** That amazing waterfall you see in some of the scenes from Disney's animated film *Up* was inspired by Angel Falls in Venezuela. **33.** Captain America's shield can withstand death rays, bullets, and Wolverine's claws. **34.** Mickey Mouse was almost called Mortimer. It was Walt Disney's wife who came up with the name Mickey. **35.** It takes 4 to 5 years to make an animated movie like *Monsters University* or *Brave.* **36.** In the early 1900s, it took hundreds of drawings to make a minute of animation. The invention of celluloid—sheets of a transparent material—around 1913 made it quicker. **37.** Anthony Daniels, the voice of C-3PO, is the only actor to be in all 6 *Star Wars* films plus the TV

Characters from *Shrek*

cartoon series *Star Wars: The Clone Wars*. **38.** *Toy Story* was the first full-length film that was animated entirely by computers. **39.** In one Superman story line, Clark Kent and Lex Luthor were childhood friends. They didn't become enemies until Superman knocked over a chemical that caused Luthor to lose his hair. **40.** In Belgium, where the Smurf comics originated, the blue creatures are called Schtroumpfs. **41.** Pixar movie animators work in office cubicles that they design and build themselves. **42.** *Alvin and the Chipmunks* was originally recorded at half speed, then replayed at full speed to give the characters their squeaky sound. **43.** Jim Davis, the creator of the comic strip "Garfield," had a cat named Pooky, which became the name of Garfield's teddy bear. **44.** Popeye has four nephews named Peepeye, Poopeye, Pipeye, and Pupeye. **45.** Gumby was inspired by a gingerbread man; his slanted head was modeled after creator Art Clokey's dad's hairdo! **46.** The K99 ice-cream truck in London, England, which serves sweet treats for dogs, plays the Scooby-Doo song. **47.** So far, the fastest marathon ever run by a person dressed as a cartoon character was achieved in 2011 by a Charlie Brown look-alike, who finished in 2 hours, 46 minutes. **48.** The 1962 premier of *The Jetsons* came 7 months after John Glenn became the first American to orbit Earth. **49.** For 59 years, Bazooka Joe gum came wrapped in a tiny comic strip. In 2012, the comics were replaced with puzzles and brainteasers. **50.** A 1958 *Action Comics* revealed that Superman has 2 birthdays: As Superman, it's the day he landed on Earth; as Clark, it's the day he was adopted by the Kents. **51.** The *SpongeBob SquarePants* opening song is inspired by the old sea chantey "Blow the Man Down." **52.** Tweety Bird's original name was Orson. **53.** The creator of "The Incredible Hulk" based the Hulk on a combination of Jekyll and Hyde—the original good guy/bad guy character—and Frankenstein. **54.** "Peanuts" has been published in newspapers in 75 countries. **55.** A Comics Code Authority was created in 1954 to make comics more kid friendly by cutting down violence. **56.** In the comic books, Tony Stark—later Iron Man—is said to have been admitted to the Massachusetts Institute of Technology at age 15. He graduated with 2 master's degrees in engineering. **57.** In Japan, the first season of the *Transformers* cartoon show was called *Fight! Super Robot Life Form Transformers*. **58.** Wonder Woman's tiara is not just an accessory—it is razor sharp and can harm anyone who is otherwise immune to injury. **59.** Originally, "Batman" took place in New York City, U.S.A., but later it was placed in the fictional city Gotham. Some say Gotham is in New Jersey. **60.** When Peter Parker first got his Spider-Man powers, he didn't swing from buildings to solve crimes, he competed against a professional wrestler and won. **61.** Aang, the main character in the cartoon show *Avatar*, is a vegetarian. **62.** In the cartoon show *Phineas and Ferb*, the organization Agent P belongs to is called the OWCA—the Organization Without a Cool Acronym. **63.** With a budget of $260 million, *Tangled*, the Disney film about Rapunzel, is the most expensive animated movie ever made—so far. **64.** The original Avengers were Thor, Iron Man, the Hulk, Ant-Man, and Wasp. Captain America joined in issue 4, but a 2011 movie was called *Captain America: The First Avenger.* **65.** Captain America's first shield wasn't round. It was shaped more like one used by a medieval knight. **66.** SpongeBob was originally going to be called SpongeBoy. **67.** The members of the Fantastic Four were exposed to cosmic radiation and acquired superpowers. One of them turned into the Thing. **68.** "Little Orphan Annie" started out as a newspaper comic strip in 1924 and later became a Broadway musical and a movie. **69.** Despite his name, Squidward, in *SpongeBob SquarePants*, is an octopus—according to the show's creators. **70.** Originally, Robin was going to be in only one issue of the "Batman" comic because one of the editors didn't think Batman needed a kid sidekick. **71.** The creators of the "Teenage Mutant Ninja Turtles" comic were brainstorming and thought the contrast of a slow turtle and the quick grace of a ninja would be a clever setup. **72.** Captain America can lift Thor's hammer, not because of his strength, but because he is "worthy." **73.** A scientist estimated that Thor's hammer would weigh as much as 300 billion elephants. **74.** There is a Buzz Lightyear action figure on the floor in the dentist's office in *Finding Nemo*. **75.** A Nemo doll appears in *Monsters Inc.* as one of Boo's toys. **76.** In the movie *Wall-E,* you can spot the Lightning McQueen car and other toys from Pixar movies in Wall-E's trailer and in the trash on Earth. **77.** The last name of Auguste Gusteau, Remy the rat's idol in *Ratatouille*, is mixed-up letters of his first name. **78.** *Superman* and *Spider-Man* have been Broadway musicals in New York City, U.S.A. **79.** *Brave*, Pixar's 13th film, was its first to feature a girl as a lead character. **80.** The New Jersey, U.S.A., license plate on the penguins' car in *Penguins of Madagascar* reads, "I ♥ BNJVI," referring to the New Jersey rock singer Jon Bon Jovi. **81.** A man fixing up a house in Minnesota, U.S.A., found a copy of the first comic book that featured Superman behind a wall. He sold it for $175,000 even though it was missing the back cover! **82.** A near mint edition of the first issue of *Action Comics,* which was published in 1938 and featured Superman, can sell for more than $2 million. **83.** *Shrek* was the first movie to win an Academy Award in the category Best Animated Feature. **84.** In the early "Superman" comic books, Superman didn't have the ability to fly. **85.** "Shrek" means "monster" in Yiddish. **86.** The people who do the voices for animated films often record their parts separately and never even meet each other. **87.** In the first issue of the "Incredible Hulk" comic, printed in 1962, the Hulk was gray, not green. **88.** None of the main characters in the movie *Madagascar*—a giraffe, lion, zebra, and hippo—are housed in the real Central Park Zoo in New York City. They just live there in the movie. **89.** The animators for *Kung Fu Panda* took a kung fu class to get prepared for the action parts of the film. **90.** A small, toothy mammal resembling the fictional saber-tooth squirrel Scrat from the *Ice Age* films was recently discovered in Argentina. **91.** *Star Wars: The Clone Wars* takes place between Episode II and III of the *Star Wars* saga. **92.** In early comic strips, Popeye got his strength from petting a type of lucky hen, not by eating spinach. **93.** Lightning McQueen's number 95 in the movie *Cars* is a nod to the year (1995) that *Toy Story* was released. **94.** Ben Tennyson, the main character on *Ben 10,* discovered a total of 20 Omnitrix aliens by the end of the original series. By the end of the *Ultimate Alien* series he discovered 63. **95.** The evil counterparts to the Powerpuff Girls are the Rowdyruff Boys. **96.** Each character in the U.K.'s *Wallace and Gromit* films is moved at least 12 times per second to make the animation look life-like. **97.** A study found that chimps yawn when they watch a cartoon chimp yawn! **98.** The first movie adapted from a comic book was *Adventures of Captain Marvel,* which was released in 1941. **99.** He-Man was a popular action figure before he got his own cartoon show: *He-Man and the Masters of the Universe.* **100.** Superman has been in continuous publication since he originally appeared in *Action Comics*—that's more than 75 years!

# 35 FACTS ABOUT PARASITES THAT WILL FREAK YOU OUT

**1** PARASITES GET THEIR FOOD FROM HOSTS—organisms, such as animals, plants, and even humans, that they live on or in.

**2** Going barefoot can be hazardous to your health. HOOKWORMS ENTER THE BODY THROUGH THE BOTTOMS OF PEOPLE'S FEET and live in the small intestines.

**3** There are over 1,500 SPECIES OF TAPEWORMS—also known as flatworms—but only 25 are known to infest humans.

**4** Tapeworms don't have a stomach or digestive system. THEY LIVE IN AN ANIMAL'S INTESTINES, taking in already digested food through their skin.

**5** The Meguro Parasitological Museum in Tokyo, Japan, is the only museum of its kind in the world. It has about 60,000 PARASITES in its collection.

**6** The WORLD'S LONGEST TAPEWORM was living in a 40-year-old man. At 29 FEET (8.8 M), it was longer than a giraffe is tall.

**7** Tapeworm eggs were found in 270-MILLION-YEAR-OLD SHARK POOP.

**Lamprey**

**8** People infested with *Loa loa* can feel and **SEE THE PARASITE MOVING IN THEIR EYES.**

**9** *Plasmodium falciparum,* a parasite that causes malaria, can duplicate itself **40,000 TIMES IN 1 WEEK.**

**10** Need something soft and cuddly? One company sells **PLUSH PARASITES,** like bedbugs, *Plasmodium falciparum, Trypanosoma bruce* (causes sleeping sickness), and more.

**11** Nematodes— microscopic and mostly parasitic worms—**ARE THE MOST NUMEROUS MULTICELLED CREATURES ON EARTH.**

**12** Some scientists believe nematodes make up **90 PERCENT OF ALL LIFE ON THE OCEAN FLOOR.**

**13** The oldest known nematodes are about **400 MILLION YEARS OLD,** but some scientists think these worms may date back 1 billion years.

**14** The prescription for getting rid of a parasitic worm in ancient Egypt was to **EAT A CAKE MADE OF SALT, HERBS, AND COW BILE.**

**15** Some parasitic isopods—a type of crustacean—**INVADE A FISH'S MOUTH, DEVOUR ITS TONGUE,** and take its place!

**16** After stinging a cockroach in the brain, **A PARASITIC WASP CAN LEAD THE ROACH TO ITS BURROW,** where it becomes food for the wasp's babies.

**17** One kind of parasite gets inside **BLACK ANTS AND TURNS THEIR BUTTS BRIGHT RED.** Birds eat these red "berries," giving the parasite a place to reproduce.

**18** Rodents infested with *Toxoplasma gondii* are **ATTRACTED TO CAT PEE, MAKING THEM EASY PREY FOR CATS.** When a cat eats the rodent, the parasite has a place to reproduce.

**19** Humans can get *Toxo* from cats. Some scientists believe that the **PARASITE CAN ALTER BEHAVIOR,** making a person more trusting or outgoing, for example.

**20** In rare cases, *TOXO* **MAY CAUSE SCHIZOPHRENIA**— a severe brain disorder— in people.

**21** A lamprey uses its sucker mouth to attach itself to a fish, then **USES ITS TONGUE TO BORE A HOLE IN ITS PREY** and suck the blood out.

**22** Asian **LADYBUGS CONTAIN FUNGAL PARASITES** that kill any insect that eats them.

**23** Bloodsucking lice have probably been around for **130 MILLION YEARS**—long enough to have infested feathered dinosaurs!

**24** One kind of parasitic worm infests **GREATER WAX MOTH CATERPILLARS AND MAKES THEM GLOW.**

**25** Once a male anglerfish finds a mate, **HE LATCHES ON TO HER BODY AND BECOMES PART OF HER,** eventually losing his eyes and most of his internal organs!

**26** A female anglerfish can carry **6 OR MORE PARASITIC MALES ON HER BODY.**

**27** Some birds, like the **CUCKOO FINCH,** are known as brood parasites. They lay their eggs in another bird's nest to be hatched and raised.

**28** Even though the medical term for ringworm is *tinea*—Latin for "growing worm"—**THIS SKIN RASH IS CAUSED BY A FUNGUS,** not a parasitic worm.

**29** A tick is "questing" when it stretches out its front legs, **READY TO JUMP ONTO A PASSING HOST.**

**30** Some ticks make a cement-like substance to anchor their heads firmly in a host's body as **THEY DRINK THE BLOOD.**

**31** In the United States, ticks can transmit over **10 DIFFERENT TYPES OF DISEASES,** including Lyme disease.

**32** Female guinea worms can **GROW UP TO 3 FEET (1 M) LONG INSIDE A HUMAN BODY.** They cause painful sores as they force their way out of the body.

**33** The Bible talks about **GUINEA WORMS,** calling them "fiery serpents."

**34** **HORSEHAIR WORMS INFEST GRASSHOPPERS AND CRICKETS.** The name comes from a legend that says hair from horses fell into water and came to life.

**35** There is a parasitic worm that burrows into a snail's eyestalks, causing them to **GROW INTO COLORFUL, PULSATING TARGETS** for predators.

**1**
Backgammon is likely the **WORLD'S OLDEST BOARD GAME**. In 2004, a 5,000-year-old set was unearthed in Iran's ancient Burnt City.

**2**
The shortest possible game of Monopoly—with the right rolls and cards—is **21 SECONDS**. The scenario is likely only once every 253,899,891,671,040 games.

**3**
In 2013, **MONOPOLY FANS VOTED** to replace the iron game piece, which has been part of the game since 1935, with a cat.

**4**
In a **LEGENDARY ROYAL CHESS GAME**, the Persian king won and was rewarded with 90 elephants and 1,200 camels loaded with treasure.

**5**
Go is the **MOST POPULAR GAME** in China, Japan, Korea, and Taiwan. It was believed that playing Go helped one become an educated gentleman.

**6**
When chess came to China about 1,000 years ago, people there called it *xiangqui*, or **"THE RIVER GAME."**

**7**
Parcheesi evolved from the **ANCIENT ASIAN GAME** of Pachisi, which was often played on a cloth "board" shaped like a cross.

**8**
Each hour, **30,000 SCRABBLE GAMES** are started around the world.

**9**
In the 1500s, one Chinese emperor was so obsessed with Pachisi that he turned his palace courtyard into a **LIFE-SIZE BOARD** with people as the game pieces.

**10**
In 1970, British Petroleum sponsored a game called Offshore Oil Strike that **EERILY DESCRIBED** events in BP's 2010 Deepwater Horizon oil spill in the Gulf of Mexico.

**11**
Diplomacy, **PLAYED ON A MAP** of pre-WWI Europe, doesn't have dice, a spinner, or cards. To win, you must negotiate, eavesdrop, and form alliances with other players.

**12**
Chess players once believed that **PUTTING STONES** on the corners of the board kept anger created during a match from spilling out into the real world.

**13**
During WWII, the British hid **ESCAPE KITS** inside Monopoly games sent to soldiers in German prisons. The kits included compasses and maps of the area around a prison.

**14**
An early British version of Chutes and Ladders features a schoolboy trying to get to the **TOP OF THE CLASS.** Canes—used for punishment—are the chutes.

**15**
The original name of Clue, a popular murder-mystery game, was **MURDER!**

**16**
A wealthy Canadian couple **INVENTED A GAME** to play on their yacht in the 1950s. We know it today as Yahtzee.

**17**
In the 1970s, a game came out that was based on the **SINKING OF THE TITANIC.** Players raced to get on lifeboats, then traveled to islands to find food.

**18**
One board game was **BASED ON A REAL SNOWSTORM.** Various versions of The Blizzard of '77 Travel Game were set in different U.S. cities.

**19**
A competition called Grid turned part of **LONDON, ENGLAND,** into a game board where players had to do a lot of running to find clues that would lead to prizes.

**20**
Senet is a **3,000-YEAR-OLD** board game from Egypt. Historians have come up with rules for modern versions by studying ancient drawings.

**21**
The Game of LIFE was one of the first board games to **HAVE A 3-D BOARD** and a built-in spinner.

**22**
In 1861, Milton Bradley made **POCKET-SIZE BOARD GAMES** for Civil War soldiers to take with them to play between battles.

**23**
The game Sorry! is also known as The Game of **SWEET REVENGE.**

**24**
Classic board games have found a home in technology. Scrabble is one of the **MOST POPULAR GAMES** on the iPad.

**25**
King Tut was buried with 4 senet boards to **PLAY IN THE AFTERLIFE.**

**26**
When Battleship—a game where players try to find and destroy each other's ships—came out in the 1930s, it was played with **PAPER AND PENCIL.**

**27**
A Japanese island turned itself into a **GIANT VERSION** of The Game of LIFE. Players used fake money, maps, and buses in place of game pieces.

**28**
An Illinois, U.S.A., man has a collection of over **1,500 DIFFERENT BOARD GAMES**—the largest in the world.

**29**
More board games are **SOLD IN GERMANY** than anywhere else on Earth.

**30**
A winding street in San Francisco, California, U.S.A., was turned into a **REAL-LIFE CANDY LAND** board for the game's 60th anniversary.

**31**
A film company is planning on creating **MOVIE VERSIONS** of some board games, including Candy Land, Monopoly, and Ouija.

S₁ C₃ R₁ A₁ B₃ B₃ L₁ E₁

HOME

# 50 PLAYFUL FACTS ABOUT BOARD GAMES

**39**
Cartoonist Rube Goldberg—famous for putting together random things to "invent" something that performed an everyday task—created the game MOUSE TRAP.

**45**
Settlers of Catan, a game where players create a civilization, is an example of a German-style—or Euro—game, which emphasizes STRATEGY rather than luck.

**46**
In some countries, the Scrabble dictionary allows for SLANG WORDS. In Great Britain, the dictionary includes words like "grrl," "thang," and "blingy."

**40**
In the largest game of Mouse Trap, a bank safe CRUSHES A CAR, not a mouse. The designer shows off his 25-ton (23-MT) contraption at fairs and other events.

**47**
In 1904, when Elizabeth Magie patented what we know as Monopoly, she called it LANDLORD'S GAME. Players bought plots of land like Lonely Lane and Easy Street.

**41**
To play MONOPOLY IN THE PARK, a life-size Monopoly board in San Jose, California, U.S.A., players wear helmets with the game pieces on top.

**36**
Twister wasn't selling until TV show host Johnny Carson played it on air with actress Eva Gabor. It's still one of Hasbro's MOST POPULAR games.

**48**
The popularity of the board game Risk, where players compete to conquer the world, has led to SPIN-OFF GAMES such as Martian Risk, Nuclear Risk, and Revolution Risk.

**42**
The WORLD'S LARGEST Scrabble game was played outside with table-size game pieces.

**37**
The ORIGINAL NAME of the game Twister was Pretzel.

**49**
Pandemic is ONE SICK GAME. Diseases have broken out all over the world, and players must work together to wipe them out.

**32**
*Jumanji*—a Zulu word that means "many effects"—is a movie based on a story about a man who BECAME STUCK INSIDE a board game for 26 years.

**34**
The game Othello, played with 2-sided black-and-white pieces on a checkered board, was CALLED REVERSI when it was invented in 1880.

**43**
Two men set a world record for the longest continuous play of a board game. They played 116 games of simulated baseball for 61 HOURS AND 2 MINUTES!

**50**
Ouija boards are supposedly a way to COMMUNICATE WITH THE DEAD. But it is muscle, not spirit, responses that move the Ouija across the board.

**33**
The 2012 movie *Battleship* is based on the board game. The movie team engineered some of the weapons to look like the BOARD GAME'S PEGS.

Ludo aka Parcheesi (The game Sorry! is based on Ludo.)

**35**
The WORLD'S LARGEST CHESS SET is in Canada and has pieces up to 4 feet (1 m) high that weigh a total of 870 pounds (395 kg).

**38**
One elaborate backgammon board takes competition to a new level. It's made with over 60,000 black, white, and yellow DIAMONDS. That's one sparkly game!

**44**
Scrabble was invented in the 1940s by architect and statistician Alfred Butts, who had a mind for math, NOT SPELLING.

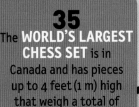

* YOU HAVE LEARNED **2,984** FACTS

**1**

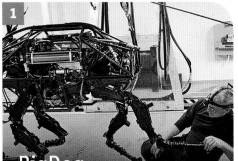

**BigDog** is the most advanced all-terrain robot in the world. The size of a small mule, its 4 animal-like legs are able to carry up to 340 pounds (154 kg).

**2**

SEARCH-AND-RESCUE TEAMS CAN THROW THE BOUNCE IMAGING EXPLORER—A BASEBALL-SIZE PROBE EQUIPPED WITH 6 CAMERAS—INTO DANGEROUS PLACES TO TAKE PICTURES AND TEST FOR POISONOUS GASES.

**3**

Ever played Angry Birds on water? The Displair is a touch screen made of mist that needs up to a half gallon (2 L) of water every hour to keep it going.

**4**

Smartwatches let users read their email, listen to music, check social media, and even monitor their health.

**5**

A company makes a **HARRY POTTER–LIKE WAND** that can learn up to 13 commands that will turn up the volume, change the channel, and do more on your TV.

# 25 CUTTING-EDGE FACTS ABOUT EXTREME

**6**

LEARN TO PLAY GUITAR ON YOUR T-SHIRT. The electronic guitar T-shirt lets you play all major chords while the sound comes from a mini-amplifier attached to your belt.

**7**

PLUG AN IPHONE INTO A TECHPET ROBOTIC DOG FRAME, AND THE PUP COMES ALIVE! THE CAMERA AND MICROPHONE LET THE ROBOT ANIMAL RECOGNIZE HAND SIGNALS AND SIMPLE COMMANDS.

**8**

A company is attempting to bring the Internet to remote parts of the world by launching jellyfish-like balloons that will beam down a connection from 12 miles (19 km) above Earth.

**9**

**GOOGLE GLASS** is a headset that uses voice commands to chat, take pictures, video, and more. It vibrates bones near the ear to generate sound, so earphones aren't needed.

**10**

THE RED SCHUMACHER MI3 IS THE FASTEST REMOTE-CONTROL CAR IN THE WORLD, ZOOMING AT A SPEED OF 161.76 MILES PER HOUR (260.32 KPH).

**11**

A company has developed drones—unmanned robotic helicopters—that can deliver food, medicine, mail, and more where roads don't go.

**12**

One of U.S. President Lyndon Johnson's favorite gadgets was his **AMPHIBIOUS CAR.** He surprised unsuspecting riders by yelling that the brakes didn't work as he drove straight into a lake.

**13** JetLev is a water-propelled jetpack that pumps 1,000 gallons (3,785 L) of water a minute through a backpack, launching the wearer 30 feet (9 m) into the air.

**14**
## EVER WISH YOUR CARPET WAS ALIVE?
The soft "moss carpet" bathroom mat is made out of real moss—kept alive by the bathroom's humidity.

**15** Who knew potty training could be so high-tech? iPotty is a plastic, orange-and-green *MINI-TOILET WITH AN IPAD ATTACHED TO THE FRONT.*

**16** SMART LOCKS ARE CONTROLLED BY YOUR SMART-PHONE, NOT KEYS. SOME LOCKS CAN TELL WHO'S ENTERING YOUR HOUSE AND EVEN TAKE A PICTURE.

**17** A car company created a self-driving model car called Shelley that allows the company to test performance at speeds up to 155 miles per hour (249 kph).

**18** The BeBionic3—the world's MOST ADVANCED PROSTHETIC ARM—mimics real hand and wrist movements and is controlled by the wearer's actual muscles.

# GADGETS

**19** There's a basketball that records every dribble and shot you make, then transmits the data to your mobile device to help you achieve the perfect game.

**20** Shaped like a shark, dolphin, or orca whale, the Seabreacher watercraft jumps, dives, rolls, and speeds across the water at up to 55 miles per hour (89 kph).

**21** You can order a Tree Tent, a sphere-shaped tent that hangs from a tree, equipped with a woodstove, sink, bed, table, and more to satisfy your tree-hanging needs.

**22** FOR $26,000, YOU CAN RIDE AROUND IN YOUR VERY OWN MONDO SPIDER, AN
## 8-legged, 1,600-pound
(726-kg) ROBOT ARACHNID THAT MOVES AT 5 MILES PER HOUR (8 KPH).

**23** A DISAPPEARING TELEVISION COULD SOON BE A REALITY. ONE CONCEPT IN DEVELOPMENT IS A SEE-THROUGH TV, WHICH USES TRANSPARENT LCD TECHNOLOGY TO LOOK LIKE GLASS WHEN TURNED OFF.

**24** The HAPIfork aims to manage weight loss by measuring how often you raise your fork to your mouth and vibrating when you eat too quickly.

**25** Portland, Oregon, U.S.A., has four 17-foot (5-m)-tall street lamps that look like colorful CARNIVOROUS PLANTS. Solar panels allow them to glow for 4 hours after dark.

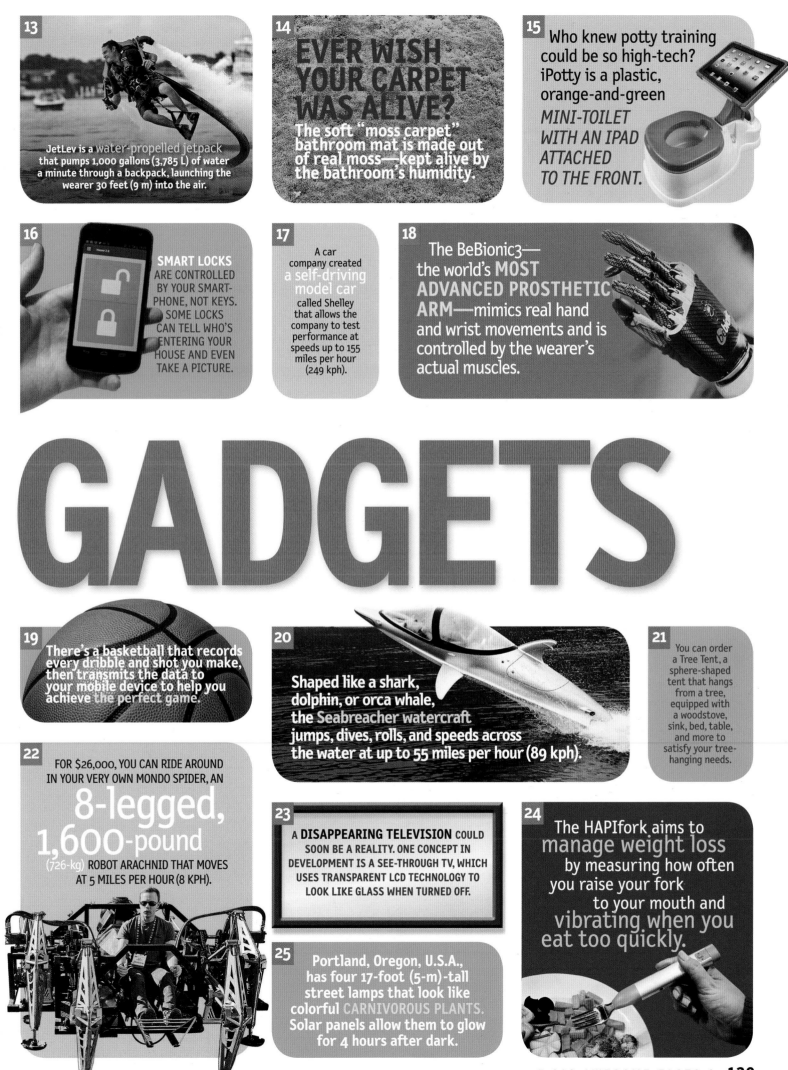

# 15 SPORTY FACTS ABOUT

**1** **DOGGIE SURFERS** catch waves and hang 16 at the Loews Coronado Bay Resort Surf Dog Competition in San Diego, California, U.S.A., which welcomes around **40 POOCHES FROM AROUND THE COUNTRY** each year.

**2** In horse soccer, horses—ridden by humans—go for the goal by **KICKING A GIANT BALL** up and down the field.

**3** A dolphin at a sanctuary in Cuba shoots hoops by **BALANCING THE BALL ON ITS NOSE** while jumping out of the water.

**4** What does a **BEAR DO WHEN IT'S BORED?** A 2-year-old black bear named Eli likes to bat around a **TETHERBALL!**

**5** Hudson, a 3-year-old Belgian Malinois, **LEAPED THE LENGTH OF A STRETCH LIMO** into a pool during a dock-diving competition for dogs.

**6** A bunny named Lykkes Fancy Faith **CLEARED A HURDLE TALLER THAN A FIRE HYDRANT** to win a Danish rabbit-hopping contest.

**7** At the Pig Olympics, which so far have been held in China, Russia, and the United States, pigs compete in events like **PIG RACING, PIG SWIMMING, AND PIGBALL—**a game like soccer except the porkers chase a ball covered in fish oil.

# ANIMAL ATHLETES

**8** In the Indonesian sport of Pacu Jawi, **FARMERS RACE COWS** across muddy rice fields while trying to hold on to their harnesses.

**9** A French **SHEEPDOG NAMED NORMAN** broke a scooter-riding world record after **COVERING 100 FEET (30 M) IN JUST 21 SECONDS.** He can ride a bike, too.

**10** In order to lose weight, Holly, a 13-year-old **CAT THAT WEIGHS 18 POUNDS** (8 kg), uses a life vest to swim laps for up to 30 minutes at a time in a pool at a pet resort in Virginia.

**11** More than 35,000 people come out to watch California's Calaveras County Fair & Jumping Frog Jubilee each year. To win the top prize of $5,000, **A JUMPER HAS TO BEAT THE LEAP SET BY THE LEGENDARY ROSIE THE RIBETER:** 21 feet, 5.75 inches (6.55 m).

**12** Each year, dozens of snails line up to "race" a 13-inch (33-cm)-long course at the **WORLD SNAIL RACING CHAMPIONSHIPS** in Norfolk, England. The prize? A trophy filled with lettuce!

**13** Bolt, a **CHAMPION RACING PIGEON** named after the Olympic gold-medal-winning Jamaican sprinter Usain Bolt, recently **SOLD AT AUCTION FOR $400,000.**

**14** A man in Australia has trained his **PET MICE** to "catch air," zoom down ramps, and **SOAR THROUGH A RING OF FIRE ON TINY SKATEBOARDS.** They can surf too!

**15** In certain parts of the world, **ELEPHANT POLO** is a popular sport. **TWO PEOPLE RIDE EACH ELEPHANT**—one steers the animal while **THE OTHER SWINGS AN EXTRA-LONG MALLET** to try to hit a ball toward the goal.

**1** South Africa has not 1 but 3 capital cities: Pretoria, Cape Town, and Bloemfontein. Each city is home to a different branch of the government.

**2** Eight different cities served as the capital of the United States before Washington, D.C., became the permanent seat of government in 1800.

**3** Lancaster, Pennsylvania, was the U.S. capital for the shortest period of time—1 day: September 27, 1777.

**4** BEAVER, OKLAHOMA, U.S.A., IS THE COW CHIP THROWING CAPITAL OF THE WORLD. EVERY YEAR THERE IS A CONTEST TO SEE WHO CAN TOSS A MANURE PATTY THE FARTHEST.

**5** The national capital city with the lowest elevation is Baku, Azerbaijan. Located on the shore of the Caspian Sea, the city is 92 feet (28 m) below sea level.

**6** In Beijing, the capital of China, an underground city covers almost 33 square miles (85 km²). Construction on the city, which was built as a nuclear fallout shelter, began in 1969.

**7** Antarctica is the only continent without a country or a capital city.

**8** Damascus, Syria, is considered to be the world's oldest capital city. It has been inhabited since at least the third millennium B.C.

**9** All the copper used to make the dome on the state capitol building in Phoenix, Arizona, would make 4.8 million pennies.

**10** Both Stockholm, Sweden, and Copenhagen, Denmark, claim their cities to be the Capital of Scandinavia. Scandinavia hasn't had an official capital city since the 1500s, but both countries consider the title good for business and tourism.

**11** According to a famous travel guide, the Culinary Capital of the World—as of 2012—is Japan, not France. It gave its highest rating of 3 stars to 29 restaurants in Japan and only 25 in France.

**12** The subway system in Moscow, Russia's capital city, has 12 lines of travel and more than 180 stations.

**13** Rides on the merry-go-rounds in Binghamton, New York, U.S.A.—known as the Carousel Capital of the World—are always free. Instead of paying a fee, riders are asked to pick up a piece of litter.

**14** The Vikings called Dublin, now the capital of Ireland, Black Pool. The name came from the dark bog water that feeds into the River Liffey, which flows through the city.

**15** In 2011, South Sudan became an independent country, making Juba the newest capital city in the world.

**16** The nickname for the Sydney Harbor Bridge in Sydney, the capital of New South Wales, Australia, is the coat hanger because that's what it looks like to some people.

**17** San Salvador, the capital of El Salvador, is located at the base of the active San Salvador Volcano, which last erupted in 1917. The city is home to more than 1.6 million people.

**18** Denver, the capital of Colorado, U.S.A., is nicknamed the Mile High City because it is located 1 mile (1.6 km) above sea level.

**19** VATICAN CITY IS BOTH THE NAME OF AN INDEPENDENT COUNTRY AND ITS CAPITAL CITY.

**20** The Thai name for the capital city of Bangkok is Krung Thep Mahanakhon Amon Rattanakosin Mahinthara Ayuthaya Mahadilok Phop Noppharat Ratchathani Burirom Udomratchaniwet Mahasathan Amon Piman Awatan Sathit Sakkathattiya Witsanukam Prasit—or Krung Thep for short!

**21** More than half of the world's top retail stores are located in London, England.

**22** THE METROPOLITAN AREA OF JUNEAU, CAPITAL OF THE U.S. STATE OF ALASKA, IS BIGGER THAN THE STATE OF DELAWARE!

**23** Anoka, Minnesota, which calls itself the Halloween Capital of the United States, has held a Halloween parade every year since 1920.

**24** L. Frank Baum, who wrote *The Wizard of Oz,* may have been inspired to name the capital of Oz the Emerald City in honor of his mother's homeland of Ireland—the Emerald Isle.

**25** Perforated toilet paper was invented in Albany, the capital of New York, U.S.A.

**26** Cairo, Egypt's capital city, is known as the city of a thousand minarets.

**27** Established in 1610, Santa Fe, New Mexico, U.S.A., is the oldest capital city in the United States.

**28** Ottawa, the capital of Canada, got its name from the native Algonquin word *adawe,* which means "to trade."

**29** For 6 months of the year, the average high temperature in Nuuk, Greenland, is below freezing. *Brrr!*

**30** Danville, Virginia, was the third and final capital of the Confederate States of America, but only for 8 days.

**31** Quito, Ecuador, is the closest national capital to the Equator.

**32** Montpelier, the capital of Vermont, is the only U.S. state capital without a McDonald's.

**33** If you lose your luggage on a flight, it might end up in Scottsboro, Alabama, U.S.A., the Lost Luggage Capital of the World.

**34** Athens, the capital of Greece, is considered the place where Western civilization began. In ancient Athens, the juries for court trials could have 500 or more people.

**35** MEXICO CITY, MEXICO, IS SINKING! OVER THE PAST 100 YEARS, THIS CAPITAL CITY HAS SUNK 30 FEET (9 M), AS WATER HAS BEEN DRAINED FROM UNDERGROUND RESERVOIRS FASTER THAN IT HAS BEEN REPLACED.

**36** The largest urban colony of bats is located in Austin, capital of Texas, U.S.A. At dusk each evening, approximately 1.5 million bats fly out from their shelter underneath the Ann Richards Congress Avenue Bridge.

Baku, Azerbaijan, on the shore of the Caspian Sea

# 75 POWERFUL

## FACTS ABOUT CAPITAL

**37** The capitol building in Boise, Idaho, U.S.A., is heated by a hot spring located 3,000 feet (914 m) underground.

**38** One of the widest avenues in the world is in Buenos Aires, Argentina's capital city. Called Avenida 9 de Julio in honor of the country's independence day, it stretches across 12 lanes.

**39** THE FIRST SUBWAY SYSTEM IN THE UNITED STATES STARTED OPERATING IN 1897 IN BOSTON, MASSACHUSETTS, U.S.A.

**40** When viewed from up in the sky, the layout of the roads and buildings in Brasília, the capital of Brazil, resembles a bird, an airplane, or a bow and arrow.

**41** Trees, forests, or other shrubbery cover one-fifth of the land in New Delhi, India's capital city.

**42** Avon, Ohio, U.S.A., is the Duct Tape Capital of the World. Every year the city has a festival over Father's Day weekend with parades and sculptures—made of duct tape, of course.

**43** There are more than 300 different islands surrounding Helsinki, the capital of Finland. City dwellers escape to them for sunbathing, picnics, and swimming.

**44** During the U.S. Civil War, defeated Confederate soldiers set Richmond, Virginia—the capital of the Confederacy—on fire so the attacking Yankees wouldn't find much of value.

**45** The Coconut Palace in Manila, Philippines, is an extravagant guesthouse made from coconut trees. It was built for Pope John Paul II's visit to the country in 1981, but he declined to sleep there because too much was spent on it.

**46** The largest women's university in the world—Princess Nora bint Abdulrahman University—is located near Riyadh, Saudi Arabia's capital city.

**47** More than 400 species of birds are found in Nairobi National Park, which is named for Kenya's capital city.

**48** The most ice cream made by a single company (Blue Bunny) is produced in Le Mars, Iowa, U.S.A., making it the Ice Cream Capital of the World.

**49** BELGIUM IS KNOWN AS THE CHOCOLATE CAPITAL OF THE WORLD. THE COUNTRY HAS MORE THAN 2,000 CHOCOLATE SHOPS.

**50** The mint green–colored CFM Railway Station in Maputo, Mozambique's capital, is considered to be one of the world's most beautiful railroad stations.

**51** Albertville, Alabama, U.S.A., is considered the Fire Hydrant Capital of the World. In honor of its one millionth fire hydrant, a company built a 4,800-pound (2,177-kg) hydrant-shaped monument.

**52** After seeing the world-famous ancient sites of Rome, Italy's capital city, you can visit the National Museum of Pasta Foods.

**53** Two famous Georgians—Martin Luther King, Jr., and President Jimmy Carter—were each awarded the Nobel Peace Prize. The medals are on display in Atlanta, the U.S. state's capital city.

**54** There is a statue of John Lennon of the Beatles rock group in Havana, Cuba's capital.

**55** The Canadian province of Manitoba is known as the Slurpee Capital of the World. More Slurpees are bought there than anywhere else in the world.

**56** Known for its diners, New Jersey, U.S.A., is sometimes called the Diner Capital of the World.

**57** The most visited attraction in Paris, France's capital city, isn't the Eiffel Tower or the Louvre—it's Disneyland Paris.

**58** According to legend, a lake in Hanoi, Vietnam's capital city, is home to a turtle that came out of the water to steal a sword from a 15th-century king, then dived back into the lake.

**59** Sactown, River City, the Camellia Capital of the World, and the Big Tomato are all nicknames for Sacramento, the capital of California, U.S.A.

**60** The Restaurante Botin, in Madrid, the capital of Spain, calls itself the oldest restaurant in the world. It uses a wood-fired oven dating back to 1725, the year the eatery opened.

**61** Since 1960, Bloomer, Wisconsin, U.S.A., has held an annual jump-rope contest, making it the Jump Rope Capital of the World.

**62** The city of Amsterdam, capital of the Netherlands, has more bicycles than people.

**63** If the boards from the permanent seats at the Indianapolis Motor Speedway, which is named for the capital of Indiana, U.S.A., were laid side by side, they would stretch almost 100 miles (161 km).

**64** London, England, has more multi-millionaires than any other city in the world, but New York City has the most billionaires.

**65** THE WEATHER CAPITAL OF THE WORLD IS PUNXSUTAWNEY, PENNSYLVANIA, U.S.A. IT'S WHERE THE FAMOUS WEATHER-FORECASTING GROUNDHOG LIVES.

**66** Male, capital of the island nation of the Maldives, is protected from the sea by a wall that surrounds the island where the capital city is located.

**67** Because the District of Columbia is a federal district and not a U.S. state, it doesn't have a vote in Congress. Its nonvoting delegate can only enter into debates and serve on committees.

**68** THE START OF HUMAN MIGRATION CAN BE TRACED BACK OVER 100,000 YEARS TO ONE LOCATION: ADDIS ABABA, THE CAPITAL OF ETHIOPIA.

**69** Believe in Bigfoot? Willow Creek, California, is known as the Bigfoot Capital of the World. The town is located near wooded areas where the creature reportedly has been spotted.

**70** Tokyo, Japan's capital and most populous city, was once a small fishing village named Edo.

**71** The star Arcturus always rises directly above Honolulu, the capital of Hawaii, U.S.A., and the Hawaiian islands.

**72** Accra, the name of Ghana's capital city, comes from a native word that means "an army of ants"—probably a reference to the many anthills in the area.

**73** St. Paul, the capital of Minnesota, U.S.A., was once called Pig's Eye after the nickname of Pierre Parrant, the French-Canadian trader who established the city.

**74** The Casa de Aliaga is the oldest house in Lima, capital of Peru. Eighteen generations of the Aliaga family have lived there.

**75** Nauru, a small island country in the Pacific Ocean, does not have an official capital city.

# CITIES

**1**

There are more than 290 MARSUPIAL SPECIES in the world.

**2**

A kangaroo mom makes 2 DIFFERENT KINDS OF MILK—one for her newborn and another with more fat for when the baby gets older.

**3**

TAMMAR WALLABIES that live where fresh water is scarce get their liquid by eating sea plants or even drinking salt water.

**4**

The YAPOK, or underwater opossum, has a WATERPROOF POUCH that keeps its babies safe and dry.

**Kangaroo joey peeking out of mother's pouch**

**5**

Young KOALAS ride piggyback on their moms and stick close by until they are about 2 years old.

**6**

The special pouch that marsupials use to raise their babies is called the MARSUPIUM.

**7**

Marsupial babies are tiny. Some are the SIZE OF A JELLY BEAN, but others are smaller than a grain of rice.

**8**

ONLY ONE KIND of marsupial lives in the United States—the Virginia opossum—but more than 200 different types live in Australia and New Guinea.

**9**

The FASTER a kangaroo hops, the less energy it burns.

**10**

The Virginia opossum can survive being bitten by a RATTLESNAKE.

**11**

Koalas, wombats, and kangaroos are HERBIVORES, meaning they eat only plants. Others, like the Tasmanian devil and marsupial mice, are meat-eaters.

**12**

A western gray kangaroo is as TALL AS AN AVERAGE 13-YEAR-OLD BOY—5.25 feet (1.6 m)!

**13**

When A.A. Milne wrote Winnie-the-Pooh, he created mom and baby kangaroo characters named KANGA AND ROO. Kanga is the only female character in the stories.

**14**

Gray kangaroos are great hoppers. They can hop FASTER THAN A HORSE can run.

**15** Male red kangaroos are sometimes called **RED FLIERS**, while females are called blue fliers because their color is more bluish gray.

**16** Kangaroos belong to a family called **MACROPODIDAE**, which means "big feet."

**17** Taz, the **TASMANIAN DEVIL** from *Looney Tunes*, is currently voiced by Jim Cummings, who also provides the voice for Winnie-the-Pooh.

**18** Australia and New Guinea have **MORE MARSUPIAL SPECIES** than other kind of animal species.

**19** The long-tailed **PLANIGALE**, which looks like a small mouse, is the world's smallest marsupial. It's about as long as your finger.

**20** **WOMBATS** don't have claws on their big toes because they use these toes to wipe their eyes and other sensitive places.

**21** How do you know when a Tasmanian devil is excited or stressed out? **ITS EARS TURN RED.**

# 35 MARVELOUS FACTS ABOUT MARSUPIALS

**22** Sydney, Duncan the Daredevil, and Dunk were all names for the kangaroo that appeared on packages of **DUNKAROOS**—cinnamon cookies that you dunked in icing.

**23** Some kangaroos that lived 12,000 years ago were the **SIZE OF RHINOCEROSES.**

**24** An Australian company makes **KANGAROO SCULPTURES** out of recycled car, bus, motorbike, and truck parts.

**25** **MARSUPIAL MOLES** are blind and live in desert areas in underground holes, which they close off. They breathe the air that is trapped between grains of sand.

**26** The **SUGAR GLIDER** can jump from a limb and glide through the air for as far as 325 feet (100 m)—the length of 8 school buses.

**27** Wombats dig **ELABORATE BURROWS.** Although they have only one entrance, the maze of tunnels can stretch for 650 feet (200 m).

**28** Male sugar gliders—marsupials that live in Indonesia, Australia, and Papua New Guinea—are **RIGHT-HANDED;** females are **LEFT-HANDED.**

**29** Baby koalas **EAT A FORM OF THEIR MOTHERS' POOP** called pap, which gives them the bacteria they need to digest the toxins in eucalyptus leaves.

**30** Baby Australian marsupials are called **JOEYS,** but there is no special name for baby opossums—the only kind of marsupial in North America.

**31** Most marsupials are **NOCTURNAL** animals. The rufous bettong (or rat kangaroo) usually wakes up after it gets dark.

**32** Opossums will sometimes **BLOW BUBBLES** when they are playing dead.

**33** A koala is only **AWAKE FOR ABOUT 4 HOURS** during the day.

**34** The **BOODIE**, which is about the size of a rabbit, is also known as the burrowing bettong. It lives in the desert and uses its burrow to stay cool.

**35** Paleontologists found a mouse-size marsupial in China that lived 125 million years ago, making it the **OLDEST MARSUPIAL FOSSIL** found so far.

**1.** Nature deficit disorder is a term for people who spend too much time indoors. **2.** Going outside in the natural light may help people heal faster after surgery. **3.** Researchers think spending time outside can improve distance vision in kids. **4.** Nishi Rokugo Park, a playground in Tokyo, Japan, has giant sculptures of Godzilla and a robot that are made out of old tires. **5.** You can explore a beached pirate ship and a castle at St. Kilda Adventure Playground in Australia. **6.** Stockholm, Sweden's Fruit and Scent Playground has banana-shaped slides, cherry swings, and a watermelon jungle gym. **7.** In 2011, 340,200 people set a world record by planting nearly 2 million trees across India in just 1 hour. **8.** Hyperion, the world's tallest tree, is located somewhere in Redwood National Park in California, U.S.A. Scientists won't reveal its exact location to protect it from tourists. **9.** Mexico's El Árbol del Tule, a Montezuma cypress, has the largest circumference (distance around) of any tree—119 feet (36 m). **10.** California's Grove of Titans, home to some of the largest redwood trees on Earth, wasn't discovered until 1998. **11.** The grove's Del Norte Titan has the most wood of any tree in the world. It has the same mass as 15 blue whales. **12.** The oldest living redwood trees are thought to be between 2,000 and 3,000 years old. **13.** Redwood trees get about 30 percent of their water supply from fog. **14.** Roosevelt elk, named for U.S. President Theodore Roosevelt, roam the West Coast's redwood and coastal forests. **15.** When Teddy Roosevelt was President, there were about 300,000 white-tailed deer in the United States. Now, there are 30 million.

# 100 WILD

## FACTS ABOUT

**16.** In 2011, 702 people in the United Kingdom set a world record for being the largest group of people hugging trees. **17.** In 2011, geographers, using new mapping technology, measured the many bays and inlets of Norway's coastline and added 11,000 miles (17,703 km) to the old total. **18.** American Indians used the tough leaves from California's Joshua trees to make baskets and sandals. **19.** Petrified Forest National Park in Arizona, U.S.A., isn't home to terrified trees. Instead, the logs scattered throughout the park have petrified, or turned to stone! **20.** A firenado is a tornado that's partially on fire because it has sucked up flammable gases and debris. **21.** The temperature inside a firenado can reach up to 2,000°F (1,093°C). **22.** In the United States alone, some 40 million people go camping every year. **23.** Some tents are now equipped with solar or electrical systems so that campers can charge a range of electronic devices. **24.** Glamorous camping, or "glamping," is a trend where campsites offer special amenities such as indoor bathrooms, heated pools, and free Wi-Fi. **25.** Visitors to New York City, U.S.A., can sleep in the AKA Central Park hotel's rooftop "outdoor room" for about $2,000 a night. **26.** Tiny Wilson Island, on Australia's Great Barrier Reef, can be rented out by glampers. It has 6 tents, all of which include hammocks, wood floors, and housekeeping service. **27.** The Human Nest, in Big Sur, California, is a bed made from woven wood suspended in the trees. **28.** A company in Belgium has built wooden shelters along waterways for campers traveling by canoe. **29.** At France's Maisons Bulles, guests spend the night in a nearly 10-foot (3-m)-tall transparent tent, or "bubble," complete with a carpeted floor and heat. **30.** Staying in Dream Domes in New Brunswick, Canada, might not feel like camping at all. The transparent domes have a kitchen, bathroom, and Japanese-style hot tub. **31.** The recipe for s'mores, a popular fireside snack, first appeared in a 1927 Girl Scout handbook. **32.** One out of every 10 people lives close enough to a volcano to be in a danger zone. **33.** In arborsculpture, people grow and shape trees to look like decorative or everyday objects. Some people have even grown living chairs! **34.** Chêne Chapelle is an ancient oak tree in France that's big enough to have 2 chapels built into it. **35.** Solar winter refers to the 3 darkest months of the year: November, December, and January in the Northern Hemisphere. **36.** You can see North America's autumn leaf colors from space. **37.** The word "fall" meaning the season didn't come into use until around 1500. **38.** Scientists think that microscopic gold particles discovered in the leaves and twigs of eucalyptus trees growing in Australia were sucked up from the soil by the roots. **39.** If you can hear thunder, you are within 10 miles (16 km) of a storm. **40.** Thirty people set a world record for largest outdoor BASE jump by skydiving from a tower in Moscow, Russia, in 2004. **41.** In 2009, 6 Australian bowlers set a world record for the longest outdoor bowling marathon: 170 hours and 3 minutes. **42.** The most seafood ever prepared for an outdoor event was 13,978.94 pounds (6,340.74 kg) of grilled sardines. **43.** The world's largest outdoor mural spans almost 2 miles (3 km) along the Arkansas River in Pueblo, Colorado, U.S.A. **44.** New York City's Central Park covers 843 acres (341 ha). It has 26 baseball fields, 30 tennis courts, 21 playgrounds, a carousel, and 2 ice rinks. **45.** After the holiday, Christmas trees in New York City are collected and chipped into mulch that is spread across Central Park and city flower beds. **46.** In 2010, a Christmas tree at the Emirates Palace in Abu Dhabi, United Arab Emirates, was decorated with jewelry worth over $11 million. **47.** Trees in a Japanese forest hold particles that scientists think reached Earth during a cosmic event more than 1,000 years ago. **48.** Nightshades are often thought of as very poisonous plants, but tomatoes, eggplants, and potatoes are all part of the nightshade family. **49.** The tallest sunflower stood more than 25 feet (8 m) high—that's taller than a giraffe! **50.** Magnolia trees have been used for over 5,000 years in traditional Chinese medicine. **51.** The Appalachian Trail (AT) stretches 2,180 miles (3,508 km) through 14 eastern U.S. states. **52.** Maryland and West Virginia contain the easiest sections of the AT, while New Hampshire and Maine have the hardest. **53.** The total elevation gain over the entire AT is equivalent to climbing Mount Everest 16 times. **54.** The Pacific Crest Trail runs from Mexico to Canada. **55.** When completed, the Continental Divide Trail will be the world's longest hiking trail, spanning over 3,100 miles (4,989 km) in North America's Rocky Mountains. **56.** There's an AT stop on New York City's Metro-North Railroad that lets people ride from Grand Central Station out into the forest and hit the trail. **57.** In 1955 at the age of 67, Emma Gatewood—nicknamed Grandma Gatewood—became the first woman to hike the entire AT alone. **58.** The oldest person ever to hike the entire AT was 81 years old. **59.** The Appenzell region of Switzerland is famous for its naked hikers. **60.** The Bibbulmun Track, a 600-mile (996-km) trail in Australia, was inspired by the Australian Aboriginal tradition of the walkabout, where people hike into the bush for months. **61.** Speed hiking requires light shoes, hydration backpacks, and a superfast pace of about 4 to 5 miles per hour (6–8 kph). **62.** Nepal's Great Himalaya Trail, which runs about 1,000 miles (1,609 km), has been speed hiked in less than 50 days. **63.** Out of respect for the 5 religions that consider it sacred, no one has ever climbed to the summit of Tibet's Mount Kailash. **64.** An American woman climbed California's 9,400-foot (2,865-m)-high Mount Baden-Powell on stilts. **65.** Visitors to America's Great Smoky Mountains National Park, on the Tennessee-North Carolina border, can enjoy more than 800 miles (1,280 km) of trails and 1,000 campsites. **66.** A book written in the 1800s described a monster tree from Central and South America that can eat humans! **67.** When touched, the leaves of a touch-me-not plant will fold and droop. Scientists still don't know how or

# THE GREAT OUTDOORS

why! **68.** The species name of the touch-me-not is *pudica*, Latin for "shy." **69.** The eastern skunk cabbage smells like its namesake animal. Flies drawn to the scent help pollinate the plant. **70.** Eastern skunk cabbages can generate heat that melts surrounding snow. **71.** Most of the *Hydnora africana* plant lives underground, but its aboveground flower smells like poop. **72.** Despite its stench, the flower of the *Hydnora africana* will develop into an edible fruit that reportedly tastes like potato. **73.** The corpse flower, named after its unfortunate smell, can take up to 6 years to bloom—thankfully! **74.** The black cat flower is maroon-black and has "whiskers" that can extend up to 28 inches (71 cm), nearly brushing the ground. **75.** São Paulo, Brazil, bans billboards and other outdoor advertising. **76.** A study found that people who grow up in rural places and spend time outside are less likely to develop allergies. **77.** The 206-year-old Congressional Cemetery in Washington, D.C., U.S.A., rented 58 goats to "mow" the lawn. **78.** A large, moving sand dune in Tunisia, Africa, is swallowing a movie set built to film planet Tatooine scenes in *Star Wars: The Phantom Menace*. **79.** The Poison Garden at Alnwick Castle, the setting for Hogwarts in the Harry Potter films, has over 100 toxic plants. **80.** In 2007, a man made a stone skip 51 times in a row on a body of water, setting a world record. **81.** During France's Lily of the Valley Festival people give bouquets of the flower to friends to wish them good health and happiness. **82.** At the Wilderness Awareness School, in Washington, U.S.A., classes include wolf tracking, survival, and bird calls. **83.** In 2009, a world record for the largest picnic was set by 22,232 people at a park in Lisbon, Portugal. **84.** The world's longest picnic table is over 320 feet (98 m) and was created by Hellmann's to celebrate the mayonnaise maker's 100th anniversary. **85.** The largest picnic blanket would cover 4 professional basketball courts. **86.** In standup paddleboard yoga, participants perform yoga atop wobbly platforms floating on water. **87.** Mountainboarding is similar to snowboarding only it's done on grass, dirt, or pavement—not snow—and the board is on wheels. **88.** The world's longest fishing rod measures more than 73 feet (22 m). That's longer than a humpback whale! **89.** A German man holds the world record for catching the most fish with 1 hand in 1 minute—38 salmon. **90.** At New Zealand's Hot Water Beach, where sand is heated by volcanic activity, people dig "hot springs" on the beach at low tide. **91.** The world's largest bird feeder holds 760 pounds (345 kg) of birdseed. **92.** It takes 12 hours to finish the world's longest zip line course in Georgia, U.S.A. The course has 135 lines and is over 7 miles (11 km) long. **93.** GORP, a nickname for trail mix, stands for "good old raisins and peanuts." **94.** In New Zealand, trail mix is called scroggin or schmogle. **95.** A Zipflbob is a special plastic sled that can be used on snow, grass, sand, and water. Its top speed is 86 miles per hour (139 kph). **96.** In one Ukrainian city, hundreds of students celebrate the new year by gathering together for an outdoor pillow fight. **97.** Croatia's Velebita Cave contains the longest straight-down drop. The 1,683-foot (513-m) shaft is longer than New York City's Empire State Building is tall. **98.** The longest continuous game of beach volleyball lasted 25 hours and 39 minutes. **99.** Scenic 1,119-foot (341-km) Honokohau Falls in Hawaii, U.S.A., was featured in the 1993 film *Jurassic Park*. **100.** Austria hosts the world's longest downhill ski race. So far, the fastest skier to complete the nearly 16-mile (26-km)-long race took just over 50 minutes.

**1**

The baby whose face has appeared on all **GERBER BABY** food jars since 1928 grew up to be mystery writer Ann Cook.

**2**

Every baby has a **BELLY BUTTON,** but only 10 percent have "OUTIES."

**3**

African-American, Asian, and Hispanic babies usually are born with **DARK EYES.** Caucasian babies have blue or gray eyes that can **CHANGE COLOR** several times before their first birthday.

**4**

The 2010 French film *Babies* **DOCUMENTED** the first year of life for **4 BABIES** from very different cultures around the world.

**5**

Nadya Suleman became famous as the mother of **OCTUPLETS** in 2008. That's like having 4 sets of twins at once!

**6**

At 5 weeks, a developing baby is only the size of a **PEN TIP.** At 6 weeks, its heart is beating.

**7**

**DANCING BABY** became an Internet sensation in 1996, as people watched a 3-D model of an infant move to the beat.

**8**

Ten years later, **LAUGHING BABY** was viewed by at least 109 million viewers. Even Britain's Queen Elizabeth II watched the real infant with the infectious giggle.

**9**

A **BABY ELEPHANT IS CALLED A CALF,** just like a baby cow.

**10**

**BABY CARROTS** are usually not really young carrots; they are carrots that have been trimmed down to their tiny size.

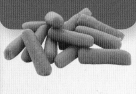

**11**

In 1962, the birth of Packy, the first elephant born in a U.S. zoo in 44 years, was celebrated with gifts of **GOLD-PLATED SAFETY PINS,** handmade clothing, and record crowds.

**12**

The disappearance of aviator **CHARLES LINDBERGH'S BABY** in 1932 is one of the most famous kidnapping cases of the 20th century.

**13**

According to legend, Rome was founded by twin baby boys named **ROMULUS** and **REMUS.**

**14**

Those two soft spots—called **FONTANELS**—on a baby's head allow the brain to grow during baby's first year.

**15**

More Americans watched the birth of **LITTLE RICKY** on the TV show *I Love Lucy* in 1953 than watched the Inauguration of President Eisenhower.

**16**

**NATIVE AMERICANS** often carried their babies on cradle boards strapped to the mother's back.

**17**

In 2013, Chinese artist Ai Weiwei created a map of China using **1,800 CANS** of baby formula to call attention to the problem of China's contaminated **BABY FORMULAS.**

**18**

Pop singer **JUSTIN BIEBER'S** song "Baby" hit the charts in 2010 and by 2013 had become the best-selling digital song ever released.

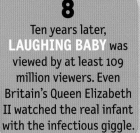

# 50

## ITTY-BITTY FACTS ABOUT BABIES

✱ YOU HAVE LEARNED **3,284** FACTS

**19**
A just-hatched **KIWI CHICK** weighs one-half of its mother's weight. That's like a 100-pound (45-kg) woman giving birth to a 50-pound (23-kg) baby!

**20**
New Zealand has a list of 77 unacceptable baby names, including—believe it or not—**TALULA DOES THE HULA FROM HAWAII!**

**21**
Germany, Sweden, Japan, and Iceland also have **RULES ABOUT BABY NAMES.**

**22**
Even though the top baby names change from year to year, **MARY** for girls and **MICHAEL** for boys have been the most popular over the last 100 years.

**23**
Human babies **CANNOT TASTE SALT** until they are 4 months old.

**24**
A baby will use almost **3,000 DIAPERS** on average in the first year.

**25**
Baby Jessica became famous when she was **RESCUED FROM A WELL** in Texas, U.S.A., after being trapped for 2½ days in 1987.

**26**
In Japan, it is traditional to eat *osekihan*—red rice with red beans—to **CELEBRATE THE BIRTH** of a baby.

**27**
A baby dog, a **BABY BAT,** a baby seal, a baby gerbil, and a baby shark can all be called pups.

**28**
While it normally takes 9 months for a human baby to develop and be born, **ELEPHANTS TAKE 22 MONTHS.** That's longer than any other mammal.

**29**
A baby's brain more than **DOUBLES IN SIZE** during the first year, making it about half its adult size.

**30**
Since ancient times, some babies have been delivered by **CESAREAN SECTION,** a surgical procedure possibly named after the Roman emperor Julius Caesar.

**31**
Albert Einstein, Charles Darwin, Pablo Picasso, and Pierre-Auguste Renoir were all **PREMATURE BABIES,** meaning they were born at least 3 weeks early.

**32**
In 2013, the public voted to name the baby panda born at the National Zoo in Washington, D.C., U.S.A., **BAO BAO,** which means "treasure" in Chinese.

**33**
Even though **POLAR BEARS** are one of the largest carnivores in the world, a baby weighs only about **2 POUNDS** (0.9 kg) at birth.

**34**
The only primates known to **SMILE** at their parents are human babies.

**35**
Just like a human baby, a baby monkey is called an **INFANT.**

**36**
Every year, nearly 500,000 **PREMATURE BABIES** are born in the United States.

**37**
A **NEWBORN HUMAN'S EYES** are roughly 75 percent the size they eventually will be as an adult.

**38**
**EVERY 3 SECONDS** a baby is born somewhere in the world.

**39**
A **BABY'S HEAD** weighs about one-quarter of its total weight.

**40**
In ancient Rome, an olive branch was hung on the door as a sign that a **BABY BOY** had been born.

**41**
A woman in Russia gave birth to **69 BABIES** between 1725 and 1765. Her children included 16 sets of twins, 7 sets of triplets and 4 sets of quadruplets.

**42**
Former president Bill Clinton, Jesse Jackson, and Daunte Culpepper were **ALL ADOPTED AS BABIES.**

**43**
Just 3 days after giving birth, a mother can **PICK OUT HER BABY'S CRY** from a roomful of other crying babies.

**44**
A 2-day-old human baby can recognize his or her **MOTHER'S VOICE** from a recording of just one syllable spoken by her.

**45**
A baby giraffe is about **6 FEET** (1.8 m) tall when it is born.

**46**
A natural response called the **DIVE REFLEX** causes babies to hold their breath and open their eyes when they go underwater.

**47**
About **80 PERCENT** of babies are born with a **BIRTHMARK.**

**48**
Babies aren't born with **KNEECAPS.**

**49**
A baby bird is often called a chick, but a baby peacock is called a **PEACHICK.**

**50**
A human baby is more likely to **TURN ITS HEAD TO THE RIGHT** than to the left when it hears a sound.

**1**

**BEEF TONGUE** is a popular flavor of ice cream in Tokyo, Japan.

**2**

For hundreds of years, people in the parts of Asia, Europe, and Africa that made up the Ottoman Empire have enjoyed salep—a hot drink of sweetened ground orchid root.

**4**

**Oreo cookies** TASTE—AND LOOK—DIFFERENT AROUND THE GLOBE. IN INDONESIA, SOME ARE FLAVORED LIKE **blueberry ice cream.** IN ARGENTINA, OREOS "x 3" HAVE **3 cookies and 2 layers of filling.**

**3**

During Roman times, people ate dormice—as appetizers and for dessert!

**5**

In the Czech Republic, you can buy **CHOCOLATE** in the shape of **KITTEN TONGUES!**

# 25 ZANY FACTS ABOUT WEIRD

**6**

**THE ICE-CREAM CHEESEBURGER,** served at the state fair in Florida, U.S.A., has a scoop of fried ice cream for one of its layers.

**7**

Civet coffee is made from coffee beans that have been eaten by the catlike civet of Southeast Asia and **picked out of its droppings!**

**8**

Rocket Fizz Soda Pop offers up soda flavors ranging from peanut butter and jelly to buffalo wings to bacon!

**9**

Silkworm larvae are steamed or boiled and sold at street markets in South Korea. In China and Vietnam, they're fried.

**10**

YOU CAN BUY A **PANCAKE-AND-BACON-** FLAVORED CUPCAKE AT A BAKERY IN SEATTLE, WASHINGTON, U.S.A.

**11** In Singapore, people order sweet corn–flavored ice-cream sandwiches.

**12** A restaurant in Japan sells the Napoli Panda Burger: **A HAMBURGER PILED WITH SPAGHETTI AND SAUCE.** Two panda bear faces are stamped on the top bun.

**13** **BIRD'S NEST SOUP,** a Chinese delicacy, is made with a swiftlet's nest floating in broth. Swiftlets make their nests entirely out of sticky saliva.

**15** Bananas, curry, and mashed potatoes are all **TOPPINGS** served on pizza in Sweden.

**14** THE "FAT ELVIS ON-A-STICK" IS A DEEP-FRIED, BANANA-BATTERED PEANUT BUTTER CUP WITH BACON.

**16** **TUNA EYEBALLS** are served up with garlic and soy sauce in Japan.

**17** You can find "Sunday Best Roast Chicken" and "Chilli & Chocolate" **POTATO CHIPS** in Great Britain.

**18** Chocolate and strawberry are **TASTY TWISTS ON PLAIN MILK,** but the latest milk flavor to hit U.S. grocery store shelves is root beer.

**19** You can buy jam infused with sand from the Great Pyramid at Giza, Egypt.

# FOOD

**20** Fairgoers in Arizona, U.S.A., can buy caramel apples dipped in **MEALWORMS!**

**21** At a restaurant in Taiwan, food is **SERVED IN MINI-TOILETS.**

**22** You can order **FRIED WILD EEL SPINE** at a restaurant in New York City, U.S.A.

**25** Fried Kool-Aid balls— MADE WITH A DEEP-FRIED COMBO OF FLOUR, WATER, AND KOOL-AID MIX—ARE SOLD AT SOME U.S. COUNTY FAIRS.

**23** WASABI-INFUSED **KIT-KAT** CANDY BARS ARE SOLD IN JAPAN.

**24** IF YOU THINK YOU'VE TRIED EVERY KIND OF POPSICLE, THINK AGAIN: YOU CAN BUY A **pickle-flavored** ONE IN THE UNITED STATES!

# 15 BLACK -AND- WHITE

❶ You can watch pandas **24 HOURS A DAY** on the Smithsonian's National Zoo "Giant Panda Cam."

❷ Pandas **EAT SITTING UP,** not standing on all fours.

❸ For his 22nd birthday, a panda at the San Diego Zoo in California, U.S.A., was **GIVEN A 215-POUND (98-KG) CAKE** made of ice, bamboo, apples, and yams.

❹ Pandas **BARK** to scare away an enemy.

❺ **PANDAS CAN SWIM!** To escape predators, they jump in the water and paddle.

❻ Unlike other bears, pandas have evolved a **LARGE WRIST BONE** that looks like a thumb to help them hold on to bamboo.

❼ **PANDAS DON'T HIBERNATE.** In the wild, they travel to lower elevations where it is warmer in winter.

❽ *Daxiongmao*— the Chinese word for "panda"—means **"LARGE BEAR-CAT."**

# FACTS ABOUT PANDAS

**9** Male pandas do a **HANDSTAND WHILE PEEING** to mark trees.

**10** **ALL WILD PANDAS LIVE IN CHINA.** Those that live in zoos around the world belong to China—they are just on loan.

**11** A few pandas **ARE BROWN AND WHITE**—but they're very rare.

**12** To keep pandas at a nature reserve in China from getting used to humans, scientists **DRESS UP LIKE PANDAS.** This helps the cubs survive when they're released into the wild.

**13** You can eat a **SUSHI ROLL THAT LOOKS LIKE A PANDA!**

**14** To show how few wild pandas there are on Earth, a conservation organization displayed **1,600 PAPIER-MÂCHÉ PANDAS IN PARIS,** France.

**15** It is Chinese tradition to wait to name a panda cub until it is **100 DAYS OLD.**

**1** George Eastman, founder of the Eastman Kodak Company, came up with the name Kodak out of the blue because he liked the letter *k*.

**2** Eastman created the Kodak camera and the rolls of film it used.

**3** Eastman worked with Thomas Edison to make the first moving pictures.

**4** IT TOOK SO LONG TO MAKE A PHOTOGRAPH ON COPPER PLATES DURING VICTORIAN TIMES THAT MOTHERS SOMETIMES WERE DISGUISED AS CHAIRS TO HOLD THEIR CHILDREN STILL FOR THEIR PORTRAITS.

**5** A camera was invented in the 1940s that could photograph nuclear bombs milliseconds after they were detonated.

**6** Today, we take as many pictures every 2 minutes as were taken in the entire 1800s.

**7** A rare 1923 Leica camera sold for $2.8 million at auction in 2012.

**8** Astronauts had to leave 12 expensive Hasselblad cameras on the moon so that they had room to carry more lunar rocks back to Earth.

**9** Funny pictures of cats didn't originate on the Internet. During the 1870s, Harry Pointer became the first photographer to capture cats in ridiculous poses.

**10** The word "photography" is derived from the Greek words *photos*, meaning "light," and *graphien*, meaning "to draw."

**11** In the 1830s, French artist and inventor Hercules Florence was the first to use the word "photography" for the process of making pictures.

**12** The first Kodak camera cost $1.

**13** The first digital camera cost $10,000.

**14** In the mid-1820s, a specially treated pewter plate was exposed to light for over 8 hours to make "View from the Window at Le Gras"—the world's first snapshot.

**15** The British physicist James Maxwell is credited with creating the first color photo in 1861.

**16** Dilish Parekh of India has the largest collection of antique cameras—4,425 specimens!

**17** Louis Daguerre created the daguerreotype—a photograph produced directly on a silver-coated sheet of copper—by accident in 1835.

**18** Smiling faces weren't common in photographs until about 1920. That's when people started taking their own pictures of friends and family.

**19** Before color photography, photos were hand-tinted with watercolors.

**20** Early 20th-century Italian photographers rode to work on bicycles loaded down with all their equipment.

**21** On his first wilderness trip in 1920, Ansel Adams carried 30 pounds (14 kg) of photographic equipment; his burro, Mistletoe, hauled almost another 100 pounds (45 kg).

**22** In 2013, it took photographers 3 days to shoot a 360-degree view of London, England. If printed out, the photo would almost cover the front of Buckingham Palace.

**23** IN 1920, 2 GIRLS TOOK PHOTOGRAPHS THAT THEY CLAIMED PROVED FAIRIES EXISTED. IT WAS LATER REVEALED THAT THE SO-CALLED COTTINGLEY FAIRIES WERE PAPER CUTOUTS.

**24** Dorothea Lange's powerful 1936 photo "Migrant Mother" helped show the American public the plight of Depression-era farm workers.

**25** President Franklin Roosevelt believed that seeing photos of dead U.S. soldiers would strengthen Americans' determination to win World War II, so he lifted the ban on their publication. It worked.

**26** About 20 percent of all photos taken end up on Facebook.

**27** Facebook contains 100,000 times the number of photos in the collection of the Library of Congress.

**28** In 1855, Roger Fenton became the world's first war photographer, during the Crimean War in Europe.

**29** Dr. Edwin Land invented a 1-step process for developing film. In 1948, his Polaroid camera went on sale.

**30** Photographer Alfred Stieglitz encouraged the growth of modern art in America by showcasing the works of Picasso, O'Keeffe, and other newcomers in his gallery in the early 1900s.

**31** Some artists search out vintage Polaroid cameras and alter images on the film using a variety of techniques.

**32** William Wegman, famous for his photographs of his dog Man Ray, has created film segments for *Saturday Night Live* and *Sesame Street*.

**33** THE RED-EYE EFFECT IN PHOTOS IS STRONGER IN BLUE-EYED PEOPLE THAN IN THOSE WITH BROWN EYES BECAUSE BLUE EYES ABSORB LESS LIGHT.

**34** The first webcam, developed in 1994, is still transmitting photos of fog at San Francisco State University in California, U.S.A.

**35** For 3 weeks in 2013, photographers camped outside a London hospital to get the first photos of the newest heir to Britain's throne.

**36** Paparazzi, photographers who aggressively pursue celebrities, are named after a character in the Italian movie *La Dolce Vita*.

**37** In 2008, more than 20,000 photographers took part in photographing a week in the United States for Rick Smolan's America at Home project.

**38** Rick Smolan was the founder of Day in the Life, a photo book phenomenon that captured life around the world in the 1980s.

**39** The Hubble Space Telescope took its one-millionth observation in 2011. Each is a snapshot of the sky in a particular wavelength.

**40** When Kodak stopped making its iconic Kodachrome film in 2009, National Geographic photographer Steve McCurry was given the historic last roll to shoot.

**41** The last frame of McCurry's Kodachrome roll was of a cemetery statue with yellow and red flowers, symbolic of the colors on the Kodachrome film box.

**42** Platinum prints, known as platinotypes, have the greatest range of tones in black-and-white photographs and are a favorite among collectors.

**43** According to one study, the most photographed city in the world is New York City. The most photographed building there is the Empire State Building.

**44** Edward Steichen's photos of evening gowns for a 1911 magazine are considered the first fashion photography shoot.

**45** Seventeen years after Steve McCurry took his now famous photo of a 12-year-old Afghan refugee, he was finally able to track her down and learn her name.

**46** Annie Leibovitz's famous *Rolling Stone* cover photo of John Lennon and Yoko Ono was taken just hours before Lennon was shot and killed.

**47** The Wright brothers used photography to record their scientific experiments with flight.

**48** A photo of Venus the cat may look like a terrible Photoshop job, but it's not. The cat's face really is half black and half orange, and each eye is a different color.

**49** THE 2013 OXFORD DICTIONARIES WORD OF THE YEAR WAS "SELFIE," A SELF-PORTRAIT TAKEN WITH A SMARTPHONE OR WEBCAM THAT CAN BE UPLOADED ONTO SOCIAL MEDIA.

**50** The Blue Earth Alliance uses photography to raise awareness about the environment, endangered cultures, and social concerns.

**51** During the 1989 Tiananmen Square showdown in China, photographer Jeff Widener took a picture of a demonstrator standing in front of a line of tanks. Widener paid a stranger to smuggle the film out of the country so it could be published.

**52** *Time* magazine later listed the man in Widener's photograph, "Unknown Rebel," as one of the 100 most important people of the 20th century.

**53** A study shows that photographs of the left side of the human face are more pleasing to look at—possibly because the left side shows more emotion than the right.

**54** A photography contest for kids sponsored by National Geographic in 2011 drew 12,000 photographs from around the world.

**55** Pinhole cameras—devices that use a tiny hole to let light expose the film—can be made from almost any container.

**56** David Urbanke picked up his first camera around the age of 12. By age 16, he was a professional fashion photographer!

**57** Taking pictures is restricted in museums for fear it could damage light-sensitive art or cause copyright issues.

**58** PIGEONS CARRYING TINY CAMERAS SNAPPED PHOTOGRAPHS DURING WWI AS THEY FLEW ABOVE ENEMY TROOPS.

**59** The first photograph that includes a person was taken in 1838. It shows a Paris street scene with a man getting his shoes shined.

**60** In 2013, Instagram had 150 million users sharing 16 billion photos and posting 1 billion likes every day.

**61** DSLR stands for digital single-lens reflex camera.

**62** The first cell phones with cameras became available in 2002. Since then, they have become so powerful they can rival a DSLR for clarity.

**63** Joel Sartore's Photo Ark documents plant and animal species threatened with extinction. More than 2,800 species have been photographed over a period of 8 years.

**64** It is estimated that only 2 out of every 10 photographs taken are ever printed on paper.

**65** You don't have to carry a bunch of fancy camera lenses to take great photographs. Multi-award-winning photographer Jay Maisel is known for using just 1 lens and taking simple photos.

**66** NEARLY 1 MILLION PHOTOS OF HURRICANE SANDY TAKEN WITH CELL PHONES WERE UPLOADED TO INSTAGRAM USING #SANDY.

**67** A 1933 photograph supposedly of the Loch Ness Monster was proved to be a hoax in 1984, but it was not until 1994 that the "monster" in the photo was revealed to be a toy submarine with a sea-serpent head.

**68** Photographer Daniel Seung Lee and art director Dawn Kim created Crayola Theory, a series of photos that depicts the crayons' color names.

**69** The 1858 Exhibition of the Photographic Society of London, in England, was the first of its kind in a museum. More than 1,000 photos were displayed.

**70** The first aerial photograph was shot from a hot-air balloon over Paris in 1858.

**71** Auguste and Louis Lumière are credited with inventing the first motion picture camera in 1895.

**72** Paul Simon released "Kodachrome"—his song about the iconic film—in 1973.

**73** Photoshop, a computer program first released in 1990, has revolutionized photography by making it possible to alter a photograph on a computer instead of in a darkroom.

**74** Edward Steichen's 1904 photograph "The Pond-Moonlight" sold for close to $3 million in 2006, making it one of the world's most expensive photographs.

**75** Features like autofocus make point-and-shoot cameras easy to use. All you have to do is aim and push the button.

# 75 PICTURE-PERFECT
## FACTS ABOUT PHOTOGRAPHY

**1**
Montreal's Underground City, which **STRETCHES FOR 20 MILES** (32 km), has shopping malls, banks, hotels, movie theaters, offices—even a cathedral—up to 4 floors deep.

**2**
To build an underground, earthquake-proof highway in Seattle, Washington, U.S.A., an $80,000,000 tunnel-boring machine named **BIG BERTHA** is being used.

**3**
A group of 33 miners survived being trapped 2,257 feet (688 m) below-ground in a mine in Chile for **69 DAYS.**

**4**
Paintings of birds and mountain sheep still decorate the cliff dwellings carved into canyon walls **700 YEARS AGO** by ancestors of today's Pueblo people in Mesa Verde, Colorado, U.S.A.

**5**
Agonizer, a heavy metal band from Finland, once held a concert for a small audience in a **MINE ALMOST A MILE (1.6 KM) BELOW SEA LEVEL.**

**6**
Japanese researchers seeking extreme life-forms have **DRILLED A HOLE IN THE PACIFIC OCEAN** floor that's at least 2,000 feet (610 m) deeper than the Grand Canyon, U.S.A.

**7**
**PAINTINGS OF ANIMALS** and human hands on the walls of Altimira Cave in Spain date back 25,000 to 35,000 years.

**8**
Buddhist-style paintings dating back more than 1,000 years can be seen in the Mogao Grottoes, a network of **492 CAVES** carved into the cliffs above China's Dachuan River.

**9**
Pink-, peach-, and rose-colored stalagmites and stalactites **GROW BY THE HUNDREDS** from the ground and ceilings of the Caverns of Sonora in Texas, U.S.A.

**10**
The oldest known water on Earth—some **2.6 BILLION YEARS OLD**—has been found 2 miles (3 km) below Earth's surface in a mine in Ontario, Canada.

**11**
An **UNDERGROUND MANSION** in Los Angeles, California, U.S.A., features 9 bedrooms, 25 bathrooms, an indoor pool, and a tennis court—on 5 subterranean levels.

**12**
Up to **7 MILLION ANTS** can live in just 1 of this insect's vast underground colonies.

**13**
A trapdoor leads to an underground village in Vietnam. A **SECRET HIDEOUT** during the war, it includes a hospital and sleeping chambers, all connected by tunnels.

**14**
More than a million people a year check out the **WIELICZKA SALT MINE** in Kraków, Poland, which has underground chapels, statues, and even chandeliers, all sculpted from salt.

**15**
**IBERIAN FROGS** are the only known kind of frog that can spend their entire lives underground in cavelike chambers.

**16**
During the cold war, which lasted from 1945 to 1990, the U.S. government built a **TOP-SECRET BUNKER** beneath the Greenbrier Hotel in West Virginia, U.S.A.

**17**
A man recently uncovered **ICE AGE BONES** belonging to bears, bison, snakes, and other prehistoric animals in a cave in Indiana, U.S.A.

**18**
Researchers have discovered animal burrows in South Africa that date back **250 MILLION YEARS**—that's before dinosaurs walked on Earth.

**19**
The Great Pyramid of Giza would fit inside Oman's Majlis al Jinn — **THE SECOND LARGEST CAVE CHAMBER** in the world.

**20**
The world's largest cave, located in a remote Vietnamese jungle, is as high as **25 DOUBLE-DECKER BUSES**. It's so big that it holds an entire forest.

# DIGGING UP 35 FACTS ABOUT LIFE UNDERGROUND

**21** There are close to **400 LAKES UNDER THE ICE** in Antarctica, including one with an area nearly as big as North America's Lake Ontario.

**22** A massive body of water the size of the Arctic Ocean lies **LOCKED IN LAYERS OF ROCK** hundreds of miles (km) beneath eastern Asia.

**23** **MEERKAT** burrows, which serve as homes for 20 to 30 animals on average, may have 90 entrances and be over 6 feet (2 m) deep.

**24** A **2,000-YEAR-OLD, HUMAN-MADE CAVE** in Israel—believed to have served as a quarry, then possibly as a monastery or a Roman army base—is almost as big as a football field.

**25** Flashlight tours of **SLAUGHTER CANYON CAVE** in Carlsbad Caverns National Park in New Mexico, U.S.A., reveal formations like Christmas Tree, a crystal-covered column.

**26** A 95-mile (153-km)-long river flowing through a cave in Mexico is believed to be the **WORLD'S LONGEST UNDERGROUND RIVER.**

**27** For about $600, you can **SPEND THE NIGHT 509 FEET (155 M) BELOW-GROUND** in a luxury hotel room that is accessible only through a mine shaft elevator.

**28** It takes a total of 2 hours for trucks to go in and out of a 1,722-foot (525-m)-deep **DIAMOND MINE IN SIBERIA**— one of the world's deepest man-made holes.

**29** **GIANT CRYSTALS AS LONG AS A SCHOOL BUS** can be found 1,000 feet (305 m) underground in Mexico's Cave of the Crystals.

**30** The floor of the Ice Caves in New Mexico is covered by a 20-foot (6-m)-thick layer of ice, which **GLOWS GREEN** from the algae growing beneath it.

**31** Parts of the 365 miles (587 km) of caverns in Mammoth Cave in Kentucky, U.S.A., started forming more than **10 MILLION YEARS AGO** as streams began carving out the limestone.

**32** Thirty-five hundred Australians **LIVE IN UNDERGROUND HOMES** in the town of Coober Pedy, which features subterranean shops, churches, and hotels.

**33** Rabbits live in a **NETWORK OF BURROWS** called a warren that can stretch for thousands of feet (m) underground.

**34** **FOUR-THOUSAND-YEAR-OLD EARS OF POPCORN** have been found in a cave in New Mexico.

**35** The **DEEPEST-LIVING ANIMALS** yet discovered are roundworms that live 0.8 miles (1.3 km) beneath Earth's crust.

Climber scaling the
Great Wall of Vietnam

1. Unlike wars, which can last for years and are made up of many battles, battles usually last a few hours or a few days. 2. Some battles stretch on for months. The Battle of Verdun lasted over 9 months during World War I. 3. During the American Revolution, the Battle of Moore's Creek Bridge, fought between North Carolina Patriots and Loyalists—people who supported Great Britain—lasted just 3 minutes. 4. Battles are fought on land, in the air, at sea, and even in cyberspace. 5. When no one wins a battle, it's known as a stalemate. 6. Ten-thousand-year-old cave paintings in Spain show men fighting with bows and arrows. 7. A battle that took place around 5,500 years ago is the first in recorded history. The fighting centered on the ancient city of Hamoukar in what is now Syria. 8. Roman soldiers used a defense tactic called *testudo* (meaning "tortoise"), where they'd lock their shields together over their heads for protection and inch slowly toward the enemy. 9. The first known use of bronze weapons was in 1600 B.C. in Greece and Sweden. 10. At the Battle of Cajamarca in 1532, 80,000 Inca armed with bows were defeated by 168 armored Spaniards with guns and riding horses. 11. Ancient Egyptian soldiers drove war chariots—2-wheeled, bucket-like vehicles pulled by galloping horses. 12. Some historians credit the Egyptian war chariot with revolutionizing the way battles were fought. 13. Soldiers drove chariots through enemy lines, scattering the troops before the main Egyptian force attacked. 14. Around 1300 B.C., the largest chariot battle in history took place between the Egyptians and Hittites. Some 5,000 chariots carrying 30,000 troops fought at the Battle of Kadesh. 15. Roman troops often traveled in legions—groups of 5,000 soldiers. 16. Highly trained Roman legions, wearing strong armor and using sharp, metal weapons, were undefeated for 500 years. 17. The first known battle at sea saw the Hittites, who controlled what is now Turkey, defeat a fleet from the Mediterranean island of Cyprus in 1210 B.C. 18. In ancient Rome, soldiers who refused a command were often beaten, stoned, or beheaded. If a soldier left his post, his fellow soldiers could pummel him to death. 19. In ancient Rome, a red flag was a signal for battle to begin. 20. During the Battle of Marathon in 490 B.C., the Greeks surprised the Persians by charging, rather than marching, toward them. 21. According to legend, a Greek soldier named Pheidippides ran 26 miles (42 km) nonstop from Marathon to Athens to share news of the victory before dying of exhaustion. 22. The modern 26-mile (42-km) marathon race honors this epic run. 23. For protection, Greek soldiers carried shields made of wood and wore metal helmets and leg guards. 24. Crests—usually made of horsehair—were placed on Greek soldiers' helmets to make them look taller and fiercer. 25. In 480 B.C., more than 1,000 ships were used by both the Greeks and the Persians in the Battle of Salamis, the first great naval battle in recorded history. 26. Spartan soldiers—the warriors of the ancient Greek city of Sparta—began training for battle at the age of 7. 27. By the time Spartan boys turned 12, they were deprived of all clothes except for a cloak and forced to sleep outside to ready themselves for life on the battlefield. 28. Spartans wore red so bloodstains from wounds would not show. 29. Instead of wearing metal armor, some soldiers in ancient Greece wore body armor made from layers of linen glued together to make a stiff shirt. 30. After a victory, some Greek warriors thanked the gods by hanging their armor in trees near the battlefield. 31. Greek soldiers marched into battle to the sound of flutes. 32. Between battles, Greek soldiers snacked on barley, cheese, salted meat, and onions. 33. Some soldiers in ancient Greece carried spears that were over 19 feet (6 m) long. That's longer than some streetlights are tall! 34. Victorious Celtic warriors—soldiers considered barbaric by the ancient Greeks and Romans—would chop off the heads of their enemies and take them home. 35. The bows of Roman ships were equipped with sharp points called rams designed to smash holes in enemy boats. 36. Roman ships had triangular sails that gave them greater speed and mobility in battle

# 100 FIGHTING

than square sails. 37. Roman battleships called triremes were powered by oars as well as sails. Some had as many as 170 rowers, 1 for each oar. 38. During ancient and medieval sea battles, sailors launched pots of burning oil at enemy ships. 39. In the 14th century, catapults—giant slingshot-like weapons—were used to fling boulders at castle walls. 40. The first use of cannons in battle is believed to have been by English troops in 1346, during the Hundred Years' War. 41. A cannon commissioned by a 15th-century Turkish sultan was said to be 27 feet (8 m) long and able to hurl a giant stone ball 1 mile (1.6 km). 42. These early cannons were so powerful that they often killed the soldier who fired them. 43. Napoleon Bonaparte, the emperor of France, was the first to divide calvaries—troops on horseback—into heavy and light units. 44. The heavy cavalry would smash through the enemy's front line, while the light cavalry performed scouting and patrolling duties. 45. Some elite members of Napoleon's heavy cavalry were required to ride on all-black horses. 46. The last king to be killed in battle in Britain was James IV of Scotland at the Battle of Flodden, 500 years ago. 47. The Hundred Years' War between France and England actually lasted 116 years—from 1337 until 1453. 48. In the Revolutionary War, Americans sometimes called British soldiers redcoats because they wore red uniforms into battle. 49. The "minutemen" soldiers of the American Revolution got their name from the fact that they were ready to fight at a minute's notice. 50. Food became so scarce for some American soldiers during the Revolution that they ate the leather from their own boots. 51. Starving American troops boiled lichen, an algae-like growth found on rocks, to make a soup they called rock tripe. 52. For her work attending to the wounded during the U.S. Civil War, Dr. Mary Edwards Walker was awarded the Medal of Honor. She is the only woman ever to receive it. 53. Some 570 tons (517 MT) of ammunition were fired during the 3-day Battle of Gettysburg during the U.S. Civil War. 54. As part of the 150th anniversary of the Civil War, over 12,000 "soldiers" and 400 horses gathered in Gettysburg, Pennsylvania, in 2013 to reenact the famous battles fought there. **55.** The U.S. Civil War, which lasted from 1861 to 1865, cost about $6.7 billion in 1860 money— nearly $25 trillion in today's dollars. **56.** On September 17, 1862, over 23,000 soldiers died or were injured in the Battle of Antietam, making it one of the bloodiest days in American history. **57.** All told, more than 620,000 people died in the U.S. Civil War. **58.** During the Civil War, the monthly pay for a white Union soldier was $13. Black Union soldiers were paid $7. **59.** The oldest soldier to fight in the Civil War was 80 years old. **60.** In 1884, the Maxim gun—the first automatic weapon—was invented. It could fire 600 rounds per minute. **61.** In the Battle of Little Bighorn, fought in 1876 in what is now Montana, U.S.A., Native Americans fought against the U.S. Army to keep whites from settling on their sacred lands. **62.** The 1876 battle is also known as Custer's Last Stand because George Armstrong Custer led the U.S. charge in which he and all the men under his direct command were killed. **63.** The battle, which lasted under an hour, is considered the most decisive Native American victory and the worst U.S. Army defeat in the decades-long Plains Wars. **64.** The U.S. Army took its revenge in 1890 when it massacred 200 Sioux at the Battle of Wounded Knee—the last battle in the Indian wars. **65.** Great Britain was the first to use the tank in battle—in 1916 during World War I. **66.** Trench warfare—fighting from inside giant ditches in the ground—was introduced during World War I. Before that, soldiers battled each other in open fields. **67.** Soldiers dug long and deep trenches in the ground to shield themselves against flying bullets. **68.** The battlefields of Europe were scarred with 12,000 miles (19,312 km) of trenches. **69.** In the trenches, rats said to be the size of cats were known to gnaw at the bodies of soldiers—living and dead. **70.** World War II lasted from 1939 to 1945, with battles fought in Europe, North Africa, Asia, and in the Atlantic and Pacific Oceans. **71.** During some of the desert battles in North Africa, German troops camouflaged their tanks with sand and thorny shrubs and plants. **72.** In 1943, over 6,000 tanks were involved when the Germans and Soviets (Russians) fought at the Battle of Kursk, making it the largest tank battle in history. **73.** With nearly 2 million casualties, the 7-month-long Battle of Stalingrad—fought between the Soviet Union (now Russia) and Germany—is among the bloodiest battles in history. **74.** By eating rats and drinking soup made from wallpaper glue, Soviet soldiers managed not only to survive the harsh Stalingrad winter but also to force the starving Germans to surrender. **75.** The Battle of the Coral Sea, fought between the Japanese Navy and U.S. and Australian naval and air forces during World War II, was the first air-sea battle in history. **76.** During World War II, battles fought on land or sea in the Pacific Ocean were said to take place in the Pacific Theater. **77.** During the Battle of Leyte Gulf in 1944, Japan deployed kamikazes—suicide bombers—against American ships for the first time. **78.** All told, kamikaze attacks on U.S. ships during World War II sank 34, damaged hundreds of others, and killed almost 5,000 sailors. **79.** In one of the hardest fought battles of World War II, U.S. Marines captured the Pacific island of Iwo Jima from the Japanese in 1945. **80.** The famous photo of Marines raising the American flag on Iwo Jima inspired the Marine Corps War Memorial near Washington, D.C., U.S.A. **81.** The mass destruction caused by the atomic bombs dropped on the cities of Hiroshima and Nagasaki by the United States forced Japan to surrender in 1945, ending World War II. **82.** Many battles in World War II were decided by speedy fighter planes, outfitted with machine guns as well as torpedoes or

# BATTLES

bombs. **83.** Pilots and crew often painted pictures or messages on their planes. **84.** The Battle of Britain, when the German Luftwaffe (air force) bombed England for several months in 1940, is the only battle ever fought entirely in the air. **85.** The air attacks failed to get Britain to surrender. They cost Germany nearly 2,000 aircraft compared with about 1,000 for Britain. **86.** During the Vietnam War, U.S. soldiers fought battles with a tactic called hit and run that relied on helicopters to enter enemy territory, attack, and then take off quickly. **87.** The first laser-guided bomb was used in battle during the Vietnam War in 1968. **88.** Using lasers to guide bombs to their targets made the bombs more than 100 times more accurate and effective. **89.** Drones—unmanned, remotely operated planes—are the latest weapon in aerial defense. **90.** The first known U.S. use of a drone was in 2004 over Pakistan. **91.** In 2007, the U.S. Army deployed 3 robots armed with machine guns into Iraq—the first time robots carried guns into battle. **92.** At more than 20,000 feet (6,100 m), the Siachen Glacier, a disputed region in the Himalaya between India and Pakistan, is considered the world's highest battlefield. **93.** The first use of poisonous gas as a weapon was at the Second Battle of Ypres, Belgium, in 1915 during World War I. **94.** German forces shocked enemy soldiers by unleashing more than 150 tons (136 MT) of lethal chlorine gas in the Belgian town. **95.** Chemical weapons are still being used in modern battles, even though they are banned under international law. **96.** During a 2009 Battle of the Bands event in Buenos Aires, Argentina, 439 bands set a world record by playing nonstop for 160 hours and 35 minutes. **97.** Mechanical horses weighing 200 pounds (90 kg) were used to film the epic battle scene in the 1995 movie *Braveheart*. **98.** In 1968, the U.S.S. *New Jersey* had the top speed ever recorded for a battleship: 35.2 knots (65.2 kph). **99.** It took almost a year to construct the set and then film the Battle of Helm's Deep in *Lord of the Rings: The Two Towers*. **100.** Today's soldiers can prepare for missions virtually by using simulated battlefields, vehicles, and aircraft.

# LISTEN UP!

# 50 FACTS ABOUT SOUND

**1**
Sound is a **FORM OF ENERGY** made from air molecule vibrations. It moves in a pattern called a **SOUND WAVE.**

**2**
Sound waves that vibrate slowly produce **LOW SOUNDS;** those that move fast create **HIGH SOUNDS.**

**3**
Most people can **HEAR SOUND WAVES** that vibrate between 20 and 20,000 times a second.

**4**
Hearing is the **FASTEST HUMAN SENSE.** A person can recognize a sound in as little as 0.05 seconds.

**5**
Scientists think our speedy hearing developed from **PREHISTORIC ANCESTORS** who had to recognize predator sounds quickly in the dark.

**6**
Sounds surround us all the time. So humans have developed a **"VOLUME CONTROL" SYSTEM** that allows us to ignore unimportant sounds.

**7**
Lasers, typically made of light, can be made from sound waves, too. Initially called **SASERS,** they are now popularly known as **PHASERS.**

**8**
Scientists hope phasers can one day be used to replace the **QUARTZ CRYSTALS** that power clocks in many electronic devices. Phasers require **LESS ENERGY.**

**9**
The first movie with an **OFFICIAL SOUND TRACK** was Disney's *Snow White and the Seven Dwarfs,* made in 1937.

**10**
The speed of sound at sea level is 761 miles per hour (1,225 kph). Traveling faster than the speed of sound is called **BREAKING THE SOUND BARRIER.**

**11**
The Bell X-1 plane that **CHUCK YEAGER** flew to break the sound barrier in 1947 hangs in the National Air and Space Museum in Washington, D.C., U.S.A.

**12**
In 1997, **ANDY GREEN** drove 768 miles per hour (1,236 kph) to become the first person to travel faster than the speed of sound on land.

**13**
There's a **SOUND CAMERA** that uses 30 digital microphones to show where sound, like rattling in a car, is coming from.

**14**
A **FOLEY ARTIST** is someone who adds sound effects to movies.

**15**
**THUNDER** is caused by air expanding very quickly around a lightning bolt.

**16**
**ELEPHANTS SING** to each other, but you can't hear their songs. They're sung too low for the human ear to hear.

**17**
Scientists think if we could hear a **STAR EXPLODING** it would sound like 10 octillion (1 followed by 27 zeroes) 2-megaton nuclear bombs going off at once.

**18**
When **FELIX BAUMGARTNER** set a world record for skydiving in 2012, he broke the sound barrier, reaching a speed of 833.9 miles per hour (1,342 kph).

**19**
BUSH CRICKETS, small insects from South America, can chirp as loud as a POWER SAW.

**20**
There are some 30 places around the world where SAND DUNES "SING." Explorer Marco Polo heard the sound while crossing the Gobi desert.

**21**
The common COQUI is the loudest amphibian. When groups of these tree frogs croak together, they can be as loud as a lawn mower!

**22**
The common coqui's 2-PART CROAK sounds just like its name: *co kee*. Males respond to the *co* sound, while the *kee* attracts females.

**23**
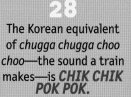
BLUE WHALES can hear each other up to 500 miles (800 km) away!

**24**
Scientists can make small beads LEVITATE—rise from a surface—using SOUND WAVES.

**25**
CAVE-DWELLING OILBIRDS are the loudest birds on Earth. A colony can contain thousands of birds, each as loud as a hand drill.

**26**
The LOUDEST INSECT—a type of mole cricket—digs a megaphone-shaped home that helps project its loud chirps.

**27**
The loudness of sound is measured in DECIBELS. Normal conversation is about 60 decibels. Sounds of about 80 decibels can cause hearing loss.

**28**
The Korean equivalent of *chugga chugga choo choo*—the sound a train makes—is *CHIK CHIK POK POK*.

**29**
The VEGETABLE ORCHESTRA, based in Vienna, Austria, plays instruments made from fresh veggies, like pumpkin drums, celery guitars, and carrot flutes.

**30**
*Buzz* and *hiss* are examples of ONOMATOPOEIA—words that sound like the noise they're associated with.

**31**
The world record for the LOUDEST BARK from a group of dogs measured 124 decibels—about as loud as a jet plane taking off.

**32**
Homer Simpson's famous *D'OH SOUND* is trademarked, which means it can't be used by anyone else without permission.

**33**
In 1994, HARLEY DAVIDSON tried to trademark the sound of its motorcycles. Its request was denied.

**34**
Clapping your hands near the stairs of Mexico's El Castillo pyramid produces a CHIRPING ECHO that some say mimics the quetzal, a bird sacred to the Maya.

**35**
Researchers are developing a device that may one day allow doctors to use sound waves to ZAP CANCEROUS TUMORS.

**36**
VAMPIRE BATS find their prey by listening for their breathing sounds.

**37**
Visitors to the INTEGRATRON in California, U.S.A., can take a "sound bath" to soothe the mind and body by listening to music played on quartz crystal bowls.

**38**
STELLAR SOUND—sound that the sun produces—helps heat the chromosphere, an outer layer of the sun, as high as 20,000°F (11,000°C).

**39**
DWARF MINKE WHALES make a noise that's been compared to the sound of a light saber in the *Star Wars* movies.

**40**
There's a device that uses sound waves to PUT OUT FIRES.

**41**
Singing can BREAK GLASS! One singer shattered a wine glass by producing a 105-decibel sound. That's about as loud as a gas lawn mower.

**42**
The sound of TIE FIGHTER SPACESHIPS in the *Star Wars* movies is actually a mix of elephants trumpeting and cars driving by in the rain.

**43**
A 2012 study found that NAILS SCRAPING A CHALKBOARD is only the fifth most unpleasant sound. Number one is a knife blade rubbing a bottle.

**44**
A man who was BORN BLIND taught himself to "see" by clicking his tongue and listening to the sound waves bouncing off objects around him.

**45**
The sound of ICEBERGS MELTING and breaking apart in the ocean around Antarctica can be as loud as a few hundred supertanker ships.

**46**
The sounds that drifting icebergs make are called ICEQUAKES.

**47**
In deep space, there is NO SOUND because there is no air or other particles to vibrate to create sound waves.

**48**
Migrating birds use INFRASOUND—low-level background noise in Earth's atmosphere—as an auditory "map."

**49**
One research team uses physics and math to simulate the SOUNDS OF OTHER WORLDS, such as dust storms on Mars and lightning on Venus.

**50**
Shipping and other HUMAN ACTIVITY at sea disrupts whale communication, sometimes driving them from their feeding grounds and each other.

**1**
In the Half-and-Half race in Washington, D.C., U.S.A., participants must run 6.55 miles (10.54 km), **EAT A CHILI DOG WITH ONIONS,** then run another 6.55 miles to the finish line.

**2**
Forget arm muscles. In the **WORLD TOE WRESTLING CHAMPIONSHIPS,** you need strong feet to beat the other competitors.

**3**
In the **ZOMBIE RUN,** runners must get to the finish line before brain-hungry "zombies" chase them down.

**4**
Participants in the Pumpkin Regatta in Damariscotta, Maine, U.S.A., **CARVE BOATS OUT OF GIANT PUMPKINS,** climb aboard, and race them, using paddles or motors.

**5**
People compete against horses over a 22-mile (35-km) course in the **MAN VS. HORSE MARATHON** in Wales. A human has won the race only twice in 33 years.

**6**
A woman won the Great Face Off contest in Atlantic City, New Jersey, U.S.A., by **POPPING HER EYEBALLS OUT OF THEIR SOCKETS!**

**7**
At the **PICKLED-QUAIL-EGG-EATING CONTEST** in Grand Prairie, Texas, U.S.A., competitors down as many of the olive-size eggs as they can in 1 minute. The record is over 3 dozen!

**8**
Mountain bikers ride almost the entire length of Africa in the Tour d'Afrique—a 4-month, 7,500-mile (12,000-km) **JOURNEY FROM SUDAN TO SOUTH AFRICA.**

**9**
A man from Long Island, New York, U.S.A., ate **20 TENNIS-BALL-SIZE MATZO BALLS IN JUST OVER 5 MINUTES** to win a trophy and a $2,500 gift certificate.

**10**
Participants in Thailand's **PATTAYA INTERNATIONAL BED RACE** compete for a place on the podium by pushing colorfully decorated beds on wheels.

**11**
Runners in the **UNDERWATER MARATHON** in Hershey, Pennsylvania, U.S.A., run all 26.2 miles (42.2 km) on an underwater treadmill.

**12**
A man from England earned the title of **WORLD'S FASTEST PIZZA MAKER.** He needed just 39.17 seconds to make 3 large pizzas.

**13**
At the **WORLD BEARD CHAMPIONSHIPS,** men with wacky facial hair compete in 17 categories, including goatee, sideburns, and full-beard freestyle.

**14**
In Sanya, China, couples celebrate the New Year with a **BRIDE-CARRYING RACE.** Grooms run to the finish line while carrying their white-gowned partner on their back.

**15**
At the **POWER TOOL DRAG RACING** event in Mora, Minnesota, U.S.A., participants turn tools into makeshift motors to power skateboards, scooters, bikes, and go-karts.

**16**
Participants strap on snorkels and fins to **BRAVE SCORPIONS AND LEECHES** as they swim 2 laps in a peat bog at the World Bog Snorkeling Championships in Wales.

**17**
The 2004 winner of a **CORNED BEEF AND CABBAGE EATING CONTEST** in Milwaukee, Wisconsin, U.S.A., packed away over 5 pounds (2 kg) of the dish in 10 minutes.

**18**
At the **ROCK PAPER SCISSORS WORLD CHAMPIONSHIP** in Toronto, Canada, participants rely on strategy and a little bit of luck to throw the right signal.

**19**
At the International Birdman Rally in Worthing, England, competitors **LAUNCH OFF A 35-FOOT (11-M)-HIGH PLATFORM** in human-powered flying machines.

**20**
A recent winner of the Isle Waterloo World Cupcake Eating Championship in Iowa, U.S.A., wolfed down **42 CUPCAKES IN 8 MINUTES.**

**21**
Hundreds of people sweat it out at the **WORLD SAUNA CHAMPIONSHIPS** in Finland each year to see who can last the longest in 230°F (110°C) heat.

**22**
To win South Korea's **HANGANG HIGH WIRE WORLD CHAMPIONSHIPS**—and $10,000—you have to be the fastest to walk a half mile (0.8 km) across a 1.5-inch (3.8-cm)-wide high wire.

**23**
Less than perfect pooches show off their mugs at the annual **WORLD'S UGLIEST DOG CONTEST** in Petaluma, California, U.S.A.

**24**
For the Bar Stool Races in Wisconsin, kids and adults **STRAP SKIS TO DECORATED STOOLS,** then *shoosh* down a snowy slope. Fall off your seat, and you're disqualified.

**25**
In the Pig-Squealing Championships in Trie-sur-Baïse, France, **PEOPLE IMITATE OINKERS** with squeals, grunts, and snuffles.

**26**
On Gumboot Day, people in Taihape, New Zealand, compete to see **WHO CAN THROW A RUBBER BOOT THE FARTHEST.** So far, the record is over 150 feet (46 m).

**27**
Champion competitive eater Joey Chestnut once ate **8 POUNDS (3.6 KG) OF PORK RIBS IN 12 MINUTES** to win a contest in Las Vegas, Nevada, U.S.A.

**28**
Thousands of "airheads" participate in the annual **AIR GUITAR WORLD CHAMPIONSHIPS** in Oulu, Finland.

# 35 WINNING FACTS ABOUT CRAZY COMPETITIONS

**29**

At the annual Matlock Raft Race in Matlock, England, competitors **SAIL DOWN AN ICY RIVER IN RAFTS** shaped like fire trucks, Viking ships, and more.

**30**

In "retro running" races like the Cupcake Classic Backwards Mile in Tumwater, Washington, U.S.A., participants must **RUN, JOG, OR WALK IN REVERSE.**

**31**

In the **FROZEN DEAD GUY DAYS COFFIN RACE** in Nederland, Colorado, U.S.A., teams race through a snowy obstacle course as they slide, roll, or carry a coffin.

**32**

Soccer players get down and dirty in the **SWAMP FOOTBALL WORLD CUP,** where teams kick, scrap, and slosh it out in a muddy swamp.

**33**

At a race in Trakai, Lithuania, teams—including one member **WHO SITS ON A TOILET**—push porta potties around a track on a frozen lake.

Grasscar racer

**34**

Each year in the United States, **SOUPED-UP LAWN MOWERS** reach speeds of over 30 miles per hour (48 kph) in a highly competitive event known as grasscar racing.

**35**

In chessboxing tournaments, contestants switch between playing **CHESS AND BOXING** until there's a checkmate, a knockout, or a judge ends a round.

**1** A grain of sand varies in size from **0.0008 TO 0.08 OF AN INCH** (0.02–2 mm) across.

**2** TWO BEACHES IN THE UNITED STATES (ONE IN HAWAII AND THE OTHER IN THE TERRITORY OF GUAM) HAVE NATURAL **GREEN SAND,** MAINLY MADE UP OF OLIVINE CRYSTALS.

**3** According to legend, THE SANDMAN throws sand in kids' eyes to make them fall asleep.

**5** So-called SINGING SAND DUNES create a rumbling sound as air between grains of sand becomes squeezed, or compressed, as the sand shifts.

**4** Wind and waves eventually destroy all sand castles, but some entered into competitions are sprayed with a **MIST OF GLUE AND WATER** to help them hold their shape.

# 25 FACTS ABOUT SAND

**6** Besides buckets, artists who work with sand use tools such as forks and spoons, cake frosting knifes, melon ballers, and palette knives.

**7** Of the 5 basic kinds of sand dunes, crescent-shaped ones are the most common. They resemble a crescent moon.

**8** Quartz is the most common mineral found in sand. It is nearly insoluble in water and doesn't wear down easily.

**11** In 2010, more than 2,500 people created the largest sand painting in the world. It took up more space than **7 OLYMPIC-SIZE SWIMMING POOLS.**

**9** MALE PUFFER FISH SPEND DAYS CREATING CIRCLE DESIGNS IN THE SAND ON THE BOTTOM OF THE OCEAN TO ATTRACT MATES.

THE CIRCLES STRETCH 6 FEET (1.8 M) IN DIAMETER.

**10** IF **Earth** WERE THE SIZE OF A GRAIN OF SAND, **the sun** WOULD BE THE SIZE OF AN ORANGE.

**12** SAND DOLLARS are sea animals covered in small spines that they use to claw and dig into the sandy bottoms of shallow seas.

**13** A laundry detergent company asked master sand artist JOOheng Tan to create 3 different sand sculptures for an ad campaign, including a scene from outer space.

**14** IN FEBRUARY 2013, 684 PEOPLE BURIED THEMSELVES IN SAND ON A BEACH IN ECUADOR, SETTING A WORLD RECORD. A FLIP-FLOP MAKER SPONSORED THE EVENT.

**15** Tibetan Buddhist monks use different colored sands to create paintings called mandalas. The works are swept into a stream or river to show the temporary nature of all things.

**16** CONTESTANTS IN THE SAND CASTLE BUILDING CONTEST AT POINT REYES NATIONAL SEASHORE IN CALIFORNIA, U.S.A., DECORATE THEIR CREATIONS WITH SEAWEED, DRIFTWOOD, AND SHELLS.

**17** FIFTY-FOUR SANDY ISLANDS OFF THE COAST OF BRAZIL MAKE UP THE WORLD'S LARGEST CHAIN OF BARRIER ISLANDS, STRETCHING FOR MORE THAN 350 MILES (560 KM).

**18** At Weymouth beach in Dorset, United Kingdom, you can stay in an open-air HOTEL MADE ENTIRELY OF SAND.

# YOU CAN SINK INTO

**19** Sandboarding, which is like snow-boarding except done on sand, uses special boards with slick bottoms to enhance speed and the ability to slide.

**20** About one-third of Earth's land surface is desert, but only one-fifth of these deserts are covered in sand.

**21** In 2011, some 11,000 volunteers created a sand sculpture nearly 17 miles (27 km) long on a beach in Germany.

**22** The ideal way to create wet sand to build a sand castle is to mix 8 PARTS SAND WITH 1 PART WATER.

**23** It took Eppo Vogel 78 days to create a 7-story-tall sand sculpture. He based it on a Nigerian folktale called "Why Is the Hummingbird King of All Animals?"

**24** IN 2012, IT TOOK 600 SAND CASTLE BUILDERS ONLY 1 HOUR TO BUILD 1,939 CASTLES—A RECORD NUMBER—ON A BEACH IN DUNFANAGHY, IRELAND.

**25** The winner of the 2013 National Sand Sculpting Championship in Revere, Massachusetts, U.S.A., created a gigantic SANDY OCTOPUS and took home $5,000.

# (15) EYE-POPPING FACTS

**1** Instead of ink, **3-D PRINTING USES MATERIALS LIKE SILICONE, METAL, AND PLASTIC TO CREATE REAL-LIFE OBJECTS.** It has been around since the early 1980s.

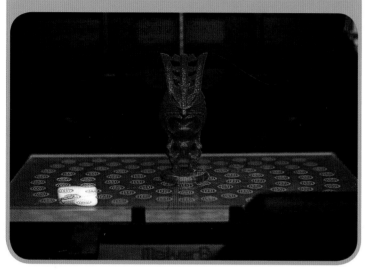

**2** Instead of printing just left to right, **3-D PRINTERS GO UP AND DOWN,** too, depositing materials in layers that eventually create the desired object.

**3** So far, 3-D printers can make **PROSTHETICS (ARTIFICIAL BODY PARTS)** and even blood vessels. One day, it may be possible to print a human kidney and other organs—one layer of cells at a time.

**4** There are 3-D printers that **USE CHOCOLATE FOR "INK"** to create morsels in the shape of your face, flowers, hearts, snowmen, and more.

**5** Soon, **ASTRONAUTS IN SPACE WILL BE ABLE TO PRINT OUT OBJECTS** like clips, buckles—even replacement parts—thanks to a 3-D printer on the International Space Station.

**6** A designer created **SHOES THAT YOU CAN PRINT OUT AT HOME OVERNIGHT.** All you have to do is download the digital files, select your size and preferred color, and hit "print."

**7** **"URBEE," THE WORLD'S FIRST 3-D PRINTED CAR,** is about half the weight of the average car and can reach speeds up to 70 miles per hour (113 kph).

# ABOUT 3-D PRINTING

**8** A Japanese artist uses a 3-D printer to make HERMIT CRAB SHELLS in the shapes of city skylines.

**9** NASA is developing a 3-D printer designed to make hot, EDIBLE PIZZA FOR ASTRONAUTS TO ENJOY IN SPACE.

**10** College students at the University of Maryland, U.S.A., used a 3-D printer to make a ROBOTIC BIRD CALLED ROBO RAVEN. It can flap its wings, dive, spiral, and backflip and is so realistic that it was attacked by a hawk while flying.

**11** Using layers of a superfine nylon powder, an engineer was able to create an ACOUSTIC GUITAR with his 3-D printer.

**12** Researchers have used 3-D printers to replicate DINOSAUR FOSSILS. The results give them a better sense of how the animals moved.

**13** A company in the Netherlands PRINTED OUT EYEGLASSES for the Dutch king and queen.

**14** A watchmaker has created a program that prints 18-CARAT GOLD by fusing bits of gold powder together.

**15** Engineers at Cornell University in New York, U.S.A., have figured out how to print replacements for HUMAN EARS that look and act like real ones.

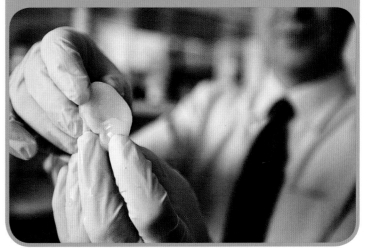

1 Professional soccer players run about 6 miles (10 km) during every game.

2 Golf balls were once made of solid wood.

3 During the 1928 Summer Olympics, a rower stopped mid-race to let a mother duck and her ducklings pass in front of his boat. He still won the race.

4 About 3.2 billion people watched at least 1 minute of the World Cup soccer tournament in 2010. That was almost half the world's population at that time!

5 A 1988 NFL game between the Philadelphia Eagles and the Chicago Bears became known as the "Fog Bowl" because the fog was so thick the players couldn't see the sidelines.

6 U.S. PRESIDENT ABRAHAM LINCOLN IS IN THE NATIONAL WRESTLING HALL OF FAME IN STILLWATER, OKLAHOMA, U.S.A.

7 Out of the 209 members of the International Football Association (FIFA), only 3—the United States, Canada, and Samoa—refer to soccer as "soccer." The rest call it football.

8 American runner Dean Karnazes once ran 50 marathons in 50 U.S. states over 50 consecutive days. He has also completed a marathon on every continent—twice!

9 Pittsburgh, Pennsylvania, is the only U.S. city where all of the pro sports teams wear the same colors. The Pirates, Steelers, and Penguins all sport gold, black, and white.

10 The very first game of basketball was played with a soccer ball.

11 Every baseball used in the major leagues is rubbed with a special mud before a game. This helps pitchers get a better grip.

12 Extreme urban climbers clamber up the sides of buildings—some 40 stories high—without the help of climbing gear or safety harnesses.

13 A MAN ONCE JUMPED ROPE 10 TIMES WHILE SUPPORTING 3 PEOPLE— WEIGHING A TOTAL OF 407.8 POUNDS (185 KG)—ON HIS BACK.

14 One study says that grunting during a tennis match may help the player win.

15 A giant soccer ball, about 20 times the size of a full-size bicycle wheel, was once displayed in a parking lot in Doha, Qatar.

16 A soccer field is also called a pitch.

17 A man in Pennsylvania has a collection of more than 36,000 golf balls.

18 At the 1896 Summer Olympic Games in Athens, Greece, swimmers competed in the 55°F (13°C) waters of the Bay of Zea, battling waves reaching as high as 12 feet (3.7 m).

19 A trip around the bases on a baseball diamond is 20 yards (18 m) longer than a run from one goal line to the other on a football field.

20 More than 2,000 years ago, people in China played a game similar to soccer, kicking a ball made of animal skin stuffed with feathers.

21 Bikers wearing scuba gear race along the bottom of the Atlantic Ocean in the annual Underwater Bike Race in Beaufort, North Carolina, U.S.A.

22 The Pittsburgh Penguins hockey team made Mister Rogers an honorary captain in 1993.

23 Fred Cox, a kicker for the Minnesota Vikings, invented the Nerf football in 1972.

24 A woman from Argentina can shoot a bow and arrow over 18 feet (5.5 m)—using her feet instead of her hands.

25 In the sport of Monster Fishing, it can take 30 minutes and the strength of 2 people to reel in supersize fish. Some weigh as much as a hippo!

26 THE OLDEST KNOWN LEATHER SOCCER BALL— DATING BACK SOME 450 YEARS—WAS FOUND HIDDEN BEHIND THE WALLS OF A SCOTTISH CASTLE.

# 75 SPORTS FACTS TO CHEER ABOUT

**27** During a race, the inside of NASCAR race cars can heat up to over 100°F (38°C).

**28** During the 1956 Summer Olympic Games in Melbourne, Australia, the equestrian events had to be held in Stockholm, Sweden, because foreign horses weren't allowed in the host country.

**29** Hand-stitched soccer balls include up to 2,000 stitches and can take over 4 hours to make.

**30** While training for the Olympics, 18-time gold medal swimmer Michael Phelps consumed 12,000 calories a day. His typical dinner? One pound of pasta and an entire pizza!

**31** Like regular hockey, Octopush involves players passing and shooting a puck into a goal. The difference? All of the action is underwater at the bottom of a pool.

**32** THE CONE ON A BADMINTON SHUTTLECOCK USED IN PROFESSIONAL MATCHES IS MADE OF GOOSE FEATHERS.

**33** Only 7 countries have ever won the World Cup in soccer: Uruguay, Brazil, Argentina, France, England, Italy, and Germany.

**34** An NFL lineman can lose up to 9 pounds (4 kg) of water weight during 1 game.

**35** From 1900 until 1920, tug-of-war was an event at the Summer Olympic Games.

**36** The sport of high-heel racing has runners sprinting in stilettos to see who's fastest—and who has the best balance—in heels.

**37** Major league baseball slugger Ted Williams once hit a ball more than 560 feet (170 m) in the air. That's nearly twice as high as the Statue of Liberty in New York Harbor, U.S.A.

**38** The average NHL game uses a dozen hockey pucks.

**39** The World Cup soccer trophy once was stolen and went missing for a week, only to be found by a dog named Pickles, who sniffed it out in a bush.

**40** In 1919, Ray Caldwell of the Cleveland Indians continued to pitch after being struck by lightning in the middle of the ninth inning.

**41** AN AUSTRALIAN WOMAN HURLED A BLUEFIN TUNA 40.19 FEET (12.25 M) TO CAPTURE THE WOMEN'S TITLE IN THE WORLD TUNA TOSSING TOURNAMENT.

**42** In the 1800s, baseball umpires in the United States sat in rocking chairs behind home plate.

**43** Each year, Major League Eating oversees as many as 100 competitive eating events across the globe.

**44** Joey Chestnut, a competitive eater known as Jaws, can consume 69 hot dogs in 10 minutes.

**45** Jai alai, a game where players throw a ball against a wall, is considered the world's fastest sport because players hurl the ball over 100 miles per hour (160 kph).

**46** The U.S. House of Representatives adjourned to watch the Preakness Stakes horse race in 1877.

**47** In 1940, the Chicago Bears beat the Washington Redskins 73–0 in the most lopsided game in the National Football League's history.

**48** A Malaysian badminton player once hit the birdie a speed of 261.6 miles per hour (421 kph). That's faster than some high-speed trains!

**49** In 2013, Arunima Sinha, an Indian woman with only one leg, climbed Mount Everest—the first female amputee to do so.

**50** About 42,000 tennis balls are used each year during the Wimbledon Championship in London, England.

**51** Most NASCAR drivers use nitrogen in their tires instead of air.

**52** IN VOLCANO BOARDING, PEOPLE ZOOM DOWN THE SLOPE OF AN ACTIVE VOLCANO ON A SLEDLIKE PIECE OF PLYWOOD.

**53** In 2012, 16-year-old Laura Dekker of the Netherlands became the youngest person to circumnavigate the globe alone in a boat.

**54** During the Man Versus Horse Marathon in Wales, United Kingdom, runners race horses along a 22-mile (35-km)-long obstacle course.

**55** On turns, NASCAR drivers face about 3Gs of force—similar to what astronauts experience during liftoff from Earth into space.

**56** In the sport of pogo-sticking, jumpers bound up to 9 feet (2.7 m) into the air—high enough to clear an SUV.

**57** The last time Olympic athletes received solid-gold medals was in 1912. Modern medals are made mostly of silver, with just 0.2 ounces (6 g) of gold.

**58** In the 2002 Las Vegas Bowl football game, Katie Hnida, a junior at the University of New Mexico, became the first woman to play in an NCAA Division I football game.

**59** Figure skating was initially part of the Summer Olympics.

**60** LEGEND HAS IT THAT BASEBALL GREAT BABE RUTH KEPT COOL DURING GAMES BY WEARING A CABBAGE LEAF UNDER HIS CAP.

**61** The longest major league baseball game went 25 innings and lasted 8 hours 6 minutes—nearly 3 times longer than an average 9-inning game.

**62** The first baseball caps were made of straw.

**63** Sixteen hundred years ago, people played tennis with their bare hands—not a racket.

**64** Held every year since 1875, the Kentucky Derby is the longest continually run sports event in the United States.

**65** In 1875, a colt named Aristide won the Kentucky Derby, taking home $2,850 in prize money. In 2013, Derby champ Orb collected $1,439,800.

**66** In 2013, fans at a packed Sacramento Kings–Detroit Pistons basketball game produced a crowd roar almost loud enough to drown out the sound of a jet taking off.

**67** In baseball and softball, hitters with brown eyes may have an advantage over those with blue eyes, which are more sensitive to glare from the sun.

**68** Participants in the Double Decatriathlon World Challenge have 21 days to complete a 47.2-mile (76-km) swim, a 2,236-mile (3600-km) bike ride, and a 524-mile (844-km) run.

**69** THE YOUNGEST FOOTBALL STAR TO APPEAR ON A WHEATIES CEREAL BOX WAS A 9-YEAR-OLD GIRL NAMED SAM GORDON.

**70** During the 1900 Summer Olympic Games in Paris, swimmers in the men's 200-meter obstacle race navigated their way under or over poles and boats, while fighting the current in the River Seine.

**71** *Yagli Gures*, or grease wrestling, is the national sport of Turkey.

**72** The World Series of Poker is one of the highest-paying sports events on the planet, with the winner receiving nearly $9 million.

**73** Emily Beaver, a senior at Missouri State University, U.S.A., recently ran a mile (1.6 km) in 5:58 while juggling 3 beanbags, setting a "joggling" world record.

**74** Synchronized swimmers keep their hair in place by slathering it with waterproof gelatin.

**75** You would need 2,500 pairs of recycled sneakers to make the surface of one tennis court.

**1** The New Zealand town of **WAIPU** is pronounced "why poo."

**2** It's a mystery how **KILL DEVIL HILLS**, North Carolina, U.S.A., got its name, but the story probably involves sand dunes, pirates, and rum that tasted so bad it would kill the devil.

**3** The British have some interesting place-names: **GIGGLESWICK**, **PUDDLETOWN**, and **PIDDLE RIVER** are just a few.

**4** **HALFWAY**, a town in Oregon, U.S.A., changed its name for a year to **HALF.COM**.

# 35 ODDBALL FACTS ABOUT

**5** A pharmacist in **WASHINGTON STATE**, U.S.A., came up with a clever name for the town he founded: **GEORGE**. Get it?

**6** **PAKISTAN'S** name is made up of letters from Punjab, Afghan Frontier, Kashmir, and Baluch**istan**—all names of regions in the country.

**7** If you want a good laugh, ride along **HA-HA ROAD** in London, England.

**8** Visiting **SODA SPRINGS BASIN**, Utah, or **SODA LAKE**, California, U.S.A., could make you thirsty.

**9** You may not want to book a flight into **MORON AIRPORT** in Mongolia.

**10** You might think anything goes if you live in **WHY NOT**, North Carolina, U.S.A.

**11** **FROSTPROOF**, Florida, U.S.A., usually lives up to its name. But in 1981, a cold snap sent temperatures plunging to a record low of 18°F (-8°C).

**12** The general store in the village of **MOOBALL** in New South Wales, Australia, is painted to look like a cow.

**13** If you lived in **MOOSE JAW**, a city in Saskatchewan, Canada, you would be called a **MOOSE JAVIAN**. Sounds sort of alien!

**14** The mayor of the Turkish city of **BATMAN** once threatened to sue Warner Bros. for using the name of his town in their Dark Knight trilogy without his permission.

**15** Hamburgers take their name from the German city of **HAMBURG**, where Hamburg steak was a popular food.

**16** **CHRISTMAS** is a popular U.S. place-name. It is used as part of the **OFFICIAL NAME** of everything from canyons and swamps to airports and towns.

**17** **BELMOPAN**, the capital city of Belize, is named after 2 rivers: the **BELIZE**, the country's longest river, and the **MOPAN**, which flows into the Belize.

**18** **ZZYZV**, a town in the Mojave Desert of California, U.S.A., is the very last name in an alphabetical list of U.S. place-names.

**19** **SAHARA, NEGEV,** and **GOBI** are all deserts with names that mean "**DESERT**."

**20** Taumatawhakatangihangakoauauotamateapokaiwhenuakitanatahu is a **HILL** in **NEW ZEALAND.**

**21** Vikings sometimes called Iceland **SNOWLAND.**

**22** Šņores is a town in Latvia, but its name has nothing to do with sleeping. In Latvian, the word for "**SNORE**" is krākšana.

**23** Don't feel bad if you live on **BOSSY BOOTS DRIVE** in Allen, Texas, U.S.A. You could live on **PEEPEE STREET** in Hilo, Hawaii, U.S.A.

**24** **THE TEXAS NO NAME NUMBER 47 DAM** sure has a long name for not having a name.

**25** Before it was officially named **HAUMEA**, this dwarf planet was called **SANTA** by the team that discovered it right after Christmas.

**26** Jupiter's moon **IO** has the **SHORTEST NAME** of any moon in our solar system.

**27** You better not **YAWN** while passing through **SLEEPY EYE**, Minnesota, U.S.A. With an area of only 1.7 square miles (4.4 km²), it's easy to miss.

**28** A town in Madagascar—an island country off Africa's east coast—has a name that just won't stop: **GOGOGOGO**.

**29** Try not to be surprised when you get to **UNEXPECTED ROAD** in Buena, New Jersey, U.S.A.

**30** **TOMBOUCTOU** (or Timbuktu) is not just a made-up name for a remote place. It's a real city in Mali, West Africa, that was a stop on the caravan route across the Sahara.

# PLACES ON THE MAP

**31** Do you think you can get takeout on **CHICKEN DINNER ROAD** west of Nampa, Idaho, U.S.A.?

**32** **"HAPPY VALLEY"** in Pennsylvania, U.S.A., is a nickname for the area surrounding Penn State. During the Depression, people there were happy because they could still work at the university.

**33** **HUMPTY DOO**, Australia, is famous for its sculpture of a gigantic crocodile wearing boxing gloves.

**34** Dogs aren't allowed on **RABBIT ISLAND** off New Zealand's South Island.

**35** If you are ready for this to end, you might want to climb **END PEAK** in the Philippines or stay at the **TRAILS END MOTEL** in Sheridan, Wyoming, U.S.A.

**The Boxing Croc in Humpty Doo, Australia**

✳ YOU HAVE LEARNED **3,769** FACTS

**50 FACTS THAT GIVE THE SKINNY ON SKIN**

**1**
Skin is the **LARGEST ORGAN** in your body.

**2**
The hard, bony plates on alligator and crocodile skin are called **SCUTES**.

**3**
Each person's fingerprints are unique. There are only 3 main patterns: **ARCHES, LOOPS, OR WHORLS.**

**4**
Frogs and salamanders can **BREATHE** through their skin.

**5**
Eating lots of fruits and vegetables can give your skin a **HEALTHY GLOW** in tones of **RED** and **YELLOW.**

**6**
Your skin has more than **2 MILLION SWEAT GLANDS.**

**7**
By trapping moisture, **WRINKLES** on an elephant's skin help keep the animal cool.

**8**
In hot temperatures, your body can release up to 3 gallons (11 L) of **SWEAT** in a day.

**9**
A **POLAR BEAR** has **BLACK SKIN.** This dark skin absorbs heat from sunlight and helps keep the bear warm.

**10**
The fingerprints of **KOALAS** look so much like human fingerprints that they can confuse even trained professionals.

**11**
**LEAFY SEA DRAGONS,** seahorse-like fish, have skin that looks like tiny leaves to help them blend in with seaweed.

**12**
It takes **ABOUT A MONTH** for the skin on your body to **COMPLETELY REPLACE ITSELF.**

**13**
Fish have **TASTE BUDS** in their skin.

**14**
A pigment called **MELANIN** helps to protect your skin from the sun's ultraviolet rays. It also makes your skin darker or lighter.

**15**
No matter how badly **FINGERPRINTS** are damaged, they will **ALWAYS GROW BACK** in their original pattern.

**16**
The skin of amphibians is very different from that of reptiles. Amphibians have **MOIST SKIN** and no scales. Reptiles have **DRY SKIN** covered with scales.

**17**
The skin on the surface of your body is actually made up of **DEAD SKIN CELLS.** New cells grow underneath this outer layer.

**18**
Drops of **SWEAT** on your skin help to cool your body. As sweat evaporates, it **PULLS HEAT OUT** of your body.

## 19
Your skin grows and **REPLENISHES** itself as you sleep. That's why "beauty" sleep is good for everyone!

## 20
**SES** are classified by the number of rings around their bodies.

## 21
Your body has **SWEAT GLANDS** all over the skin, but the highest concentrations are in your hands and feet.

## 22
The **SCALES** on the underside of a **SNAKE** are larger than those on its back. The larger scales on its belly help it move along the ground.

## 23
People who sweat in excess have a medical condition called **HYPERHIDROSIS.**

## 24
A **FLOUNDER** can change the pattern of its skin to blend in with the ocean floor and hide from predators.

## 25
The **GOLDEN POISON DART FROG** has enough venom in its skin to **KILL 10 MEN.**

## 26
The **DRAGON FRUIT**, which comes from a kind of cactus, gets its name from the odd, fleshy scales that cover the skin.

## 27
That pruny-looking skin you get when you stay in the water too long is good for something: It makes it easier to **PICK UP WET OBJECTS!**

## 28
**BOTOX INJECTIONS** can help people get rid of wrinkles. The mild toxin causes muscles to relax so that the skin looks smooth.

## 29
Those crusty things growing on the skin of some kinds of whales are **BARNACLES.** These crustaceans filter food from the water but don't hurt the whale.

## 30
Stress can make a **CHAMELEON** change its skin color.

## 31
The **ORIENTAL FIRE-BELLIED TOAD** secretes toxins from its skin as a way to protect itself from predators.

## 32
Human skin is made up of 3 distinct layers: the **EPIDERMIS, DERMIS,** and **SUBCUTIS.**

## 33
The dermis makes a kind of oil called **SEBUM.** Too much of it can lead to an outbreak of **ACNE.**

## 34
Some marine mammals, such as seals and whales, have a thick layer of **BLUBBER** just under their skin that insulates them from cold water.

## 35
People implant **RADIO FREQUENCY ID TAGS** under their skin so their medical information can be accessed quickly in an emergency.

## 36
By combining human skin cells and spider silk, scientists are making progress in creating a **SPIDER-MAN-LIKE** material that is strong enough to stop a bullet.

## 37
Pig or human? When looking at skin it can be hard to tell. Pigskin is **VERY SIMILAR** to human skin in its color, thickness, and how it acts.

## 38
**PIGSKIN** and human skin are so similar that pigskin can be used like a **BANDAGE** to protect burns while they heal.

## 39
G'day, mate, but put on your sunscreen. **AUSTRALIANS** have the highest rate of **SKIN CANCER** in the world.

## 40
The FBI has more than **70 MILLION FINGERPRINTS** of criminals and more than 34 million fingerprints of people who haven't broken the law.

## 41
**DEAD SKIN CELLS** make up part of the dust in your house. How much depends on how many people live there.

## 42
If you could count all the bacteria on your skin, you would get a number close to **1,000,000,000,000.**

## 43
Scientists have created an **ELECTRONIC SKIN** for robots that has touch sensors.

## 44
**GOOSE BUMPS** happen when tiny muscles raise the hairs on your skin to trap air. This helps you keep warm.

## 45
It can take **6 HOURS** or longer for a **SUNBURN** to develop.

## 46
The **TOUCH SENSORS** in your **FINGERTIPS** are some of the most sensitive in your entire body.

## 47
On rare occasions, people are born without the ridges that create fingerprints. This condition is called **NAEGELI SYNDROME.**

## 48
About 20 percent of the **NUTRIENTS** in a potato are in its skin.

## 49
There are at least **5 DIFFERENT SENSORS** in your skin that respond to pain and touch.

## 50
An **ELEPHANT'S SKIN** can be an inch (2.5 cm) thick in places.

**1** As the U.S. population exploded from 5.2 to 76.2 million between 1800 and 1900, people headed west to find land and opportunity.

**2** **ABOUT 1 IN 10 PEOPLE DIED** along the Oregon Trail, a 2,020-mile (3,250-km) covered-wagon journey west from Missouri to Washington.

**3** THE FAMOUS 1881 GUNFIGHT AT THE
**O.K. CORRAL**
IN TOMBSTONE, ARIZONA, LASTED ONLY ABOUT 30 seconds.

**4** *THE PONY EXPRESS set a speed record when its riders delivered President Abraham Lincoln's first Inaugural Address in 7 days and 17 hours.*

**5** Cowboys were also known as **COWPUNCHERS** or **COWPOKES.**

**6** Timothy O'Sullivan was **the first photographer** to take pictures of the Wild West. He built a darkroom in his horse-drawn wagon so he could develop his images on the spot.

**25 FACTS ABOUT THE WILD**

**7** Charley Parkhurst, one of the greatest stagecoach drivers of the Old West, lived much of her life disguised as a man.

**8** In the Wild West, "mustang runners" were cowboys who would catch, tame, and sell *wild horses.*

**9** FROM 1836 TO 1846, TEXAS WAS AN INDEPENDENT NATION CALLED THE **REPUBLIC OF TEXAS.**

**10** The average cowboy in the Old West made about **$30** a month.

**11** Jesse James, one of the most feared outlaws in the American West, led the robberies of 20 banks and trains, stealing around $200,000, mostly in Missouri.

**12** In the Wild West, the word **"DUDE"** was used to describe a city-dweller.

**13** THE PONY EXPRESS LOST ONLY 1 SACK OF MAIL out of the almost 35,000 pieces this horse-and-rider mail service carried between Missouri and California during the 19 months it existed.

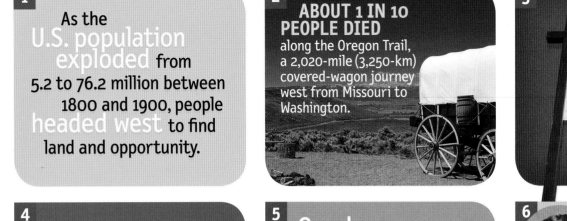
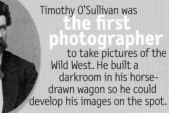

**14** In 1873, James Glidden invented **barbed wire**— also known as the "thorny fence"— to keep his cattle from roaming free. It was one of the **greatest innovations** of this era.

**15** PONY EXPRESS RIDERS— SOME AS YOUNG AS 11 YEARS OLD— TRAVELED UP TO **100 miles** (160 km) **a day,** SWITCHING HORSES EVERY 10 TO 12 MILES (16 TO 19 KM).

**16** The **"10-GALLON"** hats that cowboys wear to protect them from the sun and rain actually hold only about **3 QUARTS** (3 L) **OF WATER.**

**17 DEAD MAN'S HAND** —a pair of aces and eights— refers to the cards gunfighter-lawman Wild Bill Hickok was holding when he was gunned down in a poker game.

**18** A $500 REWARD WAS OFFERED TO ANYONE WHO TURNED IN THE NOTORIOUS OUTLAW **Billy the Kid**— DEAD OR ALIVE. THAT'S ABOUT $10,000 TODAY.

**19 CAMELS** ROAMED THE **PLAINS OF TEXAS** AFTER THE CIVIL WAR. THEY WERE ESCAPEES FROM THE SHORT-LIVED U.S. CAMEL CORPS, FORMED BY THE ARMY IN THE 1850S.

# WEST TO WHOOP 'N' HOLLER ABOUT

**20** Cowboys considered it **RUDE TO WAVE** at a man on a horse. Nodding was more appropriate.

**21** AFTER THE DISCOVERY OF **GOLD** IN CALIFORNIA IN 1848, THE NUMBER OF NON-INDIANS LIVING THERE JUMPED FROM 14,000 TO **100,000** IN JUST 2 YEARS.

**22** A shotgun belonging to **ANNIE OAKLEY**— one of the most **LEGENDARY FEMALE SHARPSHOOTERS** of the Wild West— sold for $143,000 in 2012.

**23 Ghost towns**— REMNANTS OF ONCE THRIVING AREAS ABANDONED AFTER THE GOLD RUSH STILL STAND IN THE WESTERN UNITED STATES.

**24** Jesse James was called **"Dingus"** by his friends.

**25** TODAY, HUNDREDS OF PEOPLE SHOW OFF THEIR STUFF IN WILD WEST–INSPIRED COMPETITIONS LIKE **GUN SPINNING, TRICK AND FANCY ROPING, AND WHIP CRACKING.**

# 35 EXTRAORDINARY FACTS ABOUT EXTREMOPHILES

**1** Extremophiles are organisms that can survive in the most **EXTREME CONDITIONS**, like next to deep-sea hydrothermal vents, in hot springs, and at the bottom of Antarctic lakes.

**2** "Extremophile," which comes from the Latin *extremus* and the Greek *philos*, means **"LOVER OF EXTREME ENVIRONMENTS."**

**3** Hyperthermophiles—extremophiles that thrive in heat—survive in temperatures hotter than 212°F (100°C). That's the same temperature as **WATER BOILING** on your stove!

**4** Studying extremophiles on Earth helps scientists understand how **LIFE-FORMS MIGHT EXIST AND THRIVE** in extreme conditions elsewhere in the universe.

**5** A tiny bacterium found 2 miles (3.2 km) deep in a Greenland glacier was revived after being buried in ice for **120,000 YEARS.**

**6** A type of bacteria lives in the mud of Mono Lake in California, U.S.A., **WITHOUT OXYGEN OR SUNLIGHT** and in water 3 times saltier than the ocean.

**7** Sixty feet (18 m) below the surface of a valley in Antarctica lies a lake that is home to bacteria that have survived for at least **2,800 YEARS** without light or oxygen.

**8** A type of moss growing in Siberia has been living in a **DORMANT STATE IN PERMAFROST**—a layer of permanently frozen ground—for 40,000 years.

**9** The bacteria *Deinococcus radiodurans* has been nicknamed **"CONAN THE BACTERIUM"** because it can withstand extreme amounts of radiation and repair its own DNA.

**10** A microbe (microscopic organism) that lives in the Atacama Desert in Chile **SURVIVES BY DRINKING THE DEW** that gathers on spiderwebs.

**11** Scientists discovered that **MYSTERIOUS ELECTRICAL CURRENTS** detected on the ocean floor off Denmark are created by microbes "eating" oxygen from seawater.

**12** Scientists are looking at Saturn's moon Titan, which has **LIQUID METHANE LAKES,** as a possible home to extremophiles that can live in a waterless environment.

**13** Microorganisms that can survive in extreme cold have special **ANTIFREEZE PROTEINS** that allow their cells to remain fluid when temperatures are below freezing.

**14** Organisms that can **SURVIVE EXTREME RADIATION** have protective sheaths that turn black to form a natural sunscreen.

**15** By converting chemicals given off by **DEEP-SEA VENTS** into sugars, bacteria make the food that tube-worms and other vent animals need to survive.

**16** Scientists are studying microbes found in Antarctica and Siberia to see if similar extremophiles could be found in **ICE DEPOSITS ON MARS.**

**17** Normally, acid destroys cells, but acidophiles—**ORGANISMS THAT LIVE IN SULFURIC POOLS AND GEYSERS—** thrive in it!

**18** Scientists say that whatever hit Earth and caused the **EXTINCTION OF DINOSAURS** could have blasted some extremophiles into space, where they found new places to live.

**19** A tiny, 8-legged creature called a tardigrade—or **"WATER BEAR"**—is capable of surviving in a sleep state for 100 years and then being brought back to life.

**20** BRINE SHRIMP LIKE WATER THAT IS TWICE AS SALTY as the ocean. Eggs can dry out for 10 years or longer until the right conditions revive them.

**21** Certain extremophiles found in lakes in East Africa have been USED TO IMPROVE LAUNDRY DETERGENT. Their high salt content helps loosen dirt and stains.

**22** Life-forms have been found in a LAKE OF LIQUID ASPHALT on the Caribbean island of Trinidad.

**23** Extremophiles have STRONG DEFENSES for fighting off scavengers. Understanding these defenses might lead to new antibiotics for humans.

**24** In the Gulf of Mexico and near Monterey Bay in California, U.S.A., cold seeps on the ocean floor release METHANE GAS, creating a habitat for ice worms.

**25** GIANT TUBE WORMS that live near deep-sea hydrothermal vents can be about as long as a JUMP ROPE.

**26** EYELESS SHRIMP living around hydrothermal vents in the Atlantic Ocean eat bacteria that they grow on their bodies.

**27** The mangrove killifish is an extremophile of the fish world. Native to the Americas, it is able to survive out of water for up to 66 DAYS!

**28** Before leaving Earth, LANDING PROBES ON SPACESHIPS ARE CLEANED to prevent microbes from this planet from contaminating other worlds.

**29** THE DEAD SEA is not entirely dead. Halophile microbes thrive in the salty waters.

**30** Germs can survive MILLIONS OF YEARS in ice.

**31** A microbe that lives 2 miles (3.2 km) below Earth's surface in South Africa's gold mines is the only known species that can SURVIVE WITHOUT HELP from another organism.

**32** Heat-loving bacteria color the edges of GRAND PRISMATIC BASIN in North America's Yellowstone National Park. The hot spring's center appears blue because it is bacteria free.

**33** SNOTTITES are single-celled bacteria that hang on the walls and ceilings of caves. They have the consistency of snot (mucus).

**34** The bluish "hair" that covers POMPEII WORMS, which live near hydro-thermal vents, is actually bacteria that help make the worms HEAT RESISTANT.

**35** Soft-shelled, single-cell organisms are able to live at the deepest part of the ocean—Challenger Deep—where the pressure is 1,100 TIMES GREATER than at the ocean's surface.

# 15 FANTASTIC FACTS

**❶ FUNGI AREN'T PLANTS OR ANIMALS.** They're so different from other organisms that they belong to **THEIR OWN KINGDOM.**

**❷** Fungi include organisms like **YEASTS, MOLDS, MILDEWS, AND MUSHROOMS.**

**❸** There are some **100,000 KNOWN SPECIES OF FUNGI,** living everywhere from the steamy tropics to the wood huts built by explorers in frigid Antarctica.

**❹ MOLDS ARE USED TO RIPEN CHEESES,** such as blue cheese, Brie, and Roquefort.

**❺** A colony of **TENS OF THOUSANDS OF ANTS** can live off a garden of fungus. A single ant starts the garden by spitting out a mouthful of fungus and then "farming" it.

**❻** Fungi—and the bacteria buddies that grow with them—**CAN DECOMPOSE EVERYTHING** from food scraps to blue jeans and jet fuel.

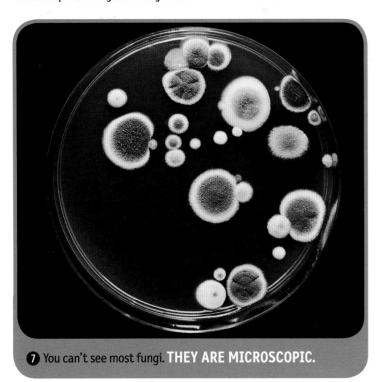

**❼** You can't see most fungi. **THEY ARE MICROSCOPIC.**

# ABOUT FUNGI

**8** Lichens are organisms made up of **BOTH FUNGI AND ALGAE.** One kind is named after U.S. President Barack Obama.

**9** According to a 2012 survey, the **SECOND MOST FAVORITE PIZZA TOPPING IN THE UNITED STATES** is a fungus: mushrooms!

**10** Some fungi not only grow but also thrive in **POLLUTED WATER.**

**11** The biggest organism on the planet is a fungus that spreads under a forest in Oregon, U.S.A. **IT COVERS NEARLY 2,500 ACRES** (1,012 ha)—an area big enough to fit almost 1,900 football fields!

**12** **WILD MUSHROOMS** can be boiled to produce **BEAUTIFUL, NATURAL CLOTH DYES.**

**13** In China's Yunnan Province, more than **100 MUSHROOM CAPS** grew on a single stem to create a gigantic mushroom top that **WEIGHED 33 POUNDS** (15 kg).

**14** The ancient Romans held an **ANNUAL FESTIVAL FOR ROBIGUS, THE GOD OF RUST FUNGI.**

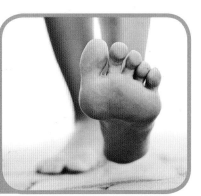

**15** The fungus that causes **ATHLETE'S FOOT** is among the dozens of different kinds of fungi that live all over our bodies.

1. The Chinese probably flew the first flags some 5,000 years ago. Made of silk, they were carried during battles or religious ceremonies.

2. During the Middle Ages, knights identified themselves in battles and tournaments by carrying flags that showed their coats of arms.

3. **DURING THE CRUSADES, KNIGHTS CARRIED FLAGS DISPLAYING A CROSS IN THE COLOR THAT REPRESENTED THEIR COUNTRY.**

4. When Canada was taking suggestions for its new flag in 1964, over 2,000 people submitted designs featuring the maple leaf. The winner was a red maple leaf on a white background with 2 red bars.

5. One red flag flown at the beach signals swimmers to use extreme caution because of high surf and/or strong currents. Two red flags means conditions are so bad that water activities are banned.

6. Grenada's flag has a nutmeg on it, one of the island's major exports.

7. The sun on Argentina's flag represents the Inca god Inti.

8. All Scandinavian countries have a cross on their flags.

9. The flag of Peru looks just like Canada's except Peru's has a coat of arms instead of a maple leaf.

10. According to legend, the double-headed eagle on Albania's flag is the symbol of Skanderbeg, the country's medieval national hero.

11. The blue, black, and white stripes on Estonia's flag are said to stand for loyalty, past suffering, and virtue.

12. The red, white, and blue colors of Iceland's flag represent the elements of the island: red for volcanic fires, white for snow and ice, and blue for the ocean.

13. **UNLIKE MOST OTHER NATIONAL FLAGS, SWITZERLAND'S IS SQUARE.**

14. The green on Bangladesh's flag stands for its fertile land. The red circle is the rising sun and the sacrifices endured to become independent.

15. The dragon on Bhutan's flag has been a symbol of the country since about 1200.

16. The design of Israel's flag is based on the tallith, a shawl worn by Jewish men during prayers.

17. Japan, known as the Land of the Rising Sun, has a solid red circle on its white flag to represent the sun.

18. Kenya's flag shows a Maasai warrior's shield with 2 spears.

# 75 FABULOUS FLAG FACTS

**19** THE TOP OF A YURT—THE TRADITIONAL HOME OF CENTRAL ASIA'S NOMADIC PEOPLE—IS SYMBOLIZED IN THE CENTER OF KYRGYZSTAN'S FLAG.

**20** The cedar tree at the center of Lebanon's flag represents eternity, steadiness, happiness, and prosperity.

**21** Purple and blue flags at the beach mean dangerous animals have been spotted in the water.

**22** The 5 points on the star on Vietnam's flag represent workers, farmers, traders, intellectuals, and soldiers.

**23** The blue in Botswana's flag represents rain. The black and white stripes symbolize racial harmony.

**24** A circle of 10 stars on Cape Verde's blue, white, and red flag represent the country's 10 major islands.

**25** Romania and Chad have almost identical flags except Chad's band of blue is slightly darker.

**26** The red and blue yin-yang on South Korea's flag represents positive and negative cosmic forces.

**27** The crescent moon and star are symbols associated with the Islamic religion and often appear on flags of Islamic countries.

**28** The star on Morocco's flag is known as Solomon's seal and represents the 5 pillars of Islam.

**29** The rainbowlike color pattern on the Seychelles flag represents moving into the future.

**30** Uganda's flag has the country's national symbol—a grey crowned crane—in the center.

**31** The blue and white wavy lines on Kiribati's flag represent the Pacific Ocean. A frigate bird—symbolizing freedom—flies over the sun.

**32** The Southern Cross, a constellation visible only in the Southern Hemisphere, appears on the national flags of Australia, New Zealand, Brazil, Papua New Guinea, and Samoa.

**33** New Zealand's flag is the only one on which the stars in the Southern Cross are red instead of white.

**34** Tonga's constitution says that the country's national flag should never be changed.

**35** The wreath of olive branches on the flag of the United Nations symbolizes peace.

**36** The vertical stripes on the Buddhist flag represent eternal peace, and the horizontal stripes symbolize all races living in harmony.

**37** THE WHITE STRIPE ON THE NATIONAL FLAG OF CHILE REPRESENTS THE SNOW-COVERED ANDES.

**38** The colors of Ireland's flag have no official meaning, but many believe the green stripe represents Catholics, the orange represents Protestants, and the white represents peace.

**39** Liechtenstein and Haiti didn't realize their flags had the same design until the 1936 Olympic Games. The next year, Liechtenstein added a crown to make its flag different.

**40** The 7 diagonal blue and white stripes and 7 red lily pads on the flag of the Dutch province of Friesland represent the 7 coastal regions that were independent in the Middle Ages.

**41** The Isle of Man flag has a triskelion—meaning "three legs of man"—symbol. Each leg is armored and has a gold spur.

**42** Moldova, Paraguay, and Saudi Arabia are the only countries that have a different design on each side of their flags.

**43** A red flag with a diagonal white stripe means "diver down." Attached to a boat or buoy, it warns that a diver is swimming nearby.

**44** In car races, a solid black flag means the driver must pull into a pit stop, usually due to a violation.

**45** There are 6 American flags on the moon, but only 5 are still standing. One blew over when the rocket carrying the Apollo 11 astronauts blasted off.

**46** The red and white colors on Greenland's flag symbolize the sun reflecting off a field of ice.

**47** The National Geographic Society flag has been carried to every continent, both Poles, the top of Mount Everest—even to the moon.

**48** The U.S. flag has 13 stripes, representing the 13 original colonies. It briefly had 15 when Vermont and Kentucky entered the Union, but in 1818, Congress set the number at 13.

**49** There have been 27 official versions of the U.S. flag, 25 of which involved changing the stars.

**50** Since 1923, the United States has had a flag code that says what you should and shouldn't do with the flag.

**51** According to the code, the flag should be lowered at sunset unless properly lighted during darkness.

**52** While the U.S. flag code says the flag shouldn't be used as an athletic uniform, a flag patch can be worn.

**53** According to the U.S. flag code, the preferred way to dispose of a worn-out flag is to burn it.

**54** FLYING THE U.S. FLAG UPSIDE DOWN SIGNALS EXTREME DISTRESS.

**55** A Mexican flag larger than an Olympic swimming pool is the biggest flag flown from a flagpole—so far.

**56** The most expensive flag ever sold is the one Antarctic explorer Ernest Shackleton rescued from his icebound ship, *Endurance*. It was auctioned for $180,600 in 2002.

**57** In 2013, 32 Texas, U.S.A., flag football players set a world record by playing the game for 52 hours, 3 minutes, and 57 seconds in California, U.S.A.

**58** Denmark has had the same design for its national flag longer than any other country. The design for the "Danish Cloth," as it's called, was adopted in 1625.

**59** In 2010, 35,000 people at a fiesta in Spain set a world record for twirling flags at the same time.

**60** The Olympic flag with the 5 colored rings was first raised at the 1920 games in Antwerp, Belgium.

**61** The first time Olympic medalists were honored by the raising of their national flags was at the 1932 Los Angeles games in California.

**62** Flags over each end of a swimming pool tell backstrokers they have 5.4 yards (5 m) to go before they touch the wall.

**63** Countries that are—or have been—part of the British Empire often have a Union Jack on their flag. The Union Jack is the national flag of the United Kingdom.

**64** Since 2011, Libya's solid green flag has been replaced with 3 horizontal red, black, and green stripes with the star-and-crescent symbol of Islam in the center.

**65** The blue on Brazil's flag is the April 1889 sky over the capital the day the republic was declared. Stars are for the states and Federal District.

**66** MANY WEST AFRICAN COUNTRIES THAT GAINED INDEPENDENCE FROM EUROPEAN EMPIRES USE RED, YELLOW, AND GREEN ON THEIR FLAGS AS A SIGN OF UNITY.

**67** Some countries, like Colombia, Ecuador, and Venezuela, have similarly designed flags that reflect their shared history.

**68** The part of a flag that is nearest to the staff is called the hoist. The outer part is called the fly.

**69** If a ship is flying a yellow flag, it means the ship is in quarantine because people on board have some kind of infectious disease, such as yellow fever or cholera.

**70** A white flag is universally used to represent truce—an end to fighting.

**71** A flag flying at half-staff is a universal symbol of mourning.

**72** Each year, the American flag is flown at half-staff on Patriot Day (September 11), Memorial Day (until noon), and Pearl Harbor Remembrance Day.

**73** The proper way to fly a flag at half-staff is to run the flag all the way to the top of the flagpole, then slowly bring it down halfway.

**74** Belize has the only national flag that depicts people. It shows a shield with 2 workers in front of a mahogany tree.

**75** Cambodia's national flag, which shows the temple of Angkor Wat, is the only national flag that uses a building in its design.

**1** The giant **MEGANEURA** dragonfly went extinct 250 million years ago. This large-eyed insect's wingspan was over 2 feet (60 cm)!

**2** Hunted for its oil and skin, a **MARINE MAMMAL CALLED THE STELLER'S SEA COW** went extinct in 1768—less than 30 years after its discovery by Georg Steller.

**3** The **FIRST HORSES WERE ABOUT THE SIZE OF SIAMESE CATS.** They were the smallest horses that ever lived.

**4** During Earth's history there have been at least **5 MASS EXTINCTIONS**—times when the majority of all living species died off.

**5** More than **9 OUT OF EVERY 10 ORGANISMS** that have lived on Earth have died off.

**6** Some **250 MILLION YEARS AGO,** more than 90 percent of all animals in the oceans and on land died off during a mass extinction.

**7** The last major mass extinction occurred 65 million years ago and **WIPED OUT THE DINOSAURS** along with half of all other species.

**8** Today, the animals most threatened with going extinct are **AMPHIBIANS.**

**9** *Aepyornis*, a giant, flightless bird that lived on Madagascar, laid huge eggs. **ONE EGG COULD HOLD 2 GALLONS (8 L) OF LIQUID.**

**10** The **FIRST WHALES LIVED SOME 50 MILLION YEARS AGO,** had 4 legs, were the size of a large dog, and lived on land.

# 35 GRAVE FACTS ABOUT EXTINCT ANIMALS

**11** A mammal from South America called a macrauchenia had a **HUMPLESS CAMEL'S BODY, RHINO-LIKE FEET, AND A TRUNK LIKE AN ELEPHANT'S.**

**12** **THE LAST REPORTED SIGHTING OF A DODO WAS IN 1662.** This flightless bird lived in Mauritius, an island country off the east coast of Africa.

**13** **BILLIONS OF PASSENGER PIGEONS** lived in North America when Christopher Columbus reached the New World. By the early 1900s, the birds were extinct—mostly due to hunters.

**14** One of the last great auks, a flightless, penguin-like bird that stood 3 feet (1 m) high, was killed in 1840 because **SCOTTISH VILLAGERS THOUGHT IT WAS A WITCH.**

**15** Plentiful in Australia more than 2,000 years ago, the last **TASMANIAN TIGER** died in a zoo in 1936. These animals looked like a dog and had stripes like a tiger and a pouch like a kangaroo.

**16** **A HORNLESS RHINO** that lived some 30 million years ago was the largest land mammal ever known. It stood 20 feet (6 m) tall.

**17** The **SABERTOOTH**, a lion-size cat that went extinct about 10,000 years ago, is the state fossil of California, U.S.A.

**18** A group in South Africa is trying to breed zebras to produce offspring with the distinct markings of the **QUAGGA**, an extinct relative. The last quagga died in 1883.

**19** South America was home to a **SUPERSIZE RODENT** between 2 and 4 million years ago. It was 10 feet (3 m) long and weighed as much as—or more than—an American alligator.

**20** The **BAIJI DOLPHIN** was last seen in China's Yangtze River in 2007. Scientists think this species is probably extinct now.

**21** **CAMELS ORIGINATED IN NORTH AMERICA** but became extinct on the continent 10,000 years ago.

**22** Some of the earliest members of a meat-eating order of mammals known as Carnivora were named **"BEAR-DOGS"** because they looked like a mix of these 2 animals.

**23** The last known **PYRENEAN IBEX** died when a tree fell on her in January 2000.

**24** Some **TRILOBITES**, sea creatures that went extinct 250 million years ago, may have buried themselves in the mud, leaving only their eyes sticking up to look for danger.

**25** The fierce-looking **ENTELODON**—or "terminator pig"—which lived over 15 million years ago, had an enormous head and strange, knoblike bulbs on its jaw and cheekbones.

**26** Although last seen in 1982, the **ALAOTRA GREBE** was not declared extinct until 2010, mostly because the bird's remote habitat in Madagascar made it difficult to study.

**27** A giant prehistoric shark called megalodon, which means "megatooth," had a **BITE THAT COULD CRUSH A CAR.**

**28** In 2009, scientists in Costa Rica "rediscovered" **HOLDRIDGE'S TOAD**, an amphibian that can't hear or make noise. No one knows how many—if any—remain today.

**29** Bringing extinct animals back to life through **CLONING IS POSSIBLE ONLY FOR ANIMALS THAT HAVE LEFT CELLS OR DNA** that scientists can use in the lab.

**30** **XERCES BLUE**, a butterfly that lived in sand dunes near San Francisco, California, U.S.A., was last seen in the 1940s. The species died off when people built on its habitat.

**31** As of 2013, **MORE THAN 11,000 SPECIES OF ANIMALS**—from corals and insects to tigers and pygmy hippos—were vulnerable to becoming extinct.

**32** A **GIANT SLOTH** lived in North and South America until 10,000 years ago. At the shoulder, it was at least twice as tall as an NBA basketball player.

**33** **BULLDOG RATS** once thrived on Christmas Island in the Indian Ocean. By 1908, they had all died, probably from a disease brought by rats that arrived with explorers.

**34** The skeleton of an armored mammal called a **GLYPTODONT** can be seen in the Natural History Museum in London, England. It looked like an armadillo but weighed as much as a car.

**35** A kind of **WALKING BAT** in New Zealand is nearly identical to a relative that died off 15 million years ago in Australia when the climate there became cooler and drier.

**1.** There are about 7,000 languages spoken throughout the world. Some 50 of them are spoken by only 1 person. **2.** The United States has no official language, but 28 of the 50 states have designated English as their official language. **3.** Some languages are only spoken, not written. **4.** About half the people in the world speak more than 1 language. **5.** The European Union has 24 official languages. **6.** Romance languages stem from Latin and include French, Spanish, Italian, Portuguese, and Romanian. **7.** A "mother tongue" is the first language a person learns. **8.** An Indian artist released the song "Golden Dreams of Gandhiji" in 125 different languages. **9.** Before early humans developed the ability to speak, they probably used their hands to communicate, just like we use hand gestures. **10.** People can speak the same language, but no 2 voices are exactly alike. **11.** More than 100 different types of sign languages are used by deaf people around the world. **12.** In many cultures, shaking your head back and forth is body language for "no." But in Bulgaria, the opposite is true: Shaking your head back and forth means "yes"! **13.** Asian pottery from 7,000 years ago provides the earliest known example of a written language: characters for the numbers 5, 7, and 8. **14.** Though scientists don't know exactly when spoken language arose, it is older than written language. **15.** South Africa has 11 official languages. Nearly a quarter of the population speaks one called isiZulu, the most common language spoken at home. **16.** In Spanish text messages, "bss" means "besos," or "kisses." **17.** Mandarin Chinese, the main language spoken in China, has about 20,000 different characters. But you need to know only about 4,000 of them to read a newspaper. **18.** Early humans probably used sounds and "clicks," like those used today by the San people of Africa, to communicate. **19.** The most written word in English is "the." "Be" comes in second; "to" third. **20.** The most frequently used noun in the English language (other than pronouns) is "time." **21.** The dollar sign ($) comes from the abbreviation for "peso," which was written in old Spanish-American books as "pˢ." Imagine the letters overlapping each other when written quickly. **22.** The longest English title of a video game is "Cthulhu Saves the World: Super Hyper Enhanced Championship Edition Alpha Diamond DX Plus Alpha FES HD—Premium Enhanced Game of the Year Collector's Edition (without Avatars!)." **23.** Some 2,000 to 3,000 people in Cornwall, England, speak Cornish. **24.** Arabic is an official language in 24 countries. **25.** The letter *j* was separated from the letter *i* and became its own letter during the Middle Ages. **26.** The Norse god Odin is said to be the inventor of the runic alphabet, which was used by people in northern Europe beginning about the first century A.D. **27.** Schoolchildren in Ireland are taught Irish Gaelic, 1 of the country's 2 official languages. English is the other. **28.** An American man who had spent some time in Sweden woke up from a coma in Florida speaking Swedish and having forgotten how to speak English. **29.** New Zealand is the only country to have a sign language as an official language. **30.** Lynx get their name from the Greek word meaning "to shine," which may be a reference to how the cat's eyes look at night. **31.** Red Square, in the center of Moscow, Russia, isn't named for its color. "Red" means "beautiful" in old Russian. **32.** A university in Moscow, Russia, teaches more than 50 different languages—the most of any university in the world. **33.** Because each American Indian nation in Oklahoma, U.S.A., has its own language, more languages are spoken in that state than in all of Europe. **34.** *Arrrr* matey! September 19 is International Talk Like a Pirate Day. **35.** "Adcomsubord-comphibspac" is a Navy term. It stands for Administrative Command, Amphibious Forces, Pacific Fleet Subordinate Command. **36.** Sliced *tu dou* means "sliced potato" in mainland China, but in Taiwan, *tu dou* means "peanut," which is decidedly harder to slice. **37.** In most people, the left hemisphere of the brain controls speech. **38.** You can use an online dictionary to translate the language of the Klingons from *Star Trek;* "nuqneH" means "hello." **39.** One out of 8 people in the world speaks Mandarin Chinese. **40.** People who live on the U.S. coasts tend to call sweet, carbonated drinks "soda," while people in the upper Midwest call them "pop." **41.** The 63-letters-long German word *Rindfleischetikettierungsüberwachungsaufgabenübertragungsgesetz* is no longer in use—not because of its length, but because it referred to a law about beef that was repealed. **42.** About 400 words begin with the letter *x* in English, including rare words and those no longer used, but not including proper names. **43.** The word for armed forces in Chinese characters is made up of the symbols for "stop" and "fighting," a nod to the military's power to prevent wars. **44.** Silbo gomero is a language with no words, only whistles. It is used on the Spanish island of La Gomera. **45.** More than 300 languages are spoken in the United States. **46.** A radio station in Finland broadcasts news in Latin. **47.** Papua New Guinea has some 836 languages. **48.** Whales who live together communicate using a distinct dialect, or regional variety of a language. **49.** A harbor seal named Hoover could mimic the phrase "get outta here." **50.** Translated, the name of Africa's Ténéré Desert means "where there is nothing." **51.** Depending on where it is spoken, Spanish can be called either *Español* or *Castellano*. **52.** "Crayola" was created by merging the French word

# SAY
# 100 FACTS ABOUT LANGUAGE

# WHAT?

for chalk, *craie*, with "ola," a shortened form of the word "oleaginous," which means "oily." **53.** The word "ocelot" comes from an Aztec word meaning "field tiger"—*tlalocelot.* **54.** Words that are spelled and pronounced alike but have different meanings are called homonyms. For example, "rock" can mean a stone, type of music, or kind of movement.

**55.** The Shona language of southern Africa has no word for green. Instead there is a word for yellowish green and a word for bluish green. **56.** People from the Ethiopian Hamer tribe have 27 different words to describe the various textures and colors of a cow's coat. **57.** Every man from the Hamer tribe has 3 names: his human name, his goat name, and his cow name. **58.** The name "Canada" comes from the word "kanata," which means "village" in the Huron-Iroquois language. **59.** *The Oxford English Dictionary* (second edition) contains 171,476 words. **60.** The Hawaiian language has only 13 letters. **61.** No words in the English language have 3 of the same letters in a row. **62.** The majority of the world's languages are spoken in Asia and Africa. **63.** When NASA launched the Voyager 1 and Voyager 2 spacecraft in the 1970s, engineers included gold discs with 55 languages on them. **64.** Esperanto, an international language that's a blend of Latin, English, German, and some Romance languages, was invented in 1887. **65.** More than 30,000 books have been published in Esperanto. **66.** People with brain damage sometimes have trouble thinking of the right words for things, a disorder called aphasia. **67.** Only about 100 people in the world speak Latin fluently. **68.** Some texting abbreviations are popular in certain regions, like "coo" for "cool" in California, U.S.A. **69.** The huamn mnid deos not raed ervey lteter by istlef, but rthear the wrod as a wlohe. **70.** During World War II, Navajo "code talkers" used words from their native language to communicate with American front lines. The hard-to-crack code kept messages secure from eavesdropping enemies. **71.** In the game of chess, the word "checkmate" comes from a Persian phrase that means "the king is stumped." **72.** Scientists think that early humans began to speak some 45,000 years ago. **73.** Dolphins use clicks, squeaks, and whistles to communicate with one another. **74.** In French, a bottle of shampoo is called "shampooing," and a tracksuit is called a "jogging." **75.** Latin is the international language of science. All organisms have a Latin name, like *Ursus maritimus* for polar bear. **76.** Hindi, an official language of India, means "language of the land of the Indus River." **77.** In Africa, the largest group of related languages, or language family, is the Niger-Congo. It contains about 1,500 languages. **78.** Chinese is the oldest continuously used language. Early words have been found on turtle shells more than 3,000 years old. **79.** Wait, what? The word "when" in English sounds like the word for "where" in Arabic. **80.** The English word "cookie" comes from the Dutch word *koekie*, or "little cake." **81.** Forty-four percent of California residents speak a language other than English. **82.** Many people believe shifty eyes are a sign a person is lying, but a 2012 study of this body language found no evidence to support the idea. **83.** If you have misheard the lyrics of a song, then you have experienced a mondegreen. **84.** Nearly 8 out of 10 people speak 1 of the world's 85 most common languages. **85.** More than 1,000 languages are very close to going extinct. **86.** A study of Olympic athletes from 37 countries found that all—even blind athletes—had similar body language upon winning: They raised their arms and puffed out their chests. **87.** The word "bagel" comes from the Yiddish word *beygl*, which has its roots in a German word meaning "ring." **88.** Sentences written in Cambodia's Khmer language don't have spaces between words. Spaces are placed only at the end of a clause or a sentence. **89.** More than 60 languages are spoken in the countries that belong to the European Union. **90.** Some 7 million people in Spain and France speak a language called Catalan. **91.** Harry Potter speaks to serpents using parseltongue, a language consisting of hisses. **92.** In 2007, 4,796 people in China performed a song in sign language at the same time, setting a world record. **93.** Though parents around the world speak different languages, they all use the same melodies, or series of sounds, to communicate with their babies. **94.** In tonal languages, the meaning of a word changes depending on its pitch, or how high or low it is spoken. **95.** Some 2,500 computer languages have been created to run the world's devices. **96.** Fewer than 4,000 people speak Blackfeet, a language native to North America. **97.** A scientist created a program to try to decipher any alien languages. It can compare them with 60 languages spoken on Earth. **98.** In Africa, there are at least 75 languages that have more than 1 million speakers. **99.** One word can have many different meanings, depending on the language. For example, "burro" means "butter" in Italian, but in Spanish it means "donkey." **100.** The Danish word *hygge* describes the feeling of sharing food and drink with family. There is no word to describe this emotion in English.

**1**
Oceanographer **BOB BALLARD** found the *Titanic* while on a secret mission for the U.S. Navy in 1985.

**2**
The *Titanic* wreckage is in 12,467-foot (3,800-m)-deep water—enough to cover almost **12 EIFFEL TOWERS STACKED ON TOP OF EACH OTHER!**

**3**
The gashes an iceberg cut into the *Titanic* were smaller than **2 SIDE-WALK SQUARES**, yet they ultimately caused the ship to sink.

**4**
A memorial built over the sunken **BATTLESHIP U.S.S. *ARIZONA*** honors all those who died during the Japanese attack on Pearl Harbor, Hawaii, U.S.A., in 1941.

**5**
Ever since it sank in 1941, the U.S.S. *Arizona* has been **LEAKING** 2 to 9 quarts (2–9 L) of **OIL** into the Pacific Ocean **EVERY DAY.**

**6**
An 18th-century ship was found during **EXCAVATION FOR THE NEW WORLD TRADE CENTER** in New York City, U.S.A., in 2010.

**7**
A man who survived the sinking of the *Titanic* **ALSO SURVIVED** the sinking of the *Empress of Ireland* **2 YEARS LATER!**

**8**
Shipwrecks are often **DISCOVERED BY FISHERMEN** whose nets get caught in sunken vessels.

**9**
The "**LAW OF FINDS**" says that the goods on board an abandoned shipwreck belong to the finder.

**10**
Some experts say the total value of the unrecovered treasure on sunken ships worldwide is about **$60 BILLION.**

**11**
In the 13th century, a typhoon sank more than 4,000 ships belonging to **MONGOL RULER KUBLAI KHAN** as he was preparing to attack Japan.

**12**
The **SKELETON COAST** is a fitting name for the rocky, foggy shores of Namibia, Africa, where 1,000 ships have wrecked.

**13**
Geologists looking for diamonds off the coast of Namibia found a 15th-century shipwreck full of **ELEPHANT TUSKS** and **GOLD COINS.**

**14**
The recovered cargo of a ship that sank in the Aegean Sea in 350 B.C. included **CERAMIC JUGS** that still had traces of oregano-flavored olive oil.

**15**
Britain's **LUSITANIA** was sunk by a German sub in 1915, killing almost 1,200 people, including 128 Americans. The attack helped push the United States into World War I.

**16**
It took the *Titanic* **2 HOURS AND 40 MINUTES** to sink. The *Lusitania* sank in 20 minutes.

**17**
In 1972, a Scottish family survived **38 DAYS AT SEA** on a rubber raft after their boat was struck and sunk by a pod of killer whales.

**18**
The **PHAROS LIGHT-HOUSE,** built in the third century B.C., helped prevent shipwrecks by guiding ships into the port of Alexandria, Egypt.

**19**
The freighter *Edmund Fitzgerald* sank in **LAKE SUPERIOR,** North America, in 1975. The cause is still a **MYSTERY.**

**20**
Some say a wreck found in the Red Sea in 1988 was just a fishing trawler; others believe it was a Russian **SPY SHIP** that had been gathering intelligence for years.

**21**
*Doty*, a U.S. steamship that sank in **LAKE MICHIGAN** in 1898, was found 111 years later with its cargo of corn still in place!

**22**
The steamship *PRESI-DENT COOLIDGE* was struck by 2 mines in the South Pacific during World War II and is now one of the top wreck-diving destinations.

**23**
At 600 feet (180 m) long, the *Bianca C*, which sank in 1961 after catching fire, was considered the **TITANIC OF THE CARIBBEAN.**

**24**
**SNORKELERS** can easily explore the *Sweepstakes*, a 2-masted schooner that sank in 20 feet (7 m) of water in a Canadian harbor in 1885.

**25**
On its maiden voyage, the *Vasa*, a 17th-century **SWEDISH ROYAL WARSHIP,** sank less than a mile (1.6 km) out in the Baltic Sea.

**26**
A deep layer of oxygen-free water in the Black Sea has **PRESERVED SKELETONS** in shipwrecks that are more than 2,000 years old.

**27**
The *Port Nicholson*, a British ship sunk by German subs off the coast of Maine, U.S.A., in 1942, may have platinum and gold bars on board worth about **$4 BILLION.**

**28**
The novel *Moby-Dick* was inspired by real-life events aboard the *Essex*, which sank after being **RAMMED BY A WHALE** in 1820.

**29**
During World War II, a Japanese destroyer wrecked U.S. Navy *PT-109,* a boat commanded by future U.S. President John F. Kennedy.

Artwork of the *Titanic* sinking

**30**
Scientists, use sonar to create **3-D MAPS** that let them "swim" through underwater shipwrecks and actually see wreckage buried under the ocean floor.

**31**
During the U.S. Civil War, the **U.S.S. HATTERAS**—a Union ship—was sunk by cannon fire from a Confederate ship pretending to be a friendly British vessel.

**32**
An anchor from **BLACKBEARD'S SHIP** was recovered in 2011—almost 300 years after the ship sank off the coast of North Carolina, U.S.A.

**33**
Explorers are still searching for **ENDURANCE,** the ship that took Ernest Shackleton on his 1914 Trans-Antarctica Expedition. The vessel sank after getting trapped in sea ice.

**34**
SOS—the international distress signal—is associated with the saying **"SAVE OUR SHIP,"** but it actually doesn't stand for anything.

**35**
Some passengers who jumped overboard as the *Royal Charter* sank in 1859 drowned because they **LOADED THEMSELVES DOWN WITH GOLD.**

**36**
In the 1700s, **LIGHT-SHIPS**—stationary ships lit up with oil lanterns—warned ships away from rocks and sandbars.

**37**
The *Victory*, which sank in the English Channel during a storm in 1744, is believed to hold a **"SECRET" CARGO OF GOLD** valued at $1 billion.

**38**
The **BARREL DIVER,** invented in 1715, was the first practical device for exploring shipwrecks. It could be lowered to 60 feet (18 m) for 30 minutes.

**39**
For centuries, the search for the final resting place of the Bible's **NOAH'S ARK** has focused on the summit of Turkey's Mount Ararat.

**40**
*GILLIGAN'S ISLAND,* the TV show about 7 castaways from the shipwrecked *Minnow*, was filmed on a studio lot with a man-made lagoon.

**41**
Jules Verne's 1870 sci-fi novel *20,000 LEAGUES UNDER THE SEA* tells of a hunt for a sea monster using futuristic submarines and diving equipment that are now a reality.

**42**
In 1965, a sponge diver discovered the *Kyrenia*—the oldest known trading ship. It sank off Cyprus about **2,300 YEARS AGO.**

**43**
The *Sultana*, a steamship designed to hold 376 people, was carrying 2,300 when she **EXPLODED AND SANK** in the Mississippi River in 1865.

**44**
Shipwrecks offer archaeologists **CLUES ABOUT ANCIENT CULTURES,** their technology, and their approach to the sea.

**45**
Today, more shipwrecks happen in the **CORAL TRIANGLE,** an area of the South China Sea and the East Indies, than anywhere else.

**46**
Visitors can scuba dive to a **"LIVING MUSEUM"** created around 2 Spanish galleons shipwrecked during a hurricane in 1724 near the Dominican Republic.

**47**
**CHINESE ADMIRAL ZHENG HE'S FLEET** has not been found, but porcelain from the early 15th-century ships has been salvaged off the coast of Kenya.

**48**
The heaviest amount of **PRECIOUS METAL** ever retrieved from a shipwreck—122,000 pounds (55,338 kg) of silver—came from a 1941 wreck off the coast of Ireland.

**49**
Archaeologists made **27,000 DIVES** to study the *Mary Rose*, Henry VIII's 16th-century warship, before she was raised in 1982.

**50**
**SHIPWORMS**—"termites of the sea"—bore into and destroy wooden ships. They can devour a medieval vessel within a decade.

# 50 SENSATIONAL FACTS ABOUT SHIPWRECKS

**1** You can buy ANTI-FLATULENCE UNDERWEAR. Some companies make undies that claim to filter out and neutralize stinky odors.

**4** Calvin, from the comic strip "Calvin and Hobbes," has a lucky pair of underwear with rocket ships on them.

**2** After a German discovered x-rays in 1895, people started to FEAR FOR THEIR PRIVACY. So some companies advertised X-RAY-PROOF LEAD UNDERWEAR. Talk about a wedgie!

**3** In 2011, Queen Victoria of England's silk underwear, also known as **bloomers,** sold at auction for nearly $15,000.

**5** THE WORD "BRASSIERE" COMES FROM A MILITARY WORD MEANING "ARM GUARD" IN OLD FRENCH.

# 25 NAKED TRUTHS ABOUT

**6** Some companies make underwear out of bamboo. It's the ultimate in going green.

**7** It's an Italian tradition to wear red underwear for GOOD LUCK on New Year's Eve. People in Latin America wear yellow to bring HAPPINESS AND PROSPERITY.

**10** According to tradition, **TRUE SCOTSMEN** do not wear underwear under their kilts.

**8** Since the 1500s, **CORSETS** have been helping women to hold in their bodies and stand straight. Girls as young as 6 have been made to wear this **RIGID** undergarment.

**9** A man in the United Kingdom holds the world record for putting on the MOST PAIRS OF UNDERPANTS IN 1 HOUR: **144!**

**11** Archie McPhee's **Instant Underpants** come as a 2.5-inch (6.4-cm) pellet, which, when added to water, **expands** into full-size underwear!

**12** Knights in the Middle Ages wore special underpants to keep their bodies from rubbing against their metal armor.

**13**

Ancient Egyptians wore underwear made of silky linen or leather that were called loincloths. King Tut was buried with lots of this clean underwear for the afterlife!

**14**

The most expensive bra-and-underwear set ever made cost **$15 MILLION** and was embedded with **1,300 GEMS,** including 300 carats of Thai rubies.

**15**

One diaper company has a sensor that attaches to your baby's diaper and sends you *A MESSAGE ON TWITTER WHEN YOUR CHILD HAS PEED.*

**16**

Members of the British military sent to very hot climates are issued **germ-fighting underwear** that can be worn for 3 months at a time!

**17**

Fruit of the Loom, one of the world's largest underwear companies, has been making cotton clothing since 1851— **before the invention of the lightbulb!**

**18**

The book series Captain Underpants features characters named Professor Poopypants, Dr. Diaper, and Tippy Tinkletrousers.

# UNDERWEAR

**19**

**WHEN YOUR UNDERWEAR BECOMES STUCK IN YOUR ... AHEM ... REAR END,** IT'S CALLED A **WEDGIE.**

**20**

DURING WORLD WAR I, THE UNITED STATES USED **28,000** TONS (25,455 MT) OF METAL FROM WOMEN'S CORSETS TO BUILD 2 BATTLESHIPS.

**21**

The worldwide underwear market is worth about **30 BILLION** —that's with a *b*— dollars.

**22**

A **UNION SUIT** consists of a shirt and pants combined into one piece of underwear. It was invented in the 1800s but is still worn today by skiers to keep warm.

**23**

**NATIONAL UNDERWEAR DAY** events take place every August in New York City, U.S.A.

**24**

Underwear can actually show how the U.S. economy is doing. **THE MEN'S UNDERWEAR INDEX** shows that when times are tough, men's underwear sales fall.

**25**

The LARGEST PAIR OF UNDERWEAR in the world has a 65-foot-7-inch (20-m) waistline—big enough to fit around 2 elephants standing end-to-end!

# 15 QUiRKY FACTS

**1** A farmer in England successfully grew **PUMPKINS SHAPED LIKE MICKEY MOUSE'S HEAD** for DISNEYLAND PARIS IN FRANCE. He used a SPECIAL MOLD early on in the growth cycle to get the gourds to sprout the famous round "ears."

**2** Although the **SHERATON HUZHOU HOT SPRING RESORT** in China is really a circle, it is called the HORSESHOE HOTEL because 2 of its floors are built underground.

**3** There's a PRESCHOOL IN GERMANY built in the **SHAPE OF A CAT.** Kids enter through the kitty's mouth, 2 ROUND WINDOWS serve as the eyes, and the tail is actually a slide.

**4** Worldwide, **PASTA IS MADE IN MORE THAN 600 SHAPES,** including wagon wheels, corkscrews—even Christmas trees, pumpkins, and hearts.

**5** There's a house in **PENNSYLVANIA, U.S.A.,** that is SHAPED LIKE A SHOE. Its original owner was a businessman who wanted to use the **HOME AS AN ADVERTISEMENT** for his shoe stores.

**6** When VIEWED FROM THE AIR, a newly formed landmass near Japan—**NICKNAMED SNOOPY ISLAND**—looks a lot like Charlie Brown's dog in the "PEANUTS" COMIC.

**7** FROST "FLOWERS" shaped like stars sometimes form in the seas around BOTH POLES.

**8** A company based in the United Kingdom sells a rubber iPhone case that's in the SHAPE OF A GIGANTIC EAR.

**9** There's a small, HEART-SHAPED LAKE in India called **HRIDAYA SARAS**—or Eros Lake, after the Greek god of love.

**10** WOMBAT DUNG is **CUBE-SHAPED**, while male turkey poop is SHAPED LIKE THE LETTER J.

**11** The **VALLEY OF THE SQUARE TREES** in Panama is home to hundreds of cottonwood trees with square-shaped trunks. Even their GROWTH RINGS ARE SQUARE!

**12** A single cornflake shaped like the **U.S. STATE OF ILLINOIS** sold at an online auction for **$1,350.**

**13** **HYPERION,** one of Saturn's 62 moons, is shaped like a **HAMBURGER PATTY.**

**14** The streetlights in Hershey, Pennsylvania, are shaped like HERSHEY'S KISSES.

**15** A woman in Florida, U.S.A., found a **STRAW-BERRY SHAPED LIKE A GRIZZLY BEAR** while shopping in her local grocery store.

1. There are billions of insects on the planet. They outnumber humans 300 to 1.

2. Some midge larvae, or babies, can survive in liquid nitrogen, which has a temperature of minus 321°F (-196°C).

3. Some assassin bugs use a tube called a proboscis to suck blood from other animals. The nymphs, or babies, are see-through, so you can watch the blood fill up in their bodies.

4. Orchid mantises are born looking like small black ants. When they grow up, they turn white or pink—just like the flowers they hide in to catch their prey.

5. Chan's megastick is the longest known insect on Earth. It measures almost 2 feet (0.6 m)!

6. Food experts say cicadas, which spend years underground sucking sap from trees, are a great low-fat snack. They reportedly taste like asparagus.

7. Some wasps hold on to plants with their teeth when they sleep.

8. **TWO BILLION PEOPLE ON EARTH EAT INSECTS AS PART OF THEIR REGULAR DIET.**

9. Adult mayflies may live for only one day, but these insects have been around hundreds of millions of years, making them one of the oldest kinds of bugs on Earth.

10. Icebugs live in near freezing temperatures. Holding one will kill it, since their bodies break down at room temperature.

11. Coneheaded katydids are named for the pointed cone on the top of their heads. Males chirp, and some even dance to find mates.

12. Dragonflies are deadly predators. They stalk their prey and can predict where it's headed. Their 95 percent success rate is nearly 4 times that of lions.

13. Pygmy mole crickets are expert jumpers. By using their paddle-shaped back legs to push off from the water, they can actually leap into the air.

14. One kind of fly lays its eggs inside honeybees. The larvae eat the insides of the bees, causing them to fly around in a bizarre way until they die.

15. Peanut bugs are named for the peanut shell–shaped bulge on the front of their heads. It's actually hollow—like a balloon—but it helps scare away predators.

16. Crazy ants seek out electrical wiring because of the heat it gives off, and they have been known to crawl inside cell phones.

17. Dung beetles use light from the Milky Way as a sort of GPS so they can roll their dung balls in a straight line from the dung pile to their nests.

18. **MALE LUNA MOTHS CAN SMELL SCENTS FROM FEMALE MOTHS FROM OVER 6 MILES (10 KM) AWAY.**

19. As sand termites chow down on grass in some areas of a desert in Namibia, Africa, they leave bare spots in the sand called fairy circles.

20. Cochineal insects are collected, dried, ground up, and added to some foods and drinks to give them their red color. The color comes from the cactus berries the bugs eat.

21. Some jewel bugs are brightly colored and even metallic looking. Scientists think some colors mimic those of toxic bugs so that predators will stay away.

22. Jewel bugs don't have teeth. To eat plants, they liquefy them with their saliva and suck up the juice.

23. Ant-eating assassin bugs pile the bodies of dead ants on their backs to make themselves look bigger than they really are to ward off predators.

24. One of the smallest insects in the world is a fairyfly called *Tinkerbella nana*. It's so small, it can't be seen by the naked eye.

25. New Zealand's giant weta— the world's largest insect—gets its name from a word that means "god of bad looks."

26. Since 1999 when the first glow-in-the-dark species of cockroach was discovered, at least a dozen other species have been found.

27. The fuzzy puss moth caterpillar may look like a cuddly critter, but watch out. It is one of the most toxic caterpillars in North America.

28. **THE QUEEN ALEXANDRA BIRDWING BUTTERFLY IS THE BIGGEST BUTTERFLY ON EARTH. ITS WINGSPAN CAN BE 1 FOOT (30 CM) ACROSS—LARGER THAN THAT OF MANY BIRDS!**

29. Water bugs look like cockroaches—only they're bigger. But in contrast to cockroaches, it is the males that carry the egg sacs—on their backs—until they hatch.

30. Atlas moths have a larger wing surface than any other kind of moth. Their name comes from the fact that their wing patterns can look like maps.

31. The 4-inch (10-cm)-long violin beetle's flat body resembles a violin. The flat shape gives the beetle the advantage of being able to easily slip under bark and away from predators.

32. Some kinds of giraffe weevils have a neck that is longer than the rest of their body. Males use their necks for fighting; females use theirs to roll leaves into nests for their eggs.

33. Grasshoppers have over 900 different muscles—more than humans.

34. Tiny scales, formed by 3-D crystals that reflect light, give some weevils their wild colors.

35. The 3-D crystals that give some weevils their flashy colors are so complex, scientists haven't figured out how to duplicate them.

36. Tarantula hawks are actually wasps. After killing a tarantula, they drag it to their burrow, lay an egg inside it, and bury it. The larva lives off the spider's body.

37. The female irritator wasp has a whiplike body part, called an ovipositor, on her rear end that she uses to bore into trees and lay her eggs.

38. The names of some U.S. towns were inspired by insects: Bumble Bee, Arizona; Bugscuffle, Tennessee; and Fleatown, Ohio.

39. Fuzzy-looking red velvet ants are wasps, not ants. But only the males have wings.

40. The neon cuckoo bee attacks from within by laying its eggs in the nests of other bees. When the cuckoo bee's eggs hatch, they kill the colony's larvae.

41. Blue morpho butterflies have territories that they regularly patrol, just like some mammals do. They chase away rivals.

42. When its wings are closed, the dead leaf butterfly is as drab as its namesake. But its open wings are colored bright blue and orange.

43. Blowflies are usually the first insects to arrive at a carcass. They'll even infest a live animal's wounds.

44. When startled, a Brazilian hawk moth caterpillar raises its head and inflates its upper body to look like a snake to scare predators.

45. A fly's wings are covered with sensors that allow the insect to smell and even taste with its wings.

46. Termite queens are some of the longest-living insects. They've been known to live for up to 50 years, but some scientists think they can live for 100.

47. Some scientists think having waterproof eggs allowed insects to be among the first creatures to move from water to land some 400 million years ago.

48. Japanese honeybee stingers can't kill a giant hornet, so the bees "cook" the hornet by surrounding it. Heat generated from their vibrating bodies can reach 117°F (47°C).

49. Water striders have legs that can be twice the length of their bodies. They use them to move quickly under and on top of the water.

50. A group of scientists raised a dragonfly that was 15 percent larger than modern species by simulating air conditions from 300 million years ago, when bugs were bigger.

51. **THE FROGHOPPER INSECT CAN JUMP HIGHER THAN ANY OTHER BUG—UP TO 28 INCHES (71 CM).**

# 75 FACTS ABOUT WEIRD INSECTS TO BUG YOU OUT

**52** The African cicada is the loudest insect on record. When you're standing about 2 feet (61 cm) away, its buzz sounds as loud as a rock concert.

**53** The 1-inch (2.5-cm)-long Jamaican click beetle emits light from green "headlights" near its eyes, making it the brightest insect on record.

**54 SOME INSECTS KEEP THEIR BRIGHT COLORS EVEN AS FOSSILS MILLIONS OF YEARS OLD.**

**55** The fastest flying insect is the desert locust, which zooms through the air at up to 21 miles per hour (34 kph).

**56** A *Hyalomma asiaticium* tick can eat 0.3 ounces (9 ml) of its favorite meal—blood—in one sitting.

**57** African driver ant queens lay the most eggs of any insect species: 3 to 4 million every 25 days.

**58** The line-like patterns on insect wings—like those on dragonflies—are veins. The patterns differ from species to species.

**59** The glasswinged butterfly uses its see-through wings to blend into any surrounding.

Giraffe weevil

**60** Ant lion larvae are called doodlebugs because in their hunt for a place to create a good sand trap where they catch their prey, they leave patterns in the sand.

**61** The United States is among the countries that are developing robotic flying insects that can be used to explode and attack military targets at close range.

**62** Normally, coloring in insects is inherited or comes from the food they eat, but pea aphids seem to steal color DNA from fungi and other microbes.

**63** Pea aphids may be the only photosynthetic insect—meaning they can turn light from the sun into food.

**64** Some butterflies love mud puddles! Puddles and moist soil have mineral salts the butterflies like to eat—a behavior called puddling.

**65** Cricket fighting has been popular since the ancient dynasties of China. One 13th-century emperor's obsession with crickets reportedly led to the downfall of his kingdom.

**66** The Mall of America in Bloomington, Minnesota, U.S.A., released 72,000 ladybugs to eat the aphids that are destroying the mall's indoor landscaping.

**67** One man gets insects to walk through watercolor paint and then create patterns on paper. His artwork includes "Black Widow on Canvas" and "Butterfly Feet and Wings."

**68 HUMAN BOTFLY LARVAE, NATIVE TO SOUTH AND CENTRAL AMERICA, LIVE AND GROW IN HUMAN SKIN. SOME INFECTED PEOPLE CAN FEEL THEM MOVING AROUND.**

**69** Planthoppers are expert jumpers! Adults can accelerate to 500 Gs in milliseconds. Just 5 Gs is enough to make some people pass out.

**70** Insectopia in Paris, France, is a series of wooden houses built at various heights. Its purpose is to attract bugs and promote biodiversity in the area.

**71** National Moth Week is held every year in July in the United States.

**72** The minute pirate bug may have a fierce, swashbuckling name, but it's actually one of the good guys. It's used in greenhouses to eat mites and other destructive insects.

**73** The hawk moth has an unusual defense against bat attacks. It rubs parts of its body together to create an ultrasonic blast that throws the bat off course.

**74** A man in Seattle, Washington, U.S.A., is known as the Bug Chef. His culinary delights include Three Bee Salad and Chocolate Cricket Torte.

**75** During metamorphosis, caterpillars break down inside a chrysalis or cocoon into clumps of soup-like cells that get reorganized and restructured to create a winged butterfly or moth.

# 35 GROOVY GREEN FACTS

**1**
Since Kermit the Frog first sang **"IT'S NOT EASY BEING GREEN"** in 1970, it has been performed by everyone from Tony Bennett to *The Voice*'s CeeLo Green.

**2**
There are over **10,000 DIFFERENT SPECIES OF GRASSES**, including some varieties—like wheat, corn, and rice—that we don't think of as green.

**3**
Unlike most needleleaf trees, the larch has needles that turn from **GREEN TO YELLOW,** then drop off during winter.

**4**
Robin Williams does the voice-over for a **FRUIT BAT NAMED BATTY KODA** in *FernGully, the Last Rainforest*, an animated film about the destruction of these green habitats.

**5**
At **FERN GROTTO,** a popular tropical wonderland in Kauai, Hawaii, U.S.A., lush, green ferns grow upside down from the cave's ceiling.

**6**
**GREEN SEAWEED,** like you find served in sushi restaurants, has been eaten in Chinese and Japanese cultures since 300 B.C. It's chock-full of vitamins and minerals.

**7**
Policeman Lester Wire of Salt Lake City, Utah, U.S.A., invented the **FIRST ELECTRIC TRAFFIC LIGHT** in 1912. It only had a red and a green light.

**8**
Beneath that perfect golf green is a **LAYER OF PLASTIC, THEN GRAVEL, DRAINAGE PIPES, AND SAND.**

**9**
Wimbledon's grass tennis courts are sown with ryegrass and **CUT TO EXACTLY 0.3 INCHES (8 MM) IN HEIGHT.**

**10**
Crayola may have retired **MAGIC MINT,** but there are at least 17 other green crayons in Crayola's standard box, including jungle green, screamin green, and inchworm.

**11**
**THE GREEN LANTERN** comic book hero may have been named after the green/red lantern that train engineers held and Aladdin's mystical lantern of green light.

**12**
On a challenge, Dr. Seuss wrote *GREEN EGGS AND HAM* using only 50 different words.

**13**
**DANDELION GREENS ARE GOOD FOR YOU.** They have double the calcium, 3 times the vitamin A, and 5 times the vitamins K and E as spinach.

**14**
Since 1970, **EARTH DAY** has been held every April 22 to celebrate the need to be "green"—or take care of the environment.

**15**
Green apple was one of the **ORIGINAL 8 FLAVORS** Jelly Belly introduced in 1976.

Movie poster from
*Green Lantern*, 2011

**16** During Nickelodeon's Kids' Choice Awards **CELEBRITIES GET COVERED IN GREEN GOOP.** Katy Perry and Jack Black are two who have been slimed.

**17** Without the **GREEN PIGMENT CHLOROPHYLL,** plants can't make food. Without plants, life as we know it wouldn't exist.

**18** **JADE,** said to stimulate creative energy and mental agility, is the **PERFECT GEM** to wear on test day!

**19** Green eyes, found in only 2 percent of the population, are **MORE COMMON IN FEMALES THAN MALES** and among celebrities than the general population.

**20** A **GREENHOUSE** traps the sun's energy to provide a warm place for plants to grow year-round.

**21** By trapping some of the sun's energy, **EARTH'S ATMOSPHERE ACTS LIKE A GREENHOUSE** to keep the planet an average 59°F (15°C).

**22** Green has come to be associated **WITH BEING JEALOUS.** Shakespeare, in his play *Othello*, calls jealousy the "green-eyed monster."

**23** A **GREENHORN** isn't a kind of cow. It's someone who is new on the job.

**24** **EMERALD** is the birthstone for May and the traditional gift for a 20th, 35th, or 55th wedding anniversary.

**25** The term "greenback," slang for U.S. paper money, came into use during the Civil War. **THE BACKS WERE PRINTED WITH GREEN INK TO MAKE THEM STAND OUT.**

**26** The **GREEN BERETS** are an elite special operations group of the U.S. military. The name comes from the distinctive hats members wear.

**27** Leonardo DiCaprio won Nickelodeon's first **BIG GREEN HELP AWARD** for his eco-focused website, his green foundation, and *11th Hour*, the eco-documentary he directed.

**28** The Green Giant character first appeared in 1925 on cans of unusually large peas. Over the years, he has become known as the **JOLLY GREEN GIANT.**

**29** Green was a **PREFERRED COLOR FOR WEDDING GOWNS** in 15th-century Europe.

**30** Habitat for Humanity uses insulation made from **RECYCLED BLUE JEANS** and other denim clothing in the "green" houses they build.

**31** **MR. GREEN JEANS,** with his green overalls, plaid shirt, and straw hat, appeared on the *Captain Kangaroo* TV show from 1955 until 1984.

**32** **GREEN ICE-CREAM FLAVORS** include green tea, wasabi, and avocado.

**33** "Greene" is one of the most common names for U.S. counties. All are named for famed Revolutionary War general **NATHANAEL GREENE—** not for any lush vegetation.

**34** **THE GREEN MOUNTAIN NATIONAL FOREST** encompasses over 400,000 acres (161,880 ha) in Vermont, U.S.A.—the Green Mountain State.

**35** *Verdi*, by Janell Cannon, **TELLS THE STORY OF A LITTLE SNAKE** who doesn't want to grow up to be a boring, old green python.

# 100 MORE COOL FACTS ABOUT COUNTRIES

**1.** The Island of Palm Trees in Lebanon is a protected ecosystem for green sea turtles and rare birds. **2.** The tiny country of Lesotho is completely surrounded by the country of South Africa. **3.** In 1822, a U.S. organization established Liberia as a colony for former African slaves. **4.** Palm dates, grains, olives (olive oil), and milk are the 4 main ingredients of traditional food in Libya. **5.** Prince Hans-Adam leads the country of Liechtenstein, but his son Crown Prince Alois handles the daily business. **6.** Lithuania, the largest of 3 Baltic States, is known for its beet soup. **7.** Of the 75 medieval castles in Luxembourg, some of the most famous are in the Valley of Seven Castles. **8.** The town of Ohrid, Macedonia, once had 365 churches, which meant a person could attend a different one each day of the year! **9.** Ninety percent of the animals and plants on Madagascar exist in the wild nowhere else in the world. **10.** Malawi is known as the "Warm Heart of Africa" because of its friendliness. **11.** Children in Malaysia don't put their teeth under their pillows when they lose them—they bury them in the ground. **12.** Out of the 1,190 islands that make up the Maldives, some 900 of them are uninhabited. **13.** Most of the buildings in Djenné, Mali, are made of mud bricks. **14.** The Upper Barrakka Lift is a 19-story elevator in Valletta, Malta, that transports people from the waterfront to the city center in 25 seconds. **15.** With little rainfall to provide fresh water, the Marshall Islands is a challenging country to live in. **16.** A circular rock formation about 30 miles (50 km) in diameter in the desert of Mauritania has earned the nickname Eye of Africa. **17.** The island of Mauritius was the home of the flightless dodo bird until it went extinct in the 17th century. **18.** Scattered across Mexico are thousands of ancient step pyramids. **19.** The Federated States of Micronesia was the 16th setting for the TV show *Survivor*. **20.** Each March, people in Moldova wear a *martisor*—a decoration of red and white—to symbolize the victory of spring over winter. **21.** The principality of Monaco is so tiny—less than 1 square mile (2 km²)—that the entire country would fit inside Central Park in New York City, U.S.A. **22.** In Mongolia, the annual Thousand Camel Festival is designed to celebrate and protect 2-humped, Bactrian camels. **23.** Even though the James Bond movie *Casino Royale* is set in Montenegro, not a single scene was filmed in that country. **24.** The red-felt fez hat originated in the town of Fez in Morocco and was worn by students as a symbol of intelligence. **25.** Visitors to Maputo, the capital of Mozambique, can enjoy the nearby Maputo Elephant Reserve. **26.** Sparsely populated Namibia has 2 deserts—the Namib on the coast and the Kalahari in the east. **27.** Tiny Nauru, an island country near Australia, was formerly known as Pleasant Island. **28.** The elevation change in Nepal between its valleys and mountaintops is the greatest in the world, thanks to record-setting peaks like Mount Everest. **29.** The Netherlands has 1,180 windmills. **30.** Kiwifruit, grown in New Zealand since the early 1900s, was not exported until the 1970s. It now can be found in most U.S. supermarkets. **31.** Lake Managua in Nicaragua is the only freshwater lake that contains sharks. **32.** Niger is the youngest country in the world. Half its population is under the age of 15. **33.** Nigeria is often called the Giant of Africa partly because it has the continent's largest population. **34.** Most images of Vikings show them wearing helmets with horns, but the only helmet that has been found came from Norway and doesn't have any horns. **35.** When children lose a tooth in Oman, they face the sun and throw it as far as they can. **36.** In Pakistan, trucks are painted with bright designs and often words of poetry, making every street an art gallery. **37.** The famous rock islands of Palau look like giant green mushrooms rising out of the

Pacific Ocean. **38.** In Panama, the dollar is called a balboa after the Spanish explorer who crossed the Isthmus of Panama to become the first European to see the Pacific Ocean from North America. **39.** Papua New Guinea has more than 800 indigenous languages. **40. Children in the Recycled Orchestra in Cateura, Paraguay, play instruments, like violins and cellos, created out of items found in landfills. 41.** The Amazon River begins its 4,000-mile (6,437-km) journey to the sea in the mountains of southern Peru. **42. The Philippines is the only country that reverses the colors on its flag during wartime, putting the red bar on top and the blue on the bottom. 43.** There is a famous salt mine near the city of Kraków, in Poland, that has been in operation for over 700 years. **44. The largest Santa Claus parade took place in Porto, Portugal, in 2010, with close to 15,000 people dressed in Santa Claus costumes. 45.** Qatar, ruled by the Al Thani family since the mid-1800s, boasts the highest per capita income in the world, due to its oil and natural gas reserves. **46. In Romania, November 30 is St. Andrew's Day, or the Day of the Wolf, when animals take on unusual powers and ghosts walk the world. 47.** Russia is world famous for ballet. The first performances of *The Nutcracker, Swan Lake,* and *Sleeping Beauty* were held there in the late 1800s. **48. The tiny nation of Rwanda is home to one-third of the world's remaining mountain gorillas. 49.** Officials in Samoa redrew the International Date Line in 2011 so that their country became the first to see the sun rise instead of the last to see the sun set. **50. San Marino, the world's oldest republic, is surrounded by Italy. 51.** The island of Sao Tome and Principe is the smallest country in Africa. **52. Saudi Arabia, the birthplace of Islam, is home to the holy shrines of Mecca and Medina. 53.** Senegal is the westernmost country on the mainland of Africa. **54. Devil's Town (Djavolja Varos) in Serbia has 202 pointy rock formations that according to legend represent everything from a petrified wedding party to ruins of churches destroyed by devils 55.** The giant Aldabra tortoise takes its name from the Aldabra Islands in the Seychelles. The reptile appears on the country's coat of arms. **56. Sierra Leone means "lion mountains." Portuguese explorers named this land along the west coast of Africa in the 15th century. 57.** When the Japanese invaded Singapore during World War II, they renamed the island country Syonan-to, meaning "light of the south." **58. Ice hockey and soccer are the most popular sports in Slovakia. 59.** Slovenia hosts a lot of food festivals, including Bean Day, Cabbage Festival, and Chestnut Sunday. **60. Evidence has been found that humans have inhabited the Solomon Islands for more than 3,000 years. 61.** Boys in Somalia are expected to attend school for only 3 years, girls for 2. **62. Although the country of South Africa takes up only 1 percent of Earth's landmass, it's home to about 6 percent of all mammal and reptile species. 63.** In South Sudan cattle are a sign of wealth and status. **64. In Spain, matadors are considered both artists and athletes when they fight bulls in the ring. 65.** In 1960, Sri Lanka became the first country in the world to elect a woman as head of state. **66. Christopher Columbus discovered the volcanic islands that make up the present-day country of St. Kitts and Nevis in 1493. 67.** In St. Lucia, you can go aboard the *Brig Unicorn.* This replica of a 19th-century sailing vessel was used in the movie *Pirates of the Caribbean.* **68. St. Vincent and the Grenadines was once known as Yurumein, meaning "the beauty of the rainbows in the valley." 69.** Children who live in cities in Sudan celebrate their birthdays with cake and a red punch made from hibiscus flowers. **70. Adults younger than age 30 in Suriname need their parents' written permission to marry. 71.** Newala, a monthlong harvest festival in Swaziland, takes place at the end of the year. **72. Although a member of the European Union, Sweden decided to continue using the Swedish krona rather than adopting the euro as its currency. 73.** Switzerland, a landlocked country the size of New Jersey, U.S.A., has remained neutral in military conflicts around the world and didn't join the United Nations until 2002. **74. Syria boasts one of the world's largest norias, a kind of waterwheel. 75.** Tajikistan, the smallest of the so-called stans—countries in central Asia that end in "stan"—is about the same size as the U.S. state of Iowa. **76. Among indigenous people in Tanzania, it is customary for a mother to be known by the name of her oldest child—Mama Jane, for example. 77.** Thailand, which means "land of the free," was once known as Siam. **78. The tiny island of Timor is made up of 2 countries. The eastern end is the country of Timor-Leste. The rest of the island is part of Indonesia. 79.** Togo's first democratically elected president was assassinated in 1963, the same year as President John F. Kennedy. **80. The famous mutiny of the English ship HMS *Bounty,* which inspired the film *Mutiny on the Bounty,* occurred off the coast of Tonga in 1789. 81.** The tropical nation of Trinidad and Tobago has competed in 3 Winter Olympics—1994, 1998, and 2002—all in the bobsled event. **82. George Lucas used the landscape of Tunisia to film scenes of the Planet Tatooine in his *Star Wars* movies. 83.** Istanbul, the largest city in Turkey, is located on 2 continents—Europe and Asia. **84. A failed attempt at gas exploration in Turkmenistan led to the creation of the continually burning Darvaza Gas Crater, also known as the Door to Hell. 85.** The name of Tuvalu, the world's fourth smallest nation, translates to "8 standing together," referring to the 8 traditional Tuvalu islands. **86. Uganda is about the same size as the state of Oregon, U.S.A., but has 1,074 species of birds to Oregon's 534. 87.** People in Kiev, Ukraine, love McDonald's. The city is home to the world's third most popular McDonald's restaurant. **88. The capital of the United Arab Emirates, Abu Dhabi, will soon have branches of 2 of the world's most famous museums—the Louvre and the Guggenheim. 89.** The United Kingdom is made up of 4 nations—England, Scotland, Wales, and Northern Ireland. **90. There are 193 member countries in the United Nations. 91.** Benjamin Franklin was a big fan of the turkey as the symbol of the United States—even after the bald eagle was chosen. **92. The official name of Uruguay is the Eastern Republic of Uruguay because of its location east of the Uruguay River. 93.** Uzbekistan is "doubly landlocked," meaning it is bordered by countries that also have no access to the sea. **94. The inspiration for the sport of bungee jumping comes from Vanuatu, where people celebrate the yam harvest by jumping off towers during the Land Diving Festival. 95.** An ancient Egyptian obelisk that stands in the center of St. Peter's Square in Vatican City acts as a sundial. **96. Venezuela was named after Venice, Italy, by 15th-century Italian explorers. 97.** Pho, the traditional noodle soup that is considered to be the national dish of Vietnam, has become popular throughout the United States. **98. The village of Shibam in Yemen boasts some of the world's oldest skyscrapers, built of mud and dating from the 16th century. 99.** Zambia was once called Northern Rhodesia. Its present name comes from the Zambezi River. **100. Zimbabwe and Zambia share Victoria Falls, the world's biggest curtain of water.**

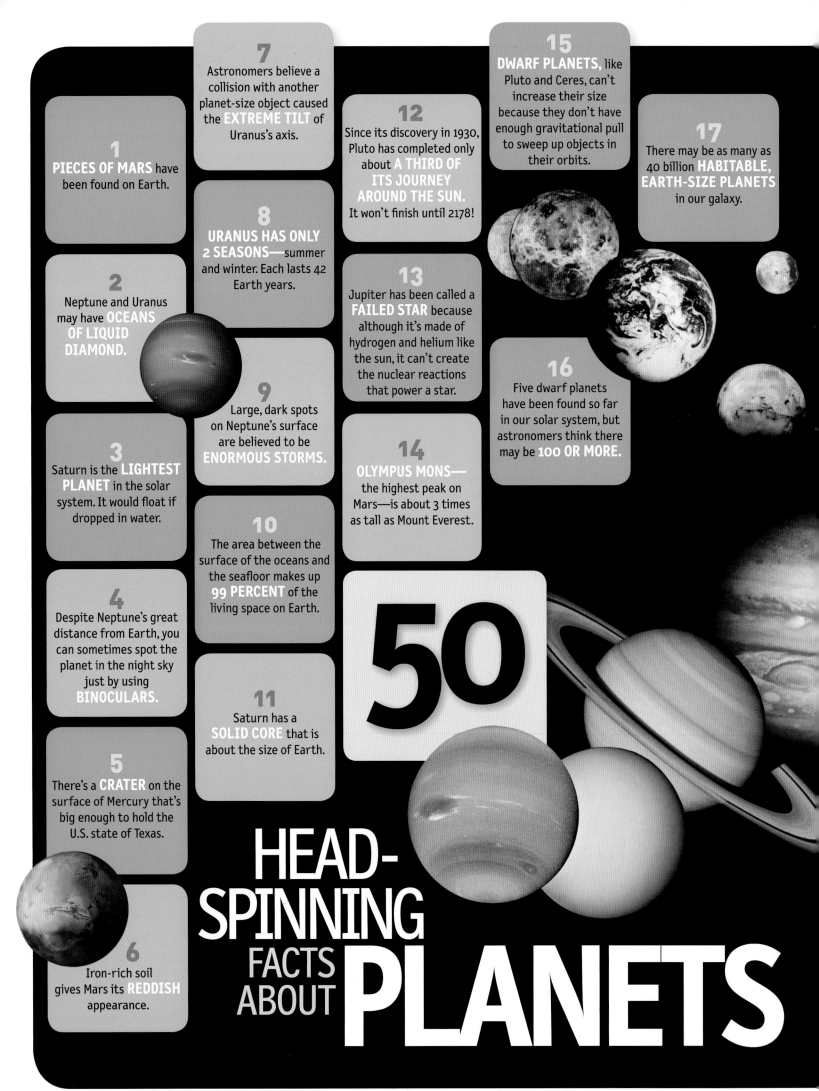

**7**
Astronomers believe a collision with another planet-size object caused the **EXTREME TILT** of Uranus's axis.

**12**
Since its discovery in 1930, Pluto has completed only about **A THIRD OF ITS JOURNEY AROUND THE SUN.** It won't finish until 2178!

**15**
**DWARF PLANETS,** like Pluto and Ceres, can't increase their size because they don't have enough gravitational pull to sweep up objects in their orbits.

**17**
There may be as many as 40 billion **HABITABLE, EARTH-SIZE PLANETS** in our galaxy.

**1**
**PIECES OF MARS** have been found on Earth.

**8**
**URANUS HAS ONLY 2 SEASONS**—summer and winter. Each lasts 42 Earth years.

**2**
Neptune and Uranus may have **OCEANS OF LIQUID DIAMOND.**

**13**
Jupiter has been called a **FAILED STAR** because although it's made of hydrogen and helium like the sun, it can't create the nuclear reactions that power a star.

**16**
Five dwarf planets have been found so far in our solar system, but astronomers think there may be **100 OR MORE.**

**9**
Large, dark spots on Neptune's surface are believed to be **ENORMOUS STORMS.**

**3**
Saturn is the **LIGHTEST PLANET** in the solar system. It would float if dropped in water.

**14**
**OLYMPUS MONS**—the highest peak on Mars—is about 3 times as tall as Mount Everest.

**10**
The area between the surface of the oceans and the seafloor makes up **99 PERCENT** of the living space on Earth.

**4**
Despite Neptune's great distance from Earth, you can sometimes spot the planet in the night sky just by using **BINOCULARS.**

**11**
Saturn has a **SOLID CORE** that is about the size of Earth.

**5**
There's a **CRATER** on the surface of Mercury that's big enough to hold the U.S. state of Texas.

**6**
Iron-rich soil gives Mars its **REDDISH** appearance.

# 50
# HEAD-SPINNING
## FACTS ABOUT
# PLANETS

**18**
The surface temperature on Venus is **HOT ENOUGH TO MELT LEAD.**

**19**
More than **1,000 ALIEN PLANETS**—planets beyond our solar system—have been found. Scientists think there may be 100 billion more.

**20**
In 1995, **51 PEGASI B** was the first alien planet (or exoplanet) to be spotted orbiting a sunlike star.

**21**
It rains **SUPERHOT GLASS** on an alien planet that's about 63 light-years from Earth.

**22**
One Earth-size exoplanet orbits around its star so fast that a **YEAR** on it lasts just **8.5 EARTH HOURS.**

**23**
Some storms on Mars **LAST FOR MONTHS** and are capable of blanketing the entire planet with dust.

**24**
A **BILLION EARTHS** could fit inside one of Saturn's rings.

**25**
**VALLES MARINERIS,** a giant canyon on Mars, stretches for about 2,500 miles (4,000 km)—nearly the distance between the U.S. cities of Philadelphia and San Diego.

**26**
Although **DAYTIME TEMPERATURES** can reach 800°F (430°C) on Mercury, its nighttime temps can dip to minus 300°F (-180°C).

**27**
Jupiter's moon **EUROPA** has an **ICE-COVERED OCEAN** that is salty like those on Earth but almost 10 times deeper.

**28**
Geysers on Europa shoot **PLUMES OF WATER** 124 miles (200 km) into its atmosphere.

**29**
The gas giants—Jupiter, Saturn, Uranus, and Neptune—are sometimes called the **JOVIAN PLANETS** after the Roman god Jove, or Jupiter.

**30**
Like the moon, **VENUS HAS PHASES.** It appears as a thin crescent when it's very close to Earth and as a sphere when it's farthest away.

**31**
There is almost constant volcanic activity on **JUPITER'S MOON IO.** Plumes of sulphur spew upward as high as 190 miles (300 km) from its surface.

**32**
A photo taken by NASA's **CASSINI SPACECRAFT** in 2013 is the first to show Saturn and its moons and rings as well as Venus, Mars, Earth, and Earth's moon.

**33**
About 13 times a century, observers on Earth can watch **MERCURY** make a trip across the face of the **SUN,** an event known as a **TRANSIT.**

**34**
There are more than **1,600 VOLCANOES** on the surface of Venus— more than on any other planet in our solar system.

**35**
NASA's **NEW HORIZONS** spacecraft is set to reach Pluto sometime in 2015. It left Earth in 2006!

**36**
The Earth moves around the sun at 67,000 miles per hour (107,826 kph)—that's more than **100 TIMES THE SPEED** of the fastest jet.

**37**
A year on some "HOT JUPITERS"— alien planets that orbit superclose to their host stars—may last only a few Earth days.

**38**
Because it is closest to the sun, **MERCURY** has the **SHORTEST YEAR** of all the planets in our solar system— just 88 Earth days.

**39**
**EARTH** is the only planet in our solar system not named for a Roman god or goddess. The name comes from the Middle English word "ertha" meaning "GROUND."

**40**
Scientists suspect that the dwarf planet **HAUMEA** got its egg shape by colliding with an asteroid or a meteoroid.

**41**
An **11-YEAR-OLD GIRL** from England is credited with naming **PLUTO** in 1930.

**42**
The **OLDEST KNOWN PLANET**—an exoplanet about 2.5 times the mass of Jupiter—is almost 13 billion years old— about 9 billion years older than Earth.

**43**
There is **NO GRAVITY** at Earth's center.

**44**
**URANUS** is so far from the sun that it receives less than 0.3 percent of the sunlight that Earth gets.

**45**
Venus **SPINS BACKWARD** on its axis.

**46**
Saturn's rings are made of **ICE AND ROCK.**

**47**
Sunsets on the exoplanet **OSIRIS** are green, blue, and brown.

**48**
**PLUTO** is just over 1,400 miles (2,300 km) across, less than half the width of the lower 48 U.S. states.

**49**
The clouds on Venus **RAIN SULFURIC ACID.**

**50**
Scientists think that a **TINY SECOND MOON,** measuring about 750 miles (1,200 km) wide, may have once orbited Earth.

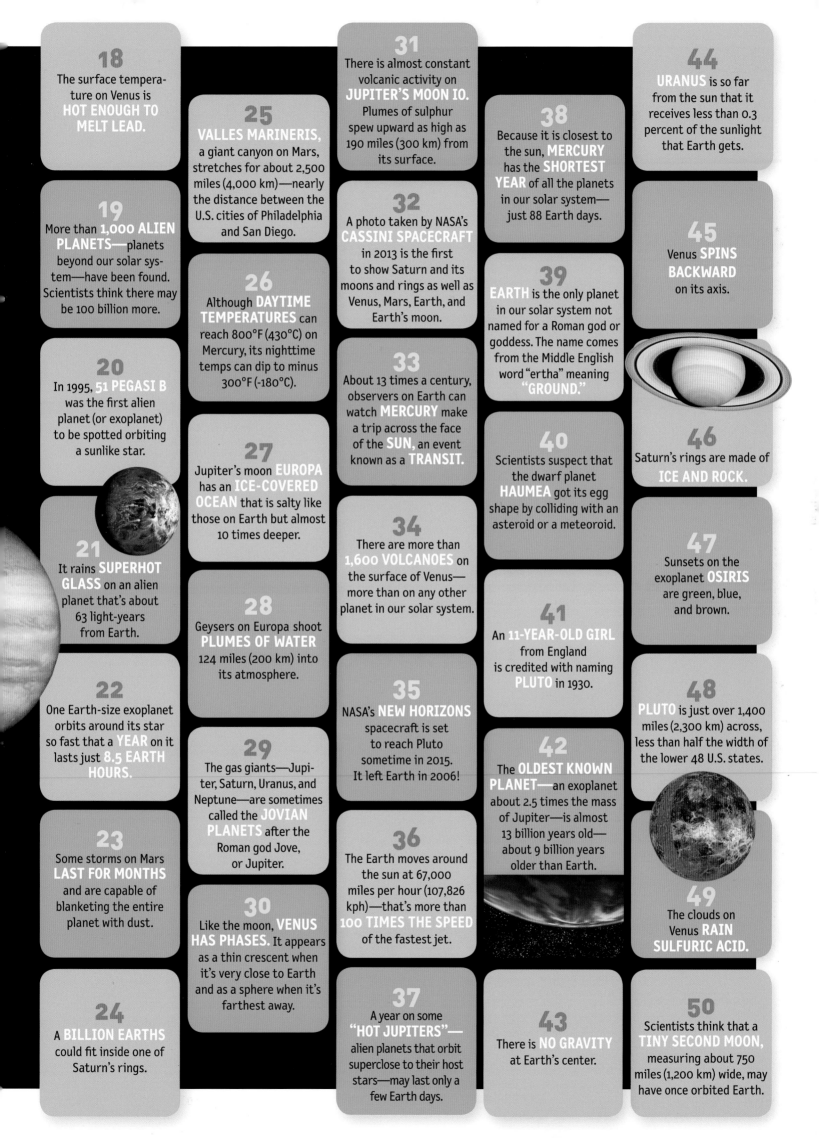

**1**

AIR FORCE ONE
isn't the name of a plane.
IT'S A CALL SIGN
—or name of the radio
transmission signal—
FOR ANY U.S. AIR
FORCE AIRCRAFT
CARRYING
THE PRESIDENT.

**2**

The need for a special call sign was realized in 1953 after commercial flight 8610 and Air Force 8610, carrying President Dwight Eisenhower, crossed paths in midair and caused confusion.

**3**

**4**

There are **2 AIR FORCE PLANES** that routinely carry the President.
They are military versions of Boeing 747 planes and are identical except for the numbers on their tails:
**28000 and 29000.**

Air Force One has 3 levels, is as tall as a 6-story building and longer than a professional hockey rink, and can hold 102 people.

**5**

NO PREPACKAGED AIRLINE FOOD FOR THE PRESIDENT. Chefs cook all meals in flight, USING BOTH OF THE PLANE'S KITCHENS IF NECESSARY.

**6**

If the President flies on a COMMERCIAL AIRLINE, the plane is known as **EXECUTIVE ONE.** A commercial plane carrying any member of the President's family is called EXECUTIVE ONE FOXTROT.

# 25 FIRST-CLASS AIR
## FACTS ABOUT

**7**

Air Force One has advanced technology that allows the aircraft to function as **A COMMAND CENTER** if the U.S. is attacked.

**8**

Talk about a long-distance flight! Air Force One can travel 7,800 miles (12,550 km) before it needs fuel. It refuels in midair.

**9**

Only the President and people accompanied by him are allowed to use the front steps of Air Force One. *Everyone else has to enter from the back.*

**10**

Air Force One
***doesn't have
an escape pod,***
despite what has
been shown in movies.

**11**

The vice president's plane is a smaller military aircraft with the call sign **AIR FORCE TWO**— unless the President is using it.

**12**

EVERY NEW U.S. PRESIDENT IS ASSIGNED A
*NEW PILOT*
TO FLY AIR FORCE ONE.

**13** For the 1997 movie *AIR FORCE ONE* starring **HARRISON FORD,** the film company painted a rented **BOEING 747** cargo plane to look like the President's aircraft.

**14** The aircraft has a medical room equipped with a SURGEON, A PHARMACY, and an OPERATING TABLE, in case in-flight surgery is necessary.

**15** *Twelve Presidents* have flown a total of more than 7 million miles (11 million km) on an Air Force One plane since 1943.

**17** The President **sleeps in the nose of the plane** in a suite that has a private bathroom, a conference room, and an office.

**18** Air Force One is due for an upgrade. In 2017, one of the planes will be replaced with a Boeing 747-8 or 787.

**16** **Franklin D. Roosevelt** was the first President to fly while in office. His plane was nicknamed the **Sacred Cow.**

**19** Air Force One zooms through the air at speeds of up to **630 miles per hour (1,014 kph).**

# FORCE ONE

**20** *Work doesn't stop* when the President is on Air Force One. The plane has **80 telephones** and over 238 miles (383 km) of cabling.

**21** IT'S TRADITION FOR PASSENGERS ON AIR FORCE ONE TO RECEIVE **a box of M&M's** AFTER THEIR FLIGHT. EVERY BOX HAS THE PRESIDENT'S SIGNATURE AND THE PRESIDENTIAL SEAL.

**22** Think you've got a lot of luggage? Air Force One can take off with over **416 tons** (377 MT) of cargo.

**23** *It costs over* **$176,000** per hour *to run* Air Force One.

**24** Lyndon Johnson was the only President to take the oath of office aboard Air Force One. He did so in 1963 after President John F. Kennedy was assassinated in Dallas, Texas.

**25** Two or more C-5 Galaxy heavy transport aircraft fly with Air Force One. They carry the President's bulletproof limousine, an ambulance, and sometimes a helicopter!

# 15 REVEALING FACTS ABOUT

**1** Julius Caesar, leader of the Roman Empire, used code to communicate with his generals. **EACH LETTER HE WROTE WAS ACTUALLY THE THIRD LETTER AFTER THE CORRECT ONE IN THE ALPHABET.** For instance, to spell out "attack" he'd write "dwwdfn."

**2** When Mary Queen of Scots tried to overthrow England's Elizabeth I, she wrote to her co-conspirator Anthony Babington using a cipher alphabet—one that substituted symbols for letters. But **MARY'S CODE WAS CRACKED, AND SHE WAS BEHEADED.**

**3** One of the earliest examples of steganography—hidden message writing—comes from ancient Greece. **A RULER HAD A MESSAGE TATTOOED ON A SLAVE'S SHAVED HEAD.** When the hair grew back, the slave was sent to deliver the message.

**4** A study found that **58 PERCENT OF U.S. TEENS USE SOCIAL STEGANOGRAPHY** in the form of inside jokes or messages that only certain friends will understand.

**5** The meaning of "OUOSVAVV," carved into Shepherd's Monument in England, has stumped code-breakers and historians for years. Some say it's a coded love letter, a biblical verse, graffiti, or even a clue for finding the Holy Grail.

O·U·O·S·V·A·V·V

**6** Composer Edward Elgar, who wrote the popular graduation tune **"POMP AND CIRCUMSTANCE,"** sent a coded letter to a young lady in 1897. It must have been for her eyes only, because no one else has been able to decode it.

# SECRET CODES

**7** During WWI, **GERMANY SENT A CODED MESSAGE TO MEXICO** promising it U.S. territory if Mexico would side with Germany. Britain intercepted and decoded the message, and soon after, the United States declared war on Germany.

**8** The Advanced Encryption Standard is used worldwide by governments and businesses to keep Internet communications secure. The program is so complex that a supercomputer would take **1 BILLION, BILLION—$10^{18}$— YEARS TO CRACK IT.**

**9** There may be a real-life secret code painted in the "Mona Lisa," Leonardo da Vinci's famous 500-year-old masterpiece. **SCIENTISTS HAVE DISCOVERED NUMBERS AND LETTERS PAINTED INTO THE EYES.**

**10** "Kryptos," a sculpture outside the CIA building in Langley, Virginia, U.S.A., contains **4 CODED MESSAGES—ONLY 3 OF WHICH HAVE BEEN SOLVED.** According to the artist, once that remaining code is deciphered, there's still 1 more riddle!

**11** The **VOYNICH MANUSCRIPT** is one of the most puzzling books on Earth. Over 600 years old, it's written in an unknown language that no one has been able to decipher.

**12** In 2011, computer scientists finally deciphered the **COPIALE CIPHER,** an 18th-century manuscript. It revealed initiation rituals performed by a German secret society that had an odd fascination with eyebrow plucking, eye surgery, and other eye-related things.

**13** With **150,000,000,000, 000,000,000 POSSIBLE COMBINATIONS,** the Enigma machine used by the German military during WWII to protect its radio transmissions was tough to crack. But the British figured it out in 1940.

**14** A journal kept by a 19-year-old Isaac Newton, later known for developing the theory of gravity, **CONTAINED A CODE THAT WENT UNSOLVED FOR 300 YEARS**—until 1964. Turns out it was a list of his "sins," such as stealing apples, making pie on Sunday, and punching his sister.

**15** U.S. presidents and their families receive code names from the Secret Service. President Barack Obama's code name is **RENEGADE** and First Lady Michelle Obama's is **RENAISSANCE.**

# 75 HEART-PUMPING FACTS ABOUT BLOOD

1. The heart is so strong it can squirt blood up to 30 feet (9 m).

2. Blood makes up about 7 to 8 percent of body weight. A 70-pound (32-kg) kid would have about 5 pounds (2 kg) of blood.

3. Blood is made of red and white blood cells and platelets, small cell fragments that float in yellowish liquid called plasma.

4. A pinprick of blood contains about 5,000,000 red cells, 10,000 white cells, and 250,000 platelets.

5. Each component of human blood has a specific job. Red blood cells carry oxygen, white blood cells fight infection, platelets help to form blood clots, and plasma carries salts and water.

6. Human blood is about 45 percent blood cells and platelets and 55 percent plasma.

7. One red blood cell is only 0.0003 inches (0.008 mm) wide.

8. A person who suffers from hemophobia has a fear of seeing blood.

9. **DONATING 1 PINT (0.5 L) OF BLOOD HAS THE POTENTIAL TO SAVE 3 LIVES.**

10. Austrian physician Karl Landsteiner won a Nobel Prize in 1930 for discovering that all human blood can be classified into 4 main groups, identified as A, B, AB, and O.

11. Every person has a blood type, and it is either positive or negative. The most common type is O positive.

12. People with type O negative blood are called universal donors because their red blood cells can be given to anyone.

13. People with AB blood are known as universal receivers because they can receive red blood cells from any of the main blood groups.

14. About 1 in every 1,000 people has a rare blood type that doesn't fall into any of the main groups.

15. In Japan, it is commonly believed that your blood type affects your personality.

An illustration of red blood cells inside the blood stream

**16** After being criticized for some insensitive comments he made, a Japanese official resigned, blaming his blood type for his lack of sensitivity.

**17** Mosquitoes use special sensors to detect heat from blood inside an animal's body. That's how they know exactly where to bite you!

**18** VAMPIRE BATS WILL SOMETIMES REGURGITATE THE BLOOD THEY DRINK TO SHARE WITH ANOTHER, STARVING BAT.

**19** Vampire spiders feed on female mosquitoes that are full of blood.

**20** In 1665, the first known blood transfusion was performed by a British doctor. It was between dogs, not humans.

**21** The medical term for a nosebleed is epistaxis. The most common causes are dry air and picking your nose.

**22** Bruises appear on the skin as red blood cells leak out of broken blood vessels and die, discoloring the skin.

**23** It takes less than 1 minute for blood to travel all around your body.

**24** In its 4-month life span, a red blood cell will travel around your body as many as 250,000 times.

**25** Sponges don't have blood. Instead, water travels through small canals in these sea creatures.

**26** Cows have more than 800 different types of blood.

**27** In 1948, a doctor invented the plastic bags used to collect and store blood. They replaced glass bottles, which were more likely to break or become contaminated.

**28** June 14 is World Blood Donor Day.

**29** In August 2010, 43,732 people each donated 1 pint (0.5 L) of blood at a 1-day blood drive in Haryana, India.

**30** More than 100 million blood donations are made every year. People in the United States, Europe, Australia, Canada, Japan, New Zealand, South Korea, and Argentina donate the most.

**31** In poorer countries, children receive the majority of blood transfusions. In wealthier countries, older people are the chief recipients.

**32** Blood cells are produced by bone marrow, a jellylike tissue in the center of bones.

**33** In a child, the marrow in most bones can make blood cells. But as people age, only marrow in the spine, ribs, pelvis, and a few other bones continues to produce the cells.

**34** The process of blood production by bone marrow is called hematopoiesis.

**35** Arteries carry oxygen-rich blood away from the heart. Veins carry oxygen-poor blood back to the heart.

**36** Oxygen-rich human blood is bright red, while oxygen-poor blood is a dull red that makes veins look blue when seen through the skin.

**37** A BLOOD-RED SKY AT SUNSET MEANS THAT THE ATMOSPHERE IS FULL OF DUST PARTICLES.

**38** People who live in the mountains and at higher elevations have more red blood cells than people who live at sea level.

**39** Bloodletting, the practice of trying to heal a patient by taking some of his blood, was used in ancient Egypt and Greece and lasted some 2,500 years.

**40** Artist Marc Quinn used his own frozen blood to make a sculpture of his head. He titled it "Self."

**41** In 1628, English physician William Harvey became the first person to accurately describe how blood circulates through the human body.

**42** A vampire rabbit is the star of the children's book *Bunnicula.* But this bunny doesn't suck blood; instead it sucks the juice from vegetables.

**43** The first successful blood transfusion in humans was in 1818 in England.

**44** Within 24 hours of donating blood, your body will replenish the plasma it lost.

**45** An average 12-year-old's heart beats about 5,000 times in an hour—more than 80 times a minute—sending out blood to all parts of the body.

**46** A camel's heart rate is around 30 beats per minute, while a bat's heart rate is around 750 beats per minute.

**47** Blood transports oxygen and other nutrients to every part of your body. It also carries away carbon dioxide and other waste products to be removed from the body.

**48** Hemoglobin is the protein in a red blood cell that carries oxygen. There are over 250,000,000 molecules of hemoglobin in 1 red blood cell.

**49** Eating iron-rich foods like spinach can help strengthen your blood: Hemoglobin needs the mineral.

**50** Circulating blood helps control your body temperature. Parts of the body that receive less blood will become colder.

**51** Leatherback turtles turn the blood flow to their flippers on and off while in frigid water to keep more blood (and heat) in their body core.

**52** The copper in horseshoe crab blood gives it a blue hue.

**53** A 13th-century Egyptian doctor was the first to suggest that blood flowed between the heart and lungs.

**54** YOU CAN LOSE UP TO 40 PERCENT OF YOUR BLOOD BEFORE YOUR LIFE IS IN SERIOUS DANGER.

**55** Giraffes have very high blood pressure—twice that of humans—in order to pump blood up through their long necks to the brain.

**56** During World War II, Germany reportedly grouped its soldiers together by blood type.

**57** Former U.S. President Jimmy Carter has donated multiple gallons (liters) of blood.

**58** If kept cool, human blood will last 42 days.

**59** In the United States, someone needs blood every 2 seconds. That's roughly 43,200 people a day.

**60** Approximately 40,000 pints (18,900 L) of blood are given to U.S. patients each day.

**61** There are 2.4 trillion red blood cells in 1 pint (0.5 L) of blood.

**62** IN 1 SECOND, YOUR BODY PRODUCES 17 MILLION RED BLOOD CELLS. THIS NUMBER INCREASES WHEN YOU'RE STRESSED.

**63** Red blood cells are shaped liked tiny doughnuts except they have a dent in the center instead of a hole.

**64** There are canine blood banks. Donating dogs receive lots of treats and special attention.

**65** In 1932, the Soviet Union became the first country to establish a blood bank.

**66** One out of every 10 people admitted to a hospital will need blood from a blood bank.

**67** Every time you stand up, gravity pulls blood to the parts of the body below your heart.

**68** Astronauts in space have bulging blood vessels in their necks because there is no gravity to help pull blood to the lower parts of their bodies.

**69** Tennis champion Pete Sampras has a mild form of a blood condition called thalassemia. It can cause anemia, or a low number of red blood cells.

**70** In people with sickle-cell anemia, red blood cells change shape and die after 10 to 20 days. Normally, red blood cells live for 120 days.

**71** Every day, your blood travels about 12,000 miles (19,000 km) through your body. That's like making 4 trips across the United States from New York to California!

**72** In 2011, doctors used synthetic blood to save a woman's life.

**73** Mary Tudor, Queen of England from 1553 to 1558, was nicknamed Bloody Mary because she ordered the deaths of hundreds of people in her kingdom.

**74** A type of vampire bat feeds on birds by climbing into trees and biting their toes.

**75** Blood makes a loop around your body more than 1,000 times a day.

**1** Some small animals, like squirrels and flies, **SEE THINGS IN SLOW MOTION** but can move fast. The combination adds up to last-second getaways.

**2** **KOALAS SLEEP** for up to **20 HOURS A DAY,** but not because they're lazy. They need to conserve lots of energy to digest the eucalyptus leaves they eat.

**3** Snails—one of the slowest creatures on the planet—move at the leisurely pace of **0.0006 MILES PER HOUR** (1 meter per hour).

**4** It would take a snail **NEARLY 4,575 YEARS** to circle Earth!

**5** Snails can't move without **SLIDING ON THE SLIME** they create. They even use other snails' slime trails to get around.

**6** Sloths —**THE SLOWEST MAMMALS ON EARTH**— spend most of their lives hanging onto trees. They have been found clinging to branches even after they're dead.

**7** Algae grow all over sloth fur, making it the perfect home for lots of insects. **OVER 900 DIFFERENT KINDS OF BEETLES WERE FOUND ON 1 SLOTH!**

**8** **INTERNATIONAL SLOTH DAY** is held every year in October to raise awareness of the dangers these slow creatures face from habitat loss.

**9** Turtles may be known as slow, but some loggerhead sea turtles have been recorded **SWIMMING AS FAST AS 15 MILES PER HOUR (24 kph)**—much faster than human swimmers.

**10** Turtles and tortoises have protective shells that look like body armor. But the **SHELL ALSO HAS NERVES AND VEINS** and will bleed if broken.

**11** Tortoises and land turtles have no need for speed. **THEY EAT MOSTLY PLANTS AND DUCK INSIDE THEIR SHELLS** when danger threatens.

**12** **ALLIGATOR SNAPPING TURTLES ARE MEAT-EATERS** but they don't chase their food. They use their wormlike tongue to lure prey into their mouths.

**13** A group of turtles is called a **BALE.**

**Three-toed sloth**

# 35 SLUGGISH FACTS ABOUT SLOW ANIMALS

**14** TORTOISES LIVE LONG LIVES. Jonathan, a tortoise that lives on an island in the southern Atlantic Ocean, is the oldest land animal on Earth at 182 YEARS OLD.

**15** On most days, Galápagos tortoises travel only about 150 feet (46 m). That wouldn't even get them to SECOND BASE ON A BASEBALL FIELD!

**16** TOP SPEED FOR A GALÁPAGOS TORTOISE is 1,000 feet (305 m) a day and happens during its annual migration.

**17** The Greenland shark is the world's SLOWEST SWIMMING SHARK. It moves about as fast as a human baby crawls.

**18** Scientists aren't sure how the pokey Greenland shark catches and eats speedy seals. Some think the SHARK SNEAKS UP ON SEALS while they're asleep!

**19** GREENLAND SHARKS are also called sleeper sharks.

**20** The small crustacean that snacks on the Greenland shark's eye tissue attracts prey to the shark with a BIOLUMINESCENT GLOW.

**21** The SWALLOWTAIL BUTTERFLY has the slowest wing beat of any insect: 300 beats per minute.

**22** SLOW-MOVING SEA COWS, OR MANATEES, swim at a relaxed speed of just 5 miles per hour (8 kph).

**23** Some manatees look brown or green because of the ALGAE GROWING ON THEIR BODIES, but their skin is really gray.

**24** SLOW LORISES, a primate related to lemurs, are named for their slow movements through Asian rain forests. They can hang on one limb for hours at a time.

**25** When they need to, slow lorises can "RACE WALK," TRAVELING UP TO 5 MILES (8 km) in one night.

**26** SEA ANEMONES attach themselves to coral reefs or rocks and stay put, waiting for prey to come close to their venomous tentacles.

**27** SEA URCHINS are spiny creatures that creep across the seafloor on tiny, tube-like feet. Some have been clocked moving only 3 inches (8 cm) a day.

**28** While creeping along the ocean floor, SEA CUCUMBERS EAT MUD. During digestion, dead organisms are filtered out of the mud and used as food.

**29** SEA CUCUMBERS MAY LOOK LIKE MOTIONLESS blobs but they can be quick to protect themselves. Some shoot out sticky threads or toxic internal organs to entangle or poison attackers.

**30** SLUGS ARE SLOWPOKES, but some do manage to escape being eaten. By flipping their bodies from side to side, these so-called jumping slugs flop away from predators.

**31** BRIGHT YELLOW BANANA SLUGS are everywhere in redwood groves. One festival in California, U.S.A., holds slug races and a recipe contest—eew!

**32** Even though they are fish, seahorses don't move like them. WITH ONLY 1 TINY FIN THAT FLAPS 35 TIMES A SECOND, they can easily become exhausted.

**33** MOST SEAHORSES PICK 1 MATE FOR LIFE. Each day, a pair greets each other by linking their tails and swimming in circles while changing color.

**34** Slowworms look and move like snakes, but they're actually LEGLESS LIZARDS.

**35** Talk about slow! SESSILE ANIMALS are creatures such as barnacles, mussels, and corals that can't move from place to place.